PENGUIN BOOKS

LOST HIGHWAY

'Peter Guralnick's *Lost Highway* combines interviews, reporting, scholarship, and nearly faultless prose to render portraits of twenty crucial but often ignored performers . . . Guralnick's book is almost too rich to take in at once . . . *Lost Highway* is less a study of musical genres, or even of individual performers, than it is a very closely observed and broadly applied study of vocation' –
Greil Marcus in *New West*

'Guralnick is a national resource. No one writes as penetratingly as he about so wide a range of our indigenous music. By contrast most of the rest of the scribes are provincials. *Lost Highway* is essential' –
Nat Hentoff

'Peter Guralnick is among that rare breed of music writers who *listen* . . . Guralnick is a thinking man's music writer . . . [This] is a book that fills a void both in subject matter and in the art of music criticism' –
Steve Morse in the *Boston Globe*

'The amazing thing is that a book about defeat could be so beautiful. In part this is because Guralnick understands so well and expresses so eloquently the forces that grind many of America's greatest artists to dust. But it's also because he never loses sight of the dream that set them all on the highway in the first place . . . He consistently gives us scenes along the road that are so strange and haunting, or touching, that they make the whole trip worthwhile' –
Lester Bangs in the *Los Angeles Herald Examiner*

'A superb source of information about American music and a perceptive, compassionate look at people at work – admittedly very special work – that is compelling even for readers who might not be primarily interest in the music . . . Inspired, honest work' –
Tom Smith in *New Haven Advocate*

Peter Guralnick has written on a variety of subjects. He has published two collections of short stories and a novel, *Nighthawk Blues*. *Feel Like Going Home: Portraits in Blues and Rock 'n' Roll*, was his first published book, originally appearing in 1971; its companion volume, *Lost Highway: Journeys and Arrivals of American Musicians*, came out in 1979. *Sweet Soul Music: Rhythm and Blues and the Southern Dream of Freedom*, the third book in this trilogy on American roots music and culture, was published in 1986. *Newsweek* called it "A stunning chronicle . . . What Guralnick has written is cultural history – a panoramic survey of a lost world . . . One of the best books ever written on American popular music." Penguin publishes all three books.

Guralnick's extended critical/biographical essay *Searching for Robert Johnson* was brought out in book form in 1989. He has been working for the last four years on a full-scale biography of Elvis Presley, to be published in 1994.

PETER GURALNICK

LOST HIGHWAY

JOURNEYS AND ARRIVALS OF
AMERICAN MUSICIANS

PENGUIN BOOKS

PENGUIN BOOKS

Published by the Penguin Group
Penguin Books Ltd, 27 Wrights Lane, London w8 5tz, England
Penguin Books USA Inc., 375 Hudson Street, New York, New York 10014, USA
Penguin Books Australia Ltd, Ringwood, Victoria, Australia
Penguin Books Canada Ltd, 10 Alcorn Avenue, Toronto, Ontario, Canada m4v 3b2
Penguin Books (NZ) Ltd, 182–190 Wairau Road, Auckland 10, New Zealand

Penguin Books Ltd, Registered Offices: Harmondsworth, Middlesex, England

First published in the USA by David R. Godine, Publishers, Inc. 1979
Published with revisions in Penguin Books 1992
1 3 5 7 9 10 8 6 4 2

Printed in Great Britain by Clays Ltd, St Ives plc

For Sam Phillips and Chester Burnett,
the real heroes of rock 'n' roll

ACKNOWLEDGMENTS

FOR THEIR continuing help and encouragement over the weeks, months, and years I'd like to thank: Bill Williams, Doug Green, Joe McEwen, Knox Phillips, Al Bianculli, Fred Click, Scott Billington, Peter Stromberg, Michael Bane, Dick Shurman, Rick Stafford, Steve Tomashefsky, Fred Davis, R. O. Curtis, Valerie Wilmer, Susan Marsh, Bruce Iglauer, Jim and Amy O'Neal, Bob Koester, Bob Claypool, David Morton, Bill Millar, Kelly Delaney, and Kit Rachlis. Grateful acknowledgment is made to all the photographers and collectors who so generously gave of their time and resources. Special thanks to Jacob, Nina, and Alexandra for their help in the difficult business of analysis and transcription. To the artists themselves I owe an incalculable debt both for the music and for their very thoughtfulness and consideration. And I would especially like to thank my editor, Harris Dienstfrey, for his insights, suggestions, and empathy as well as for turning what can be a painful process into an altogether pleasant and rewarding experience.

CONTENTS

ACKNOWLEDGMENTS vii

Introduction:
Climbing High Mountains, Trying to Get Home 1

Part One: Honky Tonk Heroes 19

ERNEST TUBB *The Texas Troubadour* 22

HANK SNOW *Still Movin' On* 37

DEFORD BAILEY *Pan American Blues* 49

RUFUS THOMAS *The World's Oldest Teenager* 57

BOBBY BLAND *Little Boy Blue* 68

Part Two: Hillbilly Boogie 93

SCOTTY MOORE *Elvis, Scotty, and Bill: A Sidelong View of History* 96

CHARLIE FEATHERS *The Last of the Rockabillies* 106

ELVIS PRESLEY *And the American Dream* 118

ELVIS PRESLEY *Faded Love* 142

SNAPSHOTS OF CHARLIE RICH 145

SLEEPY LABEEF *There's Good Rockin' Tonight* 163

MICKEY GILLEY *A Room Full of Roses* 176

JACK CLEMENT *Let's All Help the Cowboy Sing the Blues* 186

Part Three: Honky Tonk Masquerade
Or, Are They Gonna Make Us Outlaws Again? 201

WAYLON JENNINGS *The Pleasures of Life in a Hillbilly Band* 204

HANK WILLIAMS, JR. *Living Proof* 217

MERLE HAGGARD *In the Good Old Days (When Times Were Bad)* 232

JAMES TALLEY *Scenes from Life (A Triptych)* 248

STONEY EDWARDS *A Simple Little Dream* 264

Part Four: The Blues Roll On 277

THE HOWLIN' WOLF 280

OTIS SPANN *Blues Is a Man's Best Friend* 289

BIG JOE TURNER *Big Joe Rides On* 295

JUKE JOINT BLUES *Chicago, 1977* 304

Epilogue: Sam Phillips Talking 325

SELECTED DISCOGRAPHY 341

GENERAL BIBLIOGRAPHY 353

INDEX 361

Page viii: Howlin' Wolf. Courtesy of *Living Blues.* D. SHIGLEY
Page xi: Sleepy LaBeef. Courtesy of Sleepy LaBeef.

Introduction

CLIMBING HIGH MOUNTAINS

Trying to Get Home

I NEVER WANTED to be a critic. Perhaps I should amend that to explain that my initial impulse to write about music and musicians stemmed solely from a personal enthusiasm, from a conviction that what I was writing about was important and could be important to others, too. That's why I wrote *Feel Like Going Home*, primarily a collection of portraits of bluesmen, and why I wrote this book as well — which to my mind is a companion volume (with a pronounced country emphasis) to the earlier work.

Life changes, and circumstances do, too, though. When I wrote *Feel Like Going Home* some years ago, I think I still preserved, in however deliberate a way, the passionate naiveté I felt essential to the proper love of rock 'n' roll. The final words of the book in fact announced 'a swan song to my whole brief critical career,' in order to sustain that very naiveté. This is what you call definition by avoidance, a not uncommon practice, but after almost four years I started writing about music again, not only because the magic was in the music but because the music — or the impulse — was in me. I set out once more to do stories on artists I admired, people whose stories had not often been told, in some cases long-standing heroes like Bobby Bland and Merle

Mississippi, 1972. VALERIE WILMER

1

Haggard, in others recent discoveries like James Talley and Sleepy LaBeef. My aim was not objectivity; I was trying to pass along not a dry assessment but a passion. I *believed* in the people I was writing about and their art.

At the same time I couldn't help but notice the difference in tone that had crept into my work. For me, as much as for the musicians I was writing about, what once stemmed from the purest of commitments had become almost inevitably a craft. I noticed not only that I had to struggle against convenient formulations; I had learned enough so that these very formulations − which once might have passed my lips with an unquestioning air of moral authority (racism, philistinism, and big business were ruining the country)− no longer rang quite true for me any more. I reread what I once had written, and it seemed right to me, it was not that I disagreed with what I had said, it was just that I could no longer say it so simply. Moreover, there was another side to it which I frequently chose to deny to myself; I found that I was enjoying some part of my new 'professional' role. It was not that I wanted to be anything exactly, like a Doctor or a Lawyer or even a Writer; *that* I had struggled against all of my life (unquestionably I wanted to write, and did, but for me there was always an ultimate existential distinction between doing and naming); now, though, there was no question that on some level the idea of interviewing famous people, the shock of finding myself in strange airports and stranger hotels, the *image* of myself as reporter digging for a story (surely no one else could take that image seriously) appealed to me.

I had discovered what Murray Kempton has called the lure of 'going around.' 'I have done commentary,' said Kempton, 'do it still, and try to do it as best I can; but it can never be for me what going around is. The journalism that comments or pretends to explain has always been for me somehow wanting in the qualities that are most life-enhancing. . . . The province of those who go around is the immediate, the brief, and the early forgotten. But it is a province that anyone who has ceased to go around will always miss as the ground he walked with a high and an anticipatory heart when he was young.'

Well, maybe I'm making too much of it. Perhaps this is just romantic pigeonholing, and what I am doing is quite different from what Kempton was describing, but in a way I began to identify with my subjects, began to see myself like them stranded out on the highway, for brief moments anyway taking up the strangely disembodied life of the road.

Because that is how all the subjects in this book are linked − at least it is one way. For each and every one of the active performers the road has become journey, arrival, process, definition, virtually replacing in almost every instance the very impetus that set them out on the road in the first place. For someone like Ernest Tubb, the road has become almost an escape, providing him with a welcome refuge from all the nagging problems that assault him at home. On his bus he has surrounded himself with all the

*Elvis Presley. Tupelo, Mississippi, at the Mississippi-Alabama Fair,
September 25, 1956.* Courtesy of Michael Ochs Archives.

creature comforts (television, paperback novels, card-playing buddies, and
a sure relief from sleeplessness in the whirring hum of the wheels); as one of
his long-time associates says, 'I think Ernest will die right in the back of that
damn bus.' Similarly for Bobby Bland, the road has become a refuge, it has
insulated him against all the distractions of 'the street,' given him an aura
and a retinue that serve to mask his fears and insecurities, indeed his help-
lessness in the face of tasks that seem commonplace to those who live in the
square world of nine to five.

For some the road has become a kind of metaphor for all the psychic
dislocations that a career in show business necessarily entails. After an initial
blitz of personal appearances, and the acquisition of all the accoutrements of
superstardom, including an airplane and an extensive investment portfolio,
Charlie Rich shed both his manager and his roadwork and apparently sustains
himself on his records and promotions (he has been profitably connected
with Framm mufflers and Benji, the dog) plus movie and television, Las

Charlie Rich and C.J., Benton, Arkansas. RAEANNE RUBENSTEIN

Vegas and Tahoe appearances. This kind of financial security would seem to be what he was aiming for, except that he no longer has time to write music, and recognition—or perhaps it is just one more concomitant of stardom—virtually prevents him from going out of doors. As his wife, Margaret Ann, says, 'There are so many outside influences, there's so much outside pressure, there are just so many people who want things from you that it's almost impossible to cope.' Elvis's well-known retreat from the world was even more debilitating. Here was a man who started a revolution, whose irrepressible spirit still jumps out at you from records that were made twenty-five years ago, and he was wrapped up in gauze, treated as product even in death. Nowhere is the adage that America seeks heroes not for their qualities but for their marketability more brutally illustrated than in the case of Elvis, whom success first gutted, then abandoned to a twenty-year state of suspended animation.

Even scarcely known artists like DeFord Bailey or Charlie Feathers, or a blues singer like Howlin' Wolf (who never really graduated to the better class of clubs that his contemporary and rival, Muddy Waters, plays today) will live in the constant shadow of the road. For Bailey, who was a pioneer on the Grand Ole Opry, time in a sense has stood still since his dismissal from the Opry cast in 1941; in some ways he continues to see himself as a star, he still carries himself like a star, he is still holding out for the big money which he thinks is due him if he is ever to make another record. In the same way—well, in his own unique way—Charlie Feathers louses up

4

one deal after another for himself, regards the world with intense suspiciousness and not inconsiderable venom, and lives in a time warp, recalling the shows he played back in 1954, still playing the same little clubs around Memphis and Mississippi where he and Elvis and Carl Perkins all started out their careers. And Howlin' Wolf, who always spoke with the greatest mournfulness of the various roles the world had thrust upon him, who spoke longingly of retirement to his farm in Arkansas, virtually lived out his last few years on the road, frequently working himself into such a frenzy that he would nearly pass out on stage, carefully selecting his bookings so that he could check into a nearby VA hospital for the dialysis treatment he required from 1973 on. For Wolf, as for Big Joe Turner, being 'out there' was almost like saying yes to life, a proof, in Big Joe's words, that you could still 'bring some life to the party.'

Perhaps, though, the road is another kind of metaphor—one more analogue for seeking success in the conventional sense, for doing business in the everyday meaning of the term. Because what struck me most forcibly in encountering all the varied subjects of this book was not so much the vicissitudes of their lives—here they are not much different from anyone else—as the way in which the pursuit of success seriously, inevitably distorted the very core of their being, as well as the music itself. As Little Richard

Barn Dance, Pensacola, Florida, ca. 1940. Courtesy of Douglas B. Green

once sang, they all got (or didn't get) what they wanted but almost invariably lost what they had. What I am writing about is often called 'roots music'; the performers who figure in this book, black and white, sing music 'from the heart,' music that is deeply engraved in their background and experience. All make reference to this in one way or another; all recall a boyhood in the country, on the farm, a shared experience that links them inextricably not to the undifferentiated mass audience that television courts, but to a particular, sharply delineated group of men and women who grew up in circumstances probably very much like their own, who respond to the music not just as entertainment but as a vital part of their lives.

Perhaps this is self-evident. And perhaps it is self-evident to say that this is the music *business*, that for Elvis Presley, or for Stoney Edwards, stardom represented something more than middle-class iconography; music represented a way *out*. In this sense, then, it should come as no shock that the singer has lost touch with his audience, and with the very wellspring of feeling that originally gave him inspiration. In a way this argument is not altogether fair, though. Every artist, as Margaret Ann Rich says, is 'a little bit odd, I've never seen one yet you could call normal'; and in the case of Howlin' Wolf or Charlie Feathers, or even with Sun label-mates like Jack Clement and Charlie Rich—whose very first artistic impulse stemmed from their alienation from the world in which they grew up—it might be difficult to say that success has distanced them from their origins any more than traits of character or personality distanced them to begin with.

But take the case of Ernest Tubb, who identifies so totally with his audience that he seeks to keep country music 'simple enough so that the boy out there on the farm can learn it and practice it and try to play it.' What he doesn't realize is that that boy doesn't live out there any more, it has been so many years since Tubb has visited that he doesn't know the farm was long ago sold for real estate. Someone like Merle Haggard explicitly recognizes the problem and tries to resolve it by dropping out periodically or by creating situations—and sharp personal tensions—that stimulate his creativity. Waylon Jennings, on the other hand, has retreated in recent years into the fantasy world of the superstar, in which private jokes, veiled references, and incestuous self-praise have replaced the healthy anger and accessibility of the work for which he became well known. For James Talley, critical accolades, and public praise from Jimmy and Rosalynn Carter, have inevitably turned sour, as they have failed to translate into the real popularity he seeks as a practicing populist. As he says of the criticism that his writing has changed: 'What do you expect? I just write from experience and life, and my life has done a lot of changing lately.'

Elvis, of course, represents the most extreme example of a man cut off from his roots, but I think I would argue, both here and in other instances as well, that it's not just the money (or the fame or adulation); perhaps the very

Ernest Tubb: The Midnight Jamboree. J. CLARK THOMAS

process of going out solely to entertain people is, as Margaret Ann Rich says, 'unnatural. It's abnormal to have to get out and show yourself, to relate to people you've never met.' And it is a far cry from the community of which every one of these performers was once a part, a community which by and large was able to entertain itself. Oh, there may have been 'stars,' but the stars were local heroes, heroes who had developed a widely admired skill to a greater degree than any other member of the community. Demographics didn't enter into it, because you were playing for friends, neighbors, and fellow workers. It's a sobering thought to realize sometimes that this was how Hank Snow, Sleepy LaBeef, Big Joe Turner were originally perceived in their communities. Sometimes in talking to them, I felt as if they would spend the rest of their lives, in the words of an old gospel song with which most of them must be familiar, 'climbing high mountains, trying to get home.'

Every story, of course, was different. The circumstances of each meeting, as well as the details of each individual biography, necessarily lent a distinct flavor to every separate encounter. For some of the stories I found myself on the road like the people I was writing about; some were the product of hanging around for hours, or days, or weeks on end, unglamorously waiting for something to develop. Some stories I caught on the run; some, like the two on Charlie Rich, were the outgrowth of informal conversations between friends. There were certain common factors of approach to all, though. Perhaps the most significant is that I embarked upon each project wanting to do the story, admiring the person I wrote about from his work if not from prior acquaintance. What I sought to do in each case was to enter a world, a world which, as I have explored its periphery, I have come to know more and more, but from which I realize I will always be excluded. I tried to preserve, then, a sense of respectful distance, I tried to portray my own role as honestly as I could, while at the same time allowing myself to be drawn into that world (sucked in would sometimes be more like it) in a way that preempted critical objectivity. Looking back on the various stories, I find that circumstances change, attitudes may change (in the case of James Talley and Sleepy LaBeef, what started out as an assignment ripened into friendship), but I hope each story provides a specific picture of the way things were at a particular time, in a particular place.

The stories are linked in a more prosaic way as well. What I have tried to do in the pages that follow is indicate a kind of loose historical, and stylistic, progression. Certainly many of the choices are arbitrary and occasionally reflect chance as well as personal preference (it would make as much sense, for example, to do a chapter on Billy Lee Riley as on Charlie Feathers, and someone like Roy Acuff could well have stood in for Hank Snow). The book moves in a circle, though, from blues influences to the blues itself and in the end will, I hope, provide an introduction to a whole musical spectrum.

The prefaces to each of the sections will make clearer the implicit ties within each group, but briefly the book is divided into four segments. The first, 'Honky Tonk Heroes,' deals with an earlier generation, black and white, which served as an inspiration for the rock 'n' roll, soul music, and contemporary country, that would one day supplant the earlier musical forms. The second section, 'Hillbilly Boogie,' details the joining of black and white influences (among white performers almost exclusively, though black artists like Little Richard and Chuck Berry provided the inspiration for many of the music's finest moments) that became known as rockabilly, in many ways the purest of rock 'n' roll forms. The third section, 'Honky Tonk Masquerade,' deals not so much with what commercial country and western has become (Nashville after all is Muzak City, U.S.A.), as with the transmutation of the legacy of Ernest Tubb (and Hank Williams and Bob Wills) in the aftermath of the revolution wrought by rockabilly. This 'outlaw music' covers a good deal of territory, but it does embody two basic attributes. It honors traditional influences in a way that has not been seen since Ernest Tubb's generation; moreover, it extends those traditions, neither embracing nor bypassing contemporary rock 'n' roll—so that what comes out is like a skewed, technically advanced version of modern-day rockabilly, assimilating black and white roots. Which is what brings me back to the blues, my first love, with 'The Blues Rolls On.' The blues, it's true, has fallen out of fashion in recent years, has been decimated by deaths and illnesses. It remains, however, a vital living force and is in fact the underpinning for nearly all the music written about in this book. As Elvis Presley said, in neat summation: 'Rock 'n' roll music stems basically from gospel music or rhythm 'n' blues. That's where I actually got my style of singing from, was rhythm 'n' blues and gospel mixed with country and western.'

Or, as Jerry Lee Lewis remarked: 'I played on them. What the hell else do you need to know?'

SOME THINGS I'VE LEARNED

I have learned that people for the most part want to talk. Often I'm asked, isn't it difficult to get people to talk about themselves, to reveal themselves in print? I know that on the one or two occasions when I've been interviewed, a terrible self-consciousness has crept into my conversation. I'm all too aware of how it may appear or of the false enthusiasm with which I might try to reanimate an often-repeated tale. None of this *seems* to have created a problem in talking with figures who generally are used to being in the public eye. Oh, the tape recorder in some cases has been an inhibiting presence—which is why I rely for the most part on taking notes, a far meeker form of intrusion for some reason. And it has sometimes been quite a feat just getting to the people with whom an interview has been set up (fame, as may perhaps be deduced from the Merle Haggard story, sometimes does strange things to people, and certainly erects barriers that were never there before).

In some cases you talk for hours about matters that turn out to be irrelevant, or finish what was intended to be a formal interview before you catch—on the street, in a diner, or most likely driving along in a car—the casual revelation that snaps it all into focus. Some people tell you no more than they want to, most a great deal more than they mean to. The problem in fact comes more in sifting through the sprawling mass of opinion and background information to create a portrait; the challenge lies in respecting the spirit, or the naiveté, with which certain confidences were volunteered, in learning to make the determination (never easy) as to whether inclusion of a particular detail furthers the portrait or simply provides a headline that would throw the whole picture out of focus. You learn quickly that anyone you interview, anyone in life, really, could be portrayed in exactly the opposite manner with exactly the same information. It would not be difficult to mock or dismiss any of the figures in this book, or to treat the reader to a bravura display. Of course it would be, as former President Nixon pointed out, wrong. And it would only further emphasize another application of the Heisenberg Principle: the way in which the examined object changes simply by virtue of coming under examination. In this case the interview acts as a distorting lens, causing all attention to focus so exclusively on the subject that revelations are perhaps in order, things sum themselves up neatly in a way that denies the casual sprawl of real life. I go with James Talley, for example, when he is invited to perform at Jimmy Carter's Inauguration, and the story focuses on the moment itself. It tends to ignore, however, the crush of confusion, the misplaced automobiles, and the bone-chilling letdown at four o'clock in the morning, when all the excitement has fled, the exhilaration drained away, and all you're looking for is an all-night restaurant to grab something to eat.

The point is that each of these moments—which for a performer like Howlin' Wolf or Sleepy LaBeef admittedly occur on an almost nightly basis at that instant when they hit the stage—is only one high point in a wearing succession of days and nights to which the presence of a recording secretary (me) inevitably lends an additional significance. I try to remember this, naturally, and to employ it as a corrective to the glamorized picture that struggles to emerge. I try to provide a snapshot, accurate, flat, evocative in its detail, suggestive in what is included and what is left out.

I have discovered, too, a little bit about the facts of commerce in the last few years. When I first started writing about music, I wrote about blues almost exclusively, and blues was so far outside the pale of the commercial experience (most of the people I wrote about were not even professional

10

Street fiddler, September, 1935. Courtesy of the Library of Congress.
F.S.A. BEN SHAHN

musicians, or, if they were, existed beyond the furthest periphery of the
'record industry') that it led an almost blissfully unexamined life. Few of
the artists I wrote about even had a major record label, let alone a public
relations department that was anxious to see a story written, happy to provide
the writer with information and expenses and offer incentives in the way of
advertising to the magazine that would run a story. So it was possible for me,
as well as my subjects, to maintain a kind of amateur status for a long time.

In the course of doing this book, however, I came up much more against
the economic facts of the music life. In order to do many of the stories that I
wanted to do (on Charlie Feathers, for example, or a label-less Rufus Thomas
or the Chicago blues), I had to find not only a magazine to publish me but a
way of underwriting the trip. Because the odd fact is that very few of the
magazines for which I have written are at all anxious to pay expenses. Even a
counterculture escapee like *Rolling Stone* actively solicits record company
support on many of its major stories. Which is why—or one of the reasons
anyway—you hear the same artists on the radio, why in a more sophisticated
sense you find Bruce Springsteen on the cover of both *Time* and *Newsweek* at
the same time, why you will notice a particular artist covered with a blitz of
media attention upon the release of a widely promoted album, when his or
her work is no more or less important now than it was six months ago or will
be six months from now. There have been many protestations of virtue on

11

the part of the magazines (no story has ever been dictated by financial con-siderations or potential loss of advertising revenue, editors will trumpet again and again), but the basic relationship between the industry and its critics is so fundamentally corrupt, and so obvious, that I'm surprised more protest has not been raised.

For me it was a crash course in economic pragmatism, as I learned to finance one story with another, to use, for example, my trip to Memphis for an interview with Charlie Rich, to do stories on Thomas and Feathers as well, and even take a Capitol-financed side trip to Oklahoma with James Talley. Like the magazines, I have my rationalizations. I have turned down a dozen stories for every one I have done. I have initiated—that is, I have suggested the subject of—nearly every story I have undertaken. I have always written about the artists I wanted to write about. Still, it's a sad commentary that the artists most covered are the ones who generate most advertising income. Of course it's merely 'product' to the record companies, and seldom has a commodity been more aptly named.

There are other things I have learned, or had reinforced, in the course of writing this book. Perhaps the most basic—and it is a tenet that underlies all of my writing—is that the music is out there. It is, as Robert Pete Williams says, in the air. It has nothing to do with records or radio or trends. This may not seem so startling a discovery, but in an age when each month seeks a new hero, when everything has to be assigned a convenient washable label, and punk is forgotten as quickly as bossa nova, it's an important truism to keep in mind. More than that, in the case of nearly every artist that I have written about, I have discovered that what they have put down on record has only the most tenuous connection with what their music is really all about. In my earlier state of naiveté I had always imagined an album as a kind of statement, a summing up that the artist listened to over and over again, just as I once pored over my published work. That isn't exactly the way it is. A record is for the most part an accident, a confluence of particular circumstances on a particular day (the singer had a cold, the bass player got busted, the drummer couldn't get the beat, one song was never included) with production technique designed to mask the very nature of that moment. Perhaps that is all a work of art ever is, but in the case of a record—which is primarily a commercial vehicle by which an artist may become better known, a cooperative effort in which the person in charge (the producer) is not at all necessarily in sympathy with the artist's intentions—the existential nature of the moment is particularly in evidence. Some records, it is true, escape this sense of random accomplishment. Elvis's first records for Sun, for ex-ample, captured a sense of timelessness and passion, just as his television special some thirteen years later escaped altogether the bounds of the medium. But this is the rare exception. You can listen to the records of Charlie Feathers or Stoney Edwards or Sleepy LaBeef and never hear much more than a hint of the greatness of their music. Even in the masterpieces that Merle Haggard or Bobby Bland has recorded, there is still something undeniably missing. Much as I treasure the recorded work of Howlin' Wolf, I would surrender it all for just one moment of him on stage, passionately involved, fiercely committed, genuinely open to whatever caprice might happen to take him.

Another thing I've learned is to distrust critical canons, to suspect the sweeping critical pronouncement. For one thing there is no telling, of course, what the future may bring, and all the endless prognostications and analyses only spoil the fun of the surprise anyway. Over the twelve or thirteen years I have been writing about music, I have heard one Singing Sensation after another touted as the next something, and no doubt have added to the list myself. None of this is relevant, though, except to racehorse handicappers. All the figures in this book have contributed work of solid worth. So have scores of others, from Van Morrison to Gene Austin, from Bing Crosby to Big Mama Thornton or Elvis Costello. The point that must never be lost sight of is that it's all music, again perhaps a truism, but one that bears repeating amid all the absolute dictums that thunder down from Olympus. When I spoke to Son Seals, he expressed an admiration for Kate Smith; Jerry Lee Lewis cited Al Jolson; and Elvis aspired to be the next Dean Martin. Again and again I've had my own preconceptions challenged (both musically and within a broader social framework), over and over I've had my own frame of reference expanded to the point where critical purism now seems an altogether stiff and inappropriate response. Criticism, it seems to me, should expand, not narrow horizons, but it cannot do that if one artist is continually being played off against another, if achievement is measured not on its own terms but against some arbitrary, unreal standard, if the critic does not listen with his or her ears (and emotions) rather than from some abstract ideological commitment. Like E.M. Forster, I like to imagine the various artists that I admire 'seated together in a room,' or in this case perhaps playing, *quietly*, together in a room, forming a kind of creative continuum in which time and classification become irrelevant in the face of what they so clearly share, the common process of creation.

The most important thing I've learned, though, does not have as much to do with music as it does with every aspect of life in this country—or maybe life in the twentieth century—and that is the terrible danger of voyeurism. I guess on one level it could apply to the simple fact of journalism itself, but that isn't how I mean it exactly. Every one of the individuals that I met is bright, venturesome, engaged. Every one exists within a world which is complete in itself, in which there are—or were—connections, in which the individual performer plays a real and functional role. It is a world which is threatened, though, not so much by highways and technology (though these are contributory) as by a very human capacity for seeking to huddle under one blanket.

Television, of course, is the blanket—television and an age of conglomerates, agribusiness, franchises, and monopolies (thought and otherwise) that could never have been envisioned when America was casting about for universal symbols, when Jimmie Rodgers was the Father of Country Music and Babe Ruth was the Sultan of Swat. It's an argument that is perhaps both too familiar and too extended to go into here, but it has to do with the transformation of people into consumers (what could be a more fitting symbol of the seventies than the *consumer* movement?) and the voracious need of business to sell a product—not just to me and you, but to *everyone*. Every artist in this book has an audience, every artist in this book has a *mass* audience—whether of five thousand, fifty thousand, or even half a million—but that is not enough. In order for a record to be successful, it has to sell millions. In order for a performer to be successful, he has to appear on the Johnny Carson Show. In order to appear on network television, it is necessary to appeal to the lowest common denominator; all regional identification must be smoothed over. So—and this is the final step in my simplified syllogism—what is entertaining people on a mass level is no longer genuinely popular culture—in which the audience at whom the entertainment is aimed, out of whom the entertainment has sprung, continues to have a real input—but a pale evisceration, a pathetic dilution of a rich cultural tradition. If Elvis came along today, you have the feeling, he would not get the airplay, simply because he was, well—too strange, too out of the ordinary. ('Sings hillbilly in R&B time,' said a DJ of the period. 'Can you figure that out?') Top 40 radio has been closed for years to any regional, aberrant, or disturbing creative input, due not so much to strictures of popular taste as to marketing strategies and Arbitron ratings. We have been reduced to a nation of voyeurs for whom baseball, which was once the national pastime, an innocent diversion, has become just another jewel in NBC's crown. It seems sometimes as if we have all been convinced that we owe it to ourselves, we *must* be entertained by whatever entertainment is most readily at hand. Is this the legacy of Elvis Presley? Is this the legacy of rock 'n' roll?

And yet I have seen clearly, I have *witnessed* that there are deep pockets of culture which are resistant to homogenization, there are still polyglot elements in our melting-pot land. Over and over again I have had it brought home to me how different the various worlds that I have been permitted to enter really are. The music that I am writing about touches some nerve in its audience which does not allow that audience to remain passive. The musicians that I am writing about take a very different attitude towards their work than that of the nine-to-five studio musicians you hear on most popular records today. To them music is as much an article of faith as their (often lapsed) religious background. As Sleepy LaBeef has said, 'The money's nice—don't get me wrong, there's nothing wrong with it. But I was doing this before I even knew you could get paid for it. And I think I'd still be doing it tomorrow, if there wasn't any money in it at all.' To appreciate that kind of commitment, though, you have to be prepared to make a commitment of your own. What is involved is a kind of leap of faith on the listener's part, a willingness to extend his or her own horizons and break out of the passive restraints that a technologically evolving society has imposed upon us. What is involved is *engagement*.

More than anything, I consider the opportunity to do this book a kind of privilege. It's given me a chance to associate with people I like and admire, it's opened up exotic realms to me, and given me the feeling sometimes, for a brief moment, that our experience—mine and that of the person I am writing about—has merged. That moment explodes, of course, when I leave, when I wrench myself away from the small sealed-off world to which I have been at such pains to gain entrance. It is tested, too, by the role in which I am sometimes cast by the person I am writing about, a role that seems as

Bobby 'Blue' Bland. DAVID MELHADO

Fourth of July near Chapel Hill, North Carolina, 1939.
Courtesy of the Library of Congress. F.S.A. DOROTHEA LANGE

exotic and strange to me as any aspect of my subject's life. It is only natural that there have been situations where I have been seen as the vehicle by which the performer is finally going to achieve stardom. No, I have tried to explain, it doesn't work like that. I'm not sure how it *does* work, but it's not quite like that. My situation, I venture, is a little bit like their own. I have as much trouble placing stories as they do making records. Editors by and large are as unsympathetic a breed as producers. My influence is no greater than theirs, it's just in a slightly different sphere. And I hope this doesn't sound disingenuous, because on some level – for me – it represents an even closer identification with my subject. Perhaps it's romantic, but it extends Forster's continuum just a little bit further and gives me a small but legitimate sup-porting part in an ongoing drama.

An epistolary friend (than whom there are no better) wrote to me recently: 'The thing about you is that you retain the enthusiasm — or seem to — that you had when you wrote *Feel Like Going Home*. It's something I seem to have lost somewhat, though I know it hasn't gone forever and just needs a little prodding. People in this country just don't seem to have that kind of enthusiasm. . . .' Well, I hope that's true of me, though I know (and this introduction probably proves) on some level it isn't. Still, as Gulley Jimson (the irrepressible hero of Joyce Cary's *The Horse's Mouth*) said: 'Get rid of that sense of justice, or you'll feel sorry for yourself, and then you'll soon be dead — blind and deaf and rotten. . . . Go love without the help of anything on earth; and that's real horse meat.' I listen to his advice, and the whisper of my grandfather who always said not to let the bastards get you down and signed his letters (in bemused recognition of Adam Clayton Powell), 'Keep the faith, baby!' Well, I've tried to keep the faith, I still dream of making the big leagues, I love the music as much as I ever did, but at thirty-five I have a public confession to make: I don't want to be a rock 'n' roll star any more.

The Singing Bra

Part One

HONKY TONK HEROES

COUNTRY MUSIC (the commercial brand) was in its infancy when Ernest Tubb and Hank Snow—separated by nearly a continent—first heard the singer who would change their lives. Not too surprisingly it was the same singer—for Jimmie Rodgers has been widely hailed as the Father of Country Music, and his influence not just on musicians but on a whole rural generation was perhaps equaled only by such figures of contemporary myth as Babe Ruth and, later, Elvis Presley. As Tubb has said, 'I know we're not supposed to worship anyone in this life, but I'm afraid to say I did worship Jimmie Rodgers.'

Rodgers was first recorded by Ralph Peer, the pioneering RCA Victor talent scout, on August 4, 1927, in Bristol, Tennessee. It was an auspicious week for country music, for not only did Peer discover Rodgers, a former railroad man who had been working in vaudeville, but the Bristol sessions also yielded the first recordings by the Carter Family, an almost equally influential force on the commercial development of country. Like Rodgers, the Carter Family unquestionably incorporated both black and white traditions in their music, and they remain a seminal influence on present-day gospel,

Jimmie Rodgers. Courtesy of Douglas B. Green.

bluegrass, and folk music. It was Rodgers's simple blues songs, however, that captured the contemporary imagination and set the stage for the rock 'n' roll revolution thirty years down the line.

Self-accompanied by a simple guitar strum, Jimmie Rodgers introduced the first of his Blue Yodels (the still-popular 'T for Texas') in November of 1927. Though he would go on to record every type of song, including novelty numbers, story songs, train songs, of course, and the most sentimental of ballads, it was 'T for Texas' that was his single biggest seller (it sold more than a million copies) and the Blue Yodels — with their combination of traditional blues verses and Rodgers's adaptation of a Swiss yodel — with which he remains most identified today. A veteran of the minstrel show and blackface tradition, Rodgers never sang in anything like a 'blackface' style, and in fact, like the best contemporary white blues singers (Elvis, Merle Haggard, and Charlie Rich come to mind), was most convincing for the very reason that he employed his own relaxed and natural vocal style. His records were wildly popular (he is said to have sold more than twenty million records in his lifetime), and though his blues songs undeniably borrowed from black sources, he proved in turn to be nearly as influential on black styles, his own blue yodel providing the basis for Howlin' Wolf's patented howl.

Jimmie Rodgers made most of his appearances at schoolhouses, crossroads, movie and vaudeville theaters (like the Columbia Theater in Hammond, Louisiana, where I would see Hank Williams, Jr., perform some fifty years later). By the time that Ernest Tubb had begun his career, Rodgers was dead, and the Grand Ole Opry, which had only started up in 1925 as a vehicle for Nashville radio station WSM to sell National Life and Accident Insurance (the WSM call letters stand for National Life's motto: 'We Shield Millions'), was flourishing. The Opry in a sense institutionalized a music that had up till then developed along purely regional, 'folk-tradition' lines. It was not so much a vehicle for personal stardom at first (the situation of black harmonica player DeFord Bailey, who was an Opry regular but relied on a shoeshine stand to support himself, is a case in point); it was the vehicle by which country music itself was transformed into a commercial product and in turn became a kind of industry.

The effect of the Opry on listeners, black and white, was incalculable. As Waylon Jennings recalls, 'Everyone in those little country towns used to listen to the Opry; I mean, there wasn't *anything* happening in them little small towns.' On Saturday night, any established country music star will tell you, every radio within the broad range of 50,000-watt station WSM (a clear channel that traveled thousands of miles) would be tuned in to the Opry. What has often been overlooked is the influence of the Opry on the black community. Ray Charles recalls listening to hillbilly music every Saturday night. Rufus Thomas, a staunch bluesman who grew up in the same medicine-show tradition that spawned Jimmie Rodgers (save that Thomas went out with its black branch), credits the Opry with providing some of his earliest musical inspiration. And Bobby Bland, one of Thomas's protégés, whose smooth but funky way with blues ballads helped inspire much of contemporary soul singing (obviously Sam Cooke and Ray Charles, not to mention James Brown, deserve equal credit here) has said: 'I used to listen to the radio every morning, to people like Roy Acuff, Lefty Frizzell, Hank Williams, and Hank Snow. I think hillbilly has more of a story than people give it credit for.'

The music that was recorded, black and white, represented a rural style gone to the city. It was the first step in an inevitable process. 'It has been said,' writes Tony Russell in *Blacks, Whites and Blues*, 'that the advent of phonograph recording in rural areas spelled the death of folk traditions, because the record ironed out regional characteristics and killed off all the forms which did not have widespread popularity.' Russell goes on to argue that this is not altogether true, because regional characteristics did survive for a decade or two. Nonetheless, the fact is that virtually all of the musicians in this section of the book, all traditional performers, really, started out playing for friends and neighbors in a clearly defined regional style. None, with the possible exception of Rufus Thomas, had explicit professional ambitions. It was only as the recording industry emerged as a major economic factor, first for whites, then for blacks, that such ambitions could crystallize in conjunction with other commercial trends. National Life soon realized the money to be made from sponsoring the Opry, and Ernest Tubb for his part sold flour with his songs, as the Gold Chain Troubadour. The juke joints and honky tonks where Tubb and Snow and Bland developed their music were also an outgrowth of a recognition of the music's commercial potential (in this case to sell liquor), and the very amplification of the music derived from the simple need to be heard in this new and noisy setting.

When Ernest Tubb was introduced to the Grand Ole Opry in 1941 and subsequently became one of its first big 'stars' (following in the wake of Roy Acuff), it was the realization of a lifelong ambition. When in 1950 he introduced Hank Snow to the Opry (who in turn would play a part in introducing Elvis Presley to the world), the circle in a sense was complete, and Snow, a Nova Scotian, felt finally vindicated in his long-time pursuit of professional success. For Bobby Bland, once B. B. King's valet and driver, Las Vegas (the Big Payoff) still beckons up ahead at the end of a long and winding road.

ERNEST
TUBB

The Texas Troubadour

When you call me hillbilly, just smile.

IT IS SOME MINUTES past midnight, and out at the plush new Opry House
—clean, modern, spiritually and geographically removed from the seedy
waste of downtown Nashville—the Grand Ole Opry is running overtime.
Down on lower Broadway, in the heart of the tenderloin district, the crowd
that fills the Ernest Tubb Record Shop across from a darkened Ryman Auditorium (the Ryman was until very recently, until March of 1974, the site of
the Opry itself) only half-listens to the radio broadcast. The record shop,
which Tubb established in 1947 as a kind of Opry annex and which provides
his principal Nashville base (it does probably the largest country and western mail-order business in the country), has been transformed, as it is
every Saturday night, for the live broadcast that immediately follows the
Opry. A makeshift stage has been set up at the front of the store, record
bins have been slid aside and expertly stacked, and the audience—made up
for the most part of grave-looking men and women, well mannered, respectful, polite—contents itself with snapping pictures and looking for familiar
faces.

There is Jumping Bill Carlisle, an Opry star since 1954, and there's leather-
jacketed Little Tommy Collins, the man who wrote many of Merle Haggard's
hits and gave up a moderately successful career of his own to go back to
preaching. Veteran announcer Grant Turner confers with Ernest's oldest son,
Justin, a twenty-year veteran of the Opry himself, who, for all of his song-
writing and performing credits, looks out of place in this hardtack setting
with his tinted aviators, thick mustache, and sleek well-fed look. Two of
Ernest's children from his recently dissolved second marriage are here as
well—twenty-year-old Ernest, Jr., 'Tinker' to his family and his father's fans,
and Karen May, soon to be sixteen. A toothless old lady in a red kerchief,
who has ridden the bus all night from Michigan just to see the show, greets
Karen May and is greeted warmly in turn, posing with Karen for an Instamatic

Ernest and Justin. J. CLARK THOMAS

shot. At the front of the store the latest set of Troubadours, resplendent in their tight-fitting blue western suits, joke easily with each other and fiddle with their instruments, while Ernest Tubb, the original Texas Troubadour himself, fresh from a conference/reunion with Justin, booking agent Hayes Jones, store manager David McCormick, and whoever else can squeeze into the crowded office quarters at the back of the store, peers over his reading glasses and acknowledges the greetings of well-wishers, acquaintances, fans who may not have seen him in twenty years but who remember (and recite) the exact circumstances—the time and place and words exchanged—of their last meeting.

He listens patiently, nods, adds his own recollections. At sixty-three, Ernest Tubb is something like a mirror image of these fans. Although his hair is still dark and he continues to hold himself erect in his turquoise suit, white Stetson, and gleaming brown boots, the once-lean frame has filled out, and the bags under the eyes, wattles under the chin, and slow crinkling smile all give him the look of the plain hard-working men and women who come out to see him. It is almost as if, having cheated fate once when he escaped the bleak West Texas farmland on which he was raised, he has only met it in another guise further on down the line, as his origins make themselves plain in the worn weathered features, the honest creased roadmap of his face.

At last the Opry goes off the air, Grant Turner hauls himself with difficulty up the rickety stairs to the stage, and a cheer goes up as the Midnight Jamboree direct from the Ernest Tubb Record Shop in Nashville, Tennessee, goes out into the night over the powerful WSM airwaves. Ernest Tubb steps up to the microphone, and for the third time that evening (he has already done two Opry shows) and perhaps the thirty-thousandth time in his performing career, launches into the song he first recorded in 1941, the one number with which he will always be identified, 'Walking the Floor Over You.' There is a response of genuine delight; the toothless old lady, well-known to other regulars, nudges her husband in a leather hunting cap; a grizzled-looking old man in overalls tugs at the hand of his grandson, who has fallen asleep on the floor; seventy-eight-year-old Fiddlin' Sid Harkreader, an Opry pioneer who predated Ernest Tubb *and* Uncle Dave Macon (a symbol of the Opry from its earliest days) on WSM, moves lightly on his feet, dignified, erect, smiling a dazzling store-bought smile and using his cane to orchestrate the crowd's response.

It is like a gathering of the faithful, a family reunion. The flat, plodding quality of the singer's voice, so often imitated in honky tonks and barrooms (Ernest has often insisted that part of the basis for his popularity is the very modesty of his talent, encouraging the guy in the tavern who hears an Ernest Tubb record to say, 'Heck, I can sing as good as that,' and then go ahead and try) only underlines the bond between Ernest Tubb and his audience, and when he goes off the air with get-well greetings to Roy Acuff, apologies for having to omit the closing hymn, and a warm 'Be better to your neighbors, and you'll have better neighbors, doggone you,' you are tempted to believe that everything you have ever heard about Ernest Tubb—his loyalty, his fabled kindnesses, his concern for others—may well be true. There is little time to linger, however. Even as the crowd is being dispatched with hand-shakes and good wishes from Ernest, instruments are packed up, goodbyes are exchanged, arrangements are made with Little Tommy Collins to do a Midnight Jamboree guest shot in a couple of weeks, and Ernest Tubb and his Texas Troubadours, Opry Stars, enter the waiting bus outside. There are two shows to do tomorrow in Clarksville, Indiana.

At this stage in his life Ernest Tubb is an authentic legend. Stories about him abound—from his sporadic attempts to reform the bums of Lower Broad-way by presenting them not with money but with a charge account at a local restaurant, to the time he shot up the lobby of radio station WSM—and no one in the industry is any more revered. A member of the Country Music Hall of Fame, an Opry star since 1943, he is the father of honky tonk music and patriarch to a whole Texas clan which extends in a direct line to Waylon Jennings and Willie Nelson. ('A lot of people reacted to me as a rebel when I first started out, because I did what I felt like doing. I think Willie Nelson and Waylon Jennings are doing exactly the same thing.') Ernest Tubb is the man credited with having removed the 'hillbilly' label and 'hillbilly' stigma from country music; he was among the first to bring the electric guitar to the Opry stage; along with Red Foley and A&R man Paul Cohen he helped to establish Nashville as a recording center just after World War II. In addition he is renowned for his good deeds both in and out of the industry, brought country to New York when he gave Carnegie Hall's first honky tonk recital in 1947, and along with fellow aficionado Hank Snow helped keep the spirit of Jimmie Rodgers alive—in his music, in his work to establish the city of Meridian's annual Jimmie Rodgers Day in 1953, and through his constant badgering of RCA until the company finally released the first in what turned out to be a voluminous series of Rodgers reissue LPs. Along the way he has found the time to help such diverse figures as Hank Williams, Johnny Cash, Elvis Presley, and Charley Pride, and to create, in such standards as 'Walking the Floor Over You,' 'I'll Get Along Somehow,' and 'Tomorrow Never Comes,' a body of work that remains the very definition of hard country.

He has above all showed an extraordinary loyalty to his fans, and they to him. ('To his fans there'll never be anybody to replace him,' says his son Justin. 'He has a genuine rapport with these people.') Like John Wayne he is almost the last of his kind, the embodiment of a whole set of values—of loyalty, stoicism, unspoken honor—that seem almost to have passed from the present-day scene. And at a time when most of his musical contemporaries are giving thought to retirement, when Roy Acuff confines himself largely to Opry appearances and Hank Snow has cut back drastically on his performance schedule, Ernest Tubb's customized Silver Eagle touring bus is still out there for 220 show dates and 120,000 miles every year.

Nightclubs, high school auditoriums, the famed Texas ballroom circuit, of which a musician might make a whole career—it is not really so very far removed from the flatbed stages and car roofs, the crossroads and schoolhouses where Ernest Tubb, the Texas Troubadour, who sold beer town to town for Travis, Blatz, the Southern Brewing Company, started out in the mid-1930s. It was a hard, nomadic existence then and remains so. 'You give up a lot,' says Ernest somewhat ruefully today. 'Most of all you give up your home life.' There is little time as well for any of the frills or amenities that most people enjoy in their day-to-day lives. In the short time that I am with him Ernest has managed to squeeze in tax conferences with the IRS; a court appearance over support payments to his second wife, Olene; visits to children, grandchildren, and friends in the hospital; preparations for an ACE (Association of Country Entertainers) benefit concert in Memphis next month. On top of that there are additional family and business problems to straighten out; a bad back to be looked after; a golf game that needs constant attention; the recruitment of a Fan Fair softball team whose first practice Ernest cheerfully oversees amid Little League contests behind the suburban Goodlettsville Elementary School. Plus, of course, the Opry, two interviews, the Midnight

Jamboree, and the last painful details of a sudden release from MCA, his label of thirty-five years, to be worked out.

Why? Why does Ernest Tubb stay on the road at a time when it would seem that he should at last be getting some respite from its burdens and pressures? 'The years and the miles are catching up with him,' concedes Justin, who is taking an increasingly active role in his father's life. At one time, Justin admits, it hurt never to be introduced as anything but Ernest Tubb's son. ('He used to have little suits made up for me when I was a kid; they'd call me the Little Texas Troubadour.') But more and more he has sought to guide his father professionally and has come closer to him personally in recent years. 'He's not in the best of health, but, you know, that bus is home to him. He's got his books, his papers, his tapes, he's got a little bed in the back. He'll eat a bowl of chili, play a little poker, and wake up in a fresh town. He loves it.'

'It's just something in you,' says one-time sideman Jack Greene, an Opry star in his own right. 'There's a void that you can't fill. Some of us find diversions that we really love, but Ernest does not diversify. I think Ernest will die right in the back of that damn bus.'

Other observers are more caustic. The industry has been going through some painful changes lately, of which the relocation of the Opry and the opulence of its new setting are only the most visible signs. There is at the moment in Nashville a kind of cultural schizophrenia in which the present can no longer come to terms with a past it has always at least nominally venerated. Money is the stumbling block, of course, and with a demonstrated potential for the crossover success, with an audience increasingly suburban in nature and demographics, country music has moved further and further away from its roots, dismissing almost with embarrassment the continued presence of figures like Roy Acuff, Ernest Tubb, Bill Monroe. In the week that I am in Nashville, MCA – Decca when Ernest first joined the label – drops nearly every one of its traditional acts, presumably because they do not sell, an assessment that cannot help but feed on itself, since not a penny is spent on production or promotion (Ernest Tubb's last MCA album was cut in three nights). The result is the road. 'You do not find Ernest Tubb records on the rack today,' says one well-known performer who is unable to get a record contract himself. 'So – one way to move product is to move product on the road. For someone like Ernest it's one of his main outlets.'

Justin seems pretty much to agree. 'The things he did for Decca thirty-five years ago don't mean a thing to them today – and that was when they were only paying a penny a record. Now if they'd just pay him the other four and a half cents, we'd be all set.' To Ernest, predictably, it seems more a question of honor. 'They never even recognized me with being on the label for thirty-five years.' Decca, says Hank Snow – who never speaks out of turn, is always boosting the industry, and has himself recently signed a lifetime contract with RCA, his label of forty years—'Decca are being very unfair with a man who has contributed what Ernest has contributed to the label. It's a harsh thing to say, but friendship doesn't mean a thing in this business any more. I think it's a very shitty deal.'

ERNEST TUBB was born on Febuary 9, 1914, on a farm outside of Crisp, Texas, and grew up around Benjamin and Kemp on the West Texas plains, where his father was an overseer and the Tubbs tenant-farmed on a succession of large plantations. As a boy he hated the work, got his schooling between growing seasons, and shuttled back and forth between the homes of various relatives after his parents split up in 1926. He grew up working with blacks in the field, listening to phonograph records of Ethel Waters and Bessie Smith, and particularly admiring the cowboy songs of a local singer and humorist, Jules Verne Allen, who had not only published books but was one of the earliest recorded singers of western songs. With the encouragement of his mother Tubb wrote poems and sang at dances in Benjamin occasionally, though he didn't have a guitar. The thought of being a professional musician never entered his mind, however, until he heard Jimmie Rodgers's first Blue Yodel, which came out on the Victor label in 1927 when he was thirteen. From that day on he knew exactly what he wanted to be. Everything he did was aimed at emulating his idol, and frequently his father would ask if a certain well-known celebrity had paid them a visit that afternoon. 'I'd never know what he was getting at, I'd get fooled every time, but then he'd say, "You know, I could have sworn I heard Jimmie Rodgers yodeling down by the barn." Well, you know, I took a lot of kidding from my family, and it took two years of hard practice, but after two years I got pretty good at the yodeling myself.'

It wasn't until 1933, the year that Jimmie Rodgers died, that he got his first guitar. He was hitchhiking from his sister's house in Benjamin to San Antonio, where his mother lived, when he saw a guitar in a store window in Abilene for $5.95. With only $5.50 in his pocket, he managed to talk the man down some and thus acquired his first instrument. The same year he moved permanently to San Antonio, where after digging ditches for the WPA he got married and went to work managing a drugstore. The owner of the store belonged to various local service clubs, and on his half-hour lunch break each day Ernest Tubb would peddle his bicycle out to one of the clubs and entertain its members with his repertoire of Jimmie Rodgers songs ('I knew the words to every one of his songs'). It was by dint of this kind of hard effort that he eventually landed a fifteen-minute radio show twice a week on 250-watt radio station KONO. He was on the air from five-thirty in the morning till quarter of six, sold his own commercial spots to local merchants, and received no pay for his efforts. He did achieve a measure of local celebrity, though, and with this he was content until, in October of 1935, two months after his son Justin was born, he idly looked in the phone book one day and to his astonishment discovered the name of Mrs. Jimmie Rodgers, who he always presumed had moved back to Mississippi when her husband died.

'I picked up the phone and called her right away, cause I didn't have a decent picture of Jimmie, just a little wallet-sized one, and I thought she might help me to get one. I said, "Is this *the* Mrs. Jimmie Rodgers?" She said, "Yes, it is." After I got my tongue, I explained that I was a singer and how much I admired her husband, and she invited me out to the house for the next Sunday. She was just wonderful to me. She showed me his guitar, his boots, his brakeman's cap. I told her, "You're probably never up at that hour, but I'm on the air on KONO at five-thirty two mornings a week, and I'd be honored if you'd listen, cause really all I sing is Jimmie Rodgers songs."

'About four months later she called me and said that she had been listening to me sing and had some ideas. That was the beginning of our friendship, a friendship that lasted right up until her passing in 1961. Had it not been for her, I probably would have given up. In fact, whatever success I've had I believe I owe to Mrs. Jimmie Rodgers.'

It's hard to say what Mrs. Rodgers saw in Ernest Tubb that differentiated him from the host of Rodgers imitators, from Gene Autry to Nova Scotia's Yodeling Ranger, Hank Snow. One thing she did not see in him, Ernest told reporter Ed Linn some years ago, was a vocal similarity to her husband. '"You don't sing like Jimmie at all," she said. "You're amateurish. But you do have feeling in your voice. The audience knows how you feel about the song you're singing, and Jimmie always thought that was the most important thing of all." And then she said, "Ernest, I'd like to do what I can to help you."'

Help him she did, from setting up a tour and introducing him from the stage to lending him Jimmie's tuxedo and Jimmie's $2000 guitar (it was later presented as an outright gift), which he treasures to this day. She also arranged an audition with RCA, and for the subsequent recording session got her sister, Mrs. Elsie McWilliams, who had written or co-written some of Rodgers's best-known tunes, to write some original material for Tubb.

Even with this much of a boost the records didn't sell, and Ernest continued his unsettled existence, moving to San Angelo in 1937, Corpus Christi in '38, back to San Angelo and then to Fort Worth in 1940. Along the way he became the Texas Troubadour for the Texas Brewing Company and the Gold Chain Troubadour when he switched over to flour. In the beginning he was making $25 or $30 a week from his singing, with his reputation gradually expanding as a result of radio exposure. He would make another $25 a week as a salesman to the beer drive-ins ('90 percent of them wouldn't drink nothing but my beer'), at each of which he would put on a little show. It was a discouraging life, most of all because it was so uncertain, but, as he told Nashville reporter Red O'Donnell, 'Mrs. Rodgers was always in my corner.

The Gold Chain Troubadour, ca. 1940. Courtesy of the Country Music Foundation Library and Media Center, Nashville, Tennessee.

She was a constant support in my early efforts. I remember one situation in particular. It was back in 1940. I was selling mattresses for a company in San Angelo, Texas, and earning commissions up to $140 a week. Then I got an offer to join station KGKO in Fort Worth at $20 a week. I had been doing some singing for four or five years before that time and was doubtful of my future as an entertainer. Mrs. Rodgers advised me to accept the offer. I did, and I suppose it was then that I actually turned pro.'

It was shortly after that, in April of 1940, that he cut his first sides for Decca Records. Mrs. Rodgers lent him Jimmie's limousine, and he drove to Houston, where he recorded 'I'll Get Along Somehow' and 'Blue-Eyed Elaine,' two compositions he had written himself in quite a different style from the six sides that he had recorded for RCA. This change came about, oddly enough, not altogether by choice but because of an operation. Ernest Tubb had his tonsils taken out in 1939, whereupon despite the doctor's assurances his voice changed so that he could never yodel again.

'Well, you see, I tried to sing too quick, and then I thought I was finished. I was even gonna sue this doctor. But it was at this time, without hardly realizing it, that I began to come into my own style and write my own songs. A friend of mine said, "You know, you ought to put that doctor on a pension instead of suing him. Because he's the one that got you started making money from writing your own songs." Whereas had I still been yodeling, I would still have been a Jimmie Rodgers *imitator* instead of getting a style of my own.'

With his new outlook and his new voice—you have only to listen to the first Decca release to hear the difference, and it is not difficult to understand why Tubb should feel that he did his best singing prior to being accepted by the public—he had a good-sized hit right off the bat with 'I'll Get Along Somehow.' There were five more releases after that, all employing the same patented Jimmie Rodgers-style two-guitar accompaniment, none really making much of a splash. Then in July 1941 he wrote a song of which he was particularly proud. He cut it in August in Bunny Briggs's tiny studio in Dallas, and it was released in September. Ironically he was without the services of Jimmie Short, his regular guitarist and the man on whom the whole Troubadour style—with its succession of inventive, jazz-influenced lead guitarists, from Short to Billy Byrd to Leon Rhodes—would be based. As a result the accompaniment had to be learned note by laborious note by KGKO studio guitarist Fay Smith, a good reading musician but one who was incapable of even the most rudimentary improvisation. A&R man Dave Kapp ('The producer's main job in those days,' says Ernest, 'was to decide if a take was good enough to keep') was not particularly impressed with the record, but Ernest thought it was the best thing he had ever done. 'I begged him to release the record. "Just do this one thing for me, and if I'm wrong I'll never ask for anything again."' Against his better judgment, Ernest says, Kapp put the record out. It was, of course, 'Walking the Floor Over You.'

The Opry on tour, 1930s. Courtesy of Douglas B. Green.

Broadcasting over WSM. Courtesy of Douglas B. Green.

On the strength of that one success – the record sold over 400,000 copies in the first year alone, despite wartime shellac rationing – Ernest went to Hollywood and made the first of several westerns with Charles Starrett. The experience still rankles, both 'because it was such a racket out there' and because of what he saw as the filmmakers' complete lack of concern for authenticity. 'I was supposed to be a foreman on the ranch in this picture. It was all new to me. I didn't know a thing about it. But they had me wearing clothes that just weren't natural, they weren't right. On the hat, I told them, "Ernest Tubb always wears a good Stetson hat." Then they tried to get me to sing some song Autry had recorded four or five years before – it was one of those old cowboy songs like Jules Verne Allen used to sing. I told them, "I used to sing 'em, but those kind of songs are dead. Why bring me out here in the first place, if it wasn't to sing 'Walking the Floor Over You'? That's the reason you brought me out here, and that's what my fans are going to expect."'

With his newfound success he was now something more than a local attraction. He was still broadcasting on KGKO in Fort Worth, he was still the Gold Chain Troubadour singing from a platform on top of a brand-new 1941 Plymouth, but on the weekends he was being booked further and further afield. An old friend, Happy Hal Burns ('I knew him,' says Ernest, 'when he was singing in a beer joint in San Antonio. He was never a great singer, but he was a good mixer'), had gone into the booking business with the resourceful Oscar Davis, who got into country music when an ice show he was promoting went broke in Atlanta. Davis booked Tubb into a show in Shreveport for $50, then paid him $75 plus plane fare to fly into Birmingham for a concert that Roy Acuff was headlining. That was where Tubb met Joe Frank, who

31

Family portrait. Courtesy of the Country
Music Foundation Library and Media Center,
Nashville, Tennessee.

had previously managed Gene Autry, had brought Roy Acuff to the Opry,
and was still associated with his then son-in-law Pee Wee King, author of
'The Tennessee Waltz.' Having persuaded Ernest to stay over, Frank booked
him into Gadsden, Alabama, and Chattanooga at $100 and $150 apiece. The
next step was a guest shot on the Opry; Ernest got three encores when he
sang 'Walking the Floor Over You.' His guest shot turned into a four-week
audition; Frank became his manager on the basis of a handshake; and in
January of 1943 he joined the Opry as a regular member, moving his family
to Nashville later that year.

   'When I got to Nashville, I needed a band to make personals. My producer
Dave Kapp wanted to keep me like I was, with just the two guitars. His
attitude was, why change a formula that's so successful?' Ernest did change
it, though; he never hesitated to move ahead with the times. Having added
amplification two years earlier when he sent guitarist Jimmie Short a pickup

with instructions to learn how to use it, he now created a band ('You needed the drums for dancing') and a musical trademark that enabled him to compete with the raucous good times of the barrooms and dance halls in which he played. That was the real start of his fulltime professional career, a career which has proceeded at a steady unhurried pace to this day. He has never forgotten how Mrs. Jimmie Rodgers helped him, though, nor has he forgotten the struggle along the way. 'It was really tough. I mean, you just had to want it so bad,' he will say in a surprising burst of emotion. 'It has to be the only thing for you—the one thing in your life.'

TWO GIANT BUSES idle outside the Clarksville, Indiana, high school gym. Their fumes choke the parking lot, but it is chilly for April, there are no dressing rooms inside, and hardly enough energy or curiosity among the musicians to get off the bus to watch someone else perform. By four in the afternoon Ernest has already been on and off stage. He stayed up most of the night reading and playing cards and was awakened only minutes before going on for the first show. 'I wish they had woken me up earlier,' he grumbles as he grabs for his Stetson and his guitar case and confesses to the audience that he hasn't had a chance to see the acts that have gone on already because to tell the truth he was sleeping till just a few minutes ago in the bus, but he's sure that they were good, so let's give them a big hand. Then he goes ahead and does his show and afterwards retires to the bus once again until driver Hoot Borden lets him know that Del Reeves (known at one time, complimentarily, as the Dean Martin of country music) has finished up and it is time to go back and autograph albums, programs, souvenirs, meet the fans who file up to the stage one by one.

Between shows Ernest rests. The Troubadours, ranging in age from twenty-five to forty, drift in and out, mix with members of Del's band, go out for pizza, and exchange stories of the road. They have a real affection for Ernest, who they say 'makes the rules but is always the first to break them,' explain their kangaroo court with its elaborate system of fines (so much for drinking within two hours of a show, so much for drinking in public afterwards), and seem genuinely interested in the story of the early years. Like other Troubadours before them they are looking for the break and the opportunity to go out on their own, but there is little barrier of age or formality to separate them from the man they will occasionally, if circumspectly, refer to as Wolfman Ernie. In the front section of the bus where they sleep there is a sign that says 'Slave Quarters,' and in the back compartment it says 'Establishment: Do Not Disturb . . . Texas Ernest.' That's about as close as you get to class distinction, though, that and the familiar business aphorism, 'The boss isn't always right, but he's always the boss.'

33

One of the Troubadours asks Ernest if he has had a chance to listen to the tape a hometown friend of his has sent to him. 'You better tell him to keep his job,' says Ernest with a reluctance that seems almost pained. 'You know it's not really bad, it just ain't nothing special. At least that's the way it sounds to me. It just ain't special.' Another Troubadour comes back to say that they will be closing the second show, not going on stage until at least nine-thirty after Del has finished. Ernest, who wants to get rolling and has already vowed that he isn't going to close, just nods and leans back in his seat. There's about four and a half hours to kill.

'To me singers are stylists,' Ernest says. 'You don't have to be a great singer or have a fine voice. I've heard a lot of fine singers who couldn't draw fifteen people, because what they were singing just had no feeling in it. I'm not saying I'm a good singer, but I sing like I feel, I think you can tell the feeling is there. Some of this music today is fine in its way, but it's just too complicated. I want my music to be simple enough, so that the boy out there on the farm can learn it and practice it and try to play it.'

It has gotten dark outside, and the second sellout show is getting under-way. The Troubadours drift back one by one, joke with the boss, and suggest what a good spoof it would be if Ernest appeared in the middle of Del Reeves's Ernest Tubb imitation. Ernest demurs at first but then seems taken with the joke himself, and we sit in the bus waiting for Hoot Borden's thirteen-year-old son, Jerry, to let us know when Del has reached that part of his act. At last Jerry appears, Ernest draws himself up, and ambles stiff-legged up the cement walk. As he enters the gymnasium, flanked by a band member on either side, he removes the trademark Stetson, cradling it carefully at his side.

From the stage wings we can see the audience on folding chairs set up on the basketball floor and bleacher seats. It is, like the Opry, a family show, with three generations nodding in comfortable recognition to the familiar music. As Del Reeves embarks on the first of his various imitations, there seems some question whether he will include Ernest, but the Troubadours egg him on. 'Is he on the bus?' Reeves asks of head Troubadour Wayne Hammond. Wayne nods vigorously. 'Y'all sure he's on the bus?' The Troubadours' heads all bob up and down. Just as Reeves launches into his Ernest Tubb medley, Ernest clamps his hat on his head and strides out onto the stage. A great roar of recognition goes up, and Ernest doffs the hat to acknowledge the laughter and applause. Reeves looks crestfallen, though for all I know they have been through this charade many times before. 'But you said he was on the bus,' he pleads helplessly with assorted Troubadours, who are doubled over with laughter. 'WE LIED,' comes the reply. Ernest shakes hands with Del, waves to the crowd, and once back in the bus recalls with amusement his first advice to Del Reeves to restore the Franklin Delano Roosevelt portion of his name. 'That's where you fucked up, son,' he told Reeves. 'He was the greatest president we ever had.'

At last at 9:50 Tubb reappears on stage. In the wings he whispers for the name of the local DJ and then thanks him graciously for his introduction. The show that he puts on is virtually identical to the first show – the same familiar standards, the inevitable Jimmie Rodgers selection, even the country-boy jokes with the Troubadours fall in the same places – and if it were not for the evident sincerity of his manner it might almost seem perfunctory. The Troubadours themselves are competent but not equal to legendary bands of old. There are no new songs, there are no new compositions ('Oh sure, you lose enthusiasm on a song like "Walking the Floor Over You" that you've been singing every night for thirty-five years. But I tell the boys, "I know we all get tired of them, but this is what the people want"'), and he goes off after about forty-five minutes, leaving the audience, as an old vaudevillian taught him in 1943, 'wanting one more piece of pie.'

Afterwards he sits on a folding chair at the front of the stage, signing autographs, leaning over to catch a heartfelt greeting, being proudly presented to children and grandchildren. The talk is mostly of the past, of World War II or the show that Ernest did twenty-five years ago in Korea, or the Texas

Taking care of business. J. CLARK THOMAS

35

dance halls he played when husband and wife first met. Indeed, so strong is the bond between audience and performer, the reality which they share is so intertwined, that after Ernest wrote 'Our Baby's Book' about the death in infancy of his second son, Rodger Dale, he could scarcely play a dance for years without being introduced to at least one Rodger Dale, named in his son's honor. 'I still average about one a week, and you know something? They didn't have any way of knowing it was a true story, I didn't announce it or anything. But they could tell it was true because the feeling was there. It's the only hundred percent real song I've ever written.' It is the song, needless to say, of which he is proudest, the one song above all which bears out his contention that there is nothing frivolous about his music. 'Country music,' he insists, 'is music with a meaning,' a real meaning and a literal truth which sets it apart from every other music but the blues.

The line grows smaller, the auditorium slowly empties out and Del Reeves's bus is long since gone, but Ernest stays patiently, as his publicity says that he does, until the last autograph is signed. There are some stars, Hoot Borden says enviously, who would allow him to sell ahead of their signature; he knows of many performers who don't even sign every item that is sold; but Ernest won't permit him to get even one or two ahead, and as a result some fans who get tired of waiting in line just go off without buying anything. Ernest loses a lot of business that way, Hoot grumbles, as he and his son pack up albums, calendars, and other souvenirs.

Ernest meanwhile sits slumped in the chair. His face is lined and weary, and for a moment all the good cheer seems to have drained out of it. There is no question that the road has taken its toll, but Ernest Tubb is a survivor. Hank Williams is long dead, Billy Byrd, his most celebrated guitarist, has recently been working at Shakey's Pizza Parlor, alcohol has cut down many a good man, but Ernest looks as if he will just keep on, staying out on the road as long as there is anyone who wants to listen. He rouses himself at last and makes his way back to the bus, where he says his last courteous good nights.

Then the bus roars off, and as I watch it I am reminded of Jack Greene's description of going out on his own after the Top 10 success of two records he cut while still a Troubadour. 'Ernest gave me the best advice I ever had. Of course he probably don't know it, but he told me, "Son, I've lived through the Beatles, I've lived through Fats Domino, Elvis, and all the rest. Son, you just stay what you are, hang on with it, and if it's not your time now, it'll come your time again. So, you just go out there and try to make your money, and if it don't work out, well, you can always come back and be a Troubadour."'

HANK
SNOW

Still Movin' On

IT IS 1978, and Rainbow Ranch is in the Nashville suburbs now, out I-65, past the tract housing and the brick apartment buildings, in a neighborhood with churches seemingly on every corner. The white wrought-iron arch with a chain-link security gate proclaims the name in bright-colored letters, but inside the gate you see no expanse, only a modest red-brick ranch house with red and white awnings, a two-car garage with antlers mounted above the doors, and a blue Flexible bus with yellow wheels gathering dust in the yard.

Inside, Hank Snow, once Canada's Yodeling Ranger and then — when his voice deepened and he could no longer emulate his idol, Jimmie Rodgers — just the Singing Ranger, is sitting behind a desk covered with knickknacks and mementos (curios, dog figurines, wooden hillbilly sculptures, a crystal ball, a miniature guitar, a model train, and oddly enough an early picture of Elvis, Scotty, and Bill) dispensing coffee and hospitality and well-considered statements about his future, which will be largely devoted to the Hank Snow Fund for the Prevention of Child Abuse and Neglect in America, and his past, which covers most of the recent history of country music. He is courteous, polite, precise in his responses, and yet you get an unmistakable impression of the fierce combativeness which must have carried him through a loveless childhood and a thoroughly improbable career, in which, battling against all odds, including background, lack of stature ('I've always had a complex about my heighth'), and the simple fact of being a Canadian provincial in a Texan's world, he emerged finally as one of the great country music stars of the fifties. You sense, too, the incongruity that was evident at the Opry the night before, where despite twenty-eight years of stardom he seemed somehow detached, pensive, his movements oddly mechanical, his screaming rhinestone-studded suits in sharp contrast to his meticulous musicianship, the driving rhythms of his music seemingly at odds with his neat gray toupee, steely-eyed gaze, and homely doughlike face, the self-assured, almost cocky stage presence scarcely suiting a personality which Hank Snow himself describes as 'reserved, very reserved.' He prides himself clearly on his organization and efficiency and

37

perseverance ('I always worked very hard at my business. Some of 'em don't') and is apologetic for not being able to show off more of his collection of memorabilia—inlaid wallets, country comedian Rod Brasfield's boots, a Jimmie Rodgers guitar, his mother's own guitar, his first royalty statement—which has been dismantled for spring cleaning.

'That bio did help you, didn't it, Peter?' he says in response to one of my questions. 'Cause you didn't know all these things you're asking me.' I acknowledge that I didn't and that the biography was indeed useful, a 12,000-word official summary of the life of Hank Snow, written in the third person most of the time, but clearly bearing the imprint of the artist's personal authorship. It is a curious document, a mixture of humility, hard-won lessons learned, and understandable pride, that meticulously records not only the facts but the flavor of a life spent pursuing goals that have today been fulfilled storybook-fashion, '1000 times over.'

Clarence Eugene Snow was born on May 9, 1914 in a small town in Eastern Canada called Liverpool in the province of Nova Scotia. He lived with his parents and three sisters and went to school there until he was eight years old. At the age of 8 Hank became the victim of a broken home, two of his sisters were sent to an orphanage and the third and oldest sister went to work in a shoe factory. Hank was more or less the fortunate one and went to live with his grandparents, but the increasing longing for his beloved mother caused Hank to run away from his grand-

Hank with memorabilia. MARSHALL FALLWELL

parents and go live with his Mother who at this time was employed as a housekeeper in Liverpool.

Shortly after this move, Hanks Mother re-married, and with his Mother, Hank moved to a little fishing village 75 miles away known as Lunenberg, but Hank soon found out he was not very popular with his Stepfather and to keep peace in the family and at the age of 12 frail little Hank made his first trip to sea as a cabin boy.

He refers to these years often. They are the basis for his commitment to the child-abuse crusade ('I came from a broken home myself with a stepfather who was very very cruel. So I've been down that road before') and to the work ethic that has shaped his whole life. It was his mother who served not only as his model ('My mother was completely organized all the time') but who started him in music as well. 'My mother years ago, I guess even before I was born, my mother was a piano player. She used to play for the silent pictures, you see. She was very talented.' She was a Vernon Dalhart fan, too (Dalhart, who recorded under a multiplicity of names, was country music's first recording star in 1924), and one day sent away for a mail-order guitar and a fifty-two-lesson course on how to play it. 'That was for her, but it came in handy for me, too.' Was the music an escape, then? 'No, my escape from all the turmoil and poverty of that particular time was going to sea. That was my escape at that time. Which took care of about four years of it.'

It was at the end of those four years, when he was sixteen years old, that he heard the song, and the singer, that would change his life.

Hank was practicing with the guitar when his Mother came home one day with a new record but the singer was not Vernon Dalhart. It was a New American singer and the label on that Victor record told him that the singer's name was Jimmie Rodgers. When Hank put that record on and started it playing and first heard Jimmie Rodgers singing 'MOON-LIGHT AND SKIES', he knew that nothing short of a singing career would ever please him.

That seems to have been the case. Like Ernest Tubb nearly a continent away Hank Snow decided not only to try to sing like Jimmie Rodgers (each practiced his yodel, despite the protests of family and friends), but to try to be as 'near like Jimmie Rodgers as he could possibly be.' It's difficult to credit the impact that Rodgers had on a whole generation of farm boys and workingmen; today it seems virtually unimaginable to take statements like Snow's or Ernest Tubb's at face value. And yet the isolation that marked the growing up of boys like Ernest Tubb and Hank Snow may be equally unimaginable today. In any case so strong was the admiration of both men for Rodgers that they would begin to correspond in the early forties, solely

Jimmie Rodgers Memorial Day, Meridian, Mississippi, mid 1950s.
Mrs. Jimmie Rodgers, Ernest Tubb, Hank Snow, Dizzy Dean.
Courtesy of Les Leverett.

on the basis of this shared passion. Eventually it was Ernest who introduced Hank to the Grand Ole Opry in 1950, just three years before they originated the annual Jimmie Rodgers' Memorial Day celebration in Rodgers's native Meridian, Mississippi. It was, Hank says without blinking an eye, 'a dream that came true,' and indeed it must have been a dream that could scarcely be envisioned by a boy growing up poor in Lunenberg and Halifax, Nova Scotia, working at fish plants, on boats, in the woods, as a newsboy, delivery boy, lobsterman, Fuller Brush salesman, stevedore, all in pursuit of an ambition that was palpably beyond his grasp (Wilf Carter — Montana Slim — was the *entire* Canadian country recording industry at the time).

Within a few years of discovering his calling, Hank Snow had, improbably enough, achieved a certain degree of success within Canada, first landing a radio show on CHNS in Halifax (for which initially he was paid nothing), then gaining a sponsor and a national hookup, and eventually, in 1936, on the strength of his own self-promotion coming up with a recording contract with RCA's Canadian division. He was signed by a man named Hugh Joseph and recorded two sides he had written, 'Lonesome Blue Yodel' and 'Prisoned Cowboy,' as Hank, the Yodeling Ranger. 'The one was a Jimmie Rodgers type thing, it was a blues, actually you'd think it was one of Jimmie's songs, it was written so close. Mr. Joseph was awfully good to me for all the years I recorded in Canada. My first session I did in an old church in Montreal that wasn't being used any more—see, RCA Victor at the time was remodeling their studios or something—I always thought that brought me some luck.'

The record nonetheless was not much of a hit ('My first royalty statement was two dollars and something, $2.96'), and Hank continued making personal appearances, although 'my roadwork wasn't that great. When I did the theaters, I just did a one-man act, entertaining between the movies, singing the same type of songs—story songs, a variety of songs, a lot of Jimmie Rodgers songs—that I would do today. No, I never did like to sing my own in Canada, I don't really know why.' When he got married in 1936 his wife, Min, was working as a chocolate dipper at six dollars a week, and despite the recording contract and Hank's Canadian fame their son, Jimmie Rodgers Snow, was born in the charity ward of a Salvation Army hospital. He played his first engagement at the Gaiety Theater in Halifax, he told journalist Jo Durden-Smith, 'for three dollars a day, three performances, which was a dollar each. My wife made me a little neckerchief in yellow and red, a little bandana. Took a pair of black dungarees and she sewed a white stripe of cotton up each side. And this is what I did my first performance in the theater with.'

He recalls the details of this period with little nostalgia and a good deal of astringency. 'My wife used to act as my advance man. She'd go ahead and put up the posters and arrange for the little halls that we'd play in and then join up with us and sell tickets at the door. We'd go in beforehand and line up probably ten or twelve shows in an area. You'd get those little old school-houses and halls for three and four dollars a night, charge fifteen cents admission—that was big money then. One of our top crowds would have been, oh, five hundred; we figured we were really setting the woods on fire then. Play an hour and half, two hours, just my own little group. We'd put on a show first, then we had a dance after the show. In most places. We did a lot of different songs for the dance, blues numbers and "Blueberry Hill" and things like that were big then. In my travels now, you know, I talk to a lot of the younger generation, and they've never heard of any of these songs. And it is so funny to me. Because I don't know, I expect that even though you're twenty-five years old, you ought to know everything that I know.'

No matter how big he became in Canada, though, he always had the U.S. on his mind. 'Always. I just liked the sound—America. And any movie, if I ever heard tell of a movie that showed anything. Texas was always big in my mind. Because I wrote a lot of songs about Texas, you know, I'd read about these places, seen them in the movies.'

His first trip to America, in 1944, was not to Texas but to Philadelphia, where a fan of his, Jack Howard, had lined up two weeks' worth of personal appearances. He returned to the States later that year and then off and on until finally in 1946 he landed a radio program on Wheeling, West Virginia's WWVA, where he acquired not only a considerable reputation but also a trick horse, Shawnee, who was to be part of his act for the next twenty years. 'Well, that was through Big Slim. Big Slim was a real authentic cowboy, who I had been following on the radio, because we could get that up in Canada. He had a beautiful trained horse by the name of Golden Flash, he did a whip act, and he was a good country singer. It was through him I got the program, and he learned me to trick ride, too. It wasn't easy.' No, probably not, but Hank had undoubtedly done a good deal of riding in his youth? He shakes his head. Well, how did he get the idea—'I was very determined. I don't stop at nothing. And I think that's the way you get it done. By not giving up. Don't give up.'

It was at this point, perhaps because of Shawnee, perhaps because of his long-time fascination with western movies, that Hank, the Singing Ranger, like Ernest Tubb before him, found himself in Hollywood, a career decision which he still seems to view with a mixture of perplexity and disgust. 'Here I am in Hollywood, the film capital of the world, completely unknown, not even a record released, looking for work, and with the competition as great as it was. So it was really a stupid move, but at the same time I wouldn't trade the experience. Of course,' he adds with the wisdom born of hindsight, 'the movies were never in my thoughts very much. I always felt I wasn't the type of person for the movies. I wasn't the size. I certainly don't think I'm the most handsome person in the world.' Nonetheless he went out to Hollywood not once but twice, managing to lose $13,000 in the process and, after a decade of hard work, to place himself in a position that threatened his whole professional career.

Completely disgusted and discouraged he let his band go. The ole Hollywood 'shell game' had left him broker but wiser about 'city slickers' shake downs. There was only one place in the United States he wanted to try before throwing up his hands and returning to Canada. He had a few friends in Texas, so he started off for Dallas with the Hollywood loan company breathing down his back. When he drove into Dallas in the fall of 1948, he had exactly $11.00 and no job. Besides, as always, he had his wife and son with him.

It was in Texas, of course, that he finally met Ernest Tubb, the Texas Troubadour, with whom he had been corresponding for most of the decade. He still didn't have an American recording contract, although 'I had records released in practically every country in the world. But Mr. Joseph, who started me in Canada in '36, was a very close friend of Steve Sholes, who was a big wheel in New York. He kept after him and after him, it took a long time to convince Steve, and before Steve it was Frank Walker, and he couldn't see it at all, I never made any headway with him. What they would tell me, and which I found ridiculous, they said, well first before we can release any records you got to do some personal appearances and get around and get known. Well, hell, that's what I wanted records for, was to get known. So I think it was just a brush-off.' It was only in fact after a Texas fan, Bea Terry, had persuaded DJ Fred Edwards to play Hank's latest Canadian release, and after 'Brand on My Heart' had held the number one position for sixteen weeks on KRLD's hit parade *without* American release or distribution, that RCA was finally persuaded to record Hank Snow in this country.

'The first recording session was arranged in Chicago, in which I turned out one song that became very good. I did not like the song, and I still do not like it, even though it's one of the biggest requested things that I do. I don't think I could give you any reason, but I guess it was on the strength of that record that they decided to continue to record me.' The song, 'Marriage Vow,' was released in December of 1949, and on January 7, 1950, largely through the efforts of Ernest Tubb ('He kept pestering those people, he'd drag my records from his record store, take 'em under his arm, take 'em up there and play 'em, until he finally convinced them'), Hank Snow at last appeared on the Grand Ole Opry.

Early Opry audience, Dixie Tabernacle, Nashville, ca. 1936.
Courtesy of Douglas B. Green.

Left: Hank the Yodelling Ranger, late 1930s. Courtesy of the Country Music Foundation Library and Media Center, Nashville, Tennessee. *Right: Elvis and Hank Snow.* Courtesy of John and Shelby Singleton.

Even then, it seemed, his future was scarcely assured. 'I was very skeptical of myself, and I didn't have really a lot of confidence. Because I was competing with too many established artists at the time. I wasn't looking for big things, really, and I wouldn't have lasted if it hadn't been for "Movin' On." Because Harry Stone [long-time station manager at WSM and thus, in effect, head of the Opry] was about to let me go, yeah, they was getting ready to leave me go, because actually then you had to have a hit record even to get to the Opry, so I was very fortunate. If it hadn't been for "Movin' On," though, I doubt that I would have survived.

'I think "Movin' On" was such a strong song—and I don't mean that through a braggy sense, I'm just telling you like it is—I think "Movin' On" was so strong that I think, not just any other artist, but certain other artists could have recorded that song and had the same luck I did. In other words, I don't think it was the artist, it was the song.' 'I'm Movin' On' was, ironically, a song Steve Sholes had turned down in Chicago, 'the song that I had the most faith in,' so much faith that when he recorded again in Nashville he snuck it past Sholes without the producer even recognizing it. Fittingly it was a train song, 'inspired by Jimmie Rodgers, although I didn't copy anything from anybody or any song, the whole song is original, melody and all.' With its success (it quickly went to the top of the charts and stayed there for nearly a year), and the subsequent success of 'Golden Rocket' and 'Rhumba

Boogie,' Hank Snow became the number one artist in the country and assured himself of a place in hillbilly heaven.

HANK SNOW is still on the Opry, probably even more of a fixture today than he was at the height of his popularity twenty-five years ago. Because he no longer tours, and does no more than fifteen outside dates a year, he is on the Opry every week, presiding over his segment, like contemporaries Roy Acuff and Bill Monroe, with an almost magisterial calm. The Opry has changed, though. What was once a hot-blooded occasion for open competition has become mummified and formal. 'The Opry has lost a lot of strength talentwise,' he concedes glumly. 'You can't expect artists like Faron Young, Ray Price, well, you name it, to come on and do a guest spot for scale. Hank Williams, Ernest, Red Foley, Webb Pierce, you know, you can just name a string, all of us were really going strong, when I first started. Well, you don't have that today, and you're not gonna have it, unless they start paying people some money.' Once Hank Snow introduced a nineteen-year-old Elvis Presley, whom he booked in partnership with Colonel Parker, for his first and only Opry appearance. (*Hank very seldom mentions the fact that he was very instrumental in giving this great star his big break to stardom, it all happened like this,* begins the biographical section on Elvis and the Colonel which promises that: *There is some very interesting information that I as the writer, hold confidently between Hank and I, that I would dearly love to put in print in regards to Colonel Tom Parker, Elvis, and Hank, but I do not dare print it at this time, but I feel very confident this particular information will be exposed to the international public at the right time.*) Today, instead of Elvis, it is David Houston who appears on Hank's Opry segment, doing a tired reprise of 'Almost Persuaded.'

Nashville, too, has changed. At one time it had a kind of small-town atmosphere in which 'anyone could come into this city, and if they had any talent at all—I mean, anybody can write a hit song, not just anybody, but it could come from anywhere. One of the big songs I recorded, "That's When He Dropped the World in My Hands," was written by a taxi driver. Well, it's probably still that way in a way, but it's more of a closed circuit situation, it was a lot more flexible when I got here.'

For Hank Snow, of course, the hard times are long gone, the years of taking his wife and son on the road, the drinking, the struggling, the need to slap every stranger on the back because that stranger was an important part of his 'public.' 'I think I played every honky tonk and beer joint in this country. Well, probably I'm stretching it a little bit when I say every one, but I've played with no dressing room, dirt floors, no stage, standing on the dance hall floor, you name it. And any time I played the clubs back then, you had to drink with these people. I was never a habitual drunkard, or I thankfully didn't turn out to be an alcoholic, but you had to to a certain amount, to be sociable with them you'd go to their table and have a drink with them. I quit alcohol completely almost nine years ago, the thirty-first of March, 1970. In order to go back to playing the nightclubs, or play the bases in Europe, there's no way you could do it without socializing with drinking. And I wouldn't want to go that route no more.'

And the music, it almost goes without saying, has seen alterations. It's not just the pervasive countrypolitan sound or the crossover hit that everyone in Nashville is looking for; even Hank Snow's musical signature has of necessity changed. Not so much in its elements—there's still the same unmistakable clothespin-on-the-nose quality to the voice, there is the same tasty flatpicking on almost every one of the records—as in the impact of the music itself.

It may be difficult for anyone who grew up in the wake of rock 'n' roll to imagine just how influential the Hank Snow style really was (as difficult perhaps as it is for a post-Depression generation to imagine the personal impact of Jimmie Rodgers). Nonetheless it was Snow's bright, imaginative lyrics (who can forget Madame Lasonga teaching the conga, and there was even a pre-rockabilly honeymoon in outer space), the hard-driving rhythms of fiddle and steel, the blues colorations of the guitar, even the plummy vocal tones of 'I Don't Hurt Any More,' which marked a whole generation's passage into musical maturity. This was the music that Elvis Presley was listening to as he was growing up, this is the music that everyone from Ray Charles to Chuck Berry and Carl Perkins, with their own tongue-twisting lyrics and dance-reference tunes, pressed in the pages of his musical memory book.

Without any question the distinctive styling is still there. On a 1977 album in fact it came through better than it had in years, with a good selection of bluesy material, lots of sharp clean picking, that comfortable foggy baritone, and relatively uncluttered arrangements. The difference, however, was summed up in the album title, which proclaimed survival as much as it did sustained creativity: *#104—Still Movin' On.* In the once-stable world of country music this kind of constancy would have merited great tribute; as it is, it marks Hank Snow, like Ernest Tubb, as an almost discomfiting reminder of a past that Music Row would just as soon forget.

Hank Snow doesn't really fit into the Disneyworld atmosphere of the new Nashville. He seems indifferent, however, to his reputation for being standoffish. 'I am a loner, that is so right. They have got tired of sending me invitations in this city, because they know better. I'm not conceited. I'm not stuck-up. I'm just reserved and actually a loner. I've been on my own since I was twelve. I had nobody. It was very difficult. What I went through during my early years—which a lot of people have gone through, it's just my story, you can find a million stories like that—I always said it was the greatest education, you couldn't get an education like that in no college, there's no way. It prepared me and taught me to be thrifty, it taught me to be business-minded, and it taught me to continue with being on top of everything, to be completely organized, the same as now. So I think it was a great education, and I became well disciplined through all of this.'

How does this square, though, with the celebrated panache of his stage presence, with getting up on stage at all in fact?

'When you walk out on stage, you go into a completely different world. You forget all about anything else. You are in a different world. Costumes is part of it, because, as you know, flash is part of your act. Look at Liberace. I think he's got the most colorful, beautiful show I've ever seen. Flash is fifty percent of it.'

The Hank Snow story is not one of easy success, fame did not grasp him to her bosom overnight, the past was long and disheartening, and strewn with many obstacles, but not once did he falter nor did he let anything steer him from his course. Yes, Hank has been touched by the

Rainbow Ranch. LEONARD KAMSLER

sometimes harsh, sometimes gentle hand of fame, but thru it all he has remained the same young fellow who unloaded a ship load of salt to buy his first guitar, and even now when he steps out on stage to greet the roar of applause that resounds around him, you know that he still remembers the cold wet and fearful nights of the days at sea. You know, too, when listening to the songs that pour from his heart and soul, that he remembers the helping hand of the fans the world over that have reached out to lift him up to that spot in the sun from which has flown the almost regal banner of Hank Snow — The Singing Ranger — Yes, you know he remembers and you can almost hear the prayer of thanks that echoes constantly in his heart and when his gentle voice reaches out to you at the close of his programmes — 'and for now, good luck, good health, and may the good Lord always be proud of ya,' you feel the surge of wistfulness in the haunting memories that are his — you realize that here is the same young fellow who started out with nothing but persistence, a golden voice and a deep, abiding faith in the great Almighty. This, friends, ends the Hank Snow story, but the golden arrow pointing up the mountains and thru the valleys of the future, signals toward even greater heights of success for the courageous little former Canadian and painted on the arrow in glowing letters is written — Hank Snow is still movin' on and may the Good Lord always be proud of him.

As I drive back into Nashville, I see what has become a familiar sight, two modern cowboys on the highway, one wearing a hat, each carrying a guitar, thumbs stuck out, squinting into the sun and the Nashville skyline. I think immediately of Hank Snow, but they're probably thinking of Kris Kristofferson, if they're thinking of the past at all. To them the future looks bright ahead. To Hank Snow, 'The old greats will never die. They've made their mark on civilization.'

DeFORD
BAILEY

Pan-American Blues

DOWNSTAIRS in the lobby of the public housing project, a senior citizen's high-rise less than a mile from Nashville's Music Row, the old men are watching television, all dressed up for a Saturday night in suitcoats and ties. One or two nod politely at us as we enter the elevator; the decorous murmur of conversation barely disturbs the low drone of the TV. We are met at the apartment door by a tiny, hunched-over, suspicious-looking man, wearing a carefully knotted black tie, button-up sweater, and highly polished black shoes. When he sees that it is singer James Talley and Talley's little boy, along with a friend, he flings the door open, his face relaxing in a wide grin. Inside the tiny apartment it must be eighty-five degrees, and the room is filled with pictures of trains, models of trains, a red megaphone, a child's plastic locomotive, and framed clippings and publicity shots on the wall. Talley, who has known the older man for several years—ever since Talley arrived in Nashville in 1968 and went to work as a social worker for the city—offers up a new set of guitar strings. The present is accepted with an air of almost courtly deference, as DeFord Bailey fumbles with the buttons of his newly acquired tape recorder; he is anxious to play us a song he has just recorded on harmonica the night before.

DeFord Bailey is not exactly a household name. A contemporary of Roy Acuff and Sam and Kirk McGee, and a musical contemporary of that Tennessee cutup, Uncle Dave Macon (known as the Dixie Dewdrop and thought by some to have *invented* the Grand Ole Opry), Bailey was introduced to the Opry when it was still called the WSM Barn Dance in 1925 and was quickly dubbed the Harmonica Wizard by MC George Hay, the Solemn Ol' Judge, who put the Opry on the map. In fact it was DeFord's harmonica playing that inspired the Opry's change of name. DeFord's 'Pan-American Blues' led off the broadcast on the night of December 10, 1927, contrasting sharply with a 'serious' modern piece just aired on the NBC Music Appreciation Hour that was meant to convey the sense of an onrushing locomotive. There was, sniffed NBC conductor Walter Damrosch at the conclusion of the network broadcast, 'no

The Solemn Ol' Judge, George D. Hay, with Alcyone Bate Beasley on his left and Uncle Dave Macon on his right, cutting the Opry's twentieth-birthday cake, 1945. Courtesy of Douglas B. Green and WSM Archives.

place in the classics for realism.' The Solemn Ol' Judge, not to be outdone, introduced DeFord's train blues, and the Barn Dance itself, as 'nothing but realism, down to earth for the earthy,' and then came up with the inspired tag: 'For the past hour we have been listening to the music taken largely from the Grand Opera, but from now on we will present the Grand Ole Opry.'

In the early days, according to Opry historian Charles Wolfe, 'It wasn't at all uncommon for DeFord to appear for two or even three sets in a single Saturday-night show.' In the thirties, when touring became popular, DeFord went out with little-known musicians like Roy Acuff and Bill Monroe and, according to Acuff, it was DeFord's reputation that attracted the crowd. The only thing that set DeFord Bailey apart from other early Opry stars was that DeFord Bailey was black.

DeFord Bailey was born in 1899 outside of Rome (not far from Carthage) in Smith County, Tennessee, about fifty miles east of Nashville. 'I was sickly all my life,' he says, 'that's why I never growed.' And indeed a case of infantile paralysis at three left him stunted (he attained a full height of four feet ten inches as an adult), with a slight limp and a deformed back. During the year he was forced to stay in bed with the illness, he learned to play harmonica, and mandolin, too, which was not surprising, really, since music was all around him. 'Everyone in my family played music,' he told blues researcher Bengt Olsson. 'My granddaddy was the best fiddle player in Smith County— played "Old Joe Clark," "Lost John," all them *way-back* pieces.' His father and his uncle, too, played the same kind of reels and breakdowns common to musicians, black and white, of that generation, but, DeFord says, his music didn't come from them, because 'It's a gift, can't nobody teach you.' While he was still a boy, his family moved first to Newsom's Station and then to Thompson's Station on the Tennessee Central Line. At Newsom's Station he regularly passed under a train trestle on his way to school and, he has told his friend and protector, David Morton, who works for the Nashville Housing Authority, 'I would get up under it, put my hands over my eyes, listen to the sound, and then play that sound all the way to school.' He listened to sounds, it was sounds that were always on his mind; hens, foxes, hounds, turkeys were the subjects of his imitation as well as trains. Most of all, he wanted to get the train sound right and eventually came close enough so that a railroad engineer once came up to the WSM studios to compliment DeFord on his accuracy as well as to correct his whistle pattern for crossings.

DeFord by his own account was a dreamy gentle child, just as he is today a dreamy gentle man, lost in a world of bright-eyed reverie and a sense of his own importance which places him squarely in the center of a self-contained universe. He seems to have been unusually close to his family, and perhaps they sheltered him because of his illness. 'I remember the last pair of shoes my daddy ever bought me,' he recalls. 'When I was twenty-two years old. He told me to sweep up, we was sweeping out porches, y'see, but I got to dreaming, started gabbing with the ladies, I never did sweep out no more. But he bought 'em for me anyway, though, sho' did. Well, see, I'm like a child, been taken care of all my life, did yard work for a white family, mowed the lawn and such kind of work, and they just took care of me, oh it must have been close to fifteen years.' The family was the Watson family in Thompson's Station, and when they moved to Nashville in 1918 DeFord moved up there with them.

There are a number of conflicting accounts as to how he was discovered. According to what he told Bengt Olsson, he formed a brief partnership with Bob Lee, 'a crippled, diminutive harmonica player,' writes Olsson, 'who was almost a mirror image of DeFord. "Everyone called him Tip. We was real close. He was as good as I was. Sometimes we'd ride all around Nashville on a wagon—we'd have two chairs on the platform—and play duets on our harps for the people."' By the time he ran into the Solemn Ol' Judge, though, he had already been performing on radio station WDAD (which went on the air just a few weeks before the Opry's WSM in the fall of 1925) and had taken part in a 'French Harp contest' sponsored by the station. The *Nashville Tennessean* reported on December 7, 1925, that 'the first prize in the French

Harp contest was won by J.T. Bland who played "Lost John." The second prize was won by DeFord Bailey, a negro boy, who played "It Ain't Gonna Rain No Mo'."' DeFord himself boasts proudly: 'There was 135 of them there, couldn't nobody beat me. They could be playing from now until eternity, and they still wouldn't beat me.' In any case, Dr. Humphrey Bate, a Vanderbilt-trained physician then appearing on both WDAD and WSM (music, like tennis, was still an amateur sport in those days), brought DeFord up to the brand-new WSM studios, where he went on the air without so much as an audition, and Judge Hay was so impressed he threw his steamboat whistle in the air.

DeFord Bailey was a star. He appeared, for instance, on forty-nine out of fifty-two Opry broadcasts in 1928 (the next most frequent performer appeared twenty-nine times), and this was when the Opry was like a rural religion on Saturday night. He made records in Atlanta and New York and then, in the first recording sessions to be held in Nashville, cut eight sides for RCA Victor in 1928. His first records were issued not in the 'race' but in the hillbilly series, though they were for the most part simple country blues (with sometimes complicated sound effects). RCA hedged its bets, however, by bringing out one song, 'John Henry,' in both series, coupling it with white harmonica player Bert Bilbro's 'Chester Blues' for the hillbillies, and with black harmonica player Noah Lewis's 'Like I Want to Be' for its blues audience. Race in one sense, then, was almost an afterthought, with DeFord appealing equally to black and white, and white audiences discovering his color only

Medicine Show, Huntington, Tennessee, October, 1935.
Courtesy of the Library of Congress. F.S.A. BEN SHAHN

DeFord Bailey on the air, 1930s.
Courtesy of WSM Archives.

Portrait of DeFord, 1979.
J. CLARK THOMAS

upon actually seeing him. When he started touring with Uncle Dave Macon in the early thirties, the greatest problem he encountered was finding lodgings, but that was solved when Uncle Dave, never at a loss for ready-made solutions, insisted that DeFord was his valet and had to share a room with him. He must have traveled on his own, too, because harmonica player Sonny Terry remembers seeing him in the thirties in his own home town of Rockingham, North Carolina. 'There's a fellow used to come through there named DeFord Bailey, he used to play the "Alcoholic Blues." Oh, he was a little short guy about — I reckon 'bout — four feet. He couldn't play it on blues much, but that "Alcoholic Blues," he made a record of that. His home was in Tennessee, he lived in Nashville. He was a pretty old fellow then . . . he was 'bout forty-five. He had a little boy with him. I think it was his kid. It was a little act he had, he played a harp, and this boy danced. He played the harmonica, put his hat down, people throwed him money in the hat. He say he went all around.'

It was only as the Opry became more and more the province of pro-fessional entertainers — musicians who sought to make their living not by farming like the McGee brothers or medicine like Dr. Bate but by music alone — that the anomaly of DeFord's position became increasingly evident. In retrospect he feels he was always treated in a patronizing way. 'All the time I was with the Opry and they had a Christmas tree every year, I never received as much as a tie or nothing,' he says, and he never got paid more than five dollars an appearance. In the thirties he came to be referred to as

53

'our little mascot' and his playing time was gradually reduced; when he was finally let go in 1941, the dismissal was couched in the most brutal and patronizing of terms.

> Like some members of his race and other races [wrote Judge Hay in *A Story of the Grand Ole Opry*], DeFord was lazy. He knew about a dozen numbers which he put on the air and recorded for a major company, but he refused to learn more, even though his reward was great. He was our mascot and is still loved by the entire company. We gave him a whole year's notice to learn some new tunes, but he would not. When we were forced to give him his final notice, DeFord said, without malice: 'I knowed it wuz comin', Judge, I knowed it wuz comin'.' DeFord comes to the show now and then to visit us. We are always glad to see him – a great artist.

'They said I didn't learn nothing new,' says DeFord, to whom the whole debacle remains a bitter puzzle to this day. He went to work full time at the shoeshine parlor he had started in 1933 with an uncle, on the corner just across from where the housing project in which he lives now stands. Until the shop was leveled by the Housing Authority in 1971, that was where you could find DeFord Bailey, always neat as a pin, always willing to pull a battered old harp out of his pocket and, for a small consideration, play a tune. He stubbornly refused all offers to record, or appear at the Newport Folk Festival, or make a movie with Burt Reynolds (he turned down $2500 to play the part that blues singer Furry Lewis eventually took in *W. W. and the Dixie Dance Kings*). When the Opry had an Old Timers' Night just before departing the old Ryman Auditorium in 1974, DeFord was coaxed to appear and, according to newspaper reports, stole the show. He made his debut at the new Opry House on his seventy-fifth birthday and has made intermittent public appearances since then.

It's hard to say what his attitude is exactly, whether it's the money or the recognition that he missed the most, whether he is genuinely bitter or secure in his place in history. Divorced from his wife, he lives alone in so meticulous a fashion that fame might simply be an unwanted intruder. He turned down the movie and record offers presumably because the money wasn't right, but one has the feeling that the money could never be right at this point, and probably he opens up only to young friends like Talley and David Morton. Morton, who first met DeFord in 1973 and is very much a member of the family (David's wedding pictures on the wall show DeFord in a tux) protects Mr. Bailey, cossets Mr. Bailey, gave him the guitar and the tape recorder that he has in the apartment, wrote a beautiful memoir called 'Every Day's Been Sunday,' but has so far been unable to persuade him to commit his sounds to record again. At least not for any commercial purpose.

'I want to make you up a tape some day,' says DeFord to Talley, 'yessir, sure do, so you can have it just as long as you live.' He reaches for his harmonica, runs his lips up and down the reeds, and launches into a full-bodied version of 'John Henry,' playing it first one style, then another. Little crinkles of pleasure light up his face as he does 'my grandfather's song,' 'It Ain't Gonna Rain No More,' his own 'Muscle Shoals' and 'Ice Water Blues.' The sound is surprisingly full, just as on record (only 'John Henry,' 'Ice Water Blues,' and 'Davidson County Blues' have been reissued in this country), its intricate repetitive figures and subtle shifts of tone and rhythm achieved with disarming ease as he holds the harmonica casually in one hand. After another train song he pulls down the guitar, turns it upside down, and, strumming left-handed, sings a lilting version of Jim Jackson's 'Kansas City,' fingers brushing the strings with an almost feathery touch. 'Don't nobody

DeFord at home. J. CLARK THOMAS

DeFord and David Morton. Courtesy of David Morton.

else play like that,' he says with undisguised delight. 'Y'see, I doubles up on it like a twelve-string.' A beatific smile lights up his face, the guitar echoes his voice, which, DeFord says, 'is in and out' these days. 'I never played with nobody,' he says, perhaps forgetting Bob Lee. 'You see, I played too smooth, yes sir, couldn't nobody play with me. I'd like to teach your boy there,' he says to Talley with a twinkle in his eye. 'You'd see, he'd get used to me after a while.

'See, I'm just like a child, I never growed up. I goes to sleep with that harmonica there on the floor beside me. Sometimes I may wake up in the middle of the night with an idea that just keeps gnawing at me, can't be satisfied until I tries it out. It's the last thing I see before I go to sleep and the first thing I reach for when I wake up. Yes, sir!'

Downstairs the lobby is deserted when we leave at ten o'clock.

RUFUS
THOMAS

The World's Oldest Teenager

S ELF-DESCRIBED as 'the world's oldest teenager,' Rufus Thomas looks dapper in powder-blue puffed-out cap, slick belted orange leather coat, white mutton-chop sideburns, ahd shiny red platform shoes. Roebuck 'Pop' Staples, he says, has been trying to claim his title lately. 'I'm fifty-nine, and Pop's sixty-one. But Pop just *stands* and sings, he doesn't dance and go through all of these things like I do, so I'm a couple of steps ahead of him on that.' Rufus Thomas winks good-naturedly. Despite his age and a problem with his eyes, he carries off his role with easygoing assurance, slapping hands easily with the young bloods who are hanging around his agent's office in Memphis, greeting the businessmen who have flown in to talk with him about a new record contract with decorous formality. He didn't really click in show business until he was forty-five, when 'The Dog' and 'Walking the Dog,' two dance numbers that set the mode for his subsequent success, burst unexpectedly into the national charts. Since then he's done 'The Penguin,' 'The Funky Chicken,' 'The Push and Pull,' and every sort of current dance craze, and his act consists largely of his singing about, and showing off, the latest steps, dressed in pink pedal pushers, safari suits, and all manner of outrageous costumes. His roots, however, go back over forty years in show business, and his earliest hit, 'Bear Cat,' got Sam Phillips's Sun label off the ground in 1953. While his background is different from most blues singers' in that 'they came up basically in the rurals, but I came up in the city,' his orientation and sense of tradition are very much the same, and B. B. King, Johnny Ace, Bobby 'Blue' Bland are among the great Memphis singers whom he helped to start out in the business.

I was born in Mississippi just below Collierville about five miles from the Tennessee line in a little place called Cayce, it's not on anybody's map. That was March 26, 1917, but I grew up in Memphis, I been here since I was a year old. I don't know anything about country life, to tell you the truth. Of course I went back after I was thirteen or fourteen years old and picked a little cotton in places like Claybrook, Arkansas,

The WDIA team (minus Rufus), ca. 1950. Left to right: Joe Hill Louis,
Ford Nelson (piano), Moohah Williams, B. B. King, Maurice 'Hot Rod' Hulbert,
Professor Nat D. Williams. Courtesy of *Blues Unlimited.*

which was named, incidentally, for a black man. My mother and I used
to go to a farm where you could stay on by the week. I was quite a lad
then. I never picked a hundred pounds of cotton anywhere in my life,
but I tried.

My mother, she did domestic. My father worked in different plants
and what have you. *He* was musical, but my mother was a great church
woman, beautiful, little, she weighed about a hundred ten, hundred
fifteen pounds, and she didn't have a formal education, but she had
what we call mother wit, that deep-seated kind of intelligence that you
don't get out of books. So that was how I came up.

He graduated in 1936 from Booker T. Washington High School, a black
institution from which many of the best Memphis musicians—including
Booker T. and Al Jackson, Jr., of the MGs—have emerged over the years.
While still in high school he came into contact with one of the most important
personal and professional influences upon his life.

Professor Nat D. Williams. He was a professor, history teacher at
the high school, and incidentally later the first black DJ in the South.
At the time he was also MC of the Amateur Show at the Palace Theater
on Beale Street. Nat had this part of the program where he did comedy,

and he chose me out of a bunch of kids to do comedy with him. Nat was the straight man, and I was the comic. See, I started in as a comic just fooling around at school, but Nat and I go back as far as 1931, and we've been together ever since. When Nat left in a few years, I took over the MC job at the Palace, and Nat was later the reason that I came to WDIA around 1950.

Not before he had completed his show business education, however. He went out with the Rabbit Foot Minstrels immediately after high school graduation, and for the next few summers worked the tent shows and carnivals that provided the basis for a whole tradition of black professional entertainment.

I started in actually as a tap dancer. That's how my good timing came about. I was a tap dancer, and I used to do some scat singing, like Louis, you know, all of those kinds of things. Really I did it all. If it came under the heading of show business, I did it. I went with the Rabbit Foots back in 1936, I also was with Royal American, it was owned by a man named F. S. Wolcott and it was an all-white show, but Leon Claxton had the black part and they called it Harlem in Habana.

It was a tent show under a big tent, that was the time when they had an aisle right down the center and blacks sat on one side, whites

Silas Green of New Orleans, Alabama, July-August, 1936.
Courtesy of the Library of Congress. F.S.A. WALKER EVANS

on the other. The way they would do it, they'd come in and set up the tent, and then every day at twelve o'clock we'd have a parade, you understand, to bring the people, to let the people know, and you'd have maybe a hundred people marching around the square in those little old country towns. It was a different town every day, and at night you stayed in people's homes, because there were no hotels at all for blacks at that time. You paid fifty to seventy-five cents a night, a dollar if the lady fed you. Then in the morning you catch the bus, and you're off to another town.

I wouldn't have traded the world for that foundation. Even with all the racism, all the holdbacks, all those things, it was still quite likable, people were having fun. We didn't make a lot of money, but we had a damn good time. And, of course, it was a whole education. Variety at that time was the spice of life. Nothing of the same ever followed. The show would open with the band. Then there was the chorus line, and the comic would come right behind that. Then maybe a singer, the chorus line, the tap dancers, and the comic. You don't see that kind of thing any more. If you go to any show of today, you don't see no dancers, they just aren't there. The people must have loved it, though. During the day at the parade, you'd have maybe fifty or a hundred people, but at night it just look like they come out of the cotton bolls, out of the woodworks, man! You know, I think they would still love it. I haven't included tap dancing in my show yet, but before I fall apart at the seams I think I might just go ahead and insert it.

He gave up the tent shows in 1940 to marry and settle down in Memphis. That was around the time he took over the Amateur Show at the Palace from Professor Nat D., a role that put him where he wanted to be, right in the center of the black entertainment scene. The Wednesday night shows—with the weekly participation, especially in the late forties, of entertainers soon destined to become stars—have since become legend, but the reality was a bit more prosaic.

First they had the movies and then the amateur, which was the bottom hour, and then it was back to the movies. I reached back and got a friend of mine, his name was Robert Counts, they called him Bones, and we were together for eleven consecutive years at the Palace Theater every Wednesday night. I tell you, you wouldn't believe this, but we were making five dollars a night, and you had Al Jackson's band—that was Al Jackson, Sr.—and I found out that they were only making twenty-five dollars, and they had a big band, too. Course the show was only a nickel then, but the place was packed. In the beginning we used to have $5, $3, and $2 for prizes, but then they cut that out and everybody who come up on stage would get a dollar. B.B. used to come with holes in his shoes, his guitar all patched up, just to get that dollar. There was no graduation as such, but after he made '3 O'Clock,' B. didn't come back to the Amateur Show no more. Well, you know, same with Bobby. I wrote one of the first songs that Bobby Bland ever sung, and he has promised me through the years that he would record that tune, but he hasn't recorded it yet. 'I got a new kind of loving that other men can't catch on / While they losing out I'm steady holding on.' It was a good tune. Bobby sang it on the Amateur Show and won first prize.

Rufus left the Amateur Show after eleven years in a dispute over money. 'I wanted more, but I couldn't get Bones to go ask for it with me. So the man got with Bones and asked him would he work with someone else? Mind you now, I got him the job, I gave him all his lines, I even taught him a little dance. And when the man got with him and said would he work with someone else, he said yes, and *I got fired*.' This last is almost whispered with a sense of injury that twenty-five years has done little to abate.

Never anything less than resourceful, however, Rufus already had three other jobs: day work in a textile plant; broadcasting on WDIA, where Nat D. had started in 1949 and B. B. King had come in the next year with the popular Sepia Swing Club and Heebie Jeebies shows; and another amateur show that was broadcast Saturday midnight from the Handy Theater. On this show he worked with Bones as well, and as a result of the earlier episode 'they were going to let Bones go. But I said, No, no need of letting him go. No need of separating a money-making thing. So that was it—even after he got me fired from my old job at the Palace.'

Rufus and B. B. King, backstage at the Apollo Theater, 1965.
PETE LOWRY

WDIA was something else again. Known throughout the South as the 'Mother Station of the Negroes,' it employed all black announcers ('they didn't call them disc jockeys then'), but no blacks in an executive position. 'It was resented, naturally, but it was just part of what was *then*, no one knew whether it was destined to change or not.' It was also, of course, another step up the ladder, by which Rufus Thomas gained an even more focal position in the Memphis musical community.

I played it all on my show. Every type of music. See, we had a choice then, there was no control of music like it is now. Frankie Laine, Vaughan Monroe, Nat King Cole. My family and I were raised on Grand Ole Opry. Every Saturday night we'd run home to catch the Opry on the radio. So you can understand why I was the only black jock in the city that was playing the Beatles and the Rolling Stones when they came out.

I started out just on Saturday afternoons. It was just another job when I first started out, but, you know, it was really a family station community-wise back then, it really did things for the community and such. When B. left I took over his job, it was called Sepia Swing Club, and then when we went twenty-four hours in 1954, I had Hoot 'n' Holler every night from 9:30 to 11. I had a blues thing done by McGee and somebody—you probably know who it is, yeah, that's right, Sonny Terry—that was my theme, and they said at first you don't want anything like that, but it was great.

Well, you know, when I first got into radio, we used to listen to WREC, that's one of the big radio stations around here, and they would have this big booming voice, you know—'This is WREC broadcasting from the South's finest hotel, the Hotel Peabody'—and I thought you had to be like that, too. I tried to copy somebody else, but then I found out it was all right just to be myself. I just played good music, whatever it was.

All this time Rufus was a regular fixture at the clubs in and around Memphis, sitting in and singing with the great bands of Al Jackson, Sr., Tuff Green, Bill Fort, and Bill Harvey, out of which in the fifties and sixties musicians like Charles Lloyd, Willie Mitchell, and the Stax label house band would emerge. He was writing songs steadily, too, always blues songs ('It's just a part of me, I guess, the blues'), and even recorded in 1950 at a club called Johnny Curry's for the Star Talent label. It wasn't long after that, in the spring of 1951, that he found his way to Sam Phillips's Memphis Recording Service. Phillips, who would not start his own Sun label for almost another year, leased six of Rufus's sides to Chess, as he had earlier leased sides by Howlin' Wolf, B.B. King, Little Junior Parker, and one-man-band Joe Hill Louis to Chess and RPM. Then in 1953, a year before Elvis Presley cut his first record in the Sun studio, Sam Phillips included 'Bear Cat (The Answer to Hound Dog)' by Rufus 'Bear Cat' Thomas, Jr., in his first batch of Sun releases. It occasioned a lawsuit from Duke Records, which had put out Big Mama Thornton's original version of 'Hound Dog' just a month before, but the record also made number three on the national rhythm 'n' blues charts and put Sun Records on the map. Rufus's view of Sun and the whole dawn of rock 'n' roll is a little different, though, from that of white artists like Elvis, Carl Perkins, and Jerry Lee Lewis, who came later.

Everyone was just going up there, and I found out about it, so I went, too. You could come right off the street and go in there, ain't no such thing as that now. Me and Sam Phillips? We were tighter than the nuts on the Brooklyn Bridge—then. Of course he was like all the folk at that time. You know how if blacks had something and didn't have no way to exploit it and white dudes would pick it up and do something about it, they'd just beat him out of all of it, that's all. Well, that was him, that was Sam Phillips. Oh man. I guess I lost a lot of it, too, like most black folk. And when Elvis and Carl Perkins and Cash come along, just like he catered to black, he just cut it off and went to white. No more blacks did he pick up at all.

That marked the end of Rufus's first recording career. He was not to go into the studio again for another six years. 'I think Sam had it all, there was nowhere else to go,' says Rufus, who maintained his radio show and continued playing little gigs in and out of town. Then in 1960 he cut a record with his eighteen-year-old daughter Carla for Jim Stewart's Satellite Record Company. The record was called 'Cause I Love You,' and Satellite soon changed its name to Stax. Just as with Sun, Rufus maintains, 'I was the beginning of Stax. I made the first record that made money for them, me and Carla.'

On the basis of the Thomases' success, Atlantic Records closed a distribution deal with Stax, and about six months later Carla's 'Gee Whiz' was a huge national hit. Rufus himself came out with 'The Dog,' and then 'Walking the Dog,' in 1963, and as a result finally achieved a minor kind of celebrity, one which allowed him for the first time to tour nationally, both on his own and with his daughter. He went out weekends with the big package shows and was a kind of novelty act, never receiving top billing but always well received by an audience that looked affectionately upon this bald-headed old man stomping around the stage and doing the latest dances. Rufus grew more successful, and Carla became a major star, but he kept his radio show for more than ten years, and he remains grateful to WDIA and

Rufus does the Funky Penguin; daughter Carla on left.

Rufus on stage, 1960s.

program director David James Mattis in particular (Mattis was the original owner of Memphis-born Duke Records before it was sold to Don Robey's Peacock label in Houston) for giving him the opportunity to improve his fortunes while maintaining an active home base.

This was how 'The Dog' more or less came about, because David James—who incidentally has been one helluvan inspiration to me, without the aid of David James probably, just probably I would never have gotten where I got—because he let me go out on Saturdays and Friday nights and make gigs, he *told* me to go, and when I came back I would always have my job right there waiting for me. I could go to England, I could go on tour, and when I came back I knew everything was all right, it was beautiful, man.

Well, time changes and other people come along and that feeling of involvement is not there any more. I don't know, man, I hate to have to say this, but this is true, the morals of people have changed, it just seems to be a dog-eat-dog world, and people don't give a damn any more. You know, there are people, if they read this, they're probably going to hate me for saying it, but I'm telling you the truth. You see, the truth hurts a lot of people, they don't want to hear the truth, they'd rather that you paint it up or lie about it, but I won't. David James, like I say, was responsible for a lot of things for me. After he left we had a

Family gathering. Standing: Marvell Thomas and his wife, and Vaneese Thomas. Seated: Carla Thomas, Rufus and his wife.

number of other program directors, who were all incidentally white also. Then people were saying that since it was a black-orientated station, you should have a black PD or station manager. Now I don't know why, I don't want to say jealousy or whatever, but that's when the shit hit the fan, that's when my trips abroad started to fall. You had people coming in and saying, I'm the great Mr. Goddamn, you do what I say, that kind of shit, they come in trying to pop a whip. Now believe me, these are *facts*. Finally you get a black station manager, and as of today, in 1976, I am not on the air.

His face falls, he is generally crestfallen, as he is at the thought of his mistreatment by Bones, by Sam Phillips, and by Stax, the company he was with from beginning to end, which never thought to inform him of its impending collapse until it was engulfed in a sea of litigation and foreclosures.

He is honestly troubled, like many successful black entertainers, by his conflicting feelings about race, and he weighs what he sees as personal inequities against unquestionable signs of racial progress. '*Is* it progress?' he demands. 'It's like a fellow said to me the other day, "Man, I tell you," – this is a quotation. Quote: "A white man's prejudice is not half as bad as a black man's jealousy." You know, just because you make a little more money today than you did yesterday, why should you mistreat your fellow man? *But this is what's happening.*'

He soon brightens, however. Rufus Thomas cannot wear the tragic mask for long. His agent's secretary, Jewel, comes into the room, and he defers to her with courtly charm. 'Say that during the process of this interview, Jewel—which she really is a jewel—came in and had to make some coffee. She tiptoed in the door and said, "Can I make some coffee?" I want you to get that in, cause she is definitely a part of me.'

He speaks of his worldwide tours, occasional shows with Carla, and a recent trip to South Africa, where he incorporated with great success a bi-racial response to his act. He instructs me patiently, with diction that is always precise, on his roots and his continued ability to keep up with the times. 'Blues will always be here. Words change, the style of music changes. I was just fortunate enough to be able to move along with the changes and trends. As it changed, then I just changed right along with it. Yet to me blues has always been big, and it will always be big. Of all the other music in the world, watch it—it'll tail out and always change. But you'll always be able to hear twelve-bar blues. Always. It's the backbone of American music—blues and country, cause country and western and blues are right there together, just that close, and gospel. Everything else comes from that.'

He looks back with satisfaction on a career which, while never spectacular, has maintained a steady level of success and gained him a modest degree of acclaim. He might have made it bigger, he concedes, when he was younger, but he is almost surprised at the suggestion that he might have done things differently.

I wasn't about to go anywhere, not at that time. Cause I had a family. I have a son, Marvell, he's thirty-four, he's a brilliant musician, plays piano, organ, drums, very good musician. Carla's thirty-three now, and my youngest is twenty-three, she's a schoolteacher up at Morristown, New Jersey. She teaches French, she's the intellectual one of the family. I got married in 1940. I ain't been jiving around, I been working, man, I wasn't no playboy. I was working in a textile mill, the American Finishing Company, I worked there for twenty-two years, until 1963. That ice and snow and stuff had me hampered a many day, but I went on and made it, cause I had a family.

All my life I wanted to be an entertainer. My models were Fats Waller and Louis Armstrong and a fellow named Gatemouth Moore, Dwight Moore, he came out of Memphis by way of Topeka. They were all good entertainers, very very versatile, always able to do more than one thing, and they helped, they made a way if they could, for somebody else to make it, too. Well, I believe that was my whole work, helping people. And still is. It's enough room for everybody to be on top. Ain't nothing *but* room up there. It's a big enough space up there for everybody, so why can't you share it with somebody, give him a chance to climb the ladder. He needs it. *You* got the chance, now go ahead and share it with somebody else.

BOBBY
BLAND

Little Boy Blue

You know how it feels — you understand
What it is to be a stranger
In this unfriendly land.

'LEAD ME ON'

I'm gonna play the high-class joints
I'm gonna play the low-class joints
Well, and, baby, I'm gonna even play the honky tonks.

'HONKY TONK'

PROLOGUE

TWO MIDDLE-AGED BLACK MEN waiting for an elevator in a brightly lighted downtown mall. One wears a blue denim cap, denim jacket with sequins, pre-washed jeans with an elastic waist to take in his girth. The other is neat, mustachioed, perky as a medical-supplies salesman in a brown suit and belted brown leather coat. The one in denim speaks first. 'Hey, my man.'

'Tell me about it.'

'You got to know what it is.'

'I ain't so sure.'

The elevator arrives, the doors open, for a moment nothing more is said. At last the prim-looking man breaks the silence. 'Hey, don't I know you from somewhere?'

A big smile creases the larger man's face. His face in fact is wreathed in smiles.

'Yeah,' says the man in the brown suit, 'you're a musician. What band you with?'

The big man's face falls, but he pulls himself together and draws himself up proudly. 'I'm Bobby Bland,' he says in a soft drawl.

'Oh sure,' says the gentleman, not at all abashed. 'Hey, you lost a little weight there.' Bobby Bland sucks in his gut. 'Which is good. Hey, where you playing this week? I'm in town till Friday. I just might be down to catch you.'

'Sugar Shack,' says Bobby Bland, detailing location, volunteering directions, graciously acknowledging his public.

At the fiftieth floor Bobby Bland, the promo man from ABC Records who has rounded him up for this unwonted venture into the outside world, and the unidentified gentleman all get out. Bobby Bland sails past the receptionist on his way to yet another radio interview. 'Hey, lady, hey, lover,' he says, with that warm, affectionate smile. 'Hey, man, how you doing?' The reception area is buzzing with the news. Bobby 'Blue' Bland has arrived.

EVERY NIGHT it is exactly the same. The band, a brass-heavy ten pieces with dilapidated reading stands that say 'Mel Jackson/MFs/Bobby Bland's Revue,' does a desultory thirty-minute set. Then Burnett Williams, singer, valet, bus driver, and all-around good fellow, swings affably into a succession of Al Green numbers and current soul hits. The band plays dispiritedly behind him; even the bandleader, Mel Jackson, has disappeared from the stand; but Burnett always works up a sweat, finishing out his segment with shoes kicked off, doing the barefoot to the strains of 'Love and Happiness.' This invariably cracks up Mel Jackson, who reappears precisely at this point, dapper, diminutive, very much in charge. His eyes gleam and dart skittishly about the room as he laughs out loud, proclaims, 'That boy doing some barefooting!' and gives Burnett a soul slap and quick little hug as the warm-up singer departs from the stage, his shoes held delicately aloft. Then it's Show Time, Ladies and Gentlemen, a Young Man Who Needs No Introduction, he'll Take Care of You, Further on Up the Road, won't let you Cry No More, cause when you Cry Cry Cry he just wants to Turn On Your Lovelights, well he's a Good-Time Charlie, and You're the One (That He Adores), but now The Feeling is Gone and he's Two Steps From the Blues. The string of hits becomes a litany, a numbing incantation. Audience talk becomes louder and more distracted, and then Bobby 'Blue' Bland appears, big, shambling, sleepy-eyed, a cigarette between his fingers, tongue licking at the edge of his lips. He plays aimlessly for a moment with the microphone, his eyes cast upwards as if for inspiration, the band kicks off, and that smooth, mellow, almost horn-like voice slides in among the three trumpets, trombone, and saxophone (guitar, bass, two drummers, and occasionally a piano round out the band). 'I pity the fool/ I pity the fool that falls in love with you. . . .' It is ten-thirty, and Bobby 'Blue' Bland is just going to work.

The day has begun for Bobby Bland some five hours earlier, late in the afternoon, around five or six o'clock. Until then all telephone calls have been stopped at the desk, and Bobby's wife, Marty, and six-year-old daughter,

Tahanee, accompanying him on this road trip as a rare treat, can do little more than tiptoe around the small cluttered hotel room. The blinds are drawn, the rollaway cot for Tahanee is unmade, the television set is on low, and even Mel Jackson, who has been out hustling since noon, 'taking care of Bobby's business'—making contacts, looking after the band, looking into the purchase of a new bus—has been unable to get through to Bobby all afternoon.

This doesn't seem to bother Mel Jackson ('Sometimes he be up to it, sometimes he don't,' says Mel philosophically). But then nothing ever seems to bother Mel Jackson, as he sits bare-chested, a brown bowler hat on his head, in his room two doors down from Bobby's. 'It's different being an artist and a bandleader,' he explains. 'For Bobby, I don't want him worrying about anything but the music. I want things to be just exactly right. After all, he's the one people come out to see. That's what's paying us, and I don't want nothing to bother him. When he go out there on stage, I want him in fine fettle.'

Mel Jackson is courteous, soft-spoken, conservatively hip, he always chooses his words with precision and care. He is thirty-nine years old, born into the music business, with a father, Jerry Jackson, who fronted a revue in which Mel toured the country from the time he was six years old. 'Yes, I grew up fast,' Mel says, nodding his head. 'Very fast. I came through things that usually would stop a young cat. Like narcotics and shit. But my mind was strong enough to surpass all these things, even being in the environment. I credit my background with my always trying to be on top of things and hold my business mind together.' He has been with Bobby for seventeen years, ever since the Junior Parker–Bobby Bland Revue came through Nashville in 1959 and left town with a new trumpet player. He and Bobby go back a long way together, then, and enjoy a complicated and mutually dependent relationship. Mel Jackson serves as organizer, business manager, friend, and smooth-spoken conduit to the outside world. Bobby Bland on the other hand is the mealticket, the main attraction, but also the one who, in the sealed-off world that is 'the road'—where street sense is more important than education and deals often come down to your ability to collect—seems to make the final decisions. It is not all one way by any means, and it is doubtful that either man could make a real success without the other. They have been on the road for three months solid now; the show has been out for three years without a break of more than a couple of weeks.

Bobby wakes up slowly. He is a genial, slow-moving man whose forty-five years are etched into his pouched brown face. He has high cheekbones, a broad nose, sad liquid eyes, and a warmth and compassion that come through both in his singing and in his person. He is wearing Levi pants and a black silk undershirt, from which his balloon-shaped stomach and soft, almost feminine pectorals protrude. He sits on his daughter's bed while Tahanee watches television, and brushes out his Afro stroke by stroke. When

On stage, Boston, 1970s. STEVEN STONE

he is finished his wife, Marty—playful, girlish, her own hair braided in pig-
tails that accentuate her fine West Indian features—shapes his natural with a
blower. He has had his bath, room service has brought up a perfunctory
meal, his little girl brings him a pair of shoes. He looks down at his black
socks balefully. 'No, the blue shoes, baby. The blue shoes with the black
socks.' Hanging on a portable clothes rack are at least a dozen changes of
clothing. Suits and denims, brighly printed shirts. Studded leather caps.

Over by the window is a portable hi-fi with albums and cassettes (Grover
Washington, Stanley Turrentine, light jazz, bluesy ballads) scattered all around
the room. Always there is music. Bobby Bland is playing a rough mix of
his new c&w album for his visitors. Whenever he hears something that
particularly pleases him, he points it out, singing along with the melody,
repeating a lyric, embellishing a phrase. Whenever he hears a mistake, he
winces involuntarily, and seems to make a mental note that it will have to be
corrected. 'I was sharp there,' he says. 'Yeah, I been wanting to cut a country
album for a long time. We cut it live, first time I cut anything live since the

old Duke days. I think it's going to put us across to a whole new audience.' Although there are a good many things going on in the room and a number of cross-conversations, his mind is always on the music. 'I think this gonna be my best one yet,' he says with a soft smile.

There is a knock on the door. Warm-up singer Burnett Williams, who is staying in the next room, registered under his real name of Fogg ('He likes that Fogg,' explains Mel Jackson meaningfully), pops his head in. Burnett, who started out as Bobby's valet, just as Bobby started out as B.B. King's valet and driver in Memphis some twenty-five years ago, wants to know if there is anything he can do for the 'bossman.' Some girls have asked him to go to the Museum of Fine Arts, but Burnett's mind, too, is always on the music. 'I'm not into the Museum of Fine Arts. If I was into that type of thing, I'd probably be interested. But it's not interesting to me, because it doesn't have anything to do with music. Now if it would teach me how to do something else with my voice, my phrasing, how to get over to the public, then I would be interested in it.'

Burnett, Mel Jackson explains after Bobby has dismissed him, is getting a priceless opportunity to learn the business. 'What he's getting he couldn't buy, and that's exposure. That's the way you do it. You can't develop a style in your bedroom. That's just the way it's done. That's the way Bobby came through.' Will Burnett come through the same way? Mel smiles slyly. 'If he can.'

Bobby and Mel have some unfinished business to take care of, and they go off to a corner to do so. There are few words; Mel's expressive face communicates mostly with winks and little nods, and Bobby will occasionally grunt approval. To an outsider, it's difficult to tell just what is going on, but it's evident, despite everyone's denials, that there is some trouble in the band. The night before there has been an almost silent confrontation between Mel and the tenor player in the club's dressing room, where after quietly voicing an ultimatum Mel simply stares the tenor player down. 'What?' 'I didn't say nothing,' mumbles the tenor player sullenly. A quiet smile of satisfaction plays about Mel's lips. 'But you heard me.' 'Yeah, I heard you.' 'No more of that shit,' says Mel Jackson without ever raising his voice, but with chilling effect.

Today a band rehearsal has been scheduled and called off for unspecified reasons, and Mel brings Bobby up to date on the latest developments. The band is staying in the hotel where Bobby always used to stay, but Bobby has moved downtown along with Mel and Burnett ('Anyone can stay here who wants to pay the money,' says Burnett defensively), and Mel has been shuttling back and forth all day.

'You're moving up in the world,' says the PR man, fingering Bobby's gold lighter. 'Yeah, well, you know,' says Bobby with a mellow chuckle.

Bobby looks down at his jeweled watch and stretches. His big hands are covered with jewelry of one sort or another, and he is particularly partial to diamonds. It is past time for him to make his radio appointment, and the promo man is getting nervous. Marty is worried about their daughter, who has had the flu ever since arriving from Detroit. She has been waiting to call the house doctor all day. 'Is it too late to call him now, honey?' she asks timidly. Bobby glances uneasily at the phone, then at his guests. He is obviously concerned, but decides in the end that it is too late and tomorrow will be soon enough, if indeed a doctor is still necessary. He excuses himself and sprays himself with cologne, selects one shirt, then another, shakes his head and says softly to himself, 'Damn, I ain't had a joint all day. That's bad business, bad business. You're not thinking, Bobby.' A warm grin spreads across his face as he rolls a joint, then rolls another for his guests. 'C'mere, baby,' he says to Tahanee and gives her the second joint to pass around. She sets it down on the floor with shy ceremony, and Bobby laughs. 'No, baby, bring it to him.' Someone starts to pass it to Marty, but Bobby quickly intervenes. 'No, she doesn't smoke,' he says with the special protectiveness he reserves for his wife. He won't let her go to the clubs where he performs ('They're just joints,' he explains with surprising vehemence. If it were Las Vegas, he says, then it would be a different story), and he especially values the refinement and education of this woman in her early twenties, who met him, she tells me, when she was doing an interview for the newspaper at Wayne State University, where she was an education major.

At last everything is in readiness, and Bobby puts on his denim jacket over a black turtleneck shirt, donning sunglasses and setting the denim cap carefully atop his perfectly coiffed head. 'Later, baby,' he says to his daughter at the door. 'Later,' she says. 'Right on,' says Bobby with an appreciative chuckle and gives his wife a kiss.

By now it is dark outside. Don't you ever get tired of hanging around the hotel? someone says in the elevator going down. Wouldn't you like to get out more? Bobby shrugs. 'Well, you know, Boston's still Boston. Ain't nothing in the street I haven't seen, ain't nothing I'm gonna learn out on the street.'

When he hits the lobby he is altogether changed, bluff, alert, wary, speaking before he is spoken to, aware that everyone expects something of Bobby 'Blue' Bland.

FOR THE RADIO INTERVIEW Bobby Bland is all business. The DJ is somewhat in awe of this legendary performer and asks for advice on how to conduct the show. 'Let's just rap,' says Bobby Bland. 'I'm no jock.' The DJ asks what records he'd like to have played. 'Whatever you got, it's all right with me.' The DJ insists that he'd like Bobby to choose. 'Anything you got on T-Bone Walker. That was my main man. Great guitar player and a great stylist, God bless the dead. Anything you got on him when he was hot.' The

DJ still wants Bobby to make the selection and takes him in to the record library, where there is a whole shelf of T-Bone Walker records. Bobby stares at the records blankly but makes no move to examine them or pick one out. At last the DJ pulls an album, recently recorded at Montreux, and they go back into the studio to begin the interview, when a receptionist enters and confers anxiously with the disc jockey. There is a famous jazz musician outside who was supposed to come in earlier in the afternoon. Bobby Bland picks up the name and strikes his forehead in real dismay. He is mortified. 'I thought I knew who he was,' he says out loud. 'Well have him come in, come on in. You know, we both being so goddamn honest,' he goes on as the musician appears. 'That's my error all the way. Man, I wasn't even thinking.' The jockey is mystified, and Bobby briefly explains. 'He was inquiring where I was playing. I *thought* I knew who it was. But he wouldn't commit himself, and I wouldn't commit myself either.' The jazz musician smiles. It is the little man in the brown suit.

Bobby 'Blue' Bland was born Robert Calvin Bland, on January 27, 1930, in a little town called Rosemark just outside of Memphis, Tennessee. 'Little country town. Period. Grocery store, a gin, a kind of Dr. Flipping, which has passed, he was the local doctor there. Very small. Population, let me say, five hundred. Maybe.' He got to about the third grade 'between chopping-cotton time and picking-cotton time,' and was first interested in music by a local musician named Mutt Piggee ('Don't ask me to spell it, I can't do no better than that'), who played the guitar and sang the blues. Bobby never did learn to play the guitar, he remains one of the few blues singers who has never mastered even a rudimentary instrumental skill (today he still fools around with a tenor sax), but he was fascinated by the sound and started singing and playing a jew's harp that Mutt Piggee gave to him. In 1947 he and his mother moved to Memphis because 'you see, my mother wanted me to have a little more than what Rosemark had to offer. I always would tell her that some day I would make a lot of money and be able to take care of her. One of those things. I wasn't never really too bad of a kid. I didn't like to work much, but I got a job at Bender's Garage, which was $27 a week. And I started to singing on weekends. Spirituals. Just a small amount of it. We called ourselves the Pilgrim Travelers after a group that was big at the time. Then I started hanging around Beale Street with a bunch of guys. They used to give an amateur show down by the park at the Palace Theater every Wednesday night. Naturally we came to call ourselves the Beale Streeters.'

It was a tight little scene. The Beale Streeters included at one time or another Johnny Ace, Roscoe Gordon, Earl Forrest, and B. B. King. The MC at the Palace Theater was Rufus Thomas, already a veteran of over a decade of show business but still more than a decade away from real popular success.

Bobby himself was on the fringes of a group made up of Memphis's all-star talent. 'I wasn't important at all, really. I mean, I was fortunate enough to be able to sing, but, you see, I was the one who had the car.'

The places the Beale Streeters played were not exactly the poshest spots in town. Juke joints out in the country. Cafés. Rough clubs like the Kingfish. Little towns like Mason, Dyersburg, Ripley, Tennessee. The style that was being created, though, was the seed for modern rhythm 'n' blues, with B.B. King's guitar taking off from the T-Bone Walker-styled jump blues that were prevalent at the time, Johnny Ace's softer sound patterned after Charles Brown and Nat 'King' Cole, and Roscoe Gordon's orchestra emulating the very popular shout and big-band styles of Wynonie Harris, Louis Jordan, Lionel Hampton, Count Basie. Always in the background was the presence of the church, the anchor, the bedrock of a hard-edged, always scuffling existence. 'You could go out all Saturday night and have a ball, but on Sunday church was a must.' And in church the passionate, heartfelt sound of gospel music.

Bobby made recordings in 1950, '51, and '52 that came out on three different independent labels (Chess, Modern, and Duke), always in the company of other Beale Streeters, always at the tail end of somebody else's session. It is obvious, as Bobby himself says, that he had not yet found a style of his own, and most of the songs are done in the manner of Roy Brown and more specifically B.B. King, whose wailing falsetto Bobby sought to imitate. These early sides are interesting, but they betray problems with time, intonation, and phrasing, and it seems obvious that as a conventional blues singer Bobby Bland never would have been more than just that: conventional.

Then in 1952 he got drafted into the army. He celebrated by recording 'Army Blues' and was gone from the Memphis scene for two and a half years. 'I think the army done quite a bit for me, though I didn't care for it much at that particular time. I did two years six months and twenty-nine days, I had a little bad time to make up. But it grew me up into manhood, actually.' For the most part he was stationed in Japan, and toward the end of his tour he got into Special Services, singing Nat 'King' Cole, Charles Brown, Floyd Dixon, the softer side of his blues make-up. It must have been quite a change for a country boy to whom Memphis had been the fast life up till then.

When he got out, things had changed back in Memphis. For one thing rock 'n' roll had hit, and Sam Phillips, who had recorded and then leased out Bobby's and the other Memphis bluesmen's early sides to Chess and RPM, had latched on to a white boy named Elvis Presley. What this meant for artists like the Beale Streeters and Bobby Bland was that the race market had finally broken wide open, there was now the opportunity to reach a wider market than had ever been conceived of before. In addition, Johnny Ace— up till then only a local name—was on his way to undreamt-of stardom and even more spectacular apotheosis, which would come when he shot himself

Rev. C. L. Franklin. © 1979 by Jeff Todd Titon. All rights reserved.

fatally on Christmas Eve, 1954, in a backstage game of Russian roulette. And finally, on a more mundane level, Duke Records, which held Bobby Bland under contract, had been sold to Don Robey, a black nightclub owner from Houston with rumored gangland connections who had had considerable success with his gospel-based Peacock label.

'I wasn't professionally at all, really. I hadn't met Robey. I think he had some scouts out, and he had heard my voice and what have you, but really I just kind of got in there, because I was already under contract.' It was an association seemingly never based on anything more than this but one which was to last over twenty years, through the 1973 sale of Duke to ABC and right up until Robey's death in 1975.

Surprisingly he had hits almost from the start, although there was no great difference between the songs he recorded for his new Houston label— 'Farther Up the Road,' 'I Smell Trouble,' 'It's My Life, Baby'—and the conventional blues he had recorded for Modern, Sam Phillips, and James Madis before going into the army. On all, there is a spare blues accompaniment, highlighted by Pat Hare's Memphis-based overamplified guitar and featuring

76

Memphis's famous Bill Harvey Orchestra. Production work was meticulous, and the horns (Joe Scott, trumpet; Pluma Davis, trombone; Bill Harvey himself on tenor sax) added a new and disciplined dimension to the Bobby 'Blue' Bland sound. But it was still hard blues, 'which I never did care for, really,' still sung in the same B.B. King vein.

'It was '57 before I got a style of my own. Well, I was listening to Franklin a lot at the time—that's Reverend C.L. Franklin, Aretha's daddy—and my favorite at the time was B.B. King, of course, that had the high falsetto. Well, actually I was listening to a whole lot of different things, whoever had the hottest record on the jukebox, really. See, I developed the softness by listening to different singers like Nat "King" Cole or Perry Como or Tony Bennett. Man, they have a lot of feeling in their voice, they have a lot of what I call soul. I wouldn't say they would be able to sing blues, but they do a helluva job on ballads and such. But the thing is, I'd been listening to Reverend Franklin a lot—"The Eagle Stirreth His Nest"—and that's where I got my squall from. After I had lost the high falsetto. You see, I had to get some other kind of gimmick, you know, to be identified with. So I thought that was a good thing. And the first thing I tried it was in '56, I think it was, when I tried "Little Boy Blue." And I think it paid off.'

It certainly did. Bobby doesn't sing 'Little Boy Blue' any more, because, as Mel Jackson explains, 'to be doing a tune like that would be putting him in a helluva strain. Bobby was a much younger man at the time that tune was cut, so it wouldn't be the same tune by now.' To Bobby, who looks for the 'proper' approach to every song, 'it's just too hard to do every night. You can't just stand up and do it at will. Because it takes a lot of effort to make it come out. I mean, like it supposed to.' He gets requests for the song every night, though, and its combination of quiet pleading, rueful regret, and hoarse gospel shouts came in many ways to define the Bobby Bland style.

When the record came out, he was on the road with Junior Parker, his old friend from Memphis (Parker was one of the original Memphis blues stars) and Duke's biggest seller after Johnny Ace shot himself. Bobby had gone out with him in 1955 on the strength of his own early hits. 'Junior had the band. They were called the Blue Flames. Seven pieces. Yeah, I started out, I was doing a little bit of everything. Doing the driving. Setting up the bandstand. Opening the show.' He served as Junior's valet at the beginning, too, but he exhibits no trace of self-consciousness about his role at that time. 'Yeah, I think I was doing the right thing. You see, I didn't get a big hit until 1957, and even that wasn't enough to go out on your own at that particular time. What it was, normally Junior was a good business man, and he tried to teach me what he knowed, but I didn't have good enough ears at that time.'

Astonishingly, he stayed with Junior until 1961, by which time 'I'll Take Care of You,' 'I Pity the Fool,' 'Cry Cry Cry'—some of his biggest hits, records that sold half a million to a million—had already come out. Bobby

Bland considers himself a cautious man who doesn't move until the time is right. When he did go out on his own, he took the band with him. In the band at that time were Little Hamp Simmons on bass; Bobby Forte and Sonny Freeman—both later to go with B.B. King—on sax and drums respectively; Melvin Jackson, the present bandleader, business manager, third trumpet, and alter ego; Jabbo Starks, later to go with James Brown. Nearly all the musicians came from the original Bill Harvey Orchestra, and most were to stay until the band broke up in 1968. The arranger, leader, and occasional first trumpet was Joe Scott.

No one has been more influential in Bobby Bland's career than Joe Scott, and that may even include Bobby Bland. 'According to some insiders Bobby Bland is Joe Scott's creation,' wrote Charles Keil in 1966 in *The Urban Blues*. How important was Joe Scott, really? Bobby just looks at you slightly incredulous. 'I would say he was everything.'

Don Robey and Johnny Otis, early 1950s.
Courtesy of Michael Ochs Archives.

Junior Parker, Apollo Theater, 1965. PETE LOWRY

A native of Houston about the same age as Bobby, Scott was a trained musician who served as chief A&R man at Duke almost from the beginning of Don Robey's ownership. Originally sitting in on trumpet with the Bill Harvey Orchestra, Scott had been out on the road with Johnny Ace in 1953–54, fronting the group that was accompanying Ace at the time of his death. His main work for Junior Parker and Bobby Bland up until 1961 consisted of his arrangements and his work in the studio, where he produced most of the gospel as well as the secular sessions, wrote some of Duke's biggest hits, put the finishing touches on many others, and assembled the studio group that was such an important ingredient in the Duke sound. If Robey, obviously a tough operator, deserves recognition for having the vision to create one of the first of the black-owned independent labels, Joe Scott deserves as much for having the musical inspiration to put it across.

With Bobby Bland, he must have sensed a special potential, because at the beginning anyway he was working with a style that was scarcely even formed. They spent long hours on things like diction ('Well, a lot of that I learned from Nat "King" Cole'), phrasing, how to put a particular punchline across, the proper approach to a lyric—amenities that to Bobby Bland are extremely important. Bobby had a tendency then to sing flat and to rush his time, and Scott worked with him on that, too, concentrating on a single song and working on it carefully for at least a month, breaking down lines ('I never could handle no long lines') and rewriting lyrics before he would let Bobby take it into the studio. Most of all he took the songs that Robey brought him ('Shit, Robey didn't write none of them,' says Bobby of the

T-Bone Walker, 1944.
Courtesy of Callie Spencer and *Living Blues*.

classic compositions that came out either under Robey's own name or his pen name of Deadric Malone. 'He got them from – well, there used to be a lot of writers who went through there. No, he didn't steal them! They always got what they asked for. It's not his fault that they didn't have time enough to wait') and tailored them to Bobby Bland's particular talents. In the process Scott created a style and a genre, the blues ballad, that will be marked forever as Bobby Bland's own.

This style can perhaps best be compared to that of Charlie Rich, another eclectic singer whose 'Who Will the Next Fool Be?' Bobby recorded early in his career. It combines elements of ballads, blues, jazz, country, and romantic love songs, all on a gospel base, mixing a smooth and mellow vocal quality with effortless down-home funk. Where Rich was a composer as well, however,

Bobby was like another member of the band, and it is no accident that the sound Joe Scott built around him included sophisticated big-band arrangements, intricate instrumental voicings, and brass squalls to match Bobby's gargled vocal interpolations—dramatic orchestral flourishes in sharp contrast to the warmth, intimacy, and projected vulnerability of Bobby's singing voice. The guitar was always of crucial importance in this formula ('I'm fortunate to have had two guitarists mainly, Wayne Bennett and Mel Brown today, who both have that mellow, hollow kind of sound and basically had somewhat the same idol. Which is T-Bone Walker. See, if they hear a lyric, they say, "Well, Blue probably phrase it this way," and they know how to stay out of my way, and that's the most important part'), but it was the horns that carried the sound.

'Well, you see, it was the brass that gave me a kind of an identity, right from my first biggest record I ever had. That was Joe, because Joe liked the trumpets, you know, same as I have now.' It was Scott, too, who introduced the loping Texas beat ('they turn out real good musicians out of Texas, because they play a variety of stuff, jazz and blues and it's kind of a jelling thing') and in fact put together the Bobby 'Blue' Bland sound with all the care and meticulousness of a less-celebrated Phil Spector. The fact that he was successful is attested to by the remarkable consistency of the material recorded over the ten-year period (1958 to 1968) when he was in full charge of Bobby Bland's career. Experiments were introduced, there were flirtations—some very successful—with strings and choruses, different fashions were tried on and discarded, but for the most part the work over this changing decade flows together almost as if it were a single extended composition. It is not the blues exactly. The songs project a sense of hurt and vulnerability, and a willingness to assume responsibility, that is far removed from the blues' unquestioning embrace of reality. It is not jazz, because every detail is carefully worked out, down to the tiniest vocal aside or interpolation. It is simply a seamless body of work whose song titles and sentiments ('I'll Take Care of You,' 'You're the One [That I Adore],' 'Call on Me,' 'Loneliness Hurts'), shimmering melodies, and intricately arranged effects all meld together to create a portrait of Bobby 'Blue' Bland, the masterful exponent of a sophisticated new style.

They recorded at first mostly at Robey's studio in Houston. Soon they were recording anywhere but at Duke. Why was that? you ask Bobby. Everyone in the organization smiles. 'Well, it was the sound,' Bobby says at first, then thinks better of it. 'It was Robey, really. He was always mixing in, and he didn't know a damned thing about it. It really pissed me off, man.'

They cut in Chicago, Nashville, New York, New Orleans—it made no difference, really. Scott arranged the sessions, he got the musicians and the sound he wanted, the records consistently sold, and the band was always working. Over three hundred one-nighters every year on the so-called chitlin circuit, piling out of the nightclub at three o'clock in the morning, hurriedly packing up instruments and on to the next gig. Looking back on it, there is no bitterness to speak of. You won't get Bobby to talk against the system or against Robey even, not on the record. It is almost like a family, really, and while to the insider the recollection of dimly remembered family squabbles can arouse a sly smile or an evocative Yeah, to the outsider it is a closed-off world. 'Robey,' says Bobby today, 'knew tunes that would fit me. That's one thing you have to give him credit for. He had a good ear. No, there was no ill feeling whatsoever. A lot of artists wouldn't feel this way maybe, but I was always kind of partial to Robey and the Duke label, because they had faith in me, they thought I could really sing when no one else did.'

After Bobby went out on his own in 1961, the hits came bigger and bigger. It was just shortly after his break with Junior Parker that Joe Scott came out on the road with him, leaving A&R work and the Houston studio behind. 'Why?' repeats Mel Jackson, Scott's self-styled protégé in some disbelief. 'Man, that's where the money was. You see, Bobby was a star.'

AFTER the radio interview Bobby and the famous jazz musician walk back to their hotel together. The famous jazz musician, who was perfectly polite and controlled in promoting his Friday night concert, has now worked himself into a frenzy. 'There's too many mercenary cats in this business, man. Every fucking one of us is programmed to do what the man tell us to do, to play what the man tell us to play. I'm gonna teach some of these younger players and hope one of them will get it before I die. Otherwise they'll destroy it, man. They never looked upon jazz as a creative art. Jazz, blues, that was always something that was put down in the eyes of society. I mean, I been out here for thirty-five years, man, I'm just asking for a chance, man, I ain't looking for heaven to drop in my motherfucking lap.'

The promo man is getting alarmed, but Bobby Bland just takes it all in and tries diplomatically to reassure this college-educated musician. It wouldn't hurt, he suggests, if the jazzman included some of the newer sounds in his act, but the younger musicians, he agrees, 'don't have the concern that you and I had coming up.'

Afterwards he explains wearily to the promo man, 'I know exactly what he's talking about. He's tired, and so am I. I respect what he says, but you got to have something out there if you want to talk like that. That's why I talk about keeping your ears open, about getting that hit. Then he can go out and play what he wants to play. But right now he is his own worst enemy, and he don't even know it. It's all in knowing how to approach the problem. When you're out there on your own, you got to watch what you're saying and how you be saying it. You got to wait until you get the recognition and they start coming to you. It's a dry, dry pill to swallow, but otherwise you will destroy yourself with bitterness and hate.'

Being a star is always a little bit of a mixed blessing. In the case of Bobby 'Blue' Bland, a shambling, affable country boy who never knew anything in his life except music, it was something less than that.

'I was an alcoholic for eighteen years,' he explains simply today. You look a little askance, surprised at this casual revelation. It's no surprise that one of the chief problems of the road is liquor, but surely he must be exaggerating— 'No, I mean I was an alcoholic, there's no ifs, ands, or buts about it. The reason I can say it is because I know it happened, and I'll tell you something true. There's nothing worser than a drunk. He's the sorriest ass on earth.' By his own account he never missed a show, but 'as soon as I got in the car after the show I just let everything go. I'd be in the back of the limousine down on my knees going from one gig to the other. When I got to the hotel they just pack me out and I would sleep all day long. Then as soon as I wake up around six or seven I got the bottle right beside my bed, and I would start all over again. I've only been off liquor about four years. I was drinking up to about three fifths a day, man. I'm just so happy I found out that I don't have to do that no more, that's why I can talk about it now.'

Why? Why was he reduced to this in the midst of such remarkable, and gratifying, success? Bobby shrugs. 'I don't know, man. It gets to be almost a crutch. It gets so that without that drink before you go on you just don't have the confidence in yourself. And, you know, I think I was trying to escape.'

Bobby Bland with friends, Apollo Theater, 1966. PETE LOWRY

What was he trying to escape?

Bobby just shakes his head.

'You see, it's different,' puts in his wife Marty. 'I mean, every day we get up, when we don't feel well we can just go on about our business, we don't have to laugh or joke or smile with anybody. But then, see, if he does it, being an entertainer, then they have something bad to say about him, and he can't afford enemies – you know what I'm trying to say? Every day he *has* to get up, he *has* to feel good, he has to go up there on stage and make other people feel good – you know what I'm talking about?'

Bobby nods wearily. 'Yeah. I guess that was it.'

Whatever the case, success in a way turned into a treadmill, because once you get on the road you never get off. You have to keep working just to pay off the advances and the debts you have accumulated. Like a junkie's habit, it has a compelling logic all its own, but for Bobby it meant continuing to work that three hundred nights a year minimum, continuing to play the rough clubs and honky tonks along with the better gigs, crisscrossing the country first in a succession of station wagons, then by bus.

Then in 1968 the band broke up. No one will talk of the exact circumstances, but it obviously had something to do with Bobby's drinking, a quarrel with Joe Scott, and the fact that record sales were going badly. In any case the breakup served as a kind of watershed, with Joe Scott leaving never to return, the original band scattering in various directions, and Wayne Bennett, Bobby's long-time guitarist, settling in Chicago to do session work. Mel Jackson went off with Johnnie Taylor at first, and when that didn't work out returned to Houston and Cosmetology School. Cosmetology School? 'Sure, I got my shit together. When I left, I told him, you just call me when you're ready.'

Bobby wasn't ready for another three years. The years 1968 to 1971 found him plunged into depression, drinking more and more, questioning his very commitment to music. To save expenses he tried going out on the road with a rhythm section only, but 'it's a must that you have your own tools. I found that I was always looking for the horns. With just three or four pieces I didn't feel right, I didn't feel as if I was presenting myself, Bobby Bland.' He hooked up with another bandleader, Ernie Fields, Jr., out of Tulsa. The hits started coming again somewhat sporadically in the soul market. He was still booked to appear nearly every night. It just wasn't the same. 'Ernie had a good rock-type sound, you know, but it wasn't right for me. It's kind of a different change for you to go back to this, like just plain maple syrup after you've had your taste of honey. Oh, it's a bitter pill to swallow, but like I say, you just have to learn to adjust and you learn to accept and make the best of what you have.'

Then in 1971 he quit drinking. 'Cold turkey. Why? Well, it wasn't any one thing exactly that made me stop.'

'It was when him and T-Bone Walker was together,' says Mel Jackson.

'Last time they were really out together in Chicago, they both got extra sick. That's what really woke him up. Him and Bone. You was there, you got sick, too.' He turns to Burnett Williams. 'When was that, '72?'

'Yeah, Bone was my first idol,' Bobby agrees. 'Maybe it was just seeing him fucked up the way he was. Then I met my wife, too. She was eighteen years old. She believed in me, and she helped me. She was the one got me to quit. Then she got a little drinking problem of her own, but we straightened that out. Now everything's fine.'

He called Mel Jackson. Jackson, who had played off and on with Ernie Fields, got in touch with some of the old musicians, rehearsed the band, closed up the cosmetology shop, and went back on the road with Bobby, adopting almost the same role as his mentor, Joe Scott. 'Yeah. I always have thought of myself as his protégé. I work with Bobby the same way. I'm a little different than Joe in that he didn't like to take care of business day to day. He had me do that. But I try to make things right for Bobby.' Does Bobby need that? Jackson's eyes narrow. 'Well, I think it speak for itself.'

As for Bobby, he looks back on those years with a mixture of nostalgia and regret. He always speaks of the old band with affection, and it is obvious that latter-day bands, even under the direction of Mel Jackson, have never quite achieved the sound of Scott's. He speaks lovingly of the music, calling off the names of band members past and citing their specific contributions. He speaks wistfully, too, of the spirit that prevailed, of the good fellowship and relaxed, easy-going atmosphere. 'We used to have a ball team then, too, man. We played against the guys in the particular city, the musicians, you know. We'd get into Tennessee, Arkansas, Texas, in Florida we'd play against the policemen, because we knew them all. Yeah, we had gloves and everything, me and Joe Scott and all the fellows. Oh, we had a lot of fun back in those days. We had a real, real family then.'

Being on the road today remains a succession of petty annoyances which even Mel Jackson cannot completely cushion. There are the fans, and there is the myriad of details, from checking out the club's sound system to buying a bus. There are promotions to do for the local PR man, TV shows and interviews and radio appearances. There are sessions sandwiched in between gigs, and old acquaintanceships to be renewed at four in the morning after the show. And then there are the pitfalls of the road, motor accidents, problems in the band, the clubs that combine the selling of drugs and women with their more official dispensation of music and alcohol. Most of all it is a world in which there are no real friendships, where you measure your closeness to fellow entertainers by how long you've both been out there. For the itinerant singer there is only the fraternity of the road; the fact that you embrace a fellow star who stops by the club to see you does not mean anything except that you share a similar background and experience.

On stage, Houston, 1950s. Courtesy of Michael Ochs Archives.

Mel Jackson is Bobby's buffer, his all-purpose gofer and his eyes to the world. When Bobby snaps his fingers, Mel jumps—most of the time—but you don't get to deal with Bobby without Mel around, because, as Mel says, 'he likes to see my face in the place.' This is because, quite simply, for all of his natural canniness, for all of the wit and insight that he exhibits and the intelligence and sensitivity that manifests itself in his music, Bobby does not trust his own instincts. He feels unequipped for a world in which you need more than a second- or third-grade education to catch on to the hustle. Although a natural leader, he is lost on his own and afraid to venture anything that might jeopardize survival in a business in which survival is the only goal. Because there is no question that whatever the hazards of the road, they are nothing like the hazards of the real world. Where else could you get people to open doors for you, run errands, take care of your wants? Under what other circumstances could Robert Calvin Bland, black, uneducated, untrained, unskilled, stay in a $40-a-day hotel room, sport fancy diamonds and a big roll, command a small organization of individuals no different in background than himself, who are entirely dependent upon him and his fortunes? It is a sobering thought to consider the alternatives, and one that is not without its effects.

The chief effect has been to reinforce Bobby's natural sense of suspicion and wariness. Bobby 'Blue' Bland is an extremely cautious, conservative, even fearful man, reluctant to commit himself, unable to relax in any but the most intimate social situation. This sense of insularity has left its mark on his music as well. For while his singing is a marvel of effortless fluidity and ease, while every set is a model of professional workmanship, it is no accident that every phrase, every squall, every seeming aside is consciously worked out, that the warmly charismatic presence is the result of careful calculation and every effect is gauged to eliminate as much as possible the risk-taking, both vocal and artistic, inherent in spontaneous flights of improvisation.

There is no doubt that Bobby is very much aware of the difference between the kind of slick professional show that he does and the all-out effort of the gospel singers whom he so much admires. 'I don't think you can do that kind of singing every night, man. They sing hard, very very hard. June Cheeks is a good example. He's a preacher now, but he was some type of singer, he was the same type of singer as Little Joe Ligon, and they just about ruined his voice. You see, in spirituals you just sing when the spirit hits, I guess, but I don't think you can last too long that way. You've got to think about yourself staying out here. You've got to know the shortcuts to save yourself. In a way I suppose it's a mechanical show, but you can give your good performance every time and nobody ever really knows the difference.' Doesn't he ever get tired of the same songs night after night, of the evenly paced, carefully crafted, utterly predictable show that comes out? 'Oh, it gets kind of tiresome sometimes, but you get a schedule and you just go and do your work. Because, really, that's what's paying the bills.'

This kind of outlook has in turn made of Bobby Bland a more than willing advocate of the system in which he functions and an understandable cynic about the way in which it operates. 'Sure, everybody's out for themselves,' he says, with a conviction that this is as it should be. If Don Robey beat people out of their rights, it is only appropriate, since 'they didn't have the patience.' If Bobby Bland has not yet achieved his just reward, that is almost all right, too, because 'I believe what is for you you're gonna get. I have quite a bit of patience about certain things. If it's your time it's your time. And if it's not your time, it's not going to happen.' In this world, Bobby Bland knows, only the strong survive, and he is determined for all of his warmth and natural generosity to be among the survivors. The music industry is after all a business like any other, and Las Vegas, or network television exposure, is the goal.

Only occasionally will his guard slip and allow him to express his disappointments and the bitterness to which he is understandably prey. Someone mentions the Beatles and going to Europe. Bobby's wife, it turns out, is a big fan of Elton John. 'You know, I've been established as a blues singer for over twenty-five years, but I've never gotten paid. I don't know, over here it seems like they cater to an artist from over there much quicker than they would their own, and that pisses me off, man, that really pisses me off. You know, people talk to me about going over there to Europe, but nobody ever tell me nothing about the money they make over there. It's just publicity, I guess, but why they can't make me over here? That's a lot of bullshit, man, a whole lot of bullshit. It hurts, you know, to know your good years are gone and you haven't really been recognized. I mean, I don't want to be out here in my sixties. What the fuck can you do at sixty or seventy? That's what makes you angry. That's why I wish all this had happened when I was much younger, when I was thirty-five, say—cause I was really hollering then.'

More than anything else what seems to happen to a man like Bobby 'Blue' Bland, and to so many artists in a similar position, is that he will retreat increasingly from the world, withdraw into the reassuring familiarity of rumpled hotel rooms, daytime TV, and a showbiz cordiality that rings increasingly hollow, that is at odds with the very roots that gave him nurture. 'If I go any place,' Bobby rationalizes, 'I wouldn't be able to enjoy myself, you know. Because it's always somebody will recognize you and you'll have to entertain them and answer questions or however. Truthfully I only go out on my good days, that I'm feeling good.' Is he a prisoner then? 'In a way, yeah. It makes you have different thoughts about it. Like is this the right thing for you, you know? Maybe this isn't the thing that you was supposed to be doing. You see, you have to be concerned about what you're doing. If you don't enjoy it, then really you're working against yourself. But then I say to myself, this is what you said you wanted to be all along—I never really thought of nothing else. So you just have to deal with it for what it is.'

EPILOGUE

IT IS THE MONDAY following the week-long engagement at the Sugar Shack, a bright spring day on which a picture-taking session has been scheduled for the cover of the new country album. A photographer has been flown in from New York, a few likely-looking locations have been scouted in the countryside around Boston, and everybody is in the hotel lobby waiting for Mel Jackson to show up. I ask Bobby some questions, the photographer and I exchange small talk, Marty and Tahanee go out for a doughnut, and Bobby is growing increasingly upset at Mel's continued absence. At last the diminutive bandleader strides in the door with scarcely an apology for his employer. He has a wink for me, though, as he herds everyone into the cars. 'I imagine that extra hour didn't hurt you none with your interview,' he says and chortles quietly under his breath. 'Give him a taste of what it's like to get fucked up for a change.'

We ride out in Bobby's dark blue Fleetwood, Marty, Tahanee, and I. Bobby drives easily, taking in the sights. He seems, now that he has gotten over his annoyance with Mel, relaxed, expansive, looking forward to having a few days off for the first time in months. We drive by the Café Budapest, an elegant old-world restaurant that Marty has been begging Bobby to take her to all week. 'You got it, baby,' he declares this time, flinging an arm back over the seat. He obviously feels fine.

Out at the picture taking it is a little less idyllic. The day has grown chilly. Looking for a location that could be said to be country, the photographer shoots in front of a dam and out in a bleak field beside the road. No one seems to have remembered papers, and a joint is at last produced only with difficulty. Still the mood remains genial, even when Mel and Bobby conspiratorially confer and Bobby subsequently peels several hundred dollars off his roll. It is obvious that the trouble in the band has come to a head and someone has been fired. I ask Bobby about it, and he pretends ignorance at first, then concedes that a tenor player and a drummer have been let go. 'I think Melvin done it today.' Why were they fired? 'I don't know exactly. It's lack of communication more or less. Something like that.'

Bobby Bland, 1970s. Courtesy of *Living Blues.*
BURNHAM WARE

On the way back we have difficulty with the directions, and Bobby grows more and more concerned. We should have followed the others, he says, and it is obvious that he doesn't like being up in the air about even so inconsequential a matter as this. We are clearly not far off the track, but he slows down at every road sign, looking almost helplessly to Marty and me for directions. When we get back on the highway he relaxes again and is once more in a good mood as we pass the restaurant he has promised to Marty. It is just the start of the dinner hour, a few well-dressed men and women are getting out of their Mercedes, and Bobby reiterates his promise.

He deposits me back at the hotel, amused that I am going to talk to Burnett Williams. Burnett will be delighted, he declares with genuine pleasure, and indeed Burnett *is* delighted. Soft-spoken, eager, his Afro just a little askew in a way that Bobby's would never be today, he is the image perhaps of how Bobby 'Blue' Bland might have presented himself fifteen years ago (minus the Afro) when Bobby was front man and driver for Little Junior Parker. Yes, he declares, Bobby is a good employer, and a good teacher, too. Burnett started out with Albert King, and he appreciates Bobby for his patience, for his consideration, above all for his instruction. 'I can go to him, and he can tell me anything as far as music is concerned — how to keep from getting hoarse, when I'm hitting wrong notes — and it usually come out the way he say. Because he *knows*, he's a master of music, he ain't been out here just five or ten years, he been out here a long time. As long as he's happy, I'm happy. He's the one that's got to be happy first.'

We talk about the business, we talk about the firings. 'I don't know what their purpose is. I'm with the organization,' says Burnett sensibly. 'Whatever goes down is fine with me.' Mel Jackson comes in, depositing his derby on the bed. 'I heard you did a little firing today,' Burnett ventures tentatively. Mel's eyes twinkle. 'You heard that?' 'Did you fire a tenor sax and a drummer?' 'Where you heard that from?' Both men break up. 'Who said that, Fogg?' prods Mel Jackson. 'Oh man, that ain't nothing, that ain't nothing at all. I might hear anything. I wave to 'em when they get on the plane.'

They talk about the new bus that Mel thinks he finally has nailed down. As driver and chief mechanic (even Bobby will occasionally get under the big bus, Burnett volunteers), Burnett is particularly interested in this subject. It will cost a minimum of twenty thousand and probably closer to thirty. Where are they going to get the money? I ask. Mel shrugs. 'Somebody coming up with it.' The record company? 'I don't know who it's coming from,' says Mel ominously, 'but if somebody don't come up with something we just gonna sit down until they do. They'll come up with it.'

A phone call shatters the silence that this statement provokes. It is Bobby in the room next door, and immediately Burnett's manner alters. 'No, it's good, bossman,' he declares, a tone of enthusiastic servility creeping into his voice. 'You know I wouldn't tell you no lie. They got them big old thick hamburgers, just like you like 'em. You just dial 218—Room Service.' When he hangs up it is obvious that Bobby is going to eat in his room, just as he has every night since he has been in town; the Café Budapest is forgotten.

'Well, you see, I'm well-liked in my family,' Burnett explains. 'My wife goes along with me. She say, I know what you trying to do, and I'm with you 100 percent, and that's what I need. Somebody that's with me 100 percent and wants to see me try to become something. You see, I'm willing to wait. I ain't got nothing else to do, really. I'm thirty-four, and I can sing from now until my voice give out on me. I'll be out here until I die probably. Cause I want to be a star.'

Meanwhile the present star is thinking of the future. 'I ain't got no great big goals, really, that I'm striving for. Just to keep healthy and keep singing. Just to be part of this music field—and maybe help somebody along the way.' He has had, he says, no good nights in his entire week's stay at the club. 'Like I say, when I have a good night I just feel *good*. I didn't get that this time, I don't know why, it was a nice club, nice room, some clubs just distracts me funny.' It doesn't matter, really. It doesn't even matter if the outside world is threatening most of the time. For that brief moment that he is up there on stage, he is always sure of himself, always confident, always self-possessed. He is without question Bobby 'Blue' Bland, the same Bobby 'Blue' Bland who came out of Memphis so many years ago to create a style and make a name for himself. He is Little Boy Blue.

POSTSCRIPT

This is the way it was in the spring of 1975. A few months after this piece was written a number of things changed. First of all the Sugar Shack closed down, and Bobby's country album came out without any of the pictures that were shot that chilly day. In more substantive matters guitarist Mel Brown left the band to join fired drummer Charles Polk in country singer Tompall Glaser's short-lived Outlaw Band. In an even more surprising development, Wayne Bennett, Bobby's original guitarist, briefly rejoined the band for the first time in eight years, and, strangest twist of all, Burnett Williams went off on his own to join B.B. King. Since then there have been further rearrangements and realignments. There have been attempts to break Bobby Bland in the disco market, with predictably dreary results. And when I last saw him, in the spring of 1979, Bobby 'Blue' Bland was very vocally dissatisfied with ABC and shopping around for a new label. It's all just further illustration, if illustration were needed, of the vagaries of show business, an ongoing story—bright, painful, lively, dull, but always hinting at the possibility that the big breakthrough, the inevitable ticket to stardom, lies just around the next corner.

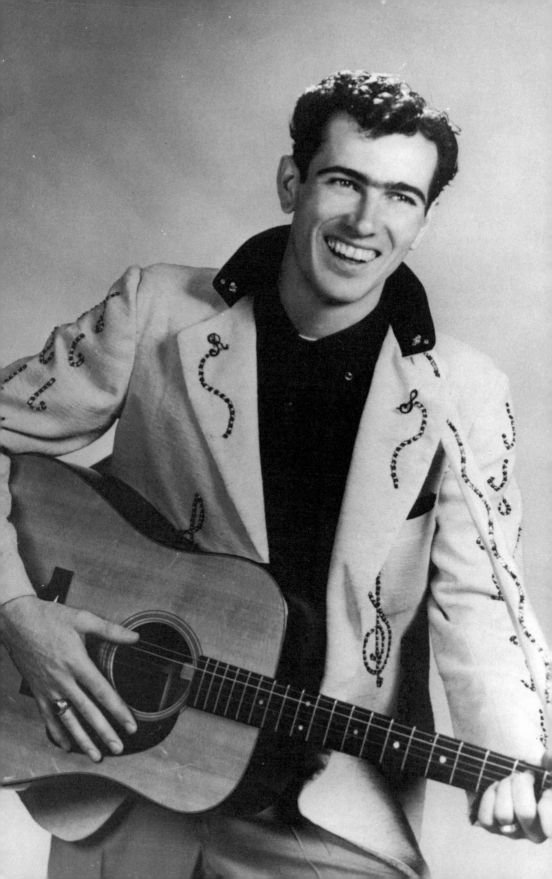

Part Two

HILLBILLY
BOOGIE

T HERE ARE MANY differing views as to when and where rockabilly (it
wasn't rock 'n' roll, but then again it wasn't hillbilly) was born. Certainly
you can hear the seeds of the style in Hank Williams's work from the late
forties, the basis, really, for almost every modern trend in country music.
Some will say that Lattie Moore, an obscure Kentucky singer born in 1924,
was singing in a rockabilly style 'before Elvis left Humes High.' And there
was a whole brief hillbilly boogie fad in the late forties and early fifties,
when the boogie woogie craze was adopted by artists like Merrill Moore
('House of Blue Lights'), Tennessee Ernie Ford ('Shotgun Boogie'), Arthur
Smith ('Guitar Boogie'), Jack Guthrie ('Oakie Boogie'), and of course the
Delmore Brothers ('Hillbilly Boogie' itself, among many others). The music
of Bob Wills, too, widely known as western swing and enjoying something
of a revival in recent years, incorporated elements of blues, big-band jazz,
country music, and boogie woogie in a style that Bill Haley would adapt and
fuse with r&b in the early fifties. The music was around, then, in the honky
tonks and beer joints, long before it ever acquired a name or label.

The Quintessential Rockabilly (in this case, Ray Smith).
Courtesy of John and Shelby Singleton.

Certainly there is no question as to who crystallized the style. Elvis Presley in many ways—visually, aurally, sociologically, sexually—captured the imagination of the country almost from the time he first burst upon the scene in 1954. To Roy Acuff and other shocked traditionalists he just 'niggerized' the music. As Sam Phillips, the founder of Sun Records, the Memphis label on which Presley first appeared, is reported to have said, 'If I could find a white man who had the Negro sound and the Negro feel, I could make a billion dollars.' Well, Phillips did find his white boy, and if he didn't make a billion from Presley (he sold his contract to RCA for $35,000), he made up for it in other ways. For just as there is no question that Presley was the focal point of a revolution in taste and style (Elvis, I think, changed forever the whole concept of the popular hero, grown bigger than life and smaller at the same time, through the process of media magnification), there is equally little question that Sun Records, and the genius of Sam Phillips, was the basis for this revolution.

What Sun did—aside from recording some of the greatest music, black *and* white, to be heard in this century—was to realize Sam Phillips's explicit vision of 'broadening the base' of American music. Once this vision had crystallized with the advent of Presley, Phillips took a number of artists who had up till then considered themselves traditionally country, and grafted on to their music the same overlay of blues and rhythm 'n' blues that had been so successful initially. For some the transition was natural. As Carl Perkins said, in discussing his own musical development as a child: 'I'd go home and take my little old guitar and try something like "Walking the Floor Over You," and I'd put me a lick in there and my daddy'd say, "Carlie, you ain't doing it right." But I loved that black rhythm and the black spirituals that I heard in the fields, and I just kind of mixed it all up together.' Sometimes the lesson had to be more forcibly applied, as in the case of Roy Orbison, who recalled, 'The one line at Sun was to bring out the old blues 78s of Arthur Crudup and others and say, "That's how I want you to sound." And I said, "Now, Sam, I want to sing ballads, you know. I'm a ballad singer."' With Orbison the process never took, and he went on to notable success with Monument Records—as a ballad singer. Sometimes the formula produced fabrications that were dry and brittle. But when it worked, it gave birth to music that was purely inspired, that seemed to feed off something that was in the air and brought some of the most talented members of a single generation (Elvis, Johnny Cash, Carl Perkins, Orbison, Charlie Rich, Jerry Lee Lewis) into one tiny studio at one time.

Whatever the reason for this astonishing phenomenon—and it was probably Sam Phillips's genius, not just for spotting talent but for drawing it out as well—the one common denominator that applied to everyone who entered the Sun studio was that you had to be crazy. 'All of 'em were totally nuts,' says publicist Bill Williams admiringly. 'They were all free spirits, they were all uniques. I think every one of them must have come in on the midnight train from nowhere. I mean, it was like they came from outer space.' 'I Wish I Was Crazy Again,' sang Johnny Cash recently in duet with Waylon Jennings; Jerry Lee Lewis's most convincing hit of the seventies was entitled 'Middle Age Crazy'; and indeed no one that I have ever met who was connected with Sun was anything less than eccentric. Everyone in this section of the book has been involved with Sun at one time or another, with the exception of Mickey Gilley—and his cousin and admitted stylistic model is Jerry Lee Lewis! Cowboy Jack Clement, a self-proclaimed legend in his time, maintains ties with nearly all of his former label-mates and in fact has plans to bring rocka-billy into the space age.

In the last few years I'm not sure that rockabilly hasn't acquired a little bit of a bad name through overexposure; like any self-consciously conceived style, it exists within the narrowest limitations and in many cases consists of no more than outright *hommage* to one of the recognized masters, or direct imitation of one of the certified classics ('Baby, Let's Play House' has probably appeared in a gross of retitled versions). I get no kick myself out of listening to one indistinguishable rockabilly cut after another, but then when I go out and hear the music of an authentic original like Sleepy LaBeef, who is still tearing up the honky tonks with a sound that refuses to die, I know un-questionably: rockabilly lives!

SCOTTY
MOORE

Elvis, Scotty, and Bill:
A Sidelong View of History

O N T H E W A L L there is a color picture of Elvis Presley, looking young,
surly, and full of confidence. Nearby is a crimson-label 45 encased in
a glass frame, proclaiming it to be the one millionth copy of 'Tragedy' by
Thomas Wayne to be sold on the Fernwood label in 1959. Other records with
gold-plated tributes to their engineer or producer are scattered about the
sparsely furnished room, and there is an eclectic selection of albums, from
Muddy Waters and Robert Johnson to Chick Webb, Cal Tjader, and Stax
soul, running the length of one wall.

The genial proprietor of this two-man tape copying and engineering
operation, situated in a converted warehouse behind the Monument studio
in Nashville, is Scotty Moore, producer of 'Tragedy,' engineer for countless
soul and country sessions, and legendary guitarist for Elvis Presley from
the very beginning (when back in 1954 it was just Elvis, Scotty, and Bill
on Sam Phillips's yellow Sun label) right up until Elvis went into the army
in 1958. Performance pictures from that period show a lean, hawk-faced,
almost expressionless guitarist standing dourly behind the featured performer.
Today the face has filled out and softened, the sharp ski-jump nose has
grown bulbous, and the manner is modest, self-effacing, and unremittingly
gracious.

'Ooh, you're making me think hard,' says Scotty Moore with a teasing
smile. 'That hurts.' He gives each inquiry careful consideration, sometimes
pauses so long before offering a response that you think he has forgotten the
question, and he is painfully scrupulous on any matter of fact. Analytic,
thoughtful, and disarmingly sincere, Scotty never seems to have a bad word
to say about anyone, but for Elvis he continues to have a particularly fond
spot. 'You know, we always had a certain bond or understanding, from day
one. We could talk to each other sometimes without saying a word, if that
makes any sense at all.' There have been periods when he hasn't seen Elvis
for years at a stretch, but he feels as if they could pick up their friendship

again right now in 1976 despite an almost total lack of contact since the 1968 TV special that served both as reunion and, for a brief time, rejuvenator of Elvis's career. 'No, no personal reason on either side,' says Scotty of the eight-year gap, 'other than just that he got into Vegas and doing tours, and I couldn't turn loose and work them. You know, he can call me a lot easier than I can see him.'

Scotty is tied up with his other activities anyway and seems perfectly content with his own modest success as a highly regarded engineer, independent producer ('A lot of it is working in a coordinating bag, setting up sessions for people, hiring musicians, putting things together'), and very occasional session man (he played on recent cuts by Sonny James and Billy Swan, although he says he no longer has the time to practice enough even to call himself a musician).

His own view of his role in history is neither overblown nor altogether self-effacing, and while he is happy to talk about the old days it does not seem to be anything he dwells on. His solos on the early records have been quoted note for note by groups like the Beatles and Creedence Clearwater, and together with Chuck Berry and Carl Perkins (and blues masters like B. B. King and T-Bone Walker), he is among the most influential guitarists of the rock 'n' roll era, but he insists candidly, and perhaps realistically, that he is not an instrumentalist. 'I don't like to sit down and learn a part. I wouldn't attempt to play sessions, because I couldn't take the regimentation. Really, I just try to find something that fits what the guy is singing, to hit on some kind of a fill or a lick that sounds right and hasn't been heard too often before.' When he first started he was 'into jazz, blues, just about all types of music,' but when Elvis became popular, and the music life became a steady procession of one-nighters and hit records, 'that's when my hopes of becoming a good musician ended.' He smiles with wry amusement at the turns that life will take and directs his attention back to interviewer's questions and reflections on the way things were and what they have since become.

He was born Winfield Scott Moore III on December 27, 1931, in Gadsden, Tennessee, outside Humboldt near Jackson. It was natural enough for him to play music, since his father and three older brothers played together in a country group. Scotty got his first guitar when he was eight years old, but he says it was probably hardheadedness that caused him to take up music. Being left out of the family group served as a spur for him to take it up on his own, and by the time he quit school in the tenth grade he was pretty well set on being a musician.

'I slipped into the navy at the ripe old age of sixteen. That's really where I got my musical education. I listened to all kinds of music, and I really got interested in jazz, Tal Farlow, Barney Kessel, that kind of stuff. I wanted to play it all. I guess probably from the country side, Merle Travis and Chet Atkins were the guitarists I listened to most. But I listened to blues things,

Merle Travis. Courtesy of Douglas B. Green.

too, all kinds of styles. We had a group in the service, just a little thing, two guitars and a steel, and we used to play on radio station KBRO in Birmingham, Washington. It was only when I came out of the service in '52 that I got back into country. You see, unless you were a schooled musician and could read and play with some of the larger groups, the small honky-tonk bands were the path of least resistance. And what they were playing then, same as they are now, was boogie music for dancing with a country-orientated beat and instrumentation.'

When he got out of the navy, Scotty never thought about going back to the farm. Instead he went to Memphis, where two of his brothers owned a laundry and dry cleaner's. After trying out a number of jobs, Scotty became a hatter in his brothers' establishment, 'because back then hats were a big thing and the guy that worked for my brothers was going to quit. So my brothers said to me, "You want to learn the hat business?" I said, "Can I make a living?" "That's about it." "Well, okay." You see, I just worked from early in the morning till two in the afternoon. That left the rest of the day to pursue other things.'

Somehow, 'by hook or by crook,' he put together a group called the Starlite Wranglers, which was fronted by a singer named Doug Poindexter, then working as a baker, and which included a Firestone Tire employee named Bill Black on bass. The group was no different from thousands of small honky tonk bands, and Scotty spent most of his time either rehearsing or booking the band. Gradually the Wranglers built up something of a local reputation, playing weekend gigs within a fifty-mile radius of Memphis, and Scotty decided 'the next thing we needed for recognition would have to be a record.' Quite naturally he gravitated towards Sam Phillips's Sun Records, one of the few recording studios, and the only real independent label in town.

The basic facts about Sam Phillips are fairly well known. He was an ex-radio engineer from Florence, Alabama, who some years earlier had opened the Memphis Recording Service, originally to record black blues singers. By the time that Scotty met him, Phillips was looking for something new. Over the past two years he had put out twenty-three records on his fledgling Sun label, all but one by black artists, all along the lines of his earlier work in blues and rhythm 'n' blues. In the spring of 1954, however, he had already recorded Michigan's Singing Cowboy Earl Peterson, white gospel singer Howard Serratt, and hillbilly boogie man Hardrock Gunter. He was also contemplating the release of a novelty number by the white blues singer, Harmonica Frank Floyd, which he had originally recorded in 1951.

'He knew there was a crossover coming,' says Scotty. 'He foresaw it. I think that recording all those black artists had to give him an insight; he just didn't know where that insight would lead. You see, Sam came from pretty much the same background as the rest of us basically, growing up listening to black southern blues and, of course, country. We were all look-ing for something, we didn't know quite what it was, just some way to get through the door. Well, Sam and I got to be pretty good friends, just by my hanging around the studio all the time. It got to be almost a daily thing in fact. I would get through work and just drift down to the studio somehow, and we would sit there over coffee at Miss Taylor's Café and say to each other, "What is it? What should we do? How can we do it?"'

Eventually Scotty persuaded Sam to record his group, the Starlite Wranglers, and the result was 'My Kind of Carryin' On.' Looking at the record today, one would be hard pressed to discover in it the seeds of revolution. The song is an uptempo novelty number; the instrumentation is straightforwardly country; the vocal is mannered and cranky; only Scotty's guitar, with its solid punchy lines, clarity of conception, and typical concise-ness and logic of approach, gives any hint of what is to come. 'It's a classic,' says Scotty, only half joking. 'I wrote it, the whole thing. I gave Doug Poindexter a third of it since he was the vocalist, I gave my brother a third of it, too, because he could read music and he wrote the lead sheet. I guess you'd have to say I was the producer in a sense, at least I was the worrywart trying to get things together, but really it was just another way to get across. It didn't cost anything, and it wasn't likely to do anything. Sure enough, it didn't.'

'My Kind of Carryin' On' was cut on the first of June, 1954. The record sank without a trace, and that might have been the end of Scotty Moore's recording career if Sam Phillips one day hadn't happened to mention a nineteen-year-old kid who had come in originally a year before to cut a birthday record for his mother ('We record anything—anywhere—anytime,' boasted the Memphis Recording Service motto) and had been pestering Phillips ever since to make a real record on the Sun label.

'You see, by doing our record, Sam and I had become fairly close, and we were going through our daily routine drinking coffee down at Miss Taylor's Café when he mentioned Elvis's name. "The best I can remember he can sing pretty good," Sam said. Well, that started me to thinking, and every day after that I would ask him, "Did you call the guy?" "No." "Did you call the guy?" After a couple of weeks of this—either Marion [Phillips's secretary, Marion Keisker] or me bothering him all the time—he finally went back to the studio one day and actually came up with the number. He told me, "You get him to come over the house and see what you think of him." Which I did. Bill Black lived just a couple of doors down, and he came down and listened, too. Well, you know, Elvis came in, he was wearing a pink suit and white shoes and ducktail, I thought my wife was going to go out the back door. We sat around for a couple of hours, going through a little bit of everything—Marty Robbins, Billy Eckstine, you name it. After he left Bill came back, and he said, "What do you think?" I said, "Well, he sings good, but I can't really say he knocked me out." This was on a Sunday afternoon. The next day I told Sam the same thing, and he called Elvis to set up an audition.'

What came next, in the accepted version of the story, was an unsuccessful preliminary audition followed by months of arduous rehearsal. Elvis, Scotty, and Bill went through every tune in their repertoire; a sorting-out process occurred; and eventually Sam Phillips decided they were ready to record. This is certainly what should have happened. According to Scotty Moore, however, it was quite different.

'A few days later, I believe it was the following Monday night [this would have been July 5, 1954, following that July 4 initial meeting], Elvis came in for the audition. Sam just wanted to see what he sounded like on tape, because quite naturally you can sound quite a bit different in the studio than sitting around the living room singing. It wasn't intended to be a session— that was the reason just Bill and I were there. Well, we tried three or four things. "I Love You Because" I believe was the first thing we actually put on

Elvis, Scotty, and Bill, 1954. Courtesy of Wayne Russell and John Morris.

tape. Then we were taking a break, I don't know, we were having Cokes and coffee, and all of a sudden Elvis started singing a song, jumping around and just acting the fool, and then Bill picked up his bass and he started acting the fool, too, and, you know, I started playing with 'em. Sam, I think had the door to the control booth open—I don't know, he was either editing some tape or doing something—and he stuck his head out and said, "What are you doing?" And we said, "We don't know." "Well, back up," he said, "try to find a place to start and do it again."'

And that, according to Scotty Moore, was the genesis of 'That's All Right,' a free-flying blues with a country beat, the A side of Elvis's first single ('Blue Moon of Kentucky,' a similar reworking of the classic Bill Monroe bluegrass tune, came about in the next couple of nights in much the same way) and the song that set the whole world of popular music in a spin from which it has yet to recover. 'That's not correct,' says Sam Phillips. 'I'm not saying Scotty's lying, because he's a very truthful person, but there was a number of rehearsals and a period of three to six months that elapsed before we recorded.' Whatever the case, when the record came out, no one knew quite what to make of it or its youthful author, not even Scotty.

'From the beginning I could see that he had a different outlook on things, just the way he dressed, the way he wore his hair. He was a rebel, really, without making an issue out of it. At the beginning he started sitting in with various bands. Then when Sam put the record out, things really started popping. At first there was some thought of making Elvis part of the group. It was along the lines of two acts in one, with the Starlite Wranglers as the regular dance band and then bring Elvis on as the special guest. Well, that couldn't last long from the friction standpoint, and very shortly after that the group just disbanded. No, there were no hard feelings, all of us were looking for the breaks, whichever way they came, and that just seemed like the best thing to do at the time. Doug Poindexter? I believe he's selling insurance in Memphis. It's been several years since I've seen him, but we still occasionally stay in touch.'

From then on it was Elvis, Scotty, and Bill, with the subsequent addition of drummer D.J. Fontana, whom they picked up on the Louisiana Hayride, a Bayou version of the Grand Ole Opry, which started booking Elvis in October. The story of those early months and years is a familiar one: high school auditoriums, one-night stands, eight-hundred-mile hops between gigs, fifteen-minute spots on talent-crammed package shows, stardom. The nervous energy, the barely controlled wildness, the certainty of aim and sureness of artistic intent are all present in the music, which stands up today as pure and timeless and irreducible as when it first appeared more than twenty years ago. At the very beginning it was Scotty who managed Elvis; then a local promoter named Bob Neal stepped in, and in November of 1955 Neal yielded to Colonel Tom Parker, snow man, heir to the whole medicine-show tradition, and one of the few people about whom Scotty Moore does not speak well. When Elvis went to Hollywood, Scotty and Bill went with him, and you can see them in such early (and notable) films as *Jailhouse Rock*, *Loving You*, and *King Creole*.

In the early days, says Scotty, the trio were 'very very close. We had to be. We practically lived together, the three of us, just months and months on end sometimes. I remember very well in the early days, there were all kinds of experiences, fights, show dates canceled, not getting paid, it was fairly rough, and every time before we would leave to go out, Elvis's mother would call either Bill or myself. "You be sure and take care of my boy," she'd say, and we'd assure her, of course, that we would. Elvis was a typical wild kid, I mean not wild in a mischievous way, but he loved pranks and practical jokes. We would have to just absolutely threaten to dump water on him sometimes to get him out of bed in the morning. I guess he was a typical teenager in that way. I mean, I wasn't that much older myself, but I had to kind of take charge.

'In the very early days he wasn't really that set on himself. At that time he didn't have the stage know-how. It was Bill who was the clown, riding that big double bass, generally cutting up, which stemmed from a lot of country acts using the bass in that way. We rarely planned anything. A lot of your black groups were choreographed back then, but there again Elvis more or less broke away from the norm. He was doing it more as an individual thing. Oh, sometimes we'd make up little goofy things we were going to do, but really there was no set plan other than that we went out on stage to entertain better than anyone else who was on the bill. At first we didn't really know what would get to them, we'd try different things, but as time went by Elvis worked into a kind of routine. He may not have known what they wanted at first, but, son, when he figured out what it was he put it to them.

'I was never the clown myself. With just the three of us, there had to be somebody to keep the beat going. We had a good time. We really had a good time. And the crowds just kept getting bigger and bigger. Half the time we couldn't even hear ourselves play. We kidded a lot of times that we were the only band in history that was directed by an ass. Because, you see, we had to take all our cues and things visually. Even with D.J. playing as loud as he could, you still couldn't hear the drums. Of course nothing was miked back then, but it was an experience that wasn't to be missed. You really got the true feeling of an audience.'

In the meantime a whole generation of rockabillies had sprung up virtually full-blown out of such southern backwaters as Pocahontas, Arkansas; Ferriday, Louisiana; Lubbock, Texas; and Tipton County, Tennessee. Within

Scotty, right, with D.J. Fontana (Elvis's drummer). CRAIG ANGLE

months of the release of Elvis's first record, the revolution had arrived, and musicians like Carl Perkins, Jerry Lee Lewis, Gene Vincent, Buddy Holly, and a whole host of lesser known but no less ardent practitioners of the art were knocking on record company doors. Indeed it was almost as if the new music had been in a stage of secret gestation, just waiting for the proper conditions to burst into full flower. Just why this should have been is a matter of some conjecture, but Scotty Moore has his own theory on the subject.

'It had been there for quite a while, really. Carl Perkins was doing basically the same sort of thing up around Jackson, and I know for a fact Jerry Lee Lewis had been playing that kind of music ever since he was ten years old. You see, from the honky tonks you got such a mixture of all different types of music, and I think what happened is that when Elvis busted through, it enabled all these other groups that had been going along more or less the same avenue – I'm sure there were hundreds of them – to tighten up and focus on what was going to be popular. If they had a steel guitar they dropped it. The weepers and slow country ballads pretty much went out of their repertoire. And what you had left was country-orientated boogie music.'

It seemed as if there might be an inexhaustible supply of talented country boys looking to make a hit, and that in fact is why Sam Phillips sold Elvis's contract for $35,000 to RCA in late November 1955. 'The only reason he sold Elvis was to get the capital to produce the others. He figured – and I think he was right – that with the money, instead of having one Elvis he could have four or five. Well, it didn't quite work out that way, but he came pretty close.'

Indeed, for a time Sun had Carl Perkins, Johnny Cash, Jerry Lee Lewis, and Roy Orbison all under contract, while also earning the distinction of never re-signing a major artist. Elvis, of course, flourished under the management of Colonel Parker. And Scotty and Bill, who had started out as more or less equal partners with their vocalist ('I was the one who had the car,' says Scotty), left several months before Elvis's March 1958 induction into the army in a dispute over money. They were getting $100 a week retainer and $200 a week when they toured, out of which all their expenses had to be paid. 'It was strictly a financial problem. After that we worked with him on a per date basis, although we didn't do but a couple of tours.' It was the Colonel, apparently, who was the root of the problem. 'We always did have problems there,' Scotty concedes, but that is all he will say. Originally Elvis had wanted to draw up an agreement that would have given Scotty and Bill one quarter of one percent on all record royalties, but that never got put down on paper either. 'It would have been nice,' Scotty shrugs with his shy, lopsided grin. It would have meant several million dollars as well, for Scotty and Bill played on 'All Shook Up,' 'Too Much,' 'Heartbreak Hotel,' 'Jailhouse Rock' – every one of the early hits.

Still, even if there had been no financial falling out, Elvis's induction into the army would have meant a temporary break. In 1959 Bill Black formed the very popular Bill Black Combo, which continues today more than ten years after its leader's death. Scotty meanwhile eased into the production end of the business, buying into the Fernwood label, which had been founded in 1956 by Slim Wallace and Sun record man Jack Clement. 'Tragedy,' Scotty's first production and Fernwood's one big hit, almost put the label out of business, as the company was forced to overextend to meet a demand for records that distributors never paid for. The label survived nonetheless, and Scotty continued to work for it and for Sam Phillips as well, both in Memphis and as head of Sun's Nashville office. He did some producing, quite a bit of engineering, and generally developed the quiet air of professional expertise by which all his endeavors have been characterized. When it became obvious that Sam Phillips's interest in the record business was not as keen as it once had been (in addition to his musical genius Phillips seems to have possessed a certain business acumen, which led him to become one of the first investors in the Holiday Inn chain), Scotty moved to Nashville permanently and established his own studio, Music City Recorders. Around 1973 he sold this, and he has been freelancing ever since. He is quite a bit in demand and is known for his professionalism, his meticulousness, and his comprehensive knowledge of the field. He remains interested in the Sun era and tries to keep up with all the books and articles that have been written on the subject. He is occasionally interviewed—although mostly about Elvis, almost never about himself—and is always glad to help out in whatever way possible.

His musical interests and inclinations remain pretty much what they have always been. If he had his way he would record everything live, but a good sixty percent of the work he does is overdubbing. He can listen to his own early work, clinkers included, without embarrassment, 'because we weren't that concerned as far as a mistake would go—I mean, unless it was just godawful—as opposed to the overall feel.' His life goes on at a slow, unhurried pace, and when the phone rings in the middle of a sentence he doesn't answer it until he has completed his thought. When asked by the caller what he is doing, he answers with a wry smile, 'Just sitting here being famous.'

CHARLIE
FEATHERS

The Last of the Rockabillies

IT IS A TYPICAL SATURDAY NIGHT at every Hilltop Lounge on the not-too-respectable outskirts of any town. Beaten-down men and women cling to each other; factory girls in tight white hiphuggers do the bump; skinny bald-headed old men in overalls jitterbug decorously with stout middle-aged women in sequined glasses; strangers huddle together against the cold.

In this particular Hilltop Lounge on Memphis's Lamar Avenue—not far from the old Eagle's Nest, where Elvis Presley first started out some twenty years ago—pandemonium reigns, as a weatherbeaten fifty-year-old patron named Stanley Johnson delivers a letter-perfect, spirited, but tuneless version of Elvis's 'Mystery Train'; the bartender, Catfish, hunches his shoulders, shuffles around the microphone, and dolefully pronounces himself 'Born to Lose'; Miss Pat King, wearing a checked western shirt and Afro-styled hair, gets up from her table to contribute a couple of country weepers; the piano player, Slick, who transports his own battered upright just to sit in, hits the keys with his elbows, exclaims 'Eat your heart out, Jerry Lee!' and does Ernest Tubb imitations. Over at the shuffleboard everyone keeps an eye on the door, because the vice squad has broken up the betting and shut down the Hilltop the weekend before.

The featured performer takes it all in with a mixture of good humor and genial contempt. 'Ain't nothing but a bunch of goddamn amateurs,' he says at one point, while claiming at another that his son-in-law, who plays rhythm guitar, does a Don Gibson number better than Don Gibson himself. Although he doesn't sing much, he is constantly involved in the performance, jumping up, grabbing for a mike, fiddling with the dials of the Peavey PA system, throwing in a bass harmony from the rickety table where he sits beside the darkened bandstand, ceaselessly expounding upon his theories of music, his plans for the future, his unending quest for the breakthrough, the hit record. He wears an open-necked white shirt, houndstooth checked coat, and his white hair is slicked back in an impeccable DA. Once in a while he will strap on his guitar and do a song or two himself, and then it is as if

Left: Charlie with Ray 'Caterpillar' Campi. Courtesy of Rollin' Rock Records.
Right: Memphis, Tenn. Courtesy of Steven Cook, Cowboy Carl Records.

the room is transformed with his energy, jumping to the rhythms of 'Good Rockin' Tonight,' 'Roll Over Beethoven,' 'Shake Rattle and Roll,' carried away by the irrepressible squeals, inspired asides, and manic enthusiasm of the singer. Everyone is having a good time, and only the featured performer, with his restless commentary, abrupt shifts of mood, and feverish memories of the past, seems to be thinking of anything but a Tennessee Saturday night. The featured performer is Charlie Feathers, sometime ambulance driver, stock car racer, semi-pro ballplayer, shuffleboard hustler, and rockabilly legend.

'You know what the secret was? You know the secret to the sound of Sun?' We are sitting in the cramped living room of the modest little house where Charlie Feathers has lived for the past ten years (since around 1966) surrounded by a tangled litter of tapes. The shades are pulled, Charlie's wife is at work, his twenty-year-old son and lead guitarist Bubba is asleep, his daughter Wanda (who doubles on vocals and tambourine) looks demure in her wedding picture on the mantel, and thirteen-year-old Ricky is at school. Outside the rain is pouring down, and the street is experiencing a minor flood, evidently a not too uncommon occurrence, since everyone has taken the trouble to pull their cars up on bare dirt lawns.

'Slapback,' says Charlie. His pale eyes light up, his handsome, smooth-skinned face takes on an animation that was not there before, and the white hair only serves to set off the youthfulness of his manner, the vehemence of his opinions.

'Now a lot of people think slapback is just somebody slapping on the upright bass, but that ain't it, cause you can take the upright bass, hit it just like they play up in Nashville. A lot of people think it was Sam Phillips. But if that was so, you tell me what happened to the Sun sound when the people that was responsible for that sound—Elvis and Jerry Lee and Carl Perkins and Johnny Cash—all left him. I'll tell you what happened, buddy. Sam Phillips just about got out of business. There wasn't nothing he could do about it when the people who knew how to get the sound wasn't there no more. Because to be honest I don't think Sam Phillips knew how to get the sound himself. Today he has a bigger studio, got lots of money, but he cannot come up with that sound again to save his life, and I wonder what the public thinks about that.'

There is no question that Charlie Feathers knows what *he* thinks about it, but exactly what that is I can't say for sure, any more than I can figure out what the true secret of slapback really was ('Aw, I don't like to talk about it some time in a way, but the way it come about, see a little old home tape recorder is what brought it about'). It's not that Charlie Feathers does not have definite views on the subject, nor that those views are necessarily inaccurate. It's just that following Charlie Feathers's conversation without previous preparation is like picking your way through a maze of veiled hints, dense allusions, and references to the obscure grudges and minute stylistic differences of twenty years ago. For Charlie Feathers was there, too, with Elvis and Perkins and Lewis and Cash, in the Sun studio at the dawn of the rock 'n' roll era.

Charlie Feathers never achieved celebrity or fame, and his role at Sun remains somewhat unclear, but everyone agrees that he was present from the beginning, that he made several of the most influential, if not popular, early rockabilly recordings, and of course that he wrote 'I Forgot to Remember to Forget,' Elvis's first major hit, a number one smash on the national c&w charts in 1955, and a song for which Charlie claims to have seen so few royalties that he eventually sold his rights to co-writer Stan Kesler. (Kesler, an ordinarily self-effacing man, says that Charlie just demoed the song, but by the terms of their partnership received half credit.) According to Charlie, he also taught Elvis his style ('I arranged all of Elvis's stuff. Definitely. Sure did. Sam's still got some things on me that he won't let nobody hear. Why? Aw, I don't know, but I reckon Sam knows the reason why. His boys heard those tapes one time, and they said I should sue. They said there was no doubt in their mind where all this stuff comes from, after listening to those tapes'), gave Jerry Lee Lewis the idea for his 'pumping' piano, developed a song called 'One Two Three,' which soul singer Joe Tex was later to popularize as 'Hold What You've Got,' and was generally Sam Phillips's right-hand man in the development of the whole rockabilly style.

All of which sounds distinctly improbable, except that throughout our conversation Charlie Feathers constantly reinforces his points with musical illustrations, detailed stylistic references, and specific examples from a tape library which he says even includes a session he cut on Elvis at a West Helena radio station in 1955. 'Some tough goddamn stuff, baby,' he says matter-of-factly with a certain glumness that seems at odds with the brash nature of his claims. That's the way it is with Charlie Feathers, though, a proud, suspicious, stubborn, and single-minded man who becomes animated only when he is talking about music. On that subject he is generous in his enthusiasms, passionate in his likes and dislikes, and fatalistic about his chances of ever setting the record straight. It seems incongruous somehow to be discussing so casually a past that is littered with the promise of great- ness, a past peopled with figures who have gone on to acquire the status of legend. With anyone else it might well sound like empty boasting, but Charlie carries it off with a tone more accepting than bitter, and even one's natural skepticism is to some extent overcome by his mastery of names, dates, tech- nical details, and all the minute particulars of the tangled history of an era. Nothing that Charlie says seems designed really to take away from the ac- complishments of artists like Elvis and Carl Perkins, whom he respects and admires, and even his feelings about Sam Phillips are decidedly ambivalent. 'Aw, you can't blame him, we were young, you know, we didn't really know what we was doing. But I'll tell you, buddy, we really did do *something*!'

CHARLIE FEATHERS was born in Holly Springs, Mississippi—actually in the country out from Holly Springs around Slayden and Hudsonville—on June 12, 1932. He grew up working the land that his parents tenant-farmed, but his sharpest memories are of music. He sang in church, listened to the Grand Ole Opry, and snuck around to the Rossville Colored Picnic, out in the woods just across the road from his family's home. He learned guitar from a local black sharecropper named Junior Kimbrough, 'the greatest blues singer in the world. Chuck Berry had nothing on him. I had him teach my son how to play, and what little I learned I got from him, too. To be honest with you, I never did do a whole lot of country. Now Hank Williams— I always liked his stuff a lot. And Bill Monroe, he used to come through Hudsonville, set up tents and all, man I thought it was the greatest thing I ever heard. Well, you see, I loved bluegrass all my life, but I never did know how to play it. There wasn't nobody around who could play that type of music, only colored artists thumping on their guitars. Oh man, there wasn't anything to beat it. Them colored get out there on the weekend, they get together anywhere there was a guitar, just tune that guitar way down and whomp on it. Man, they play and gamble and shoot dice all day long, all night long, too. Sam, he always said I was a blues singer, but I was really singing bluegrass and rapping on the guitar like I heard them colored artists

Bill Monroe and his Bluegrass Boys, ca. 1940. Left to right:
Art Wooten, Bill Monroe, Cousin Wilbur Westbrooks,
Pete Pyle. **Courtesy of Douglas B. Green.**

do. Bluegrass rock, that's what it really was, Sam called it rhythm 'n' blues, some said it was country rock, but Bill Monroe music and colored artists' music is what caused rock 'n' roll.'

At sixteen or seventeen, he left home to work on an oil pipeline with his father. He worked around Cairo and then in Texas, taking his guitar with him and playing the saloons and joints at night. After a couple of years he moved back to Memphis and got married at eighteen, driving a truck, working in a box factory, always fascinated by music. His brother-in-law, Dick Stuart, who went by the professional named of Uncle Richard, was program director at KWEM in West Memphis, and through him Charlie met Howlin' Wolf, who had a fifteen-minute fertilizer and feed spot on the air every day. Charlie still remembers going to see Wolf play out in the country—the music, the dancing, the bare dirt floor. He started hanging around Sam Phillips's studio at about that time and remembers the other great blues singers that Phillips was record-ing then as a nameless procession of colored artists who created a powerful, exciting music and received little or no pay for it. He also recalls Elvis Presley as a teenager hanging out at the Suzore No. 2 movie theater, just starting to drop by the Sun studio long after Charlie Feathers had established himself there. They were two young men desperate to become musicians, looking for a break, groping for a style. When Elvis's first record came out in July 1954, it looked as if they had found it.

Charlie insists that he did the arrangement on 'Blue Moon of Kentucky,' the Bill Monroe number that was the B side of the single. He had been working, he says, with Scotty and Bill, and even cut a demo on the song. ('If he did, I honestly don't recall,' says Scotty Moore diplomatically today.) He was ready to jump into the new style himself with 'Corinna,' 'Gone Gone Gone,' and a host of similar rocking sounds, but he never got the opportunity. 'I was just stuck doing country,' Charlie says by way of explanation. 'Sam, he was always scared to gamble. If he had two things out and one of them was going good, he just let that one kill the other dead.' Whatever the case, Charlie's first record did not appear until some eight months after Elvis's initial release. It came out on Flip, a Sun subsidiary, while the next release, a mournful country weeper called 'Defrost Your Heart,' was the only record he would ever actually have out on Sun. When he came to Phillips with 'Tongue-Tied Jill' in 1956, Sam turned him down, and he went to Les Bihari's Meteor Records, where he had a fair-sized local hit. 'It would have been number one,' he says, 'if we'd cut it at Sun.' He got the idea for the song, he explains seriously, from a telephone operator with a stammer. The title is pretty much self-explanatory, and the record is typical of all of Charlie Feathers's best material— a novelty song full of nonsense syllables, falsetto shrieks, glottal stops, and unabashed good fun. It remains the number with which Charlie Feathers is most identified today.

It served, too, to introduce him to a larger audience, and shortly there-after he signed with King Records of Cincinnati, a big name in country and rhythm 'n' blues, which saw Charlie as its answer to Elvis Presley, the newest musical rage.

'It was like getting out of a Cadillac and into a Ford,' says Charlie of the switch from Sun. For all of his grumbling about Sam Phillips, it is obvious that he recognized Phillips's contribution to the music, and the cut-rate production methods he ran into at King did not sit well with him either. He made only eight sides for King in 1956–57 and after that went back to cutting demos for Sam Phillips, doing studio work for Sam's brother, Tom, and cutting scattered singles for a wide variety of obscure and short-lived labels over the next fifteen years. Of the records that he made for King, records which are considered classics in the rockabilly mold and remain the basis for Charlie Feathers's considerable underground reputation, he has nothing but scorn. 'Aw, they was never right,' he says regretfully. 'We just didn't have the sound, man. I was dissatisfied with all of them, every one.' He muses on it for a moment. 'You just can't figure those things. You know, I never had nothing real big, but I went out, me, Cash, Elvis, and Carl, we played shows together all over the South, and I'll tell you the truth, man, we'd go out, Carl might take the show one night, next night it would be Elvis, another night it would be me, that's just the way it was.' Does he ever see any of them still? I ask, and he seems almost surprised at the question. 'I would have no reason to see them,' he explains patiently. 'I probably could if I wanted to. But they made it big, man. Why would I want to see them — unless'n it was to borrow a few thousand!' We both laugh; it is just a joke.

WHY, the question naturally arises, didn't Charlie Feathers ever really make it? Why, aside from the vagaries of fate, is he still playing the Hilltop on Lamar while the others are all commanding thousands or tens of thousands of dollars a performance? Several answers suggest themselves. 'He had the talent,' says Tom Phillips (Sam Phillips's brother), 'and he was real good on stage, too. But Charlie back then, he had to pretty much have things his own way. King promoted him pretty good, you know, but he didn't like the way they did, and he just let them know. Well, he's still pretty well like that, just not as bad. I believe if he'd had a little more patience...' 'He was his own worst enemy,' says Stan Kesler, today a Nashville producer. 'I think he had the capability, but he always had his own ideas of how things should be done, you know, and if it couldn't be done exactly that way, it wouldn't be done at all.' To Sam Phillips, Charlie Feathers was a derivative artist who took too much off too many to have an original style of his own. Which, of course, is the exact opposite of the way that Charlie Feathers himself sees it.

Most of all, though, what seems to have held Charlie Feathers back was an absence of polish, an inability to adapt, the same forthright and unsophisti-cated manner that creates a wall of isolation around him even today. He has no gift for small talk, he is deadly serious about his music, and in areas where he is uncertain of himself he draws back, creating by his defensiveness an appearance of hostility. His music, too, retains a strange parochialism and a steadfast refusal to alter either its terms or its manner. He is an un-reconstructed rockabilly in a countrypolitan age, continuing to sing about Stutterin' Cindy and Tongue-Tied Jill and never for a moment abandoning his belief in the essential craziness of a crazy music that long ago moved to the suburbs. He is, with his raw hillbilly sound, lonesome country voice, and freakish vocal effects, a traditionalist in a music that sought to overthrow tradition. He has become a rough reminder of another age and something of an embarrassment to those who would like to forget it.

Not to his fans, though. To the regulars at the Hilltop Charlie Feathers is a genius. They are no more surprised at the presence of a writer doing a story on him than they would be if an English television crew swept through the door. After all, people come from all over the world to see the legendary Charlie Feathers perform. To his brother Lawrence, a smaller, neater look-alike who will sing Charlie's songs at the drop of a hat, but who fiercely disputes his older brother's musical superiority, Charlie is nonetheless an example. 'I compare his talent to his education. I got to the third grade myself, and Charlie had less than that, cause he can't read or write. I think he's ten times better than any sonovabitch that went to school; if he was educated, you think how great he would be.' The band, which consists of Charlie's son, son-in-law, daughter, and a friend of his son-in-law's on drums, never questions the very idiosyncratic nature of his musical direction. And Charlie for his part moves about with an easy confidence and restless energy, meeting friends, greeting acquaintances, correcting the band's musical errors, and — though he doesn't drink so much as a beer in the two nights I am with

Charlie, center, with Jody (Chastain) and Jerry (Huffman).
King publicity photograph.

Charlie Feathers at the Hilltop. FRED DAVIS

him—feeding off the rising level of good spirits and good times that keeps the honky tonks and saloons in business. Charlie Feathers is in his element.

'My brother won't let me sing no more, I showed him up so bad,' Lawrence announces, after completing a set that has included both 'Tongue-Tied Jill' and 'I Forgot to Remember to Forget.'

'You see, he's just as good as Charlie,' says their niece Alice, who has gotten out of the hospital the day before and come down to the Hilltop to celebrate.

Charlie doesn't say anything. He gives no sign of having heard, but within moments has taken the stage for the first time all evening. From the very first notes, it is evident that for all their superficial similarities—the cutting tenor, the wobble in the voice, the falsetto yodel, and hiccuping style—Charlie and Lawrence are not at all alike. Charlie possesses inspiration, where Lawrence has only mastered the effects, and from the moment that he

114

launches into an impassioned version of 'Today I Started Loving You Again,' Charlie holds the room in the palm of his hand. His brief set includes 'Tear It Up,' 'There Goes My Everything,' and 'Gone Gone Gone,' but it is more like an orchestration of exuberance, passion, and feeling—an informal symphony of hillbilly soul—than it is a succession of unrelated songs. Charlie's voice is wide-ranging and powerful, his sense of what he wants to do with it is unerringly right, Bubba's guitar lead snaps into focus, and it is as if for a moment you are being permitted a glimpse of everything that might have been.

Charlie comes back to the table vaguely dissatisfied. There is always something to be improved upon; his mind is a constant whirl of new ideas, fresh approaches, different ways of doing things. The band plays for another couple of hours, but Charlie's energy never runs out. There is a torrid twenty-minute jam session in which one couple at a time holds the floor and individuals cut in with a variety of styles until they are displaced by the next dancer. Charlie shakes his head in disbelief, both at the triviality of the concept and at the blonde girl in oversize glasses who outlasts all her competition, as well as her hustling partner, by setting up and maintaining an almost perpetual shiver. At the end of the evening, while he is packing up the mikes, he allows himself a rare moment of satisfaction. 'You know, we was really playing 'em, buddy. I tell them to freewheel it. I tell Bubba, if he feels a lick, to go ahead and hit it. Cause I think that's where it all begins.'

'That's right,' the piano player throws in. 'I don't care what you say, you get the best music in the world in these little juke joints and holes in the wall. I'm telling the truth, you better believe it, buddy, because this is where they always sing from the heart. Charlie here, he's the best guy in the world, you ask anybody, because he's singing from the heart.'

Outside Charlie sits in the driver's seat of a pale late-model car and revs up the engine while the band climbs in. He rolls down the window to say his goodnights, flashes that quick, not quite certain smile, and peels out of the parking lot. He looks almost jaunty at the wheel.

ELVIS PRESLEY

*I wrote the first of these essays about eighteen months
before Elvis died. After his death (in August of 1977), it was
widely syndicated, perhaps in part because it had provided
a glimpse of the sad dénouement to come. I have changed
a few tenses but otherwise left it as it was written.
'Faded Love' was intended as an elegy and I think completes
the picture.*

ELVIS PRESLEY

and the American Dream

Have you heard the news, there's good rockin' tonight.

ELVIS PRESLEY, the Hillbilly Cat,
in his recording of the Roy Brown song, 1954

The pure products of America go crazy.

WILLIAM CARLOS WILLIAMS, from *Spring and All*, 1923

ENOUGH HAS BEEN WRITTEN about Elvis Presley to fuel an industry. Indeed a study could be made of the literature devoted to Elvis, from fanzines and promotional flack to critical and sociological surveys, which would undoubtedly tell us a great deal about ourselves and our iconographic needs. Sadly enough it is the weight of the literature itself, the very volume of information, no matter how well intended, which inevitably obscures the one quality unique to Elvis in all the pantheon of rock 'n' roll heroes: what jazz critic Whitney Balliett calls the sound of surprise. Other rock 'n' rollers had a clearer focus to their music. An egocentric genius like Jerry Lee Lewis may even have had a greater talent. Certainly Chuck Berry and Carl Perkins had a keener wit. But Elvis had the moment. He hit like a Pan-American flash, and the reverberations still linger from the shock of his arrival.

The world was not prepared for Elvis Presley. The violence of its reaction to him ('unspeakably untalented,' a 'voodoo of frustration and defiance') testifies to this, although in one sense he was merely another link in a chain of historical inevitability. His ducktail was already familiar from Tony Curtis, the movie star whose pictures he haunted at the Suzore No. 2 Theater in Memphis; the hurt, truculent stance we had seen before in Marlon Brando's motorcycle epic, *The Wild One*. His vulnerability was mirrored by James Dean,

Page 116: Elvis with Charlie Walker, Jimmie Rodgers Memorial Day, Meridian, Mississippi. Courtesy of John and Shelby Singleton.

whose first movie, *East of Eden*, was released just as Elvis was getting launched on his career in March of 1955 ('He knew I was a friend of Jimmy's,' said Nicholas Ray, director of Dean's second film, landmark for a generation, *Rebel Without a Cause*, 'so he got down on his knees before me and began to recite whole pages from the script. Elvis must have seen *Rebel* a dozen times by then and remembered every one of Jimmy's lines'). His eponymous sneer and the whole attitude it exemplified – not derision exactly but a kind of scornful pity, indifference, a pained acceptance of all the dreary details of square reality – was foreshadowed by Brando, John Garfield, the famous picture of Robert Mitchum after his 1948 pot bust. Even his music had its historical parallels, not just in the honky tonk clatter of Bill Haley and his Comets, but in the genuine popular success that singers like Frankie Laine and Johnny Ray (and Al Jolson, Mildred Bailey, even Bing Crosby) had enjoyed in bringing black vocal stylings to the white marketplace of earlier eras.

None of it seemed to matter somehow. To anyone who was alive at the time, he was, and remains, a truly revolutionary force. The recollection of country singer Bob Luman, just younger than Presley, might almost be considered a typical first reaction. 'This cat came out in red pants and a green coat and a pink shirt and socks,' he told writer Paul Hemphill, 'and he had this sneer on his face and he stood behind the mike for five minutes, I'll bet, before he made a move. Then he hit his guitar a lick, and he broke two strings. I'd been playing ten years, and I hadn't broken a *total* of two strings. So there he was, these two strings dangling, and he hadn't done anything yet, and these high school girls were screaming and fainting and running up to the stage, and then he started to move his hips real slow like he had a thing for his guitar. That was Elvis Presley when he was about nineteen, playing Kilgore, Texas. He made chills run up my back. Man, like when your hair starts grabbing at your collar. For the next nine days he played one-nighters around Kilgore, and after school every day me and my girl would get in the car and go wherever he was playing that night. That's the last time I tried to sing like Webb Pierce and Lefty Frizzell.'

It was the same for countless fans and for other performers, too. To Waylon Jennings he was 'like an explosion, really.' To Buddy Holly, 'without Elvis Presley none of us could have made it.' And to Elvis Presley, the center of the storm, it was something over which he professed to have no control. Over and over again in the course of his life he refused to speculate on the reasons for his success, putting it down to luck, blind instinct, anything but plan. 'I don't know what it is,' he said to C. Robert Jennings of *The Saturday Evening Post*. 'I just fell into it, really. My daddy and I were laughing about it the other day. He looked at me and said, "What happened, El? The last thing I can remember is I was working in a can factory, and you were driving a truck." We all feel the same way about it still. It just . . . caught us up.'

There it all is. The modesty, the deferential charm, the soft-spoken assumption of common-sense virtues (in this version even the tireless twitching and suggestive pelvic action are seen as involuntary reflex) that became the official Elvis. In many ways I am sure that the picture is accurate, and it undoubtedly conforms to the image that Elvis Presley had of himself. It tends to leave something out, however. What it leaves out is the drive and consuming ambition of the nineteen-year-old Elvis Presley, who possessed a sweeping musical intelligence, energies that could barely be contained, and a ferocious determination to escape the mold that had seemingly been set for him at birth. Even more, it ignores the extent to which his rebellion, his surly refusal of responsibility, his reaction to the stifling conformity of the time, could stand for an entire generation, taking in a social base of which he could scarcely have been aware, much less directly known. Most of all, this explanation, or lack of it, overlooks the music itself, a music which expressed a kind of pure joyousness, a sense of soaring release that in such self-conscious times as ours seems unlikely ever to be recaptured.

He was born Elvis Aron Presley on January 8, 1935, in Tupelo, Mississippi, a child of hard times but an only child, adored and pampered by a mother who would walk him to school until he was in his teens. His twin, Jesse Garon, died at birth, and he was always to be reminded of this absence ('They say when one twin dies, the other grows up with all the quality of the other, too. . . . If I did, I'm lucky'), as if he were somehow incomplete, even down to his matching middle name. An early photo shows a little boy in overalls, sober in an oversized soft-brimmed hat similar to his father's. He is flanked by parents who regard the camera with touching blank-faced looks that reflect neither expectation nor disappointment. His mother's hand rests on his father's shoulder; she is still young and pretty. And the child looks lost, waiflike, with that strange familiar hurt look in his eyes, that unmistakable, unfathomable curl to his lips. It is the picture that adorns the cover of his 1971 *Elvis Country* album, which bears the otherwise inscrutable (and totally uncharacteristic) epigram 'I was born about ten thousand years ago.'

He grew up, schooled to all the classic virtues of small-town America: diffident, polite, sirring and ma'aming his elders, hungry with an unfocused yearning which it would have been impossible for him, or anyone of his background and generation, either to explicitly admit or implicitly deny. 'My daddy was a common laborer,' he said. 'He didn't have any trade, just like I didn't have. He mostly drove trucks, and when he used to bring the truck home from the wholesale grocery, I used to sit in it by the hour.' The car radio was his first exposure not to music necessarily but to the world outside.

Music to begin with came from the Pentecostal First Assembly of God church. 'We were a religious family, going around together to sing at camp

Elvis with his parents.

meetings and revivals. Since I was two years old, all I knew was gospel music, that was music to me. We borrowed the style of our psalm singing from the early Negroes. We used to go to these religious singings all the time. The preachers cut up all over the place, jumping on the piano, moving every which way. The audience liked them. I guess I learned from them. I loved the music. It became such a part of my life it was as natural as dancing, a way to escape from the problems and my way of release.'

There is another photograph of Elvis and his parents, taken in 1956 after the phenomenal early success. In this picture Elvis is playing the piano; the mouths of all three are open, their eyes half shut. They hold themselves stiffly and are evidently singing with fervent emotion. Both parents have put on weight; Vernon is still handsome in a beefy sort of way, but Gladys has taken on the bloated, starch-fed appearance of so many poor southern whites and blacks. She is forty-four but will die in only two years time, to her son's eternal and heartfelt sorrow ('I think of her nearly every single day,' he said nearly five years later. 'If I never do anything really wrong, it's all because of her. She wouldn't let me do anything wrong'). I can remember to my embarrassment the reaction my friends and I had when we first saw the picture. We thought it was a joke. We thought that Elvis was putting us on, it seemed so clearly at odds with Elvis's rebel image and the mythology which, in our own state of self-deracination, we had erected around a pop idol. Today it is easier to recognize that out of this seeming contradiction (newness versus tradition, rebellion versus authority, sacred versus profane) arose the tension that was rock 'n' roll. Then such thinking was beyond the scope of our experience, and probably Elvis's, too.

He won a singing prize at ten, when his grammar school principal sponsored his appearance at the Mississippi-Alabama Fair and Dairy Show. The song he sang, 'Old Shep,' was a bathetic c&w ballad about a boy and his dog, which Red Foley (later to become Pat Boone's father-in-law) had popularized and Elvis would record for RCA some ten years later. It is not difficult to imagine the towheaded little boy standing on a chair so he could be seen and singing, unaccompanied, with that same throbbing emotion for which he would one day become famous. 'I wore glasses, no music, and I won, I think it was fifth place. I got a whipping the same day, my mother whipped me for something, I thought she didn't love me.'

At eleven his parents got him a guitar ('I wanted a bicycle'). Teachers and relatives remember him carrying the guitar around with him everywhere

Vernon, Gladys, and Elvis at the piano. ROBERT WILLIAMS

he went. Elvis remembered that 'it sounded like someone beating on a bucket lid.' He listened to the Grand Ole Opry, Roy Acuff, Eddy Arnold, Jimmie Rodgers's early records, and Bob Wills. He idolized the Blackwood Brothers and the Statesmen Quartet, two prominent white gospel groups. Billy Eckstine and Bill Kenny and the Ink Spots were his favorite rhythm 'n' blues performers. And he absorbed the blues off the radio and from the pervasive contact that a poor white family like the Presleys, always living on the edge of town and respectability, would necessarily have with blacks. 'I dug the real low-down Mississippi singers, mostly Big Bill Broonzy and Big Boy Crudup. Although they would scold me at home for listening to them.'

When he was thirteen his family moved to Memphis. 'We were broke, man, broke, and we left Tupelo overnight. Dad packed all our belongings in boxes and put them on top and in the trunk of a 1939 Plymouth. We just headed for Memphis. Things had to be better.'

MEMPHIS IN THE late forties and early fifties was a seedbed of musical activity. Never really much of a center for commercial country music, it had a raw hillbilly style and a distinguished blues tradition that went back to the twenties. In 1950 Howlin' Wolf and Sonny Boy Williamson were broadcasting on station KWEM from West Memphis; WDIA, the Mother Station of the Negroes, and the first black-operated radio outlet in the South, featured B. B. King and Rufus Thomas spinning records and performing daily. On Beale Street you were likely to run into such prominent figures as one-man-band Joe Hill Louis, veteran bluesman Frank Stokes, the famous Beale Streeters. In W. C. Handy Park you might hear a free concert by the legendary white blues singer and medicine show entertainer, Harmonica Frank Floyd. And at 706 Union Avenue, Sam Phillips had opened the Memphis Recording Service for 'Negro artists in the South who wanted to make a record [but] just had no place to go,' an enterprise which would evolve in 1952 into the Sun Record label. In the meantime, though, a quiet revolution had begun to take place. Many of the small independent record producers were becoming aware of it, and in Memphis, where there had long been a relaxed social, as well as musical, interchange between black and white, it was particularly noticeable. White kids were picking up on black styles – of music, dance, speech, and dress.

'They didn't let whites into the clubs,' veteran producer Ralph Bass told rock critic Michael Lydon, 'when I used to go out on the road with the black acts I was handling in the forties. Then they got "white spectator tickets" for the worst corner of the joint, no chairs and no dancing, and the tickets cost more, too. But they had to keep enlarging it anyway, cause they just couldn't keep the white kids out, and by the early fifties they'd have white nights sometimes, or they'd put a rope across the middle of the floor. The blacks on one side, whites on the other, digging how the blacks were dancing, and copying them. Then, hell, the rope would come down and they'd all be dancing together.' 'Cat clothes' were coming in; bebop speech was all the rage; and Elvis Presley, along with Carl Perkins, Jerry Lee Lewis, Charlie Rich, and all the other Southern children of the Depression who would one day create the style that was called 'rockabilly', was seeking his models in unlikely places.

In other ways Memphis was an oppressively impersonal urban dream for an only child, shy and strangely insecure. Living in a city project. Working a monotonous succession of jobs after school. Going off by himself to play the guitar. High school was a fog. He went out for football and ROTC but failed to distinguish himself in this or any other way. He majored in shop, grew his hair long, carefully slicked it down, and tried to grow sideburns from the time he started shaving, because, he said, he wanted to look like a truck driver. Which may or may not have gotten him kicked off the football team. Dressed anomalously in pink and black, he called attention only to his personal colorlessness and lived out typical adolescent fantasies of rebellion in teenage anonymity. 'Nobody knew I sang, I wasn't popular in school, I wasn't dating anybody. In [my senior year] they entered me in another talent show. I came out and did my two songs and heard people kinda rumbling and whispering. It was amazing how popular I was in school after that.'

Whether he was in fact popular even then is doubtful. Memories of rejection were inevitably clouded in the aftermath of success. Indeed it is as if in later years he set out deliberately to erase the loneliness of that time by gathering around him all the popular figures—football heroes, high school politicians, well-established Memphians—who would not even speak to him then. For some twenty years of his life, as the so-called Memphis Mafia, they made up his personal retinue, subject to his every whim and devoted to their chief. When he graduated from Humes High School in 1953, he was perceived by one schoolmate as an individual with 'character, but he had no personality, if you know what I mean. Just acted kind of goofy, sitting in the back of class, playing his guitar. No one knew that he was ever going to be *any*thing.' When he got a job working on an assembly line at the Precision Tool Company, it seemed as if his life pattern was set.

One year later he had a record out, and everything was changed.

One of Sam Phillips's sidelines was a custom recording service, where anyone could go in and cut a record for four dollars. Some time in the summer after graduation, Elvis went in and cut two sides, 'My Happiness' and 'That's When Your Heartaches Begin,' stylized ballads that had been popular for Jon and Sandra Steele and for the Ink Spots. He came back several times over the next few months to see if Sam Phillips might be interested in recording him professionally for the Sun label. Phillips put him off but held on to his address and telephone number. Elvis was not singing professionally, but he had his mind on music at the time. He was always going to the all-night gospel sings at the Memphis

Auditorium and that spring almost joined the Songfellows, a junior division of the renowned Blackwood Brothers quartet, whom he had admired for years.

In late spring, by Phillips's calculation, Sam Phillips called him to try out a demo on 'Without You,' still another ballad, which met with minimal success. Phillips was more or less undeterred. He put Elvis together with Scotty Moore, the twenty-two-year-old guitar player who had finally gotten to cut his first record with the Starlite Wranglers three or four weeks previously. Since then he had been coming around the studio looking to do something else, anxious to do *anything* else, really, and asking for the name of that kid that Phillips and Marion Keisker kept talking about. After what seemed like weeks of badgering, he finally got the information, but when Elvis showed up at Scotty's house on a Sunday afternoon, neither Scotty nor Bill Black, the bass player for the Starlite Wranglers who lived two doors down, was much impressed. Scotty called Sam and said that he thought the boy might have potential, and Sam suggested they come in, just the three of them, and see how it went in the studio in a kind of rehearsal session. That was what they did. They all came down after work the following night, and though everyone's version of this crucial moment in history is a little bit different (Sam Phillips recalls weeks, even months, of rehearsals), there is no question of the center of the story. Together they ran down song after song – pop, sentimental ballads, country weepers – in the little Sun studio on that hot night in early July. What they were looking for, no one seemed quite sure of. What they got, everyone knows.

'OVER AND OVER,' said Marion Keisker, Sam Phillips's assistant, 'I remember Sam saying, "If I could find a white man who had the Negro sound and the Negro feel, I could make a billion dollars."' With Elvis, Phillips apparently found the key, and indeed following Elvis's success he practically force-fed his formula to the succession of rockabillies – Perkins, Lewis, Roy Orbison, even Johnny Cash – who followed. That was after Elvis, though. At the time, judging by all the unsuccessful attempts (premature might be the better word) that were made to turn Elvis into a Dean Martin crooner, even Sam Phillips must have had his doubts.

'That's All Right,' a traditional blues by Crudup himself, was the first number that jelled. According to Scotty Moore, 'That's All Right' was, really, an accident that happened in the studio, something that no one could have planned, for the simple reason that no one knew Elvis had it in him. So far as anyone could tell, from both vocal style and choice of repertoire, this boy was strictly a ballad singer. So when Elvis put down his Coke, picked up his guitar, and started singing 'That's All Right' during a break ('Just jumping around the studio, just acting the fool'), no one could have been more surprised than Scotty Moore, Sam Phillips, and maybe even Elvis Presley himself.

Arthur 'Big Boy' Crudup. Courtesy of *Blues Unlimited.*

However the song was recorded, it marked a turning point in the history of American popular music.

'That's All Right' was at first glance an unlikely song to create such a transformation. A conventional blues, originally put out by a very pedestrian blues singer (if any bluesman deserves the charge of monotony, it is Arthur 'Big Boy' Crudup, who rarely escaped from one key and possessed a singular ineptitude on guitar), it consists of a string of traditional verses set to a familiar, slightly shopworn blues melody. The copy in this instance, however, bore little resemblance to the original. For even if the record was not worked out during a break, but was in fact the product of months of hard work, trial and error, and direct calculation, that isn't the way that it comes across at all.

It sounds instead easy, unforced, joyous, spontaneous. It sounds as if the singer has broken free for the first time in his life, the voice soars with a purity and innocence. There is a crisp authority to Scotty Moore's lead guitar, Elvis's rhythm is ringing and clear, the bass gallops along in slap-heavy fashion. The record sparkles with a freshness of conception, a sharpness of design, a total lack of pretentiousness, an irrepressible enthusiasm. Like each of the ten sides eventually released on Sun—evenly divided between blues and country—'That's All Right' has a timeless quality that was just as striking and just as far removed from trends of the day as it is from contemporary fashion. The sound is clean, without affectation or clutter. And there remains in the conventional lyrics—easing their way into a scat verse that was in Crudup's original leaden and deliberate—a sense of transformation, both dizzying and breathtaking, an emotional transcendence, which, if only because of the burden of knowledge, could never happen again.

And yet this is not quite literally true either. It is perhaps another self-sustaining myth, with the reality at once more straightforward and more paradoxical. The B side of 'That's All Right' was Bill Monroe's classic blue-grass tune, 'Blue Moon of Kentucky,' taken at something like breakneck tempo in the released version. An alternate take exists, however. It indicates that 'Blue Moon of Kentucky' started out its rockabilly life in a slower, bluesier version, more direct emotionally and more ornate vocally, much in the manner of 'She's Gone,' an alternate interpretation of the innocuous enough 'I'm Left, You're Right, She's Gone,' which resulted from a later session. Both unreleased versions contain surprising intimations of what is to come, with hints of the familiar vibrato, the smoky drop to a bass register, the lazy crooning style, all hallmarks, I would have said, of a later, decadent period. In fact it is a style with which Elvis is distinctly more at home than the more frantic rockabilly mold, giving vent to all the smoldering passion that was to be so conspicuously absent from his later efforts. 'Fine, fine, man,' Sam Phillips declares, as the bluegrass number disintegrates into nervous laughter and edgy chatter. 'Hell, that's different. That's a pop song now, nearly about. That's good!'

'That's All Right' was cut on the night of July 5, 1954. A dub was delivered within days to Dewey Phillips, host of the popular 'Red Hot and Blue Show,' which was a kind of Memphis Moondog Matinee, rhythm 'n' blues and hipster talk for a mixed black and white audience. Phillips, who enjoyed a close, almost fraternal relationship with his nonrelative Sam, played the record half a dozen times in a row on the first night. 'When the phone calls and telegrams started to come in,' he told journalist Stanley Booth, 'I got hold of Elvis's daddy, Vernon. He said Elvis was at a movie, down at Suzore's No. 2 Theater. "Get him over here," I said, and before long Elvis came running in. "Sit down, I'm gone interview you," I said. He said, "Mr. Phillips, I don't know nothing about being interviewed." "Just don't say nothing dirty," I told him.

'He sat down, and I said I'd let him know when we were ready to start. I had a couple of records cued up, and while they played we talked. I asked him where he went to high school, and he said "Humes." I wanted to get that out, because a lot of people had thought he was colored. Finally I said, "All right, Elvis, thank you very much." "Aren't you gone interview me?" he asked. "I already have," I said. "The mike's been open the whole time." He broke out in a cold sweat.'

By the time the record came out, there was a back order of 5,000 copies, and Elvis and Sun Records were well on their way.

Largely on the strength of this success (the record went on to sell 30,000 copies and even made number one briefly on the Memphis c&w charts) Elvis was named eighth most promising new hillbilly artist in *Billboard*'s annual poll at the end of the year. Almost immediately he began to appear around Memphis, sitting in with the Starlite Wranglers at the Bon Air, playing with Scotty and Bill (briefly billed as the Blue Moon Boys) at the Eagle's Nest, debuting at a big country show at the Overton Park Shell, even opening a shopping center. In October he appeared on the Grand Ole Opry for a one-shot appearance. He met with more success on the Louisiana Hayride, where he signed on as a regular after his second appearance and where he picked up a drummer, D. J. Fontana. And he began touring, through Texas and Mississippi and Arkansas, performing at schoolhouses and dance halls and crossroads, traveling in a succession of second-hand Lincolns and Cadillacs which were driven until they gave out.

Everywhere the reaction was the same—a mixture of shock and wild acclaim. 'He's the new rage,' said a Louisiana radio executive in a 1955 European interview. 'Sings hillbilly in r&b time. Can you figure that out? He wears pink pants and a black coat and owns a Cadillac painted pink with a black top. He's going terrific, and if he doesn't suffer too much popularity, he'll be all right.'

According to Marion Keisker, 'On that first record of Elvis's we sent a thousand copies to disc jockeys, and I bet nine hundred went into the trash can, because if a rhythm 'n' blues man got it and heard "Blue Moon of Kentucky," he tossed it away . . . same thing if the country man heard "That's All Right."'

'I recall one jockey telling me that Elvis Presley was so country he shouldn't be played after 5 A.M.,' said Sam Phillips. 'And others said he was too black for them.'

Nonetheless the records sold ('Good Rockin' Tonight,' the second release, cut in September 1954, made number three on the Memphis c&w charts), teenagers turned out in droves to hear the so-called Hillbilly Cat, King of Western Bop (his titles alone betray the cultural schizophrenia with which he was greeted), and they came away with the same dazed reaction Bob

Luman experienced in Kilgore, Texas. He stood limpid, straddle-legged at the mike, lips curled in a sneer, guitar strung negligently around his neck. One leg twitched, sending a ripple down the seam of his loosely draped pants; the other jackknifes out at the hip. Girls scream spontaneously, and he fixes them with a glance of almost scornful ease. The left leg keeps up its tireless jiggling. As the music heats up, he swivels his hips, leans forward with the mike, points his guitar like a phallic tommygun, drops to his knees, crawls to the edge of the stage, leaps back from clutching hands – will do anything, in fact, like Little Richard and Jerry Lee Lewis after him, to engage an audience's attention. 'He threw everything into it,' said Bob Neal, his first manager, 'trying to break that audience down, trying to get it with him. He'd always react to audience reaction, and in the rare instances where he'd be placed on the show early, I always felt he kind of outdid himself, making it tough for the guy to follow.'

The records followed, one after another, and although, according to Marion Keisker, 'Every session came hard,' each came out sounding like some kind of inspired accident: the unexpected falsetto with which Little Junior Parker's 'Mystery Train' trails off, the bubbly hiccuping beginning to 'Baby, Let's Play House,' the wailing lead-in to 'Good Rockin' Tonight,' the too-perfect, beautiful slow intro to blues singer Kokomo Arnold's 'Milkcow Blues Boogie,' which Elvis interrupts to declare portentously, 'Hold it, fellas. That don't *move* me. Let's get real, real gone for a change.'

Well, he got gone. The records picked up in sales, though never on a scale larger than a relatively tiny independent company like Sun could expect. The bookings increased. The cars and the clothes got fancier, the money did, too. A year after his Sun debut, in July of 1955, 'Baby Let's Play House' made the national c&w charts. By the end of the year Elvis Presley was named most promising new c&w artist. But by then, of course, he was a proven commercial commodity, for he had signed with RCA Records.

'He was greatly anxious for success,' said Bob Neal, with whom he signed in January of 1955 and went to New York, for the first time, for an unsuccessful audition with Arthur Godfrey's Talent Scouts. 'He talked not in terms of being a moderate success. No – his ambition and desire was to be big in movies and so forth. From the very first he had ambition to be nothing in the ordinary but to go all the way. He was impatient. He would say, "We got to figure out how to do this, we got to get ahead."'

Some time early in 1955, Colonel Tom Parker, who claimed to be a scion of the Great Parker Pony Circus, though he was in reality a Dutch immigrant, one-time manager of Eddy Arnold and current manager of Hank Snow, veteran of a lifetime of carnivals, medicine shows, and various enterprises of greater or lesser dubiety, entered the picture. Through Snow, then the nation's number one country star, Parker had developed Hank Snow Jamboree Attractions into one of the major booking agencies in the South, and working through Neal at first, the Colonel began booking Elvis. On November 20, 1955, Bob Neal bowed out of the management business. On November 21 Colonel Tom Parker produced a document that entitled him to represent Elvis Presley exclusively and signed a contract with RCA. Sun Records received $35,000 plus $5000 in back royalties for the artist. It was an unheard-of sum for the time.

There were many cogent reasons for such a move. For Sun Records the deal provided much-needed capital, and Sam Phillips has always staunchly defended his decision, citing the subsequent success of Carl Perkins, Johnny Cash, and Jerry Lee Lewis on his label as proof of its correctness. For Elvis Presley the benefits became obvious immediately. On January 10, 1956, he entered RCA's Nashville studio and recorded 'Heartbreak Hotel.' The rest, I think, is history. As for the Colonel, he soon divested himself of all other interests and devoted himself to advancing his boy, a devotion that took such forms as the decline of all presidential and nonremunerative invitations, the hawking and retrieving of souvenir programs at concerts, the personal dispensation of Elvis calendars at the fabled Las Vegas debut in 1970—in short, a steadfast refusal to cheapen his product. 'When I first knew Elvis,' the Colonel frequently remarked, 'he had a million dollars worth of talent. Now he has a million dollars.'

I DON'T KNOW what there is to say about the success. There are, of course, the hits: 'Heartbreak Hotel,' with its bluesy country feel, metallic guitar, and dour bass. 'Hound Dog,' with its reversed sexual imagery, savage musical ride, and spewed-out lyric ('Well, they said you was high class, well that was just a lie'). 'Jailhouse Rock,' with its frenetic pace and furiously repeated drum roll. 'Love Me Tender,' 'Love Me,' 'Loving You.' The negligent ease of 'Don't Be Cruel,' the mnemonic pop of 'All Shook Up.' The impact of hit after hit after hit, fourteen consecutive million sellers, RCA claimed, simultaneously topping pop, country, and r&b charts. The phenomenal explosion of both the mode and the music over a period of twenty-seven months until his March 1958 induction into the army. The elevation to socio/mytho/psycho-sexual status, as Elvis Presley unwittingly became a test of the nation's moral fiber.

The peculiar thing is that in retrospect it is all irrelevant. Not just in the wake of Presley's success but as the inevitable consequence of the almost total acceptance which rock 'n' roll has come to enjoy. When Elvis Presley was first recorded by Sam Phillips, he was an unmarketable commodity, an underground hero on the fringes of society and artistic respectability. Today, like every trend and tidal wave that comes along in our consumer-oriented society, with its voracious appetite for novelty and its pitiless need to reduce what it does not understand, his achievement has been subsumed, his art

Elvis and the Colonel, right, with the Duke of Paducah.
Courtesy of John and Shelby Singleton

has been converted to product, and rock 'n' roll itself has become part of the fabric of corporate America. And the music — what of the music?

For some reason Elvis Presley never recaptured the spirit or the verve of those first Sun sessions. When I say never, I don't mean to imply that all of his output for the last twenty years was worthless, nor do I mean to set up some arbitrary, pure-minded standard by which to measure, and dismiss, his popular achievement. Many of the songs that he recorded, from 'Hound Dog' to such extravagant items as 'Don't,' 'Wear My Ring Around Your Neck,'

With the Jordanaires. Courtesy of Douglas B. Green.

'A Fool Such as I,' were still classic performances, despite their musical excesses and pronounced air of self-parody (the clear, hard tenor had yielded to tremulous vibrato, dramatic swoops from high to low, and light-hearted groans). They were also fundamentally silly records, a charge that could never be leveled at the Sun sides, which, whatever else they might appear to be, were seriously, passionately, joyously in earnest. You are left with the inescapable feeling that if he had never recorded again, if Elvis Presley had simply disappeared after leaving the little Sun studio for the last time, his status would be something like that of a latter-day Robert Johnson: lost, vulnerable, eternally youthful, forever on the edge, pure and timeless.

Not that RCA would not have liked to duplicate the Sun sound. At the beginning there is little question that they tried. The echo, the slapping bass, Scotty Moore's fluid lead guitar, the Arthur Crudup blues and sentimental country numbers that appeared on the first two albums — these were the very elements that had made the Sun sides so bright and distinctive. Carl Perkins's 'Blue Suede Shoes,' Ray Charles's 'I Got a Woman,' Little Richard's 'Tutti Frutti,' all fit in admirably, and rockingly, with the five previously unreleased Sun cuts that turned up on his debut LP. Still, even RCA was aware of the difference. It was 'a new sound,' according to Steve Sholes, Elvis's RCA discoverer, because Elvis had evolved so rapidly in the months following his RCA signing. Others feel that it was a combination of technology (choruses, added instrumentation, the RCA studios could never be as funky as Sun's makeshift quarters), commercial calculation, and spiritual malaise. The fact is, I think, that Elvis was too well-suited to success. He was intelligent, adaptable, ambitious, and sure of his goals. He wanted to break loose, and music was only his vehicle for doing so.

'The way we made records,' Sam Phillips has said of the Sun days, 'kind of coincided with the studio. There was something about the looseness that rubbed off on the recordings. I had to be a psychologist and know how to handle each artist and how to enable him to be at his best. I went with the idea that an artist should have something not just good, but totally unique. When I found someone like that, I did everything in my power to bring it out.'

'Elvis never had *anything* ready,' said Marion Keisker. 'Elvis was different from the other Sun artists. He did not write his own songs. And he'd never rehearse. First thing he'd always want to cover some records he'd

Exchanging autographs with Carl Perkins. ROBERT WILLIAMS

heard on the jukebox. And Sam would have to persuade him he couldn't do that. It was always a case of the same thing — sitting down and letting him go through everything he knew or he would like to do, and we'd pick things to concentrate on.'

With RCA, it seems clear, there was too little time and too much money riding on each session to allow for so haphazard an artistic process. It was too painful for the artist as well, and Elvis soon settled on a more comfortable and formulaic approach which took advantage of his wide-ranging musical background, facility in a number of styles, real talent as a quick study, and almost total lack of taste. With the addition of the Jordanaires, a popular quartet present from the first RCA session, the sound quickly took on the trappings of the gospel and pop groups that Elvis had always admired. With the almost inexhaustible demand for material brought on by the unprecedented dimensions of the Presley success, professional songwriters were called in and invited to submit their compositions for approval (and publication, under the Elvis Presley Music imprint). Whereas a song like 'Hound Dog,' although already part of the stage act, required as many as thirty takes, after a while vocals were simply patterned on the demos that were submitted. ('He fell in love with certain demos,' says songwriter Jerry Leiber, 'and in some cases just recorded in the same key the demo was in, even when that was maybe not the most comfortable for him.') And while no session could be complete without the warm-ups and inevitable gospel sings that always remained a feature of Elvis Presley's musical life, the loose feel of the Sun studio was gone.

Events moved too rapidly even to try to comprehend. Million sellers, national tours, the triumph over Ed Sullivan's stuffy personal pronouncements (Presley will never appear on my show, said Sullivan, just weeks before he signed Elvis for a $50,000 series of appearances), instant celebrity, the promise of immortality, the rush of success. Record making in fact became something of a subsidiary interest once Elvis went to Hollywood in the summer of 1956. By the time that he entered the army in 1958 he was what Sam Phillips had foretold he would become: a genuine pop singer. A pop singer of real talent, catholic interests, negligent ease, and magnificent aplomb, but a pop singer nonetheless.

Elvis with Nudie, costumer to the stars.

I CAN REMEMBER the suspense my friends and I felt when Elvis came out of the army in 1960. By this time we were growing sideburns of our own, and in some ways his fate, like that of any other icon, seemed inextricably linked with ours. What would he be like? Would he declare himself once again? Would he keep the faith? We hadn't long to wait for the answers.

His first release, 'Stuck on You,' followed the familiar formula of 'All Shook Up,' 'Too Much,' 'Teddy Bear,' innocuous rock 'n' roll fare, but still rock 'n' roll. The second release was the monumental best seller, 'It's Now or Never,' reputedly Elvis's favorite song and loosely based on the 'Sole Mio' of Mario Lanza, one of Elvis's favorite operatic tenors. The first, and last, paid public appearance was a Frank Sinatra TV special, in evening dress. Frank Sinatra! After that he retreated from the world for nearly a decade to make movies.

We forgave him his apostasy, just as we forgave him all his lapses and excesses. His self-parodying mannerisms. His negligible gift for, or interest in, acting. His corporeal puffiness. His indifference to the material he recorded. His apparent contempt for his own talent. His continuing commercial success in the face of all these fallings away (*GI Blues* was his most successful picture; the soundtrack from *Blue Hawaii* sold an incredible $5 million worth of records). The spectacle itself of the bad boy made good.

Because that is what I think it was that gratified us most of all. Elvis's success, flying as it did in the face not only of reason but of good taste as well, seemed in a way a final judgment on the world that had scorned him and which by the sheer magnitude of his talent he had transformed. We took it as a cosmic joke. We speculated endlessly on the life that Elvis must be leading, and the laughs he must be having, behind the locked gates of Graceland, his Memphis mansion. Every fact that is presented in this essay was a mystery then, the subject of painstaking detective work, an intricately assembled collage that has since been exploded by knowledge. Most of all we labored happily in the wilderness, self-mocking but earnest, possessors of a secret knowledge shared only by fellow fans: Elvis Presley was to be taken seriously.

And, of course, we always looked for signs, which appeared occasionally, if at irregular intervals, that our faith was justified. Mostly these took the form of musical throwbacks (blues, country, rockabilly), some of which had been recorded years before their actual release date, further evidence of the secret conspiracy in which Elvis had enlisted us. The first of these found objects was *Elvis' Christmas Album*, released as early as November 1957, and dismissed at the time as sure proof of his sellout to the commercial forces that be. It turned out, like his two early gospel albums, to contain some of his most heartfelt singing as well as showcasing one of the dirtiest, nastiest (that's *bad*) blues he would ever put on record, 'Santa Claus is Back in Town.' *Hang up your pretty stockings*, we quoted the Leiber-Stoller lyrics at each other, once we had made the discovery, *Turn out de–light / Santa Claus is coming / Down your chimney tonight.*

Then there was the album Elvis put out on his return from the army, called, appropriately, *Elvis Is Back*. Basically a rhythm 'n' blues session cut with top Nashville sidemen, it charted new directions that were never followed up and featured Elvis in the uncharacteristically adventurous role of taste-maker. It, too, is crowned by a convincing blues interpretation, this time of Lowell Fulson's 'Reconsider, Baby,' which is highlighted by Elvis's gruff, 'Play those blues boy, play the blues!' long before such asides became popular with young blues acolytes.

Elvis for Everybody, a generally dismal collection, hid away not only a chiaroscuro 'Your Cheatin' Heart' and a dramatic reading of Chuck Berry's 'Memphis, Tennessee' but another r&b number that harked back to the Sun days, a really raunchy version of Sun stablemate Billy 'The Kid' Emerson's 'When It Rains It Really Pours.' The rumor that Elvis had played guitar on a Billy Emerson side (it turned out, on closer examination, that Billy was saying, Play it, *Cal*vin, not Play it, Elvis) only added to the piquancy of the association.

136

And so it went. Right up to the end. Finding evidence of life amidst marble entombment. Finding evidence of engagement, wakefulness even, in the midst of sloth and torpor. Finding treasure in the midst of dross, and faith amid an artistic inconsequentiality that is almost staggering.

There were only two footnotes to this long and continuing saga of perfect decline.

The first was the TV special that ended his eight-year retreat from the world and punctuated his long slumber in Hollywood. This came about quite simply because by 1968 Elvis had exhausted his audience, as well as himself, with movies that were no longer drawing, records that without even a semblance of commitment—they were simply lifted from innumerable, and ineffable, movie soundtracks—were no longer selling. The Beatles, the Rolling Stones, and Bob Dylan had eclipsed their one-time mentor. Elvis was begin-

Stage Show, 1956. ALFRED WERTHEIMER

ning to look dated. And so the Colonel, who had always avowed that it was his patriotic duty to keep Elvis in the 90 percent tax bracket, decided that it was time for his boy to step out. Seizing the moment with customary astuteness, he wangled a remarkable financial deal for a special to be shown at Christmas time. What could be more appropriate, the Colonel argued, than that the star should appear in a kind of Christmas pageant, dressed soberly in tuxedo and tie and singing a medley of Christmas carols and religioso numbers? For the first time in his career Elvis seems to have put his foot down. Or perhaps that is merely what the Colonel would like us to believe. In association with the show's young producer-director, Steve Binder, Elvis determined to appear in live performance, doing his old songs in taped segments, in front of a somewhat handpicked but real, live, breathing audience. A good chunk of the special was choreographed, it is true, and there remained some big production numbers, but the core of the show was just Elvis, alone on the stage with his guitar and such old musical friends as Scotty Moore and D. J. Fontana.

I'll never forget the anticipation with which we greeted the announcement and then the show itself, having the opportunity to see our idol outside of his celluloid wrappings for the first time, knowing that we were bound to be disappointed. The credits flashed, the camera focused on Elvis, and to our utter disbelief there he was, attired in black leather, his skin glistening, his hair long and greasy, his look forever young and callow. 'If you're looking for trouble,' he announced, 'you've come to the right place. . . .'

> If you're looking for trouble
> Just look in my face
> I was born standing up
> And talking back
> My daddy was a green-eyed
> Mou-ow-ntain jack.
> Because I'm evil
> My middle name is Miser—eeee . . .

I don't know if I can convey how transcendent, how thrilling a moment it was. Here were all our fantasies confirmed — the look, the sound, the stance, the choice. The voice took off, it soared, it strained, and then to our vast surprise Elvis is sweating. He is unsure of himself, he is ill at ease, he is uncertain of our reaction, and it seems clear for the first time that Elvis is trying, and trying very hard, to please us. He needs to have our attention, and it comes as something of a shock after all this time to discover that a hero whom we had set up to feel only existential scorn, a hero who was characterized by a frozen sneer and a look of sullen discontent, should need us in the end. It is his *involvement* after all that comes as the great surprise, and I don't think anyone who watched the TV show at the time will ever forget the sheer tension of the moment, the brief instant in which Elvis's and our passions, our fears, our illusions, were nakedly exposed.

I say that this is a footnote, but maybe it was more than that. Because to my mind at least it gave rise to the second brief flourishing of the art of Elvis Presley, a flourishing that could not have taken place without all that went before, but which can stand on its own nonetheless as a real and significant artistic achievement. On the strength of the success of the TV show, and the subsequent sales of 'If I Can Dream,' the inspirational single that concluded it, he went back to Memphis to record for the first time in nearly fifteen years. The singles ('Suspicious Minds,' 'Kentucky Rain,' 'Don't Cry, Daddy') and the initial album, *From Elvis in Memphis*, that came out of these sessions are true reflections of the passion and soul which Elvis invested in that rare moment of unease in an otherwise uninterrupted career. There continues to be that same sense of tension, the atmosphere remains nervous and almost self-effacing, there is that strange anxiety to please and constriction in the voice which seems a million years away from the perfect self-assurance of the nineteen-year-old 'natural' who first recorded for Sun so very long ago.

What happened after that, everybody knows. Amid much hoopla Elvis returned to live performing, first in Las Vegas, where a flock of critics, flown out to the historic opening, came back with tales of vitality undimmed, robust roots, and disarming charm. We are all fans. When it became obvious from the relative unsuccess of *That's the Way It Is*, a documentary of the Vegas act, that movies were no longer a viable commercial formula, the Colonel hustled his product back out on the road, where he appeared in coliseums and hockey rinks, the Astrodome and Madison Square Garden. There was a great deal of money made very quickly, and very soon the burst of involvement that had so briefly galvanized Elvis dissipated, the act was reduced to total self-parody, and Elvis to practicing his karate kicks on stage. When I finally saw him in person at the Boston Garden in 1971, it was like going to a gathering of the faithful, grown middle-aged perhaps in pantsuits and doubleknits, but faithful nonetheless. I sat as far away from the stage as you can sit in a big arena, but even from there you could see that he was the perfect artifact, preserved like the great woolly mammoth in a block of ice, suspended, Greil Marcus has suggested, in a perpetual state of grace, all his illusions and mine intact.

And then, sadly, the ice melted. When Elvis turned forty, the media had a field day. He was fat, and depressed about it, and didn't get out of bed all day. It seemed to be a continuing battle against creeping mortality, and Elvis was not winning. His hair was dyed, his teeth were capped, his middle was girdled, his voice was a husk, and his eyes filmed over with glassy impersonality. He was no longer, it seemed, used to the air and, because he could not endure the scorn of strangers, refused to go out if his hair wasn't right, if his weight—which fluctuated wildly—was not down. He had tantrums on stage and, like some aging whore or politician, was reduced to the ranks of the grotesque. It no longer seemed difficult to imagine where it all would end.

Don't feel sorry for him. For Elvis was merely a prisoner of the same fantasies as we. What he wanted he got. What he didn't, he deliberately threw away. There is a moment in *Elvis on Tour*, his final film and yet another documentary, in which Elvis yields the stage to J.D. Sumner and the Stamps, the gospel group in his entourage. He has just finished singing 'Lord, You Gave Me a Mountain,' a Marty Robbins song that tells in a series of dramatic crescendos a tale of separation from an only child. It could just as easily be 'My Boy' or 'Separate Ways' or even 'Mama Liked the Roses,' all dramas of broken marriage and separation from loved ones. (Elvis's daughter, whom he was said to adore, was born nine months to the day after his 1967 marriage, which subsequently ended when his wife took up with her karate instructor.) These are the only secular songs which he seems able to sing with any real conviction—painful substitutes for self-expression, artful surrogates for real life. In the film he introduces the gospel group, enlists the audience's attention ('I don't sing in this. Just listen to them, please. It's a beautiful song'), and for the first time is at rest, expression pensive, eyes uplifted, mouthing the words and shaking his head with a smile, carried outside of himself. It is as if it is intended in expiation, and it probably is. Then the music starts up, the show begins again, he launches into 'Lawdy, Miss Clawdy' without so much as a blink, and Elvis Presley is once again encapsulated in the gauzelike world from which he will never emerge.

It's all right, you want to say to him impertinently. It's all right. You did okay, even if your greatest talent did turn out to be for making money.

Earlier in the same film there are moving images from the Ed Sullivan show of 1956, where youth is forever captured, forever joyous, with a swivel of the hip, a sneer of the lip, and the full confidence and expectation that nothing will ever go wrong. 'My daddy knew a lot of guitar players,' recalls Elvis in one of the film's interview segments, 'and most of them didn't work, so he said, "You should make your mind up to either be a guitar player or an electrician, but I never saw a guitar player that was worth a damn!"' Elvis smiles. Elvis laughs. His face fills the screen. 'When I was a boy,' you can hear Elvis Presley saying, 'I was the hero in comic books and movies. I grew up believing in that dream. Now I've lived it out. That's all a man can ask for.'

Jerry Hopkins' biography, Elvis *(Simon and Schuster, 1971), has been an invaluable source of information. Several unattributed quotes have been taken from the book.*

FADED
LOVE

*It's like someone just came up and told me there aren't going
to be any more cheeseburgers in the world.*

FELTON JARVIS, Elvis's producer,
commenting on Elvis's death

I USED TO IMAGINE that Elvis would call me up some time in the middle
of the night. I would stumble to the phone, pick up the receiver, listen
blearily to the silence at the other end, and then hear that familiar voice say,
'I been reading some of the stuff you been writing about me, and it's all
right, man. It's good.' Of course it never happened, but whenever I wrote
something about Elvis – and this dates back more than ten years now – I would
always send a copy to 3764 Elvis Presley Boulevard, in those days merely
Highway 51 South. Once I got a Christmas card, a record company handout
like the yearly calendar, with printed season's greetings 'From Elvis and the
Colonel.'

More than anyone else Elvis made us all into fans. Maybe it was the
barriers that the Colonel erected around him. Maybe it was the legend to
which his own improbable removal from roots gave rise. When I first started
writing about him, it was not fashionable to admit that you were an Elvis
fan. 'For a long time,' I wrote in the middle of a Beatles era that seems curiously
more distant in time and point of view, 'to suggest that you liked Elvis Presley
only invited ridicule.' Elvis himself seemed to share in this sentiment, at
least from the evidence of his records and movies which by this time were so
perfunctory an echo of the feeling that had animated his early work as to
make the King of Western Bop seem like just another corporate success. And
yet when he emerged from his Hollywood exile in 1968 for the TV special,
the Memphis sessions, and one final burst of glory, there we all were, still
his loyal fans, eager to welcome him home, no questions asked.

It was almost too easy for him. After that first spectacular surge he didn't
have to *do* anything. He just had to be – himself, Elvis, no last name necessary.
In a way it was the classic American success story. Elvis, a desperately lonely,
desperately ambitious child of the Depression, rising from that two-room
Tupelo shack to a marble-pillared mansion on the hill. There was irony,
there was pathos, there was fierce determination, more than anything else
there was passion. There was as well a kind of unself-conscious innocence

that could never enter his music again – and for good reason. Elvis Presley was a year out of high school, and on the Sun sides he would throw in everything that had made up his life to date – all the yearning, all the unfocused resentment, all that sense of being, as he would later sing, 'a stranger in my own hometown.' And on top of it all he was imposing not so much a surly sneer as an almost contemptuous certainty that what he was doing was right, that all the rest were wrong, that it was his cat clothes and be-bop language that would eventually prevail.

Well, he was right. Elvis was, everyone has finally conceded, no overnight sensation. He was in fact one of the most phenomenal successes of our time. And he maintained the sneer; in some ways he maintained the music (to the end there were flashes of the old spirit). Most of all, though, he retained that callow adolescence of the spirit, that sense of impatient expectation that could only be staved off, never satisfied, with cheeseburgers and ice cream and peanut-butter-and-banana sandwiches. It was adolescence with a gloss on – no more pimples, no more grease, the teeth are capped, imperfect reality is replaced by the perfect dream. Because, of course, Elvis never grew up. Elvis never could grow up. For Elvis everything stopped when he was nineteen years old and knocking them dead in Kilgore, Texas, or Bethel Springs, Tennessee. After that nothing changed. He never knew anything else. And though the arenas and the money got bigger and bigger, it was inevitable that Elvis should become less important than the product he was selling. Which was – not music certainly, not even personality – perhaps it was merely economic growth and the GNP.

Everywhere you go you can see Elvis Presley as he might have been. At the ballpark eating a hot dog. Sitting at the bar with a flowered shirt hanging over his belt. Cruising along the interstate hauling a load of frozen vegetables. A heavy-set, worn-looking man with a graying ducktail and wide mutton-chop sideburns. These are commonplaces, they don't mean anything one way or another, except that the commonplace is the one thing that escaped Elvis Presley in his numbingly long stay at the top. For Elvis there was no escape in art; his original triumph was his very artlessness. He didn't write songs, nor did he aspire to anything more than success. Even his films were no more than a magnification of his image, a further reinforcement of the impossible perfection that we demand of all our public figures, and that Elvis alone fulfilled – a perfection that transformed him from a living presence into an all-purpose, economy-rate icon. Elvis, it could be said until just a year or two before his death, never made a foolish move. But then Elvis, once the Colonel got a hold of him, never made a public move at all. He didn't drink, he didn't smoke, the only time that passion ever entered his voice towards the end was in praise of the Lord. He was truly transformed from rebel into the idealized boy next door. And that was what he was doomed forever to be, trapped forever in a web of packaging in which he himself came to believe. And that was why neither he nor his followers (and I include myself) could bear to hear the faint laughter and the jeers, could come to terms with the inevitable attrition of time.

I saw him just that once, in Boston in 1971. At the end of the concert he sang 'Funny How Time Slips Away,' and when he reached the line 'Gotta go now,' a universal groan went up, mollified only in part when he followed with, 'Don't know when, but I'll be back in your town.' I don't know if it was a great performance for anything more than the ease with which he tossed it off. In many ways it was self-parody certainly, with its karate poses and vocal posturing, but it was for me and for everyone else who was there, I think, an event that would be forever memorable, and a memory which I at any rate never sought to violate by repetition.

In recent years whenever I've been in Memphis I've driven by the mansion, just one of the hundreds of thousands of pilgrims looking for a substantiation of their experience. I never saw Elvis, but Memphis friends of mine would tell of seeing him out on the highway late at night, just driving up and down the strip in a sleek new car, still impatient, still restless, still lonely. In the last few years of his life the tabloids abounded with stories to flesh out this image. Elvis the Nightstalker. Elvis hearing his mother's voice in the corridors of Graceland. Elvis, troubled and overweight, giving gifts, seeking love. They were unnecessary reminders of what we already knew.

His death represented the final violation of a jealously guarded privacy, as we learned of last words, last acts, past sins, both real and imagined. Even in death the waxy image was maintained, with pious tributes and a blurred open-coffin picture, showing Elvis at peace, on the front page of the *National Enquirer*. It doesn't matter, none of it matters. All that we are left with is a shared memory and a musical passion that could still catch fire at the most improbable moments. The last time I heard it was on 'Shake a Hand,' like so many of Elvis's best recent songs one with which he was comfortable from the past and one with strong religious overtones. As he sings, 'Shake a hand, shake a hand, shake a hand if you can,' there is nothing but the pure familiar melody and the impassioned engagement of the voice. It was this engagement that Elvis missed at the end, but when it came — in the music anyway — it seemed to overtake him all in a rush, his voice would soar, just as it always had, and he would seize on a lyric, chew on it, in the manner of the great gospel singers worry it to death, and not let go until he had wrung every last ounce of emotion from it. That was Elvis's mark; it was his only expiation. It was what rock 'n' roll first came from, and it was what doomed rock 'n' roll in the end. Because you can't manufacture that feeling any more than you can manufacture the religious belief from which it originally stemmed. As Little Richard, another evangelical soul turned once again to the ministry, summed it up, 'He was a rocker. I was a rocker. I'm not rockin' any more and he's not rockin' any more.'

SNAPSHOTS
OF
CHARLIE
RICH

W HEN I FIRST met Charlie Rich in the spring of 1969, he was playing out
at the Vapors by the Memphis airport. After nearly fifteen years, his
career seemed to be going nowhere, and he and his wife, Margaret Ann,
spoke openly about his alcoholism and their bitter disappointment and frustration with the music business. Originally signed by Sun as a kind of suc-
cessor to Elvis Presley, on record he showed a musical versatility that always
stood in the way of success, and he himself continued to incline towards jazz
in live performance.

I've never liked anyone better upon first acquaintance, and I wrote up
that meeting as a chapter in my book, *Feel Like Going Home*. I've continued
to see Charlie and Margaret Ann over the years—both as a friend and as
a journalist—and I've continued to write about him. These two stories show
him at two points in his sudden rise to stardom, first on the verge of success—
just as 'Behind Closed Doors' was about to cross over from the country charts,
to become an altogether unexpected, worldwide pop hit—and then at what
would seem to have been his peak of popular recognition. Neither occasion
saw him any more complacent in outlook or attitude than at our original
meeting. With the initial success of 'Behind Closed Doors,' in fact, Charlie
fell apart completely and drank himself virtually comatose at the taping of a
Burt Reynolds special at the Tennessee governor's mansion. After hospital-
ization and hypnosis treatment, he stopped drinking altogether, but then in
the fall of 1975 he brought further scandal upon himself on the nationally
televised Country Music Association Awards show. Slated to present the
award for Entertainer of the Year (which he had himself won the previous
year), he appeared visibly unsteady and his speech was slurred. When John
Denver turned out to be the winner, Charlie took out his lighter and burned
the slip of paper. Shortly afterwards he and Margaret Ann announced their
separation and plans for divorce. Though they got back together again, Charlie
still wasn't speaking to the press when I saw them several months later.

In Austin (which is outlaw territory), Charlie may have been a hero, but everywhere I went in Nashville, people were speaking of the disgrace he had brought to country music (forgetting Hank Williams, forgetting Ernest Tubb's escapades, forgetting where country music came from). There was a good deal of speculation — not entirely free of spite — that Charlie Rich's career was over, that he would drink himself to death before too many more CMA Awards shows were televised.

That isn't the way it turned out. Charlie and Margaret Ann stayed together, as they always have through the good times and the bad times. The hits kept on coming, even if they never again reached the platinum heights of 'Behind Closed Doors' and 'The Most Beautiful Girl.' And Charlie Rich, always the soul of sincerity, mended his industry fences, so that today it is hard to find anyone in Nashville who will say a bad word about him. He is recognized as a star, and a survivor.

Those are not the two qualities which I would have picked as his most outstanding ten years ago. The one thing that has always struck me most forcibly about Charlie and Margaret Ann is their capacity for honesty. Even when I wrote something that must have hurt, they always communicated their appreciation that it was *honest*. Both of them seem to have a faith in the truth which has carried them through the most painful times, and I like to think that this is the one thing that will always survive, whatever changes of outlook or circumstances may take place.

In the last few years Charlie's demons seem to have subsided somewhat. He has been largely off the road and managing his own career, with former manager Seymour (Sy) Rosenberg pretty much out of the picture. Financially he has reaped some enormous rewards through his association with the *Benji* series of family-entertainment motion pictures and an investment in Wendy's hamburger chain that paid off to the tune of four million dollars when he sold his shares. Then in 1978 he left Epic and signed with the United Artists label, thereby confounding industry observers who had thought him forever locked in with Billy Sherrill, and earning him another three quarters of a million dollars.

Not surprisingly the music has not gained from all these financial distractions. 'I don't really like happy music,' Charlie once declared. 'I don't think it says anything.' The blues was his natural medium, but it's as a crooner that he's best known now, a purveyor of love songs. Charlie Rich today is the Silver Fox; he's been taught to move, taught to dance, taught to toss off casual repartee (Seymour used to boast proudly that he had paid for the lessons and would ask everyone he could buttonhole, 'How do you like the *new* Charlie Rich?'), and he is at home now in Tahoe and Las Vegas.

In early 1979 I took the Gray Line tour of Memphis (actually the Elvis Memorial Tour) and to my surprise found that it stopped outside of Charlie Rich's house. There was the familiar silver Mercedes. There was the forbidding black security gate and the sprawling suburban home. 'Charlie Rich,' said John, our guide, 'is a real friendly guy. A lot different than Elvis was. He's real open, you always see him around whenever he's in town. In fact I've talked with him several times myself. He's a real nice kind of a guy.'

There are worse things that could be said about a man.

NEW YORK, 1973

GERSHWIN used to write in a little room like this,' says Charlie Rich reflectively, surveying the neatly stacked boxes in the storage area that serves as a dressing room, upstairs from Upstairs at Max's Kansas City. Waylon Jennings, who inaugurated country in New York with his engagement at Max's several months before, winks down at us conspiratorially from his poster of eminence on the wall. 'Well, you know, he used to write at night, man, he used to sit up at night and just listen to the sirens.'

The rest of the band nod politely. They are closer to Johnny Winter, androgynously eyeing their old buddy, Waylon, on the wall, than to Billie Holliday, Stan Kenton, George Gershwin — strange heroes for a man whose latest single, 'Behind Closed Doors,' has just climbed to number one on the country charts. The guitarist, David, only eighteen and still sirring and ma'aming his elders, has been on the road with Ike and Tina Turner and has some stories to tell. The bass player, John 'Cool' Vanderpool, long-haired and bearded and, like the rest, from Charlie's home base of Little Rock, has recently been a student at the University of Washington in Seattle. The drummer, Harold Murchison, bearded, too, and only slightly older than the others, is a former music teacher who has invested all his time and energy and a good deal of his money in managing this month-long promotional tour of one-nighters which has veered off course unexpectedly for a week at Max's Kansas City. Charlie's wife, Margaret Ann, his most loyal supporter and booster for the fifteen years he has been in the business, has flown in from Arkansas to be with him for the hastily scheduled opening night.

'Are you from *Country Music*?' says the bored-looking free-lance, lethargically shooting pictures and referring to the magazine. She glances over at Margaret Ann.

'Well, I don't know how to answer that,' says Margaret Ann, pretty, ambitious, but somehow fragile in this hard, jaded land. 'Charlie, you're just going to have to answer that for me.'

Charlie, a big, heavy-set man with a striking head of white hair and a broad, beefy face that might appear flabby if it were not for the curiously vulnerable set to his mouth, just sips on his Cutty and water. 'That's Charlie's wife,' Harold explains at last, and the rest of the band laugh goodnaturedly.

They obviously like and respect Charlie Rich enormously, both as a musician and as a man, but they don't consider themselves country in the least. 'Oh,' says the girl and goes back to snapping pictures.

Has he ever been to New York before? someone asks Charlie. 'Oh, sure, man,' he says, brightening up with a memory. 'I can remember when we came up with Ray Scott, it was when we were still with Sun, oh it must have been twelve years ago at least, and it was one of the grooviest things in the world, man, we walked into this little jazz club, it was just around the corner from, you know, what's the name of that famous place—yeah, the Village Vanguard—we just walked in off the street and there was Mabel Mercer, I can't really describe it, just her and a piano player, just so cool, outasight. We musta stayed in that place until three, four in the morning, I think Ava Gardner was there that night—you remember, honey. I even got a record afterwards. I wanted Margaret Ann to hear what it had been like, but it wasn't the same thing. I don't know, I guess it was the warmth, the atmosphere of that little club, whatever. I wonder if that place is still there—probably not. I don't even know the name.' What was he doing in New York? the question arises. 'Oh yeah,' he says without much interest, as if recalled to a more prosaic reality. 'We were up to see about a tour, one of those Dick Clark tours. A grand a week, a different city every night. Why not, man? . . . No, we didn't do it. God, she was outasight.'

No one should know the pitfalls of success better than Charlie Rich. A session man and songwriter for Sun before he enjoyed a brief flash of popularity with his own 'Lonely Weekends' in 1959, he has been so close so many times before that it must begin to seem like a cruelly receding mirage by now. Acclaimed from the start by such industry giants as Sam Phillips, Leonard Chess (who tried to sign Rich when his contract with Sun ran out), Jerry Wexler of Atlantic Records, and Paul Ackerman of *Billboard* — men whose aesthetic sense was exceeded only by the soundness of their commercial judgment — he has always been known as a musician's musician, with a voice that resembled Elvis's in its breadth and range and a piano style that could make the jump from Brubeck to the rocking rhythms of his more outgoing friend and contemporary, Jerry Lee. Of all his discoveries, Phillips is said to have stated, Charlie Rich alone had the potential to rival Presley.

And yet, whether because he lacked the drive, or due to the very eclectic nature of his music, or perhaps simply because he has always attached a greater value to family and friends than to the more fleeting attractions of the record industry, none of the predictions of stardom were ever fulfilled. After 'Lonely Weekends,' Charlie Rich didn't have another hit until 'Mohair Sam' appeared on the Smash label in 1965. Then . . . nothing again for almost four years, when his wife's moving autobiographical composition, 'Life's Little Ups and Downs,' first appeared on the country charts and marked the beginning of a slow climb into public awareness. Since that time each of Charlie Rich's records has done a little better than the last, and guided by producer Billy Sherrill's sure instinct for a hit ('Billy's a little bit like Sam in that respect,' says Margaret Ann, not without ambivalence. 'I think he respects money and success, in that order'), he has laid the groundwork for a solid popular following for the first time in his career. 'I've got a lot of confidence in Billy Sherrill,' says Charlie Rich, and in a way this tour is a product of that new-found confidence. For the first time, at the age of forty, Charlie Rich is going out on the road.

Surprisingly enough he seems to be taking it all in stride, with an ease and with an enthusiasm that seem almost out of character for such a private, inward-looking man. Although he is obviously weary from a month of promotionals ('Share with us the warmth of one of Epic's brighter stars for 1973 . . . in Pittsburgh . . . Seattle . . . The Little Club . . . Vic and Tony's . . . Paul's Mall'), although he just as obviously does not take to dealing with all the professional handicappers and glad-handers who populate the business, he is exhilarated, too, at for once riding the crest of the wave, at seeing himself at last the center of attention. He also enjoys finding an audience that can appreciate his own brooding, jazz-tinged compositions as well as 'I Take It on Home,' 'I Do My Swinging at Home,' or any of the latest of his country hits.

And he is full of projects, too, seemingly more excited at what his success can do for his wife's cousin, Mouse ('A lovable loser,' someone says. 'Hell, he's no loser,' protests Charlie. 'He's got the right idea. He's a real personality'), and for his son, Allan, a talented composer-pianist, than what it can do for him. 'I guess you might say they're my current projects,' he says with that generosity he reserves for those who are closest to him, spinning off plans for getting Allan recorded, for putting Mouse on tour as an opening act. He is relaxed and expansive, and it is almost as if he had been preparing for this all his life, taking it now simply as his due. 'Hey,' he says, autographing a stack of albums for a fan, an unaccustomed flicker of amusement playing about his eyes and mouth. The face on the cover changes from the self-confident young man with the obligatory sneer, hair combed back in an upswept curl, to the clear-eyed, white-haired man with wide muttonchop sideburns under a broad floppy hat who adorns the cover of his latest album. 'I hope you didn't bring too many more of these, man. I'm getting older all the time.'

The music he plays very much reflects his feeling that he is at home and among friends. In the audience at Max's the first couple of nights are Billy Sherrill and song publisher Al Gallico, flying in on their way to Vegas; Paul Ackerman, Ian Dove from the *New York Times*, and Peter McCabe of *Country Music*, all long-time fans; as well as industry flacks and a hard core of Charlie Rich aficionados who greet the opening bars of even his most obscure compositions with the excitement and scattered applause that is ordinarily reserved for the Big Hits. Charlie rewards them with a dazzling display of his virtuosity, touching on blues and soul and solid country and the kind of jazz-inflected, gospel-influenced material that he has made his special province. There are 'Lonely Weekends' and 'Mohair Sam,' of course; Margaret Ann's brilliant 'Life's Little Ups and Downs'; a rollicking boogie-woogie-styled rendition of 'Break Up,' a song he originally wrote for Jerry Lee; and an overpowering version of 'Don't Lay No Headstone on My Grave,' a blues that Lewis recently appropriated for his all-star London sessions. 'Who Will the Next Fool Be?' cuts even Bobby 'Blue' Bland's cover. There is 'Big Boss Man,' Charlie's definitive version of Sinatra's 'Nice 'n' Easy,' even a swinging 'Ol' Man River' or perhaps Lonnie Johnson's 'Tomorrow Night' thrown in for good measure, all done with a feeling and conviction that put them across, blues and rockers, ballads and r&b alike, in a manner that is absolutely incontestable.

It is a performance that no other artist that I can think of could match; there is no one, with the possible exception of a soulman like Solomon Burke, who could handle this breadth and variety of material in such an utterly

Phillips Recording Artist.

convincing and deeply felt way. Even with the looseness of the backup band, and despite the fact that his voice—a gorgeous instrument which still resembles Elvis's, but with all the energy and conviction which Elvis has lacked for years—strains occasionally on the high notes, there is no taking away from the good feeling that you get from his performance; he sings of pain and loss and suffering in such a way as to transcend all loss.

'I'm so happy for him,' Margaret Ann says, her dark eyes shining. 'God, it seems hard to believe. Sometimes I thought we'd never make it.' I nod in happy agreement. I, too, am relieved, because this is not the same Charlie Rich I interviewed in Memphis just three years ago, a thoughtful tormented man, talented, driven, haunted by the apparent gulf between the life he had chosen and a strict religious upbringing, a man for whom talk was almost painful. I had liked and admired that man very much, but I had come down to New York to renew our acquaintance with some trepidation, fearful, as I had originally written, that he simply wasn't suited for success, that he was being pushed into something he didn't really want. Instead I am confronted by this new Charlie Rich, relaxed, self-confident, a much more open and expansive version of his earlier self. I breathe a sigh of relief; Margaret Ann and I sit back and listen to Charlie, hunched over the piano and absorbed in the music in a way that is made possible by the audience's absorption in him. It is in rare moments such as these that it all actually seems worthwhile.

> Lord, I tried to see it through
> But it was too much for me
> Now I'm coming home to You
> And I feel like going home.

The next night it all falls apart. It's hard to say what it is exactly, but it seems to be a combination of a lot of little things. The turnout is somewhat disappointing, all the company men have headed uptown for a Mac Davis–Helen Reddy concert at Carnegie Hall, drummer Harold Murchison is feeling lousy from a sore throat he has been unable to shake, and Charlie has been drinking most of the day. 'You were so good last night when you were straight,' Margaret Ann pleads with him as he stands glumly in the thickly carpeted hotel hallway waiting for the down elevator and holding a glass in his hand. Charlie just answers with a shrug and a sardonic story of an established c&w artist who has recently been 'saved' by singer Connie Smith and has forsworn whiskey and cigarettes, because, he tells Charlie, 'You're taking your voice, this gift that God gave you, away from the people!' . . . 'Bullshit,' says Charlie with an unhappy laugh, downing the drink and continuing to smoke one cigarette after another on the way to the gig.

On the bandstand everyone is depressed, and it shows in the performance. The beat lags, little mistakes creep in, Charlie's voice, roughened with drinking, cracks on the high notes, and seemingly this only causes him to drink some more. 'It was bound to happen,' says Margaret Ann, almost in tears. 'That's just the way he is. It just had to happen.' As for Charlie, as he drinks he becomes more and more withdrawn; he sings with great expressiveness and feeling, but he becomes almost resentful at the presence of an audience, at the intrusion of strangers. 'You know, I've got to be crazy to be here,' he mutters, coming off the bandstand. 'I've got to be crazy, when I could be home sitting on the creek bank, fishing with my little boy, Jack.'

Between sets Margaret Ann tries to encourage him, as they sit at a table in the packed steakhouse-bar downstairs from the club, drinking coffee and talking quietly. All around them the room swirls with scenemakers of questionable gender, the sorry remnants of a real Velvet Underground. Lou Reed's 'Walk on the Wild Side' and Dylan's 'Can You Please Crawl Out Your Window?'

are on the jukebox, and for the first time Charlie Rich, hip, silver-haired, all dressed in black from his jackboots to his black·windbreaker, seems very much out of place. 'I tried to tell him,' Margaret Ann says desperately, turning to me with a pleading look. 'I mean here's a man with a number one record – after twenty years! Here's a man who's worked twenty years for this kind of success. I do everything I possibly can to encourage him – I *told* him, who else would Paul Ackerman, Jerry Wexler, people like that turn out to see? Well, you know, he's got his music, he's got something that will live on after him. I mean, it's a kind of immortality, isn't that what it's all about in a way? And he's got his *family*. Not many men in this business can say that. Oh, I don't know –'

Charlie Rich regards his wife with a puzzled frown. 'You know you're a beautiful romantic,' he says, embarrassed and a little bit angry to be subjected to such public scrutiny. 'You're a beautiful romantic, I guess that's why I love you.' Charlie reaches for his wife's hand and doesn't say anything more.

'You know,' says Harold, as he gets ready to go upstairs for the second set, 'people say all the time they want feeling in their music, they want it to be real. Well, Charlie's just about the deepest person I've ever met. Everything he does up there is real, they don't realize everything he feels goes right into the music.' Margaret Ann can't bring herself to go up with us. 'I'm sorry you had to see him like this,' she says. 'But that's the real Charlie. That's the real Charlie sure as life.' 'You know,' says Charlie, staring out bleakly at the patrons of Max's Kansas City, rouged and teased-haired, flitting about self-consciously from table to table. 'Maybe they've got the right idea. No, I mean it. Maybe we were just raised up wrong, man. A lot of different relationships, just hit and run, never get involved, never get hurt. You think it means anything to them? Maybe they've got it all figured out.' No, I try to argue with him. Maybe, I suggest, it's like the words to his songs. His lyrics are always spare, carefully chosen – as a result they carry a lot of weight.

'No, man, that's not it. That's not what I'm talking about. Now you take me. All my life, you know, my whole life it took just one – just one woman, and that's this little girl who's sitting here beside me. Just one true friend in the music business, and that would be Bill Justis, who's stuck by me when I didn't have a dime in my pocket – in a way Bill Justis has directed me through everything I've ever done. One band – and that's these boys I've got up here with me. You know, it takes me *years*, man, before I can get to the point where I can even *talk* to people. That's wrong, man.

'Now my father, my daddy, he could have walked into a place like this, and they would have loved him. They would have loved him, man, within ten minutes he would have had them eating out of his hand, just because he was who he was, he was The Original Hippie, he was . . . *The Hippie*. He was 290 pounds and *beautiful*, man, and they would have loved him. Wouldn't they?' He turns to Margaret Ann. 'Yes,' she whispers. 'They would.' 'You see, he was blessed. He could just, I don't know how to say it, he could just sit under the apple tree, he could cut a lamb—of course we never ate lamb, that was against our religion. But he had the most beautiful voice, he could *sing*—that's where it all comes from, man, it all comes from that time. Hank Williams, he was late, but all this music that we play comes from back there in my daddy's time. You know, I played him something one time, I wrote something down that he had been playing, I don't write so good, but I had him go over it for me and then I played it back, and he just thought it was the greatest thing in the world, man. He said, "Hey, man, that's all right"—except he didn't say "man," he didn't talk that shit, I picked up all that kind of jive from Margaret and my smart friends. But, you know, he was so tickled, man, can you imagine, I was supposed to be really something big because I'd been to college for a couple of years, my daddy was just so tickled, and it was *nothing*, man. What I'm trying to tell you is . . . maybe it's just not worth it.'

The last set is an almost unbearable cry of pain. The song titles alone betray what he is feeling: 'No Home,' 'I Can't Go On,' 'You Don't Know Me.' The band is unfamiliar with the arrangements, they have never played these songs before, but they gamely do their best as Charlie lingers over the lyrics and treats the small audience to an experience that they may or may not want but which they will surely never forget. The meaning of the words, the reality that lies behind the music, stands out starkly and unmistakably, as Charlie's voice, finally lubricated by the long night's drinking, takes off and soars and the piano finds those blue notes hiding between the cracks. 'I know I shouldn't say this,' says Margaret Ann, who has slipped upstairs for the final set, 'but, you know, I think Charlie drunk is better than most people sober.' I nod my head dispiritedly; it is certainly true but little consolation to any of us.

After the show there remains that feeling of restless unease. Charlie doesn't want to go back to the hotel, he doesn't want to go to the party for Mac Davis. Maybe, he suggests, as we all pile into the rented station wagon, Harold can just drop him off in the Village, he'd like to see if he can find some music. The band is puzzled but agreeable to anything, making jokes about John 'Used To Be Cool' Vanderpool's haircut, which everyone is convinced will soon have them all singing country harmony. Harold, who has been studying maps of New York City since his arrival, carefully navigates his way across town. We end up not surprisingly at the Village Vanguard, but even less surprisingly Mabel Mercer isn't there any more ('Hell, I don't even know if she's still alive,' Charlie concedes unhappily). Instead the sign outside reads Norman Connors Septet Featuring Dee Dee Bridgewater, and inside we are greeted with suspicious glances and hostile stares as the almost exclusively black clientele picks up the cracker accents of this strange party immediately. For a moment the room bristles with a mutual hostility and fear, and Charlie gets to order a drink only as the musicians finish up and start to put away their instruments, then stand by the door saying bantering

Charlie and C.J. RAEANNE RUBENSTEIN

good nights while their audience drifts out one by one. 'You see,' says Charlie, a look of utter despair on his face. 'I just wanted to show you, it's not . . . the way it was.'

I don't know what to say. No one does. Because it doesn't matter at this moment that Charlie Rich has the number one song in the country, it doesn't matter that he is surrounded by people whom he cares about and who care about him in turn. The fact that he is on the brink of a much greater success— tours, movies, television specials—is very far away right now; even the next night, when he will loosen up with a turn-away crowd that refuses to let him off stage for an hour and a half and will still keep calling for more, is far in the future. Right now there is only right now, and the words of Charlie's song, suggested, he says, by the title of the book I was working on when we first met, keep echoing in my mind:

> *Cloudy skies are closing in*
> *And not a friend around to help me*
> *From all the places that I've been*
> *And I feel like going home.*

MEMPHIS, 1976

I T'S VERY DIFFICULT. I don't think other people can understand it, really. There are so many outside influences, there's so much outside pressure, there are just so many people who want things from you that it's almost impossible to cope. It comes as a little bit of a shock, really, but after a while you realize he doesn't just belong to you any more. He belongs to whoever happens to be around.'

Margaret Ann Rich is talking about superstars, specifically about her husband, who sits opposite her, restless and smoking Salems, in the spacious living room of their Memphis home. They are surrounded by the tangible evidence of a success that until quite recently had seemed virtually unattainable. For the first nineteen years of their marriage Margaret Ann was the only one to maintain a consistent belief in Charlie's talent; for all the accolades he garnered from influential industry figures, she was the one who pushed his career, arranged personal interviews, buoyed up a sense of self-confidence that was never very strong to begin with, and contributed some of the finest songs that he recorded over the years. Today rumors swirl about them, prompted by the concern of friends, the curiosity of disinterested parties, and the malice of gossips: that Charlie is drinking again, that their marriage has at last fatally foundered after their recent, well-publicized separation, that Margaret Ann is falling apart under the twin pressures of Charlie's success and the consequent diminution of her own role in his life. Everything is normal in show business.

'I think it's almost a tragedy when you lose your enthusiasm for something that suited you. That's what happens to writers, I guess. It turns into a business, and it just about destroys your creativity. I know that's what happened to me. The biggest pleasure that Charlie and I ever had came in working together. You know, we've never been very good at communicating verbally, but through our music we're able to. I don't think I ever missed a session until quite recently, but then all of a sudden there were all these outside forces at work, it was almost as if a wedge were being driven between us, and I've never been one to push myself where I wasn't wanted. When Charlie started doing other people's songs and going to sessions alone— I never could seem to get schedules straight from Billy Sherrill—I guess I started feeling just, you know, left out. Sometimes I wish he was just playing somewhere for free, playing piano alone or with a small group, just so he could enjoy the music.'

'I did that for about twenty years,' Charlie protests softly. His broad, melancholy face always has a slightly hurt look about it. It is at once more mobile and more handsome in its private grief than in the countless grins and strained grimaces he has learned to adopt for TV appearances and ads. 'When I first started working those little clubs in Memphis, I could play anything I wanted to for ten or fifteen dollars a night. Then when I went to Sun Records I went with the idea that I would do just about anything, as long as I could keep close to the music. I thought I could work the studio gig, make a little bit, and play my jazz at home. Which is the way it worked out. But, you know, when you have a wife and a family you have to sacrifice a little bit. Well, your family has to sacrifice, too. But there comes a time when you've been working at something so long, trying so long and so hard, that you reach a point where you get scared. And you start thinking to yourself, what am I going to be doing when I'm sixty-five? And I don't think I want to be playing in the Nightlighter Club when I'm sixty-five years old. Which could very easily have been the end result. And still could be.'

It's a continuing dialogue in the Rich household and one that is almost touching in its naiveté. Margaret Ann understands the terms of her husband's success. In a way everyone does. And it's not easy, of course, to feel sorry for a superstar. But the issues that they debate without hope of resolution are issues which have application to every successful artist's life; they are the very terms of success.

'You know,' says Margaret Ann, 'everyone thinks it's a matter of pills and booze, but that's got nothing to do with it. People think I'm lying, but I've lived with that kind of thing for so long that I can cope with it. That's a familiar hell. It's the lack of privacy, I don't know, it's the sheer magnitude of the problem that's frightening. You know, we had a fence built around the property, it was a necessity, really, and when the workmen finally finished, Charlie looked out and said, "I feel like I'm being fenced in, not keeping anybody out."'

That's the way it is for Charlie Rich these days. It's a little hard to believe, but success has hemmed him in in a way that almost twenty years of relative obscurity never did. For twenty years he played his own music, wrote and performed the songs that gained him initial attention, suffered his private miseries, but at least was engaged in his own creative struggle. For almost that length of time he lived a quiet, small-town existence in Benton, Arkansas, where his best friend was a Jewish psychiatrist and his favorite occupation was going fishing. He watched his kids grow up, was supported in his bouts with self-doubt, guilt, and alcohol by family, friends, and a sense of place. Today he oversees a world that he always dreamt of, in which his importance is recognized, his music is celebrated, and he has at last achieved a measure of that success which everyone from Sam Phillips to Bob Dylan had always predicted for him. It's the dream of almost every aspiring artist, musician or otherwise, and yet somehow it's all gone sour.

'Someday I'm going to write a book,' says Natalie Rosenberg, ex-wife of Charlie's manager Seymour and Margaret Ann's publishing partner, 'about the effects of success and what's happened to all the people involved with Charlie Rich.'

Charlie Rich, Benton, Arkansas. RAEANNE RUBENSTEIN

'It's unbelievable,' says Charlie himself. 'Everyone connected with the rise of Charlie Rich and "Behind Closed Doors" is having trouble with their personal lives and with their marriage, and I don't except Margaret Ann and myself. You just can't imagine the disruption that it causes in people's lives.'

One place to start is with the music. Since the unprecedented crossover sales of 'Behind Closed Doors' and 'The Most Beautiful Girl' (in 1973 they went from number one on the country charts to million-selling pop and easy-listening success while everyone was looking the other way), a whole new market opened up for Charlie Rich, and for the first time there arose a convenient method for pigeonholing his music. Up until then Charlie Rich was a musician who defied classification, someone whose unique approach allowed him to span the most widely separated categories—blues and jazz, rockabilly, country, and gospel—while maintaining the most personal and soulful of styles. With success he was finally typed, as a country crooner, a kind of latter-day Jim Reeves, with access to the countrypolitan, easy-listening, and soft-rock audiences, and despite the subsequent sales of re-packagings of some of his earlier, and more idiosyncratic, offerings from RCA and Sun Records, countrypolitan was the label that stuck. One thing you learn in the music business is not to tamper with success.

In the beginning there was brave talk of one more hit, just one more big chartmaker and Charlie would be free to make the kind of music that he himself cared about most. He would be sure enough of his audience then to lead them a little instead of blindly following fashion. At that time he carried around a briefcase full of unpublished songs. He took it everywhere he went. 'His whole life,' said Bill Williams, Charlie's long-time friend and then Nashville publicity director at Epic, 'is in that briefcase.' Well, that may be true, but if it is, Charlie Rich's biography has yet to be written. He still carries the briefcase with him, but none of the songs have yet surfaced. Nor have any of the ideas that seemed so exciting at the time: to do a jazz album; to include a solo version of Charlie's beautiful 'Feel Like Going Home' as the final track of the album that became *Very Special Love Songs*; to cut a session with Ray Charles; to record C. J., the black sharecropper on his father's plantation who taught him blues piano. Instead, what we have had is more of the same: lush Billy Sherrill productions in which Charlie's voice is all but drowned by elaborate orchestrations, soaring choruses, and melodramatic crescendos; a preponderance of soppy middle-of-the-road material, not a small portion of which originates with Al Gallico Music, Billy Sherrill's publishing company; and a drift away from the very personal kind of music, deeply felt and almost naked in its honesty, for which Charlie Rich has always been known.

Some feel that Billy Sherrill is the root of the problem. 'I think that Charlie Rich is the only person that Billy Sherrill has ever dealt with,' says one observer, 'who has more talent than Billy Sherrill.' What this means according to this individual is that Billy Sherrill feels threatened by Charlie Rich's musical potential and as a result buries him under layers of sweetening and overdubs, presenting him as part of a prepackaged product. That's why

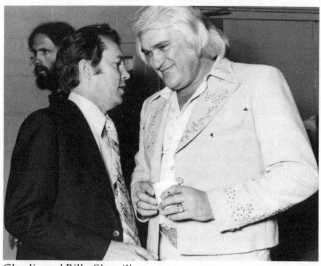

Charlie and Billy Sherrill. J. CLARK THOMAS

he took Charlie's piano away from him, preferring instead to use Pig Robbins on nearly every record since 'Behind Closed Doors.' 'I honestly think that has to be deliberate. It's almost as if he's taking his balls away from him. You can't separate Charlie Rich from his piano; without the piano it's just not Charlie.'

It isn't so, Charlie staunchly insists. Pig playing on the sessions is something that just evolved. Besides, he doesn't like the arduous process of instrumental rehearsals and working out arrangements with the session men, and his voice comes through more cleanly when it is recorded off a separate voice mike. As for song selection, he points to his own 'Every Time I Touch You (I Get High),' co-written with Billy Sherrill, the beautiful blues standard, 'Since I Fell for You', and several of Margaret Ann's compositions as evidence that some balance is being kept.

'I feel as if he could experiment more,' says Margaret Ann, whose feelings are definitely mixed and who is not at all sure that Billy Sherrill's way does not make the most commercial sense. 'I know what Billy Sherrill wants, and it's fine to a degree, but I guess it's just rather bland to my taste. I don't think Charlie has asserted himself as much as he could have, because I don't think that Charlie fully realizes that he's holding the trump card.'

Perhaps that's the key to the problems Charlie Rich has had in coping with success. Like many so-called instant stars who have been struggling for a decade or two, he was not really prepared to deal with the demands and career decisions that were immediately thrust upon him. He was not prepared for the enormous expectations that were all of a sudden riding on each new release, and he was determined not to repeat the mistake he had made on Smash in the mid-sixties, when he followed up the novelty success of 'Mohair Sam' with 'I Can't Go On,' a personal favorite and one of his finest songs, which sank without a trace. Neither was he prepared to deal with the sudden economic explosion that was attendant upon success, with its talk of tax shelters, deferred earnings, investment portfolios, growth patterns, and the like. He has had to learn all this in a hurry, and to his surprise, he has shown an aptitude for it. But not before his manager, Memphis lawyer Sy Rosenberg ('His whole idea of being a manager was to tell you not to drink on stage,' says Charlie contemptuously), extended Charlie's holdings to include real estate, hamburger franchises, a football team, cattle ranches, a personal management firm, and a payroll at one point of more than twenty, all under the corporate umbrella of Charlie Rich Enterprises. For over two years Charlie Rich had to work a grueling schedule of personal appearances just to keep this operation afloat, and it is only recently—as Seymour has become increasingly preoccupied with a messy divorce and Charlie increasingly concerned with his own home life and marriage—that he has begun to cut back to a more sensible level. Today Charlie Rich Enterprises consists of no more than six or seven fulltime employees; most of the office space, in a suburban Memphis development, is rented out; the private plane (dubbed, naturally, the Silver Fox) is due to be sold; and Charlie seems intent on making the business work for him instead of the other way around.

Even so, the life that he leads today has something of the aimless quality of the superstar's. When he is not gigging, he gets up late, goes to the office, makes a few calls, drinks a few Cokes. There may be a business meeting, and there is always some piece of paper for Charlie to sign. He concerns himself with the details of the business, how big a group he will be taking to Lake Tahoe, what the overhead will be, if it will pay to have the plane bring them back to Memphis, whether one of the musicians might give them a break on his price because of the length of the engagement. It's a comfortable life, a pleasant enough life, but everyone is sitting around waiting for something to happen.

'Here comes the Chief,' is the watchword out at Charlie Rich Enterprises when Charlie comes back from lunch with Margaret Ann. Everyone tries to anticipate his every whim, but Charlie himself, always the gentleman, seems unsure of just what form that whim should take. There are charity appearances and manufacturers who want him to try their product; there are deals in the offing, hangers-on anxious to do his bidding, maids, swimming pools, vacation condominiums, and a style of living that is generally opulent. At the center of it all are Charlie and Margaret Ann Rich, struggling to come to grips with a situation they neither actively sought nor altogether aspired to.

'I worry about Margaret Ann,' says Charlie. 'I've always liked to do the kind of things I like to do. To tell you the truth, I've never been a big mixer, so I have all the social life I want. But Margaret Ann thinks the only reason people want to have anything to do with her is because of me. Numerous people tell her different, and I tell her the same thing, but I don't know, man, as far as doing things together, that's where the problem lies.'

'We rarely ever have a good time together,' says Margaret Ann simply. 'Rarely.'

Charlie speaks of their son, Allan, who has recently put out an album of his own. 'Sometimes I envy him. He's twenty-one, he's got no ties, he's got complete and total freedom to do what he wants. He doesn't have to compromise at all. Of course I married when I was nineteen.'

'Was that a mistake?' says Margaret Ann.

'It depends on what happens from here on out,' says Charlie, who is nothing if not totally, and painfully, honest.

What is left perhaps is the music, an expression of the deepest and innermost feelings in the lives of Charlie and Margaret Ann Rich. It is the end of a long evening, and Charlie and I are sitting in Charlie's studio, designed as a projection room by the previous owners, out behind the house. The studio is sparsely but expensively furnished with a grand piano, an upright, and a little electric, a bar, a pool table, several gold records, and emblems everywhere—caricatures, monograms, designs—of the Silver Fox, Charlie's calling card. On the piano bench sits a Bill Evans–Tony Bennett album that Margaret Ann has bought but Charlie has not yet had a chance to listen to. 'I don't keep up like I used to, man,' he says. 'Somehow I just don't have the time, or take the time—' He shrugs helplessly. We are listening to an acetate of his new album, and the familiar sound of Charlie's voice fills the room with a soulfulness and sincerity that cuts through all the layers of talk and explanation. The track that is on the turntable is 'Milky White Way'; the album is a gospel album 'of old Negro-type spirituals mainly,' in which he and Billy Sherrill have invested their whole lives and backgrounds. ('Billy's father was a circuit preacher, Missionary Baptist, I think. We both practically got kicked out of the Baptist church, but I think Billy put more of himself into this album than anything else he's ever done.')

Over and over he plays the one cut, listening to the familiar words as though in a trance, transported by the sound of his voice floating free. I tell him how much I like it, and a smile wreathes his face. 'I didn't know what you'd think of it, man. I wish you could see the cover. It's something I really dig. It's got a picture of me right in the middle, and then there's a Negro woman with a handkerchief up to her face, and over in the corner there's a picture of this circuit-rider preacher on a horse. That preacher is Billy Sherrill's father. I've been telling him to put it on the back of the album, that it's his father, but I don't know if he will or not, he's funny that way. It was something we've been talking about doing for a long time now, and we just really let loose, let our hair down, it was a free, good-feeling kind of thing to do.'

'I think that's the real Charlie Rich,' says Margaret Ann afterwards. 'At first he was hesitant to play it for me, but then he played it for the whole family out in the studio, and they loved it—his mother especially. That's his background, it's completely honest, there wasn't anything faked on that at all. It's got all the guilt and all the emotion that he honestly feels. I would venture to say that that's the quintessence of Charlie Rich.'

SLEEPY
LaBEEF

There's Good Rockin' Tonight

I F YOU FREQUENT the honky tonks, you may very well have run across the
music of Sleepy LaBeef. For a number of years he worked the area around
Atlanta. Before that it was Port Huron or Kansas or the circuit of NCO
service clubs where there is three or four hundred dollars to be made for
a night's work and a string of bookings to be lined up—if you go over. When
I first met him in the spring of 1977, Sleepy LaBeef had been working Alan's
Fifth Wheel Lounge, about an hour north of Boston, for nearly three months
on a pretty regular basis. There he had been laying down the original rockabilly sounds of Sun six nights a week, five sets a night, to an appreciative
audience of truckers, regulars, factory workers off the late-night shift, and
just plain Sleepy LaBeef fans who may have caught him on talk-master Larry
Glick's two A.M. phone-in broadcasts from the truckstop.

How in the world, the question naturally arises, did a six-foot six, 265-
pound, basso profundo, first-generation rockabilly from Arkansas ever end up
at Alan's Truckstop in the northeast backwater of Amesbury, Massachusetts?
In the case of Sleepy LaBeef the answer lies in a series of mischances and
coincidences. He had spent much of the previous summer fixing up a 1948
Greyhound Silverado, which was intended to carry him on his nonstop touring
of thirty-nine states and which bore the true legend 'Sun Recording Artist.'
(Sleepy was the *only* artist then recording for that seminal label, a distinction
that he took as a compliment when new owner Shelby Singleton first proposed
to reactivate Sun for something other than reissues—'At least I thought it
was a compliment at the time. I don't know, maybe he thought I was pre-
historic.') That bus caught fire and burned up on the Maine Turnpike on
New Year's Day, 1977. Sleepy's clothes, tapes, and record collection were all
destroyed, and the bus was left a charred shell. He played his gig that night
at Alan's anyway, and when the opportunity arose, he welcomed the chance
to settle in. The result was that for the next year he would use Alan's as his
base, booking out of the club, living in the motel unit behind it, working
intermittently at restoring the bus for resale, and establishing Sleepy LaBeef
as New England's number one name in rockabilly and country music.

I'll never forget the first time I went up to Alan's to see Sleepy perform. A friend and I had noticed an item in the local paper that made reference to Sleepy's extended engagement in Amesbury, virtually next door to the small town in which we lived. We drove up to the truckstop and parked out back where the big semis were idling, then ventured into the bar with some trepidation, since Alan's had had a shaky local reputation even before its owner, Clifford Titcomb, a former Amesbury selectman, pulled a gun on an IRS agent (he was subsequently sentenced to a year's alternate service doing hospital work). Sleepy was tuning up on the bandstand, the waitresses were wearing cowboy outfits, the PA crackled with CB lingo, and we got swept up in another world.

'Call them honky tonks if you want,' wrote *Country Music* editor Michael Bane, 'but for the Saturday-night regulars, that raunchy, neon-lit bar with its cheap beer and even cheaper solace is called *home*. The honky tonk is as American as apple pie; as deeply ingrained in our collective subconscious as the prostitute with a heart of gold. A working-class pit stop between today and tomorrow; a buffer zone between exhaustion and despair; soft lights and hard country music—a good honky tonk is all that and more.

'A honky tonk is a magical place where all the rules are, however temporarily, suspended. . . . Sure, you can dance at a honky tonk, but it's more than a dance hall. You can hear live music at a honky tonk, but it's more than a listening room. And you can drink yourself blind at a honky tonk, but it's more—much more—than a bar. A good honky tonk is the American dream shrunken to beer, broads, and a bunch of loud music . . .'

To some this might not sound like much of an advertisement, and admittedly for a nondrinker and nonsmoker like myself there are distinct disadvantages to the honky tonk environment, but taken all in all, finding Alan's (and Sleepy LaBeef) was for me like finding the bluebird of happiness on my back door. I had traveled thousands of miles to hear music like this, played in just this kind of setting, and as Sleepy ran through what must have been a typical set (featuring everything from Muddy Waters to Webb Pierce to Elvis Presley and Little Richard), I turned to my friend, whose expression mirrored my own, and we both silently asked the question: could this really be for real?

Over the next few months we would come back again and again. For a while my friend joined Sleepy's band, and we became friendly with Cliff and June, who owned the Truckstop complex (twenty-four-hour diner, all-night garage, motel, and club), denounced Taxachusetts with all the zeal of the most ardent conservative civil libertarians, and eventually—despite a prior lack of experience with any aspect of the music business, save for the club, and with nothing but their unstinting enthusiasm for Sleepy and his music (which they learned was called rockabilly) to serve as qualifications—came to manage Sleepy, until the Fifth Wheel was closed down for nonpayment of

taxes. We heard Sleepy run through a good portion of the six thousand songs
he estimates to be in his repertoire. ('I don't know why, I used to just listen
to a song twice on the jukebox, and I'd have it. I don't like to boast, but I
honestly think you could put me in a room trading songs with just about
anyone you could name, and I could keep going longer than they could.') We
learned to recognize and greet the regulars in one fashion or another. We
nodded to the Bird Woman, whose slacks hung loose on her rather brittle,
skinny frame but who always seemed to find a trucker twenty or thirty years
younger than she; we always appreciated the cheerful confidence of the Glider,
a rather stout young woman who commandeered her partners around the
dance floor with a masterful stride; we even learned to enjoy the singing
of PBL (this was her CB handle—her real name was Nancy), another stout
young woman, who stepped out from behind the cash register occasionally

to warble 'You Ain't Woman Enough (To Take My Man).' There were no distinctions of age or class at Alan's Truckstop; everyone was accepted as a fellow refugee of the night. And over it all hovered the towering presence of Sleepy LaBeef.

In the space of an evening with Sleepy LaBeef you can get a short course in the history of rock 'n' roll, from Jimmie Rodgers to Jimmy Reed, encompassing Woody Guthrie, Chuck Berry, Joe Tex, and Willie Nelson as well. A multi-instrumentalist who plays the guitar with all the gut-wrenching fervor of a bluesman like Albert King, Sleepy is possessed not only of an encyclopedic knowledge of the field but of the flair, originality, and conviction to put the music across as well. At this point I can't count the number of times I've seen him perform, but I've never seen Sleepy do a set that was less than entertaining, nor have I known him to play the same set twice. You could come out to Alan's on occasion and catch what Sleepy would call a mechanical performance, but though he himself had certain reservations about the venue ('Let's face it, a lot of these truckers have one thing on their mind. They could care less about music'), a spirit of hearty informality, stubborn eccentricity, and great goodwill always prevailed.

Every night at the Fifth Wheel was a little bit different, and Sleepy always adapted to the occasion. On weekends he wore his wide-lapeled, white western tuxedo with ruffled shirt. If there was a trucker in the audience who could pick—or even one who just thought he could pick—Sleepy gave him his moment on stage. For birthdays the band responded appropriately. If the crowd was dead, it would be mainly sad songs, fast waltzes, and mournful country standards. For Monday night Fifties Night—when the waitresses exchanged their black cowboy pantsuits and hats for saddle shoes, rolled-up jeans, and sloppy shirttails—Sleepy would take on a more imposing look in T-shirt and black leather jacket, his lip curled, hair slicked back, surveying the room good-humoredly from under hooded fifties eyes.

The one constant was that Sleepy always put on a good show. The crowd might change, Sleepy's mood certainly varied, the band underwent radical changes of personnel (in the two years I have known Sleepy, only the drummer, Clete Chapman, who signed on in Iowa in 1974, has stayed for any length of time), but the feeling remained the same. He would go through phases when he would play the fiddle (actually Sleepy saws away on fiddle, which is a recently acquired enthusiasm) almost every night for several weeks running; then he might not pick it up again for months. The same with piano, which he attacks with the rough enthusiasm, if not the skill, of Jerry Lee Lewis. Some nights he might inject a heavy dose of blues; other nights it was non-stop sets of rockabilly free association in which Sleepy would shift from song to song—often after no more than a verse—with no sign to the band other than his own booming vocals and guitar, and with a decided taste for obscurity, which could make a Jerry Lee Lewis medley out of songs no one would ever think to associate with Jerry Lee, but done up in the Killer's inimitable style.

All this was great fun, as indeed it was to hear Sleepy's rumbling voice churning out rockabilly (Sleepy is probably the only rockabilly baritone, and listening to him sometimes, one is almost tempted to believe that Howlin' Wolf, a singer Sleepy admires and resembles both in stature and in physical presence, has come back to life as a rock 'n' roller), but it was nothing compared to the thrill of the rare occasions when Sleepy would really catch fire. This would generally come on older, gospel-influenced material like 'Worried Man Blues' or Roy Hamilton's 'You Can Have Her,' but there was no predicting when it would happen or if it would happen at all. When it did, Sleepy would almost go into a trance, singing and swaying in an irresistible, rock-steady groove, going on like Wolf for ten or fifteen minutes at a time, extemporizing verses, picking lyrics out of the air, savoring the moment until he had extracted every last ounce of feeling from it, and then shrugging off-handedly as he went back to his table. 'You don't,' he apologized, 'want to get too wild.' And then he might recall the first time he saw Jerry Lee Lewis, in Galena Park, Texas, when a whole football stadium walked out on Jerry Lee while the fiery piano player was chewing out his drummer. You can't get too wrapped up in your own performance, says Sleepy, who always pays the utmost attention to his audience, feeds them fast songs or slow songs depending upon their mood, but, like the consummate showman that he is, never lets them go away unsatisfied.

'When I first started off in nightclubs and things, it just scared me to death. My legs would shake, and I would be sweating all over. But then I said to myself one day, "Hey, I like this, so I've got to get through this stage fright. I've got to relax and feel out people, get to know them, get some kind of communication going." That's pretty much the way it goes. I don't plan anything. It's all trial and error, I guess. If the first two or three things don't work, then we just move around and try something else.'

HE WAS BORN Thomas Paulsley LaBeff (the family name was originally LaBoeuf) on July 20, 1935, out in the country from Smackover, Arkansas, where he grew up on a forty-acre farm, which his father eventually sold for $300 to go work in the oil fields. He remembers his mother singing 'Corinna, Corinna' as she walked behind the plow. Sleepy was the tenth of ten children and was nicknamed at an early age, on his first day of school, as a matter of fact, because—here he pulls out a frayed picture showing a six-year-old with heavy-lidded eyes almost glued shut. He started listening to Groovey Boy, a disc jockey on station KWKH out of Shreveport, who played a mixture of hillbilly boogie and rhythm 'n' blues and, according to Sleepy, developed the Bo Diddley beat years before it actually became popular, with his radio

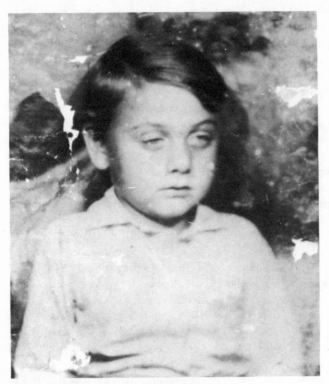

Early portrait. Courtesy of Sleepy LaBeef.

theme song, 'Hambone.' He listened to Lefty Frizzell, too, who was broadcasting on KELD in nearby El Dorado in the early forties (when Lefty himself
was only thirteen or fourteen), injecting a lot of blues into his performance.

Unlike most rockabilly singers, though, Sleepy does not cite black music
per se as being the preeminent influence on his work. He himself was well
acquainted with black music both from the radio and from selling watermelons
with his father in the black section of town. He feels strongly, however, that
rock 'n' roll, black and white, came primarily from the church, and indeed
that is both where he started out singing (United Pentecostal) and where he
lists his strongest influences: Vernie McGee, a guitar-playing deacon, and
the Reverend E. F. Cannon, pastor of his Norphlet church. He also cites Martha
Carson, whose 'Satisfied' became a white gospel standard, but above all it
was Sister Rosetta Tharpe, the great black gospel singer (she originated
'This Train,' among other classic gospel numbers), who he feels provided
the bedrock for rock 'n' roll. Jerry Lee Lewis, he is positive, derived his
piano style from Sister Rosetta's blithely bluesy guitar work, particularly on
the highly influential 'Strange Things Happening in This World' (cited also

by Johnny Cash and Carl Perkins as one of their most vivid musical memories). As far as Elvis goes, Sleepy's first reaction when he heard 'Blue Moon of Kentucky' on the radio was the shock of recognition. 'Cause I knew exactly where he was coming from. I thought, this is really something. Here's somebody singing just like we have in church for years. Only he was putting that gospel feeling to blues lyrics — *that* was what was so different about him.'

Sleepy quit school in the eighth grade over a misunderstanding with the teacher, though 'I never did give up on learning.' At fourteen he traded a .22 rifle to his brother-in-law for a guitar and 'liked it so well I was playing in church within two weeks.' Then at eighteen he left Arkansas ('Around the time it started to happen in Memphis I headed west, I guess') and ended up in Houston, where he went to work as a land surveyor, a job he has always liked (he had earlier worked for the Arkansas Highway Department and

With sister. Courtesy of Sleepy LaBeef.

Sister Rosetta Tharpe. Courtesy of Valerie Wilmer.

even after he moved to Nashville, he continued as a civil engineer for several years) because 'it gives you a chance to meditate on lots of things.' He also started singing with his first wife, Louise, in various gospel duos and quartets around town (George Jones, the current country superstar, was an occasional participant), mostly on 'family-type shows' like the Houston Jamboree. That was where he met Elvis for the first time and where his wife made the mistake of lending Elvis her guitar after he had broken the strings on his own. 'After he did the show he came back and said thank you, real nice and polite, but the front of the guitar was just about defaced, it was all scratched up and every string was broke—we sold it for, I think, $90, and that was an $800 guitar.'

It was shortly thereafter that Sleepy switched over to secular music and started making records for Pappy Daily—one of the most colorful of a colorful line of Texas entrepreneurs and George Jones's discoverer—both under his own name and under various pseudonyms, for border stations like XERF in Del Rio. The records for XERF were cover versions of popular hits of the day, sold by mail order and made to look and sound as close to the original as possible. According to Sleepy, he did everything from the Everly Brothers to Fats Domino, though it seems difficult to imagine him fooling anyone with that booming bass voice today. The records he made under his own name

Houston, Texas, ca. 1957. D. Knipe, lead guitar, and thirteen-year-old Wendell Clayton, bass. Courtesy of Sleepy LaBeef and Ron Bartolucci.

or variants thereof—as Tommy LaBeff, for example, on Wayside—included frenzied classics like 'Tore Up' and a 'Baby, Let's Play House' that came complete with Presley-like hiccuping vocals. He recorded for Gulf, Finn, Picture, Crescent—all with little or no commercial success—and crossed paths frequently with Mickey Gilley, Kenny Rogers, Glen Campbell, all of whom were hanging around Bill Quinn's busy Gold Star Studio (where Sleepy got to know blues singer Lightnin' Hopkins as well). Like Gilley (whose present drummer, Mike Schillaci, Sleepy raised from the time he was thirteen), Sleepy established a name for himself around town, investing in a couple of clubs and a hamburger drive-in and playing the rough Channel joints seven nights a week ('We didn't wear helmets back then, but it might have helped if we had'). Then one night, while he was waiting to go on at the Wayside Lounge, 'The waitress said, "There's a telephone call from Columbia Records in Nashville." I went to the phone and said hello. A man said, "Sleepy? This is Don Law. I want to sign you up." He sounded serious. It was hard to believe.'

So, while Gilley was still stuck on local labels, Sleepy signed with Columbia in 1964, moving to Nashville shortly thereafter. In 1968 he signed with Shelby Singleton, whom he had met originally on the Louisiana Hayride a decade before (this was in fact the last time that Shelby saw Sleepy perform) and who acquired the Sun catalogue from Sam Phillips the following year.

With the exception of six months he spent playing the role of a swamp monster in the movie *The Exotic Ones*, Sleepy has been on the road ever since.

IT'S VERY LIKELY that Sleepy has never made any money from any of his records. Except for 'Blackland Farmer,' a country chartmaker in 1971, he's never had anything resembling a hit ('I believe anyone could have had a hit with "Blackland." I didn't do anything special with it'), and certainly Shelby Singleton has never been lavish with his financial support. 'I have a little different philosophy than most people in the business,' declares Shelby, who has been highly successful in his own highly unorthodox way. 'My methods of merchandising are entirely different. I just print up ten or fifteen thousand copies of a record, and then if it doesn't sell I can dump it for schlock for more money than it cost me. I don't buckshot the market like the big companies do, because I believe that any artist, in the beginning at least, is the victim of the song. In other words, the song starts the artist, the artist doesn't start the song.

Unfortunately Sleepy's song hasn't arrived yet—at least not so far—and, without any promotional money behind him or income from writing or record royalties, Sleepy's whole living is on the road. Still, he manages to make the best of it in his own imperturbable way. About six months after his bus burned up, Sleepy acquired an almost-new Banner motor home through a helpful automobile dealer, just one in his legion of New England acquaintances, and between that, and a little Vega, and a high-backed trailer to bring up the rear, Sleepy's entourage (his wife Linda, a three-piece band, and occasionally his twenty-one-year-old son Harmony Paul) manage to make it from gig to gig in comfort, if not in style.

Everywhere Sleepy goes, he has what he calls his 'following.' It changes from venue to venue, but it takes in all ages and all walks of life, from policemen to wealthy businessmen to college students, truckers, Swedish rockabilly fanatics, and Navy men off the nuclear submarine base in Groton, Connecticut. There is no one with whom Sleepy is not at home and at ease, as he moves diplomatically between sets from table to table, announces the presence of an old friend from the bandstand, and placates the divergent tastes of the various segments of his audience with a characteristically eclectic and im-promptu selection of material. There's always a Big Event coming up, there's always an occasion to celebrate, even if it's only the band's imminent depar-ture for Port Huron, one of Sleepy's more frequent ports of call. Throughout the confusion of booking changes, personnel changes, automotive break-downs, and personality clashes that are bound to crop up, Sleepy remains absolutely unflappable ('You know me, I don't ever get too excited') and somewhat inscrutable besides. You can't really direct Sleepy, even towards something unquestionably to his advantage, if Sleepy doesn't want to do it himself. Whatever he does do, though, proceeds from the warmest of impulses, and Sleepy always proves the most gracious of hosts. The only qualities which he will not tolerate are drug use among band members (this has cost him a number of musicians, needless to say), bad language, dirty jokes, and racial slurs. In this, as in everything else, though, Sleepy can be so oblique in his disapproval that the offending party is sometimes not sure just what he has done — but will do almost anything to make sure he doesn't do it again.

When the Truckstop was closed down by the state tax commission in October of 1977, it seemed as if an era had come to an end. A story I wrote on Sleepy, along with numerous stories by Steve Morse of the *Boston Globe*, had generated further media interest, and Alan's had become a kind of central headquarters for all the displaced rockabillies in the New England area. I had dinner a few times with Cliff and June after the closing, and we played around with various schemes to thwart the government and get the Truckstop back in business. Sleepy's life didn't change much. June was still booking him, and he and Linda continued to live at the motel — which had also been closed down — so we would get together socially, to listen to tapes or just to talk, fairly often. Sleepy still had his books (he is an avid reader, and a born-again Eldridge Cleaver, whose *Soul on Ice* he had admired, was his great enthusiasm that winter); he had his collection of Sister Rosetta Tharpe, gospel singer Claude Ely, and, of course, his rare rockabilly records; he studied the Bible assiduously as always; and whenever he got in a tape of a new religious 'debate' (a fundamentalist dialogue between two preachers like the Reverend R. E. Bayer, a Florida evangelist known as the Walking Bible, and the Reverend Marvin Hicks of Corpus Christi), he would eagerly play us portions.

For a while, though, it seemed, he was oddly dispirited — subdued, preoccupied, some nights he seemed almost distracted on the bandstand of whatever club he was playing. We speculated that perhaps Sleepy's religious convictions were leading him to question the nature of his vocation. A long-time teetotaler, he had recently quit smoking, too (Sleepy, a man of prodigious appetites, had been smoking five packs a day for most of his adult life), and maybe, I thought, he was now giving serious consideration to his stated intention of taking up preaching some day ('I'm not a hypocrite. I don't live it, but I know it's the best thing'). I never found out what was on Sleepy's mind, and I don't think I'll ever know. He went out of town for a couple of months on tour, and when he came back he was his old self again, singing and playing with all his old vigor and enthusiasm. Only he wasn't playing at the Truckstop any more, which had reopened after eloquent testimony by Sleepy before the Amesbury board of selectmen. And June was no longer booking him. I don't think Cliff and June were ever quite sure what had happened either, but, whatever the cause of the estrangement, Sleepy patched things up socially with his former employers, and before long everyone was going out for Chinese food once again.

England, 1979—'It was like the old days.' PHILIP PARR

After that, surprisingly, things started picking up for Sleepy. He played New York and was invited to appear at England's prestigious country festival at Wembley. More stories appeared on him; he was a runner-up for *Country Music*'s Silver Bullet Award for promising newcomers (forty-seven-year-old Jack Clement won the award); even Shelby Singleton began to wonder if Sleepy's time hadn't finally come, though as far as Shelby was concerned, such thoughts were speculative only and did not necessitate any kind of rash financial commitment.

Sleepy, of course, remained calm in the midst of the storm, although 'storm' might be a misnomer for what could still turn out to be just another trade wind. Talking with Sleepy is always an education in historical perspective anyway, and his conversation is studded with references to the great and near-great, the almost weres and never wases—Charlie Rich at Houston's Sidewalk Café, Elvis at the Magnolia Garden, Willie Nelson clerking at a record store in Pasadena, Texas, Johnny Spain and Frenchy D., Rocky Bill Ford, Bobby Lee Trammell, and Charlie Busby, the guitarist from Red Shoot, Louisiana, who taught James Burton how to play. 'I think if they'd gotten the breaks,' says Sleepy ruminatively of these last, 'they could have been just as great as the ones who made it.'

I don't doubt it. At one point in our acquaintance I gave Sleepy the *Rolling Stone Illustrated History of Rock & Roll*, to which I had contributed several chapters. Sleepy found the book interesting, as I thought he would, recognizing many old friends and supplying a good number of anecdotes.

In the chapter I had written on rockabilly, though, I had included his name in a list of obscure artists I had thought as forgotten as Frenchy D. and Johnny Spain. 'They cultivated,' I wrote, 'the look, the stance, the sound of their more celebrated colleagues. All they lacked was the talent.' Had I, Sleepy asked me, puzzled and a little hurt, really meant what I wrote? No, I tried to apologize, not about *him* anyway, since I had never really had the opportunity to hear him, except on a stray cut or two, when I wrote the piece. 'I don't know,' he said with characteristic imperturbability, 'I guess you could still think that.'

Well, as it should be abundantly clear by now, I don't. In many ways Sleepy is as great a performer as I've ever seen, and when you see the way that people respond to his music, you wonder why, and if, rockabilly ever went away. Sleepy has a theory on that ('I didn't ever see it change. The people were still digging it, and the musicians liked playing it, but the big companies figured it was a fad and they took it away from the kids'), but in any case it is no exercise in nostalgia for the people who have come out to see Sleepy LaBeef at Alan's Fifth Wheel or the Hillbilly Ranch; they couldn't care less that it was John Lee Hooker who originated 'In the Mood' or Scotty Moore whose licks Sleepy duplicates note for note on 'Milkcow Blues Boogie.' Sleepy's records may not do him justice, but Sleepy knows how good he can be.

'I never sold out,' he can say with pride. 'Nobody owns me. I know I'm good. I wouldn't be honest if I didn't tell you that. I've been around long enough to know that if I get the breaks I can still make it—Charlie Rich was older than me when he finally did. And if I don't get the breaks—well, when I started in this business I didn't even know you could make a dime out of it. And I think I'd still be doing it tomorrow, if there wasn't any money in it at all. That's just the way I feel.'

MICKEY GILLEY

Room Full of Roses

MICKEY GILLEY was a name that was always vaguely familiar to me, but the first time I heard him on the radio, I was certain, like just about everyone else I knew, that it was Jerry Lee Lewis. He's back, I said exultantly to myself, hearing Jerry Lee's familiar piano arpeggios, the flat-out confidence in the voice. This was mid-1974, and I was really excited, because Jerry Lee, who was in the midst of a period of artistic doldrums at the time, was singing and playing better than he had in years. Then the announcer's voice came on and corrected my error. The song was 'Room Full of Roses,' and the singer was Mickey Gilley. . . .

FERRIDAY, LOUISIANA, on a Saturday afternoon. The war is over. It's market day in a small farming community, and there's an assortment of old Fords and pickups in front of Gilley's grocery store on Mississippi Avenue. There's a line of kids at the Arcade Theater on Fourth Avenue. In the line are three cousins, all within a couple of years of each other, all of whom play the piano occasionally in the little Assembly of God church on Texas Street. The movie is a cowboy picture—Gene Autry or Roy Rogers or Johnny Mack Brown. One week Lash LaRue appears in person to do tricks with his whip. 'If it was a double feature, oh man, the place was packed with kids. It was fifteen cents for the movie, a nickel for popcorn. Of course we weren't allowed to go to the shows, because our parents didn't hold with that, but we went just the same. I wasn't quite as wild as Jimmy and Jerry Lee. Jimmy had hopes of being a professional fighter. Next thing I knew he had went into the church.'

Jerry Lee Lewis, Mickey Gilley, Evangelist Jimmy Swaggart—'the three piano pickers from Ferriday,' which also gave Howard K. Smith to the world. Jerry's mother and Jimmy's mother were sisters; Mickey's mother Irene and Jerry's father Elmo were brother and sister, and their other sister Ada was Jimmy's grandmother. The three boys grew up like brothers. Jerry Lee started playing piano when he was eight or nine years old; he was living in Indian

Mickey and Jerry Lee. Courtesy of Sandy Brokaw.

Village outside of Clayton up on the Black River, and his parents mortgaged their home to buy an old Starck upright, which Jerry Lee still has today. 'Jerry's family was even poorer than mine, and that was bad. My father didn't even have an automobile. My mom worked in a café for $18 a week and bought me a piano, I must have been ten or eleven. Boogie woogie—that was the thing. We used to play in church a little bit, but the only one to even think about playing professionally was Jerry. The first time he ever played in public was when the Ford dealership came into town. Jerry got up and picked and sang on the back of an old flatbed truck. Then he got a little radio show. Once in a while he'd ask me to go with him, and we'd sing duets. "Don't Be Ashamed of Your Age" was one of the songs we used to do.'

Mickey Gilley grew up very much in the shadow of his older cousins. If you ask him today where he got his style—the same classic mixture of boogie woogie, country gospel, and blues that electrified the world from the moment Jerry Lee Lewis first stepped into the Sun recording studio—he'll credit it unabashedly to Jerry Lee. It was Jerry and Jimmy Lee Swaggart—later to become one of the leading radio and television ministers in the country—who snuck into Haney's Big House, an all-black roadhouse in the colored section of town where B.B. King and Memphis Slim and a host of nameless but equally well-remembered bluesmen and boogie woogie piano players held court. By the time they were in their teens, Jimmy Swaggart says, 'Mickey had developed into a fine musician, and Jerry Lee suggested we form a trio. "I'm not interested," Mickey answered when the idea was brought up. "I'll play with you guys in church, but I'm not interested in leaving town and playing in clubs." Aunt Rene's strong influence was still working in Mickey's life.'

It was only when Jerry Lee's first record came out in 1956 that Mickey Gilley even thought about becoming a professional musician. He was living in Houston at the time (he had moved there two years earlier after running off at seventeen to get married), working in the parts department of an engineering company, when 'Crazy Arms' came on the radio. 'I ran around telling everyone, "Hey, that's my cousin."' He went around to all the radio stations, too, unofficially promoting the record, and even helped publicize Jerry Lee's first Houston appearance at Dement Field in Galena Park (this is where Sleepy LaBeef saw Lewis for the first time). 'It was the same exact thing, same style we had always played when we were kids, just changed around a little bit. So I said, "I can play that." It was very easy for me to pick up. Next thing I knew, I had decided to cut me a record. After all, Jerry had made it, why not me? The only thing was, I was terrible. The first record I ever recorded is just plain embarrassing. I thought it was going to be a smash. I enjoyed doing it, though. And I've never liked to admit defeat. You know, if you stay with something long enough, I guess you have to either improve or get out.'

Mickey Gilley stayed with music long enough — for almost twenty years in fact — before he ever had anything even resembling a national hit. At first every record that came out was going to be the big breakthrough, every single on the Minor, Potomac, Lynn, Sabra, Princess labels was going to put him on the national charts. He cut his first record at Bill Quinn's Gold Star studio in Houston; he did sides for Crazy Cajun Huey Meaux (discoverer of Freddy Fender and Sir Doug Sahm) and played with back-up by Johnny Bush ('the Country Caruso') and Kenny Rogers. Once he came close to a hit with 'Call Me Shorty,' a good rocking number in the Jerry Lee vein that came out on the Memphis-based Dot label. Once he went to Nashville to cut the slickly produced 'Three's a Crowd' and bought a whole new wardrobe because 'I knew when this record came out we were going to be a hot act.' He went to New Orleans and Biloxi and Mobile's Azalea Grille and ended up in a little club called Ray's Lounge in Lake Charles, where he got paid $150 a week as a single at first, then — when he continued to pack the eighty-five-seat club — added a drummer as well.

Towards the end of 1959 he moved back to Houston, where he had a local hit with Warner Mack's 'Is It Wrong?' He got a job playing at the Ranch House across the Channel in Pasadena and spent the next fourteen years out on the Spencer Highway, first at the Ranch House and then at the Nesadel next door from 1960 to 1970. After that he went out briefly on his own at the Bel Air across town, then finally settled in at Gilley's with his new partner, Sherwood Cryer, just down the road from where he had started out. He was by this time very well established in Houston; his name was on a bright new eye-catching sign; he had a television show that aired on two channels, plus his own label, Astro, on which he had his biggest hit, 'Lonely Wine'; he had resigned himself at this point to never being anything more than a strong local club act.

What seems to have held him back was the problem that had dogged him throughout his career: his stylistic resemblance to his better-known cousin, Jerry Lee. What little success he achieved in the first place he probably owed to this very resemblance. It was Jerry Lee and His Pumping Piano, Jimmy Lee Swaggart and His Golden Gospel Piano—and Mickey Gilley and His Rocking Piano. A great deal of his later career, however, centered around his attempts to escape being labeled as just another imitator. It got to the

Gilley's. Courtesy of Sandy Brokaw.

point where he went to Nashville and recorded an album for GRT on which he didn't play piano at all, simply to establish some fresh territory of his own. 'I let it bug me to the point where it just about drove me nuts, man. I didn't want to sound anything like Jerry Lee at all, even though I knew that the type of music that he played was the type of music that I feel.' By 1974 'I had given up. I mean, I was successful. My personal appearances were good. The club and TV show were going great. But I couldn't sell records. I think I had the attitude, Why should I care? No one else does.'

The story of Mickey Gilley's 'overnight success' has been told so many times (and is so patently a real-life fairytale), it wouldn't bear repeating if it were not for the insight it affords into both Mickey's character and the sheer flukiness of fate. Minnie Elerick, the ticket-taker at Gilley's, also has title to the vending concession, both at Gilley's and at several other clubs around the city in which Mickey's partner, Sherwood Cryer, has an interest. As a favor she asked Mickey to record 'She Called Me Baby,' one of her favorite songs, for local jukebox play. Just by chance Mickey put 'Room Full of Roses,' an old George Morgan hit that he and Jerry Lee had fooled around with back in Ferriday, on the B side. Really, he didn't want to do 'Room Full of Roses' at all, partly 'because I had no confidence in the song, since Jerry had overlooked it' and also 'because it sounded too much like Jerry.' The engineer on the session convinced him that it was going to be the back side of a record that would never get played, so Mickey went ahead and cut it, overdubbed steel, and then forgot all about it for a few months. When he finally heard the engineer's mix-down, 'She Called Me Baby' sounded fine. 'I thought to myself, well, I finally got something. Then I flipped the record over. All I could hear was that damn steel guitar, the echo was just bouncing off the walls. I called up the engineer, I said, "Why's it so loud?" He said, "Man, I just mixed it the way I felt it." "Well," I said, "I'm just going to have to remix it. This is terrible." I went and got the tape, I actually cued the tape up, then I said, "Hey, I don't want to take the time to mess with this. It's just a local record, it's only going to be played on the local jukeboxes."'

When the record came out, it was a runaway hit in Houston, the pressing plant couldn't keep up with the orders, but it was the B side, 'Room Full of Roses,' that was getting the play. Finally it reached the point that Mickey could almost smell national success. He flew to Nashville, presented the song to all the major labels, and was turned down by every one. As a last resort he turned to Playboy Records, which didn't even have a Nashville office, flew out to the Coast, and leased the record. After that it was as if the dam had burst. Mickey Gilley had half a dozen number one hits in a row and was acclaimed Most Promising New Artist, Best Male Vocalist, Entertainer of the Year, by *Record World*, *Billboard*, and the Academy of Country Music.

'You can imagine how excited I was. Here I had been pushing, I'd been trying all those years, and it was only when I got to the point where I just didn't care, that I could really do something. I guess sometimes you want something so bad, you strive so hard for a certain goal, that you don't even realize it's within your grasp. I just had to get the idea of getting *away* from the style of Jerry Lee out of the back of my mind and start thinking about Mickey Gilley. You know, when I sang those two songs, I *knew* there wasn't nothing that was going to happen. I almost wasn't even trying, and they came out better than anything else I ever recorded.'

MICKEY GILLEY today is a far cry from the insecure, self-doubting entertainer who struggled for so long in his older cousin's shadow. Although he retains a strong element of self-deprecating good humor, at forty he has finally gained confidence in himself and his music. Easy-going, unpretentious, still boyish-looking in a pudgy, slightly buck-toothed, old-fashioned sort of way (his newly styled hair looks as if it should still be neatly parted on the side), Mickey Gilley gives the impression in everything he does of a sober kind of competence. You encounter in the man the same affable good-natured sort of enthusiasm that you find in his music.

At Gilley's Club, where he is an infrequent attraction nowadays, he is in his element, meeting friends, greeting old acquaintances, showing off his new twenty-four-track studio next door, winking at the pretty girls. At one time he used to hustle pool at the clubs where he played; in fact at the Nesadel, he says, that was his principal living. Although he hasn't got much time for pool today (after every set there are autographs to sign, pictures to be taken with fans, who line up at five dollars a throw, reminiscences to be exchanged), he isn't above playing a friendly game either, and he ascribes at least part of his success to his continued ability to relate to the people who pay to hear him play. 'These people love someone who don't give 'em a big-star attitude. I mean, you got to understand, you're something special to them, especially when they see you on TV, shooting the breeze with Dinah or Betty White or Ken Norton. And then when they see me out at the club, "Man, I can't believe I know him. He's just like us. He's a hometown boy. Hey, Gilley, you still play pool?"'

Gilley's Club itself sometimes seems more like an extended family than a business enterprise and is certainly one of the most unusual places I've ever been. Not so much for its atmosphere, though this is unusual enough, with its quonset hut decor, multiple screens flashing advertisements and warnings ('Ladies: Beware of Thieves at Work'), parquet dance floor filled with couples of all ages, shooting gallery, pool tables, and drunken cowboys elbowing up to the sledgehammer strength test or the mechanical bucking bull which no one rides for long. All of these features are, I suppose, standard Texas ballroom to one degree or another. What isn't standard anything is the unique spirit of Gilley's, where you find a kind of easy intimacy and

Honky Tonk Hardwood Floor, Gilley's. Courtesy of Sandy Brokaw.

tight-knit feeling hardly characteristic of a wide-open club. There's Minnie at the door, always cited as the catalyst for Mickey's unexpected success. Then there are Betty and Ann behind the souvenir counter, which is stocked with Gilley paraphernalia—T-shirts, sweatshirts, records, pictures, buttons, posters, bumper stickers, and just about anything else you can think of (and a few other merchandise items besides). Mickey's wife, Vivian—who met her husband fifteen years ago at the Nesadel when a girlfriend who liked his music dragged her out to see him—is in charge of the fan club, whose surplus wares occupy an entire stockroom of what Houston reporter Bob Claypool calls 'Gilley's K-Mart.' At the center of it all is fifty-year-old Sherwood Cryer, weatherbeaten, dour-looking, who started out as a welder at Shell and who surveys his giant club with an invariably woebegone expression, invariably clad in mechanic's zip-up coveralls.

Sherwood Cryer is a story in himself. Because of the coveralls and because you will frequently find him taking out the trash or pushing a broom, he is frequently mistaken for the janitor in his own club. According to Vivian Gilley, 'That club is his whole life,' and watching him take care of business, personally attend to every detail, dive into every fray, one is inclined to agree. He doesn't drink, he doesn't smile much, Gilley's Club seems to occupy all of his attention. That and Mickey Gilley. 'You see, Sherwood was never close to anyone before,' says Vivian. 'He's closer to Mickey than he is to his own brothers.' 'Everybody I ever talked to before was just bullshitting,' says Mickey.

Sherwood first called him when Mickey had gone out on his own in 1970 to take over the Bel Aire. At first Mickey was leery of him 'because everybody thought he was part of the Mafia,' both because of his extensive holdings and because he patrolled his property at night with a loaded shotgun. It was only when the Bel Aire looked as if it was going under and Mickey had seen no money in three weeks that he agreed to meet with Sherwood and take a look at the club Sherwood had been boasting about. The club turned out to be Shelley's, an open-air drive-in that Mickey had been past a million times. 'It was trashy. I just shook my head. "Well, what do you think?" "It wouldn't work." "What does it need?" I told him, "It could use a dozer to clear the lot off, to start with."'

Sherwood wouldn't drop the subject, though, and, after being badgered for suggestions, Mickey finally gave him a list of nonnegotiable conditions, ending with a fifty-fifty partnership and a $1000-a-week guarantee for Mickey and the band. '"Okay, you got it. When do you want to come to work?" I said to myself, "He's gonna just give me $1000 a week and put in all these changes? No way." He said, "What do you want to call the club?" "Let's just call it Gilley's." Three weeks later I drove out there. I figure he's forgotten all about it by this time. First thing I saw when I drove up was that big sign — it was beautiful! I mean, it was the same sign we got now, but it was brand-new at the time. I never seen anything so flashy. They was going full blast, paneling the ceiling. I just walked in and looked around — no one knew me from Adam. And I thought to myself, "This has got my name on it." And it really made me feel like something. So I finally got in touch with him. "Well, what do you think?" "Well," I said, "it's looking pretty good." "When do you want to open?" "Wednesday." "Fine, I'll have it ready by then." And he did. The club became an almost instant success.' And expanded, first doubling its capacity of 750, only recently adding on another wing that increased its floor area to nearly four acres, its capacity to more than 5000. When Mickey finally hit it big, it seemed to mean as much to Sherwood as it did to Mickey.

'One of the things that really intrigued me,' says Mickey, 'was that he really believed in me, he just loved my music. Everybody else was blowing smoke, but Sherwood really liked what I was doing.'

'When Mickey started going on the road,' says Vivian, 'it really killed Sherwood. He couldn't leave the club, that's his baby, but it like to broke his heart, he just missed having Mickey around so much. He got to where he started flying in to do all the TV shows. And you know Sherwood, I don't think he ever wore a suit in his life, but when he went to the CMA Awards, he went out and got himself a tux. I really wish you could have seen him in his tux.'

For every hit record that has come out, Sherwood has bestowed an expensive gift, and Mickey in turn has placed his wholehearted trust in Sherwood. 'He just loves for me to call him and shoot the breeze, say, "Hey, boss, it's Mickey." I'll tell you the reason why Sherwood admires me so. Because I'm the first person that he's met in this business, when I say I'm going to do something, I actually sit down and figure things out in my head and do it. I direct the TV show, I write the ads, and I really study it, I watch it religiously to learn from my mistakes. That's the reason why everything I tell him, he listens; he takes it serious because he knows I'm serious about it.'

Mickey and Sherwood — maybe their names will be in the headlines tomorrow with news of a lawsuit, but I doubt it. It was Sherwood and Vivian who backed Mickey up right along, told him he was important when he himself seemed to doubt it, helped give him the same sure sense of self that sustains him today. It was Sherwood who provided the push that really put Mickey over. Sherwood looks out for Mickey's career, and Sherwood pays the bills, even going so far as to put up some of the money for producer Eddie Kilroy's Nashville offices when Playboy Records wouldn't come up with it themselves. 'Once he saw that I had a chance to make it nationally,' says Mickey, 'he put everything he could behind me. He wanted everything first class.'

Mickey Gilley has had more than a dozen Top 10 hits in the last few years and has in the process finally become a well-established star. When he went out on the road he was nervous at first, but he's since developed a full-scale show with dramatic special effects, his accompanying group, the Bayou Beats, have become the Red Rose Express, and Las Vegas is on the horizon. He seems to be taking it all in stride. The astronomical jump in his income in just one year may have thrown him a little, because, as he says, 'I had nothing to spend it on.' He still lives in the same modest house with Vivian and their son Greg and seems almost embarrassed at the unpretentiousness of their surroundings. He shows me a publication of the Paint Horse Association, which profiles him as a new member of the horsey set, and he thinks at some point he might like to buy a small airplane, a four-seater (he got his pilot's license a few years ago). His only other primary concern has to do with the careers of his featured singers: Johnny Lee, who's been with him for seven years and recently had three or four hits on GRT, and Toni Holcomb, whom he has been producing on his own. He wants to handle Toni in such a way that 'she will never have anything to be embarrassed about. If I had had someone to look out for me, then my career wouldn't have been embarrassing to me.'

He even seems to have come to terms with the specter of his more flamboyant cousin, and though he never expects to surpass Jerry Lee ('I never thought that as a piano player I was anywhere near as good as him'), he no longer seems to feel so acute a sense of inferiority and worries instead about

Mickey and Sherwood. Courtesy of Sandy Brokaw.

Jerry's health and truculent attitudes ('He didn't love music any more than me, and one thing I got him beat on, I admire and love people more').

Sometimes you get a glimpse of a darker side, as when he contemplates his strict religious upbringing and the life he leads today. 'I know I don't live like I was raised to live,' he says. 'I was taught it's wrong to drink, and I drink some. I used to smoke, even though I quit smoking a few years ago. But I don't never try to put myself down. I take care of my family. I take care of my mama and daddy. I think I do what's right for me.'

In fact Mickey Gilley seems to have it all together, and in this sense he is clearly a rarity among the popular entertainers I've met. As we drive along in his pickup, he points out the landmarks of his life of the last twenty years. There's the Ranch House, and there's the Nesadel. Here are Cheri's Drive-In and Charley's Liquor and a whole block of other property that Sherwood owns. Dement Field is deserted, but we stop for a moment to look at the stands where thousands of screaming fans saw Jerry Lee kick back the piano stool for the first time. It was practically unpopulated when Mickey first came out here, it was just bleak open land. Now it's been all built up. You can smell the industry and the oil in the breeze that comes off the Channel.

'I think that whatever people do, it has to be something they're interested in and love. I think what finally did it for me,' says Mickey Gilley, 'was determination, not giving up, finally taking a good hard look at myself and saying, "Hey, you have to be yourself. Anything less, and you're only fooling yourself and the public. And the public is real, real hard to fool." Hey,' he says, rolling down the window of the truck, 'I don't think I'd be bitter if the whole thing stopped tomorrow. You know, I accomplished what I set out to do. You can't do any better than that.'

185

COWBOY
JACK
CLEMENT

Let's All Help the Cowboy Sing the Blues

He does a little Shakespeare, and he sings
He plays the mandolin and other things
He looks for love and beauty and IQ
And that's what makes the Cowboy sing the blues.

I HAVE DISCOVERED,' says Cowboy Jack Clement, songwriter, producer, ex-brother-in-law of Waylon Jennings, Sun confrere of Sam Phillips, one-time Arthur Murray dance instructor, discoverer of Don Williams and Charley Pride, and would-be recording star, 'the third universal truth.' The first, of course, is that all people from Memphis speak in parables. The second is that women don't like steel guitars. And the third? 'You can't sing a three-minute song in a minute and a half. You'd be amazed at how many people try. You see, when the creative thing hits, you can't hurry it.

'You know,' he goes on, in no particular order, but following a stream of association that in life has taken him from the heights (when as president of JMI, his own label, he was proprietor of three studios, a couple of publishing companies, a graphics arts studio, the Dipsy Doodle Construction Company, and had forty-six people on his payroll) to the depths (when as producer of *Dear Dead Delilah*, a full-scale, sub-Hollywood epic starring Will Geer and Agnes Moorehead, he lost it all, save for Jack Publishing, his main song catalogue, and in the process became one of the prime examples in Nashville legend of the perilous paths of genius). 'You know,' he repeats, 'I always wanted to make movies, ever since I was a little kid. Then I turned into one. I've been making real-life movies for the last seven years—they just don't go by in an hour and forty-five minutes. So now I've just got to find the story. I was always gonna write a book. Now I may not, because I don't know if I got anything to say. When you're young, you've got lots to say, but you don't know how to say it. Now I'd like to write a novel, but I ain't got a story. I got everything but a story. Which is why I want to make a movie.'

Jack Clement strokes his pepper-and-salt beard and runs his fingers lightly through his recently peroxided hair. Despite his appellation, Cowboy is dressed in country-club casual, with dark-colored slacks, an untucked sports shirt smoothed out over a ballooning stomach, and black patent-leather loafers ('I can't wear cowboy boots,' says Jack, 'because they hurt my feet. I'm what you call one of them drugstore cowboys. But I can ride a horse pretty good. Well, a Shetland pony anyway').

Around him in the fabled house on Belmont Avenue, only recently converted into a recording studio, there is a whirlwind of activity. The secretary is typing letters. The business manager is taking care of business. Singers and musicians pop in and out. Stoney Edwards is hanging around waiting for Cowboy to cut some sides on him. Townes Van Zandt, a singer-songwriter from Texas with a folk-cult following, arrives with the acetate of his new album and anxiously awaits Jack's verdict. A Pitney Bowes copying machine sits in one corner. The telephone connects to California. In the kitchen someone is frying up a Clementburger. And Jack is playing tapes of his latest band (recorded in his attic studio) at the professional console that sits in what was once Pat Boone's grandparents' dining room.

Despite the constant entrances and exits, projects taken up and projects abandoned, sometimes it seems as if nothing is really happening — but that, according to Cowboy, is something of an illusionist's trick, too. 'It's all happening right now,' he explains with an expansive gesture, his fingers trailing lazily in the air. He gets up out of his seat, pirouettes in plump and stately fashion, and sits back down again. 'It's like poetry. You just don't see it. Most people think if they don't see it, it's not happening, but that's not true. You know, I'm a lot more serious than I tell people. I quit being nostalgic a long time ago. I decided I was ready for the space age.'

Jack Clement was probably ready for the space age long before most people. Certainly his credits attest to the fact that he was ahead of his time, and he has received tributes to his genius from sources as far removed as Chet Atkins, Hank Snow, Johnny Cash, and Louis Armstrong. 'I've got a bunch of people who say I'm a genius,' he once told writer Lola Scobey. 'That don't make me a genius. But you've got to be pretty smart to get all them people to say that on cue.' He has even received the ultimate accolade, praise from Jerry Lee Lewis, who a few years ago, in a moment of excess zeal, jumped up on a studio console and as a result no longer drops by to visit ('Not lately,' says Cowboy, who takes his machines seriously. 'I don't dig people jumping up and down on my console while I'm trying to make records. It's a little distracting'). Jerry Lee for his part has lumped Cowboy with Sam Phillips and the Killer himself, 'nutty as a fox squirrel, ain't got no sense. Birds of a feather flock together. It took all of us to get together to really screw up the world. We've done it.'

And now twenty years later Jack Clement is trying to do it again, having spent the last year and a half making his very own record album, his first, which, he proclaims with magisterial calm, will probably be 'kind of like when Elvis hit and the bottom dropped out of country music. A lot of stuff that's popular now will just kind of vaporize; it can only happen once in a generation.' Well, all right, but why did he wait all these years? He is forty-seven now, an unlikely age for a matinee idol, even so unlikely a matinee idol as this drugstore Cowboy. 'Well,' he explains, his eyes narrowing, 'it's something that's easy to put off. You know, it's a lot of work to cut an album. Although it's something I was intending all along. You see, it's a little dis-

The Marine Corps Drill Team salutes Princess Elizabeth, 1951. (Corporal Jack Clement is at far right.)
Courtesy of Jack Clement.

heartening when you write a song, and then nobody ever sings it right. You don't need a voice to be a singer. Singers are just something to make my machines sound good. I never really wanted to be a songwriter. I've written songs for years and had 'em butchered by a bunch of real talented people. I got tired of fooling with all them hogcallers. Singers are a bunch of uptight ego-driven people, can't deal with them anyway except by trickery. And, you see, I can become invisible real quick. I guess I'm privileged in a certain sense. I've never done anything but music in my whole life. I guess I was protected in a sense, but now I'm old and wily as a fox, and I feel like I can go back – either that or fly, or float about six inches from the ground – I feel like I can go back in time or forward in time. Because the future's already happened.'

JACK HENDERSON CLEMENT was born, not on Krypton or on Alpha Centauri, the planet he somewhat whimsically hopes to colonize some day ('All I got to do is get a billion dollars together, find some other nuts who have a billion dollars, and then get myself a spaceship. Is it possible for me to ride in a spaceship? You never know. I'm just not going to get in no hurry about it; that's the whole thing about outer space'), but in Whitehaven, a suburb of Memphis, where his father was choir director and worked in a jewelry store, and his mother, who lives with him today, was, then as now, a pillar of the community. He would have become a dentist like his grandfather and uncles if his father had had anything to say about it, but instead he enlisted in the Marines at seventeen and was eventually stationed in Washington, D.C., where he remained until 1952, when he was twenty-one. In Washington he was a member of the Marine Corps drill team, and he still has the picture that appeared in *Life* magazine of a young Jack Clement standing at attention, the dimple in his chin clearly visible, as Princess (soon to be Queen) Elizabeth passes by.

It was while he was in the Marines that he started playing music professionally, forming a bluegrass group (Jack Clement and the Tennessee Troupers), along with Buzz Busby and various members of the Stoneman family ('Pop' Stoneman was originally recorded by Ralph Peer in the 1920s). They played all around the D.C. area, and then, when Clement was discharged, he and Buzz went first to Wheeling and then to Boston, for the WCOP Hayloft Jamboree, as Buzz and Jack and the Bayou Boys. When he returned to Memphis in 1954, on what was intended to be a brief vacation, he enrolled instead at Memphis State on the GI bill, through a friend became a dance instructor at Arthur Murray ('I hadn't ever danced a lick in my life. I came in on Waltz Week'), fronted a big dance band at the Eagle's Nest, where the floor show was that brand-new Memphis sensation, Elvis Presley, and hooked up with Slim Wallace, truck driver, country music fan, and fledgling record-company mogul, whose label, Fernwood, would shortly take its name from his home on Fernwood Drive. Jack got Wallace to buy a tape recorder from Sleepy-

Eyed John, proprietor of the Eagle's Nest and a well-known disc jockey in West Memphis, and cut a record on a local singer named Billy Lee Riley. He took the record over to the Sun studio to be mastered. Sam Phillips liked the tape, leased it from Fernwood—still only a name—put it out on his own label, and hired Jack Clement as his first engineer-producer at $90 a week.

From the beginning it was a heady experience, cutting Roy Orbison on the first day, getting Jerry Lee's 'Whole Lotta Shakin'' down on tape almost as an afterthought at the end of a session, writing 'Ballad of a Teenage Queen' and 'Guess Things Happen That Way,' pop hits for Johnny Cash, and recording quite incidentally a couple of singles of his own that went absolutely nowhere.

'After I was there three weeks, Sam never came to the office again,' Cowboy says occasionally today. Or: 'I learned something from Sam all the time. Of course I thought he was full of shit when I worked for him. He still is. But he had this little thing I didn't understand then—' What that was can vary from account to account (Sam's ear, his gift for psychology, his willingness to just let things happen, the proximity of a café to the studio, the absence of an office, the 'live' sound of the records, though in retrospect Sam was too much into highs, there never was enough bass), but whatever it was, when Jack went off on his own he claims he put all these lessons into practice. He went off on his own rather abruptly when Sam fired him over what Cowboy claims, in typically elliptical fashion, was 'a silly little misunderstanding' ('Well, maybe Justis had had a little bit of liquid refreshment'). He had already been evicted from his apartment for diving off the roof into the swimming pool, and after briefly starting his own label, Summer ('Summer hits, summer not, hope you like the ones we got'), he went to work as a producer and staff writer for Chet Atkins at RCA in 1960.

Next came a move to Beaumont, Texas, in 1963, where he and Bill Hall and Sun alumnus Allen Reynolds ran a record label and publishing firm that saw, among other things, the success of fellow Memphian Dickey Lee with 'Patches' and the entrance into the Clement catalogue of Lee's 'She Thinks I Still Care,' which became an all-time country standard. It also saw the permanent ensconcement of the nickname Cowboy, which—along with its built-in advantage of always allowing him to refer to himself in the third person—has given Clement instant identification in a world of first names. It derives, he sometimes says, from a Memphis-concocted radio show in which he, Dickey Lee, and Allen Reynolds (currently Crystal Gayle's producer) created the fictional John Deaux Trio and referred to each other as 'Cowboy Waliaski from Trenton, New Jersey, Red River Sylvester, we played around with all different kinds of names. It was kind of—*cute*. In Beaumont everybody got to be Cowboy Something but mine stuck.'

Finally, with his new monicker firmly entrenched, Cowboy Jack Clement moved back to Nashville for good, where—before starting up the JMI label in 1971, building two of the most successful studios in town, and becoming

Boston's WCOP Hayloft Jamboree (Jack Clement in bow tie at microphone).
Courtesy of Jack Clement.

one of the most sought-after independent producers around—he came across
Charley Pride and produced the first of thirteen gold record albums that
became the basis for his commercial reputation.

Up to here it is a conventional enough story by Music City standards.
Jack Clement as a producer was probably best summed up by his one-time
protégé, Dickey Lee. 'I thought he was a real bastard,' said Lee of the Sun
days. 'We would go into the studio feeling like heroes, and Jack wouldn't
pay much attention to us. While we were recording he would be sitting there
reading a comic book or something, and it really deflated me.' 'You don't
want to be too proper,' says Jack. 'You've got to keep the singer right on
the edge of anger, because singers sing their best when they're thinking of
anything but the song. You see, I got 'em so they think I like mistakes. Then
if they think I like 'em, they won't give 'em to me. You've got to use two or
three kinds of reverse psychology in this game.' As a businessman, too, he
seemed to have things well in hand, as witness this 1970 description by
Nashville writer Teddy Bart. 'Jack Clement is a songwriter, an independent
record producer, owner of several publishing companies and his own building, which houses his operation plus a modern new recording studio. His
many-faceted life is managed successfully in a subdued, quiet manner. . . .
Jack Clement doesn't talk, but his silence has style.'

What happened then? Is this the very same Jack Clement who has been
raving on nonstop about Shakespeare, space travel, the videotape revolution
and the need to install new order in his life? ('We've got to get some systems
into this crazy business. We've got to establish some disciplines.') It would,
I think, be useless to speculate just what caused the transformation, but
suffice it to say it may have had something to do with his discovery of a
world that even today upsets his Baptist sense of propriety. 'I've got books
and documents,' he tantalizes, 'I just might show some writer, if he promised
he wouldn't write nothing about my throwing parties or drinking beer or
smoking Turkish cigarettes or any other little thing my mother might read.

191

Of course I think she knows it all already; she just don't want to read about her son doing those kinds of things.'

And then there was the movie. It must have seemed like a good idea at the time. John Ferris, a classmate at Whitehaven High and best-selling author of *The Fury*, among others, wanted to make his directorial debut after writing a number of film scripts. Jack Clement, Renaissance man, wanted to get into the movies himself, putting up all the money ('It didn't even occur to me to be funded. I'm into that now'), handling all the production chores, and eventually taking over the final edit, which involved cutting out twelve minutes of story line because of an inept cinematographer. 'So the story is a little confusing,' says Jack, who insists that if it hadn't been for that director of photography, he might have pulled it off. In any case, to hear Cowboy tell it, he does not really have any regrets. He may have been forced to divest himself of nearly all his holdings. He saw the empire he had so carefully assembled crumble and disappear in one swell foop. He has spent the last five years digging out of the financial mess in which his unwise investment left him. But he still owns the movie and the rights to one other. And all those material possessions were weighing on him anyway. Now that he's got his debt whittled down to a more manageable $100,000, he can speak with equanimity of past travails and declare without a blush, 'I never really lost any money. All I did was spend it. I think I'm gonna get to where I don't need money anyway.' Unless he seriously decides to go into the spaceship business, in which case he may have to mint it.

Listen to the Cowboy talk.

When I was making the movie, I could tell you everything except what the story was about. Next time I make a movie I'm gonna get the story taken care of real quick, in a couple of lines. Then I won't shoot it — but it will have one. I want to win an Academy Award for directing a picture, but it'll never have a script. Well, it's a game, I like games, anything for a laugh. I've got a bunch of gold records over on the shelf. To cut a record, I've got to feel good about it. If I don't, I don't put it out. I put out what I want to hear, and I hope the people want to hear it, too. I don't know why they wouldn't. I'm a people, too. I regard it as moving portraiture. I want all my pictures to be pretty. I want all my stories to have happy endings. I got a thing against reading. If it were up to me, I'd burn every book. Sure, all of 'em, why not, just start over. You could remember the best parts, a line or two, a couple of chapters. When I was young, I read all the time. It would take me a book just to write a letter to Johnny Cash.

I've been working on a new version of Shakespeare. I call mine *As You All Like It*. I know all there is to know about Shakespeare; of course I ain't never read what he wrote; well, I may have read one play part way through. But I got his act down. I read all of P. G. Wodehouse. My mother read the whole set. And I saw *Othello*, the movie with Orson Welles. All I ever needed to know about Shakespeare I got from Kurt, my engineer. Before I taught him to be an engineer, he had just graduated from Wesleyan as an English major. So I taught him, naturally, to be an engineer. I'm particularly interested in *Hamlet*, of course. I've written a new version, where Hamlet takes a different approach, where he's decided to *be* rather than not to be, he's kind of a happy-go-lucky sort. Everything I do would be a musical, because being a writer or poet is not a valid thing to be nowadays unless you're a singer, too. There's one conversation I wrote between Shakespeare and me, and he says, 'What do you think of this, Cowboy?'

> *To be or not to be — that is the question:*
> *Whether 'tis nobler in the mind to suffer*
> *The slings and arrows of outrageous fortune,*
> *Or to take arms against a sea of troubles,*
> *And by opposing end them? . . . Etc., etc.*
> *Soft you now!*
> *The fair Ophelia! Nymph, in thy orisons*
> *Be all my sins rememb'red.*

And Cowboy says, 'Shit, Shakespeare, don't hand me all this shit about all my sins re-member-ed. I want my sins forgot.' I got other chapters and acts of me talking to Shakespeare, changing things around a little bit.

I'm gonna find me a cassette cowboy and cut a Betamax hit, cut it for peanuts but make it so it would stand up under repeated viewing. It would have to be a perfect magic performance, cut in a real good-sounding nightclub. We'd get the best performance on the best night, but without ever repeating a set. I mean, you can't do it anyway, so why try? Now I ain't gonna make no pretense of trying to repeat myself. If I decide not to count off, I just ain't gonna count off, the band'll catch on after a while, they'll make up for it afterwards. I ain't worried about getting my record played. I'll attend to that personally. No more of this wishy-washy business, no iffy propositions, there will be no pretense of decisions made by committee, there wasn't ever any hit record made by a committee, I'm gonna make all the decisions myself. I ain't particular who plays it, just as long as everyone plays it. I ain't gonna give it a name or call it nothing. I'm probably a real good promotion man myself. All you need is one radio station, that's all you need to get it going. All I gotta do is find someone somewhere who'll go out on a limb. But I'm used to taking a whole roomful of people and getting them to go out on a limb. I'm going to go out and tell them about all this bad music I hear everywhere — in Florida, in Tennessee, all over. You know, I used to be confused about other people; now I don't even know who the fuck I am any more. I'm still doing the same thing I was doing when I was fifteen, getting up a band. I remember one time in Memphis I made a whole bunch of

Cowboy and Indian.
Caption and photograph courtesy of Jack Clement.

records, all hits, about ten of them in a row, and then I went water-skiing for the rest of the summer. I had a good time and made a lot of good records. I'd kind of like to do that again.

And so on. And so on. In perfect circles that never meet. 'He's crazy as a woodpecker, ain't he?' says Stoney Edwards, who has been sitting around all afternoon waiting to make records.

'Stoney,' responds Jack obliquely, with a Cheshire-cat smile, 'can do anything he wants to do, if he can do it forty times. I'll tell you what,' he says, addressing the singer directly. 'I'll cut a single on you today, and we'll have it in the Ernest Tubb Record Shop on Sunday, and it'll be a hit by Friday. You just gotta do it forty times. And you can't fake it either, cause we ain't got a control-room window — we ain't even got a control room — and if the band ain't enjoying themselves, we can tell. I ain't run nobody through this mill in seven years. Stoney can do anything he wants. I can go to Florida, and Stoney can stay in the fucking studio, so long as he's prepared to do it forty times.' Anything less, says Cowboy Jack Clement, his producer's cap on, wouldn't be proper.

It's all very amusing, and, of course, it's great copy. Hanging around Jack Clement for any length of time, you can get vaporized yourself by the endless string of one-liners, ear gags, and polished bon mots, all delivered with the practiced ease of a slightly stoned stand-up comedian. You can be dazzled by the ceaseless flow of energy and ideas, confused by the free-form structure of the monologues, amused by the double and triple reverses that make up Cowboy's normal conversational mode. And indeed it may all be a benign put-on. 'I don't read contracts,' boasts Cowboy. On the other hand, he points out, he has a business manager who is trained to read them. He doesn't read music, either, but there's always someone to write out the horn parts. 'I've got all kinds of eggheads hanging around to give me the proper answers.'

On a more prophetic plane, many of his visions of the future could well turn out to be true. Nashville may very well become a major video center. Certainly Clement's ideas on production ('I'm into a very simplistic way of making records, using space-age technology') make eminently good sense when stripped of their more poetic excesses. His intention to build a dance band ('I want to get a physical reaction from people. I want to get 'em on the dance floor before they even think about it'), with a wide-based repertoire ('Brazil,' 'Tutti Frutti,' 'Hold On, I'm Coming,' 'Alabama Jubilee') that can be reproduced live at a moment's notice, has the immediacy of an idea whose time has come — again. His firm belief that 'music is coming around to where it's gonna be natural again, it'll be a lot more acrobatic, it's too mental nowadays,' is probably not so wide of the mark. With his videotaping, his proposed concept LPs (a dance album, an 'ear show' that presents Bo Diddley, Shakespeare, barbershop quartet, octet, and clarinet polkas, all available in one colorful stereoscopic thirty-minute package), his not-so-fanciful marketing ideas ('Sell the back cover to Coca-Cola. Fuck liner notes!'), what Jack Clement clearly wants to do is to restore some of the magic that Captain Video, Jack Benny, and Sun Records brought to the world. In none of this can he be faulted. When he shows off his latest studio, his ninth — in fact, the whole house has been turned into a studio — it embodies the very concepts that he has been talking about. There are no limiters, no equalizers, no baffles, no control room — everything is cut 'live,' everything is cut flat, the whole intention is to get a true, live sound. 'Nobody can believe it,' says Cowboy convincingly, 'because recording studios are all alike. What they don't realize is that they're all wrong.' The one videotape that he has made so far to showcase his album—and his Shakespearean soliloquies—is an equally brilliant realization of his various theories, and there seems little question that if he should get the opportunity to present either his tape or himself on *Saturday Night Live* as he wishes, he could enthrall a nationwide audience as easily as he has captivated small-town Nashville over the years. Jack Clement could be the only show in every town.

At the same time, one fears that in seeking to blind the world with his fancy footwork, the Cowboy, like so many other flim-flam men, may only have succeeded in blinding himself. For lurking just beneath the surface of all the elegant show and repartee seems to be the fear that Jack Clement himself, the real Jack Clement, is a fraud, that whatever success he has enjoyed has come as the result of a misunderstanding, that he may have parlayed his talents as a novelty songwriter and entertainer into a $100,000 record contract, but that that is as far as he can go. I don't know that there's any basis in reality for this fear; certainly the real Jack Clement has had his share of solid, measurable success. And yet, like many geniuses whose theories are equally unassailable, he seems almost incapable of going out and exposing these carefully nurtured creations to an indifferent world.

The new album, for example, contains a love song so immediate, so direct, so powerful that it should be played on every radio station, country or pop, in the nation. Even Sam Phillips has pronounced 'When I Dream (I Dream of You)' an AOR (All Over the Road) Hit. Whether or not it will ever become one, though, is anyone's guess, because for all of his lofty promises, for all of his grandiose plans, it is doubtful whether Jack Clement would ever do anything so mundane as go out and work the song; like Elvis, Howard Hughes, and other superstars, he rarely ventures outside unless the air is right. Similarly, one suspects that the band—and all the tracks that they have recorded—will meet the same fate as past bands, past tracks, not because what they are doing is not worthwhile, but simply because the money will run out before the Grand Experiment is ever launched. Even the album itself, while charming in an insubstantial sort of way, was more earthshaking in its nearly two years aborning than in its somewhat timid realization (all that labor to produce a mouse). In fact it violated nearly every one of the canons that Jack Clement, producer, would impose upon many of his artists ('I had to go to Florida to realize it was finished') and in the process forfeited the very spontaneity that is the cornerstone of his new artistic credo. 'Every time I get ready to go out,' complains Cowboy, 'I lose my voice for about a month at a time,' and one fears that the audience of *Saturday Night Live* may have to wait a long time before they ever get to see Cowboy Jack Clement's Traveling Band. Sometimes it almost seems as if Jack Clement keeps talking simply for fear of what the silence might reveal.

The consequences of always having to be on can be disastrous, both for himself and for others. To Stoney Edwards, the hipster's air of casual indiffer-

With wand. BILL DIBBLE

At fifteen. Courtesy of Jack Clement.

ence can seem almost like cruel disdain. 'Charley just got scared of him,'
says a knowledgeable insider of Charley Pride's departure from the Clement
fold. 'For about two years he was just acting like a crazy man.' 'Jack Clement,'
says a veteran Nashville superstar, with no hint of judgment, 'is a fine boy.
He's brought me some good songs, and there isn't anyone smarter than Jack
when he's straight. Now if he can just lay off them funny cigarettes . . .'
Everyone wonders about Jack, everyone is concerned about Jack, everyone
secretly fears, or hopes, that behind the inscrutable mask is—not just another
impenetrable disguise, but The Truth. And who knows—maybe there is.

Maybe it doesn't matter anyway. Perhaps, as Jack insists, it's the show
that counts, and if he never does harness all those ideas and focus all that
energy to become Jack Clement, Superstar, then maybe it's just the journey,
not the arrival, that matters. In any case Jack Clement is a man in motion,
making plans, hatching schemes, spinning out harmless fantasies, preparing
for his ascension. Sitting at his executive's desk, he flashes back and forward
in time, admits to no regrets ('Oh there was some times when I wasn't having

as much fun as I thought I oughta be having at some time in the future, but I'm pretty positive all the time. It's just when I get tired that I get kind of negative'), unearths photographs to substantiate stories told hours, or days, before. Yes, there he is; sure enough, a teenage Jack Clement is standing atop a Shetland pony (remember the Shetland pony? remember the drugstore cowboy?) twirling a lariat—only it is not, an older but not wiser Jack Clement explains, really a lariat, it is a piece of wire bent into the shape of a lariat. An illusionist even thirty-five years ago—even his most fanciful claims are rooted in reality.

A friend calls from New York and asks what he's doing. 'Oh, I'm sitting around with a houseful of journalists, planning my second childhood.' He winks at the lone journalist—or does he? Sometimes it is difficult to tell, for what must once have been merely a cheerful twinkle in his eye has become instead a kind of involuntary response. How long does this story have to be? he asks idly, and then opines that it should be kept under a thousand words, a thousand *well-chosen* words so as to avoid putting undue strain on the reader. Asked another question, he winces slightly, suggests, 'Well, that's kind of a long story. It's not a particularly interesting one either. Why don't you just make up another?', then relates the tale in its entirety.

As I am leaving, we are met by the arrival of what Cowboy has come to refer to as 'my latest album.' This is the first time he has actually seen it in its jacket, and he spends a good deal of time admiring its slightly Dickensian Portrait of the Middle-Aged Artist on a Swing (with Top Hat and Mandolin), turning it over a couple of times, his languid air unable to mask a real excitement. 'Well,' he says in his W. C. Fields drawl to no one in particular, 'there really is a Jack Clement album.'

His only other current project, he says later, is to cut another forty or fifty sides on his band and then to go water-skiing for the rest of the summer. 'We'll rehearse it and perform it and release it. If they don't sound like hits, then at least we had a good party.' And if his own record doesn't sell? Then, he says, maybe he'll sell all his equipment, pack what's left in his Chevrolet Caprice (Tennessee license plate R2D2), buy a boat, and go water-skiing anyway. Jack Clement winks and concludes with the greatest good humor that he doesn't think that this will happen. 'It ain't that my record is all that good,' he explains. 'It's just that everything else is so bad.'

Part Three

HONKY TONK MASQUERADE

*Or, Are They Gonna
Make Us Outlaws Again?*

O UTLAW' IS THE WORD that has been used, and abused, to describe the
'new' country music, music that deviates from the Nashville norm.
The principal way in which this music deviates, ironically enough, is that it
is traditional music, which honors roots, black and white, which recognizes
Jimmie Rodgers, Ernest Tubb, Hank Williams, and Lefty Frizzell—the pure
lineage that runs in an unbroken line of descent through country music.
Willie and Waylon started it all—Willie and Waylon and Tompall Glaser,
who has since fallen out with Waylon in a bitter legal dispute. Together in
1976 they put out an album called *Wanted! The Outlaws*, a spotty collection of
previously released material that served as a marketing device for a label that
up till then had been a kind of joke (you don't find Waylon talking about
'outlaw music' in the interview I did with him in 1974). The record went
platinum. The label stuck.

The basis for the Outlaw rebellion was the plasticity of the contemporary
Nashville sound—referred to for a while favorably as countrypolitan—which
prompted even Chet Atkins, its originator, to wonder if he had done more
harm than good, when he resigned as production head of RCA in 1974. This

Hank Williams. Courtesy of Les Leverett.

plasticity stemmed from several frequently cited factors, and one of them was *not* the political conservatism of Nashville (I only mention this because there is often a tendency on the part of outsiders to equate political 'correctness,' or liberalism, with musical adventurousness). Mostly it was the sound that Nashville came to be known for, a sound that owed more to the studio than to artistic inspiration – the very thing that rockabilly in its infancy, and latter-day rockabilly of the Jack Clement variety, rebelled against. Songs were written to order by professional songwriters (one of the things that had always set country music apart, as a kind of folk music, was the personal repertoire of its artists); sessions were marked by the bored competence of studio musicians and the determination of producers to take country 'uptown.' The survival of staunch individualists like George Jones or Jerry Lee Lewis could only be ascribed to anachronistic impulse.

This is an oversimplification, of course. Although it is the official Outlaw view, often promulgated by official Outlaw spokespersons, it does not take into account several complicating aspects. One is that while it's true that Willie Nelson had quit Nashville and repaired to Austin (the epicenter of Redneck Rebellion) before he ever achieved anything like mass recognition, it should not be forgotten that he was an enormously successful songwriter, in a highly commercial vein, for more than a decade before *that*. And Waylon himself, for all of his expressed dissatisfaction, managed to sustain a profitable enough career for a good half-dozen years before gaining the artistic freedom that he felt to be more consonant with his musical lifestyle. Nor does the official mythology leave any place for Merle Haggard, who never had anything to do with Nashville but went his own way from the very start and made records that were number one hits from his own enclave in Bakersfield, California. True, Haggard was never recognized by the country music establishment and still has not received his due in the Nashville-dominated Country Music Association awards. His record sales and sustained popularity from 1965 on, however, attest to the long-standing appeal of the rebel image. And more than anyone else, Haggard upheld the proud historical tradition of country music, releasing brilliant tribute albums to Jimmie Rodgers and Bob Wills, establishing his own band, The Strangers, as a premier recording unit, and always holding in living memory the spirit of Hank Williams.

Because it is Williams's spirit after all which hovers over the entire landscape of country music in much the same way that Elvis Presley still bestrides the world of rock 'n' roll. Born in Georgiana, Alabama, in 1923, Williams wrote more than a hundred songs in his brief lifetime (he died in the back seat of his Cadillac on the way to an engagement on New Year's Day, 1953), including such standards as 'Hey, Good Lookin',' 'Cold, Cold Heart,' 'I'm So Lonesome I Could Cry,' and 'I Can't Help It (If I'm Still in Love With You).' If you listen to George Jones, you'll hear the thin cutting tenor of Hank Williams. To Waylon Jennings, 'Hank was the first outlaw. He was the only one.' For his son, Hank Williams, Jr., the songs and presence of a man he never really knew have proved a haunting legacy. For James Talley, a more eclectic musician who has cited heroes ranging from John Steinbeck to B. B. King and probably considers himself more in the tradition of Merle Haggard or Willie Nelson, Williams embodies the very creative freedom he is seeking to establish. And to Stoney Edwards, a black man raised in Indian territory, in the words of his hit song, 'Hank and Lefty raised my country soul.'

Perhaps as extraordinary as his musical influence, the *image* of Hank Williams has dominated the mythology of contemporary country music. Driven, desperate, as haunted as the doomed blues singer, Robert Johnson, Williams has come to symbolize both the lure and the nightmare of the honky tonk world ('Live fast, love hard, and die young,' in Faron Young's descriptive phrase). His son, Hank junior, very nearly matched his father's fate when he fell off a mountain after years of addiction to alcohol and pills. Waylon Jennings, who served as a role model to Hank junior, proudly boasts that he was the inspiration for *Payday*, a movie about the life and death of a pill-popping country music idol (others claim that it was Jerry Lee Lewis or Merle Haggard who offered the example). Jennings and Haggard in fact both seek to recreate the roaring and innocence of their younger days, while James Talley, quite different in temperament from these self-proclaimed ne'er-do-wells, poses the political question, 'Are they gonna make us outlaws again?' and reveals the outraged sense of social conscience of a latter-day Woody Guthrie.

It is, then, a variegated legacy, in which the one constant is a fierce insistence upon individuality. Perhaps what most connects all the figures in this section is the strikingly personal way in which they express themselves, with all the feeling and the flavor of the blues (Hank Williams's greatest songs were almost without exception blues-inspired), even when the blues form is missing.

WAYLON
JENNINGS

The Pleasures of Life in a Hillbilly Band
(in Boston, in 1974)

It's a measure of people who don't understand
The pleasures of life in a hillbilly band
I got my first guitar at the age of fourteen
Now I'm over thirty and still wearing jeans.

WAYLON JENNINGS repeats the words of the song reflectively in a motel room decorated in pale convention colors ('Being on the road it's hard, you know, to keep up your writing. Like here, it's not the most in-spiring place exactly. Green and yellow are just not really inspiring colors'). He's rumpled, slightly blowsy, his dramatic stage presence and Mephis-tophelean leer thrown out of focus by lack of sleep and a bad cold. His face is framed by unkempt bangs and a bristling black goatee. 'Yep, that kind of pictures me,' he says, still thinking of the song, 'Amanda.' 'Really. Basically. That's just about it.' He nods, as if to add emphasis to his point. 'You know, I've got to be able to get into a song, I've got to be able to relate to it before I can get up and sing it on a stage. I'll tell you something, hoss, I listen to all kinds of music, and there's a lot of songs that really are country that just aren't arranged that way. It's the singer, not the instrumentation. Hell, if it was the instruments, Dean Martin would be the biggest thing in country music today.'

Maybe so. And perhaps, in a not quite literal way, 'Amanda'—a song he didn't write, but like so many songs in his repertoire, one he sings with deep personal conviction—does capture some of the truth of Waylon Jennings, some of the loose easy feeling that he conveys while on stage and, paradoxi-cally, some of the painful convolutions that he's gone through in his private struggle to define himself and his music. He didn't get his first guitar at the age of fourteen. Actually his parents gave him a guitar when he was around ten, a good while before he was to meet Buddy Holly and years before he

Fiddling. MARSHALL FALLWELL

Playing bass for Buddy Holly, January 26, 1959, Eau Claire, Wisconsin. Tommy Allsup is in center. Photograph taken by Joan Svenson, © by Don Larson, Evergreen, Colorado.

went out on the road with him, playing bass and singing backup in the group that was playing behind Holly at the time of his plane-crash death in 1959. To Waylon Jennings that looked like the end of the line. He renounced professional ambitions and moved to Phoenix, where he only gradually eased back into the business. And now in 1974, at the age of thirty-seven, he is part of the vanguard that is said to be revolutionizing country music. Or at least making inroads by reinjecting the maverick element into a music that was populated to begin with by such maverick, unpredictable, and slightly unsavory spirits as Jimmie Rodgers, Bob Wills, and Hank Williams.

His songs present a picture of the raffish hero in love with the essential seediness of twentieth-century America, the unregenerate rebel who looks back with a mixture of pride and regret on all the loves he's lost and all the hell-raising fun he's had. The movie, *Payday*, which starred Rip Torn, employed his friend Shel Silverstein as technical adviser, says Waylon, so they could get all the real-life details straight. His landmark album, *Honky Tonk Heroes*, reflected the same hell-raising image. The defiant stance suits Waylon Jennings. You get the feeling that in another life he might have been a buccaneer. And yet you sense somehow that this is oversimplification. If there were no more to the self-described 'lovable losers and no-account boozers and honky tonk heroes' who make up Nashville's new breed, then what can account for their remarkable staying power, the perseverance that's kept them knocking around Nashville all these years just looking for a hearing for their music? And in the case of Waylon Jennings—sensitive, articulate, warm, and sardonic by turns—you look for the intelligence, the dedication, and the vulnerability that lie beneath the hard-bitten facade.

They wanted me to do 'We Had It All' sitting on a horse. I couldn't do that shit. I told them to fuck themselves. Really. Later on they came around, said they wanted to make it up to me, said the show had changed, but it looked the same to me. Same shit. It's disgusting, really. I mean, country music is just as serious as any other kind of music, if the truth be told. What the hell, to them it's just foot-stomping, belly-scratching music, to them it ain't nothing but a goddamn joke.

Waylon Jennings was born in Littlefield, Texas, about thirty miles northwest of Lubbock (population 150,000, birthplace of Buddy Holly) on June 15, 1937. Both parents played the guitar, his father had entertained at country dances when he was younger. From the time that they taught him how to chord a guitar, he wanted to be a professional musician. At the age of twelve he got his own radio show, fifteen minutes on the local radio station, KVOW. He and a friend, a guitar player, had been playing a box supper, the station manager heard them, and they got their own spot.

Scene from Payday, *with Rip Torn.*

'Strictly country music, Hank Williams, Carl Smith, you know, all that kind of stuff. We used to listen to the Grand Ole Opry on the radio every Saturday night. Oh sure, the whole family. Everyone in those little country towns like Littlefield used to listen to the Opry. You know that *Last Picture Show*? Well, I'll tell you something, hoss, he's got it pegged, that's just like it was. I mean, there wasn't *anything* happening in them little small towns, they was just dying, that's really the truth, hoss, let me tell you. Who listens to the Opry nowadays? Ain't nobody out there listening any more.'

He quit school junior year ('it seemed like a good idea at the time'), got married for the first time shortly afterwards, and started working for his father, who was by then running a feed store. By this time he had formed a band and was playing at amateur shows in theaters and on the radio all over West Texas. That was how he met Buddy Holly in 1954.

'Well, you see, we played a lot of those shows together, Buddy and his band, I had my band, a different theater every Saturday afternoon. Sometimes the same band would win it two or three weeks running. We were still playing country – Buddy, too – hell, there wasn't anything else, really. I saw Elvis Presley in 1955, I guess it was, in Lubbock. Well, it changed things in a way. I think it changed Buddy, too, at least I think it had a bearing. Actually it changed almost everything, really. Country music almost died at that time, rock 'n' roll killed off just about everything. It was like an explosion, definitely, you know it was actually like that. I think it was the beginning of kids really starting to think for themselves, figuring things out, realizing things that they would never even have thought of before.'

Holly and Jennings stayed in touch over the next few years. Waylon moved to Lubbock in 1955, deejaying there for the next three years, while Buddy became one of the hottest rock 'n' roll acts in the country. 'Oh yeah, I was still playing, I was still aiming to be a singer, I was just using radio as a kind of stepping stone.' Then in 1958 Holly came back to Lubbock for a show, he heard Waylon's singing and he liked it. 'I was his protégé more or less. He cut the first record on me, you know, for Brunswick in 1958. Got King Curtis to play on it, just called him to come down, he was really hot then, too. We did an old country thing [actually Cajun] called "Jole Blonde," we did it upbeat, with the saxophone on the lead part. We didn't even know the words. No, she-it, it didn't do nothing.'

It must have been eye-opening to go out on the road with Buddy Holly at that time; the shows were wild, and Waylon Jennings had never been far outside of Lubbock, Texas, before. When he went to New York, he says, his neck got stiff from looking up at the skyscrapers. He admired Holly, too, obviously, and this is a side of his life about which he has been uncharacteristically reticent. When Buddy died, he was devastated. It was his seat that the Big Bopper, J. P. Richardson, had taken on the flight that crashed. 'After that I just kind of quit. I went back to radio. Back to Lubbock for a couple of years. I wasn't even interested any more. It was just such a ridiculous waste.'

I think right now that the country's in the best shape for the future that it's ever been, because the kids are thinking and worrying about things that never even occurred to me. They're concerned about politics, they're concerned about rights and wrongs, they're concerned about all kinds of problems I know I never even thought about when I was a kid, I mean, did you, man? And, you know, I think music is the only thing, really, basically it's one of the big hopes the country has. I mean, politics and religion ain't never gonna bring people together, but music could help. At least I think it could do something.

The first thing that strikes you about the music of Waylon Jennings is its sincerity. Drawn from a surprising diversity of sources – Dylan, the Beatles, Chuck Berry, and rockabilly, as well as flat-out country – its one unifying factor has been Jennings's patent integrity, and like the work of his friend and ex-roommate, Johnny Cash, it depends for its effect more on force of personality than on strictly musical considerations. From the start of his career it has been the subject, too, of considerable misreading and mis-interpretation.

At A&M Records, which signed him in 1964 through his friend, country comedian Don Bowman (Waylon had by then moved to Phoenix, where he was deejaying and fronting a three-man group who were 'busting ourselves up in nightclubs all over town'), his producer, Herb Alpert, didn't think of him as a country singer at all. 'We never could quite get it together except maybe on a couple of things. I was trying to hang on to country, but I think they kept hearing Al Martino.'

At RCA, where he arrived again through Bowman and another friend, Bobby Bare, he had almost the opposite problem: he wasn't quite country enough. 'Not old hard-core country. Never was.' Chet Atkins, who had arranged for his release from the A&M contract, produced his first RCA albums. 'Chet and I got along good,' Waylon says today with the benefit of hindsight. 'At least we came closer than any of those other producers I worked with. They had some strange ideas, man. But I wrote a lot of the early stuff I recorded, they even let me use my band on the first album. And I learned a lot about production from Chet.'

A nice enough sentiment, and one that may very well be true in retro-spect, since Waylon feels almost unutterable contempt for later producers like Danny Davis ('He was a front-office executive. He's pathetic. Really'). At the time, however, it must have been a lot more painful.

Because ironically enough, while he hit it big almost with his first RCA release in 1965 and has been a commercial force to be reckoned with ever since, there seems to have been an almost complete lack of understanding at RCA of what Waylon Jennings was all about. The label sat on what Waylon saw as potential breakthrough songs, like 'Love of the Common People' and 'MacArthur Park,' for years after they were first recorded. The albums were a mishmash of different styles from different periods—an odd situation for a musician who has always prided himself on his ability to select and mold material to his own ends. And if you listen to the hits of that era, it is only occasionally that you will hear glimmerings of the distinctive Waylon Jennings sound: the unique instrumentation, the choppy rockabilly beat, the singer's own stuttering guitar and rough-hewn, gutbucket voice. Instead you hear the Nashville sound that Chet Atkins did so much to pioneer, the whining steel, the swelling choruses, the same familiar sidemen playing the same familiar licks that are stamped on every record that comes out of Nashville today. Many musicians are indifferent to this kind of equalization; Waylon Jennings seems to have taken it personally, as if it were an attempt to smooth out the rough edges, not only in the music but in the man.

He moved in with Johnny Cash shortly after settling down in Nashville.

Waylon and wife, Jessi Colter, with brother-in-law Jack.
Courtesy of Jack Clement.

Backstage with Merle Travis. LEONARD KAMSLER

Jennings's second marriage had just broken up, and Cash was at the low point of his career. 'I guess we did some pretty wild things,' says Waylon a little ruefully today. By his own account, and by just about everyone else's, too, the year and a half with Cash was marked by broken-down doors, middle-of-the-night fishing expeditions, and lots and lots of pills. 'I don't think musically we had any influence on each other at all. We're both pretty bullheaded when it comes to music. We went through a lot together, though. We had some times.'

For Jennings it was a period characterized by frustration and despair, painful misunderstandings and bitter, self-destructive battles. It was three hundred nights on the road—a dead end of playing the same songs for the same audiences, crisscrossing the country in a bus painted black (black bumpers, blackwalls, dubbed Black Maria), playing tag with someone else's Silver Eagle, which might be headed for the same show somewhere in Ohio. The life of a country music star.

'That bus had a ghost on it,' says Waylon half seriously, and then explains that the spirit of Hank Williams caused all kinds of mischief on the bus. Perhaps to mollify it, Waylon painted the name Hank on the bathroom door (along with a little gold star) and always kept an extra bunk reserved for the ghost, which he saw as his spiritual adviser. Looking back on that period, Waylon doesn't seem exactly mellow ('Will you get me a little more of that

vitamin C, hoss? I got to shoot up some of that vitamin C for my cold'),
nor is he about to disown the good times and high spirits. He just seems
a little bemused that he and Cash have ended up where they have: Waylon
playing sophisticated new showcase clubs like Cambridge's Performance
Center and Max's Kansas City in New York, Cash selling Standard Oil on TV.
Was Cash ever part of Nashville's hopeful new scene? 'If he was, he's sold out
to religion now. I don't see John much any more, but we're still friends,
I think we always will be. We been through too much together. At one time
we were all we had left. Cause they had all alienated us from everything else.'

*Well, to me an album is like a book, you know. You go through periods of time
musically, and then you pick out where you were at at that particular time. The
last couple of albums are the only ones that have ever really gotten that for me.
I use my own band on them, that's all I'm gonna use. Oh, I'll add to them as far as
lead instruments go, but I've got the best rhythm section there is. At least I think
I do. And my steel player, Ralph·Mooney, he really plays fine. They're all pretty
much individuals, that's what I want — they're all renegades and outlaws and
what have you. They're men, you know. I don't want to do anything that takes
away from that. Because I had to take orders for too long myself not to know
what it's like.*

It's only in the last year or so (since 1972 or 1973) that Waylon Jennings
has finally achieved some measure of artistic freedom. 'Things are finally
about the way I want with the label now. I have this arrangement with my
own production company, which is totally independent of everything they do.
They pay for everything, they have certain obligations to me, I deliver 'em
an album. The deal I have, I'm happy, really. The reason I hesitate a little to
talk about it is that none of them have it, none of the other artists but me. So
they're afraid I'm gonna say something, and the others will hear about it,
and that'll mess things up for them.
   'Yeah, I think they've finally kind of accepted it now. The new breed in
other words, you know. They used to just think I was crazy, but I wouldn't
ever work under that kind of strain again. You know, they almost make you
gun-shy, man, they scare you off of doing anything that they've ever done.
Just because they done it! I mean, I haven't used a chorus since I started
producing myself — don't plan to either. They just can't understand that kind
of thinking in Nashville.'
   It's an idyllic vision (total artistic freedom, peaceful coexistence between
artist and corporation), and to some extent Jennings has realized it on record,
particularly in the work that he and Willie Nelson have contributed to each
other's albums ('Willie came in and helped me some on production on the
new one. I think it's gonna be good for him. He seems awful happy, and

it's the first time I've ever seen him like that'). There remain, however, uncharacteristic traces of self-consciousness even on his best recorded work, a stiff grandiosity of purpose that is very much at odds with the straight-forward, plain-spoken stance of his in-person performance. Here the music is looser, more ragged, but somehow more exuberant and more right. And I think that if Waylon Jennings never made another record, the personal message that he manages to convey to anyone who goes to see him perform would be record enough, a strikingly intimate and vivid memory of the occasion. On stage there is nothing to get in the way of direct communication with his audience, and as much as the great soul singers, as much as a Van Morrison or a Charlie Rich or any other such inward-looking artist, Waylon Jennings succeeds in establishing a mood, in creating an ambience that might be rejected as too rude but could never be denied.

Playing a place like the Performance Center in Cambridge, the old songs don't come up that often; the emphasis is understandably on the more recent material. 'I guess in the back of my mind I'm blocking it off. I reckon they haven't heard that much of me from the past.' Even so, there's room for many of the hits, from some of the earliest sides like 'The Only Daddy That'll Walk the Line' through the Kris Kristofferson period of 'The Taker' right up to the present day. It's a scrupulously careful winnowing of material. The songs exist side by side without quarrel or complaint, and presented in this way, each song reflecting a very personal vision from different stages of a lifetime, it is as if they are really just pieces of a larger work.

There is no question about the tone. Despite the exuberance, despite the good-timey rhythms and the wholehearted approval of the fashionably whooping Cambridge cowboys, it's the slow songs and sad waltzlike tempos that create the dominant impression, as Waylon's voice, more assured, less declamatory than on record, tells tales of far away and long ago, about a time that never was. There are no pyrotechnics. For all the amplification of the band, despite the heavy beat, the sound remains mostly muted and low-key, as the Waylors (bass, rhythm guitar, ten-year veteran Richie Albright on drums, bluesy harp player Don Brooks, and the great Ralph Mooney on pedal steel) stay largely in the background, fill in behind Waylon's heavily strummed, choppily rhythmic lead guitar, then come roaring into the chorus.

After a while the songs sound linked, not just thematically but melodically as well ('Yeah, I guess maybe they do all sound the same'). And each one is distinctively and recognizably Waylon Jennings; each song tells a different strand of a single story. A tale of pride and regret (*Where does it go?/The good Lord only knows*), bitterness and nostalgia (*Just pretend I never happened*), failure in love (*I wanted to be something you could depend on*), and beat resig-nation (*An old five-and-dimer was all I intended to be*). The songs look back with a weary kind of wisdom on a life that's still going on (*All alone all the way by myself, who's to say/I threw it away for a song/Cause I've sure come a*

Honky Tonk Heroes. Duke Goff, Billy Joe Shaver, Larry Whitmore, Waylon, Captain Midnite, Ritchie Albright, Ralph Mooney. JIMMY MOORE

long ways from home). They're songs for aging cowboys. Good-time Charlie's got the blues.

Still, after talking with Waylon Jennings for any length of time, you're bound to get the impression that something has been left out. Not that he isn't fascinating to talk to. He's courtly, diffident, polite, and attentive. He's above all uncompromisingly honest and open in a way that allows him to say, 'Hey, I love you,' to a buddy without having you suspect either his honesty or his protective machismo. He speaks easily of Willie and Tompall ('my best friend') and the outlaws' mutual aid society. He is also, of course, his own best promoter—his outspokenness always making good copy, his cheerful iconoclasm on subjects from politics and religion to the Opry and Richard Nixon ('Jesus, he's full of shit, isn't he?') a refreshing change from the smooth PR work of his Nashville compatriots. Even so, you still get the feeling that he is holding something in reserve, that this man who appears to live entirely on the surface is sizing you up better than you are him. He seems to be amused, he is certainly tolerant, he is genuinely interested in this new audience which takes such delight in his ass-busting reputation at the same time that he is moving away from it. 'You know, I've come to the conclusion,' he says, 'that you are what people think you are, no matter how hard you may try to get away from it.' That sounds like a line from a song, I suggest. 'Yeah,' he says with a crooked grin. 'Well, maybe it is, hoss. Maybe it is.'

POSTSCRIPT

I must add a confessional note, dictated by hindsight. This is not the definitive portrait of Waylon Jennings. Since our original meeting in 1974, Waylon has gone on to become a household name (a household *first* name—like Elvis, Elton, and Willie) and something of a recluse from the press. To interview Waylon Jennings today, you have to go through seven different screening operations and then (if you have somehow found favor in Waylon's eyes) sign a contract that stipulates that you will write nothing 'detrimental to SUBJECT's public image,' that SUBJECT has the right to approve the manu-script, and that publication can only be 'through media channels agreed upon mutually by AUTHOR and SUBJECT.' Really. When I spoke to Waylon, on the other hand, he was more than anxious for the publicity, was as accessible (I thought then) as anyone I'd ever interviewed, and showed, in the words of John Grissim (who wrote about him in 1970) a 'lack of guile' and a 'willingness to talk with complete candor.'

Looking back on it, I see that I was naive, and Waylon was, too. Who would ever have thought that Waylon's calculated strategy to leave the 'shit-kicker' image far behind could succeed so totally? Or that Willie Nelson, who seemed at the time like a taste destined always to remain esoteric, would the next year have the first platinum-selling country album with *The Red-Headed Stranger*? Who could have guessed that Waylon and Tompall Glaser ('my best friend') would have a falling out, almost before the revolution was won, over the very spoils of victory? And it's difficult to imagine that Waylon could so easily dismiss his old friend Johnny Cash, now that he, too, knows some of the complications of success.

My own point of view was nothing short of adulatory. The week that I spent going to see Waylon Jennings at Cambridge's short-lived Performance Center furnished some of the greatest music I've ever heard. I was won over, too, by the conviction that this was a cause in which all men and women of good will should enlist, something like the anti-war or civil rights movement in the nobility of its purpose. I didn't know Kris Kristofferson was going to end up with Barbra Streisand any more than Waylon did. The world seemed a much simpler place.

At the same time I think there is a corrective aspect to this vision. The Waylon Jennings image today is one of almost unrelieved gloom. Pain seems

With Captain Midnite (Roger Schutt), left, and Tompall Glaser.
J. CLARK THOMAS

to gnaw at him like a vulture, and even his music seems bruised and weary. When I first spoke to him, there was an openness, a bravado, a kind of hopefulness that peeped out, even if, as I suspect, he revealed no more than he wanted to reveal. He may have been 'lonesome and orn'ry,' but he certainly wasn't 'mean.' And he probably still isn't. It's just that like Charlie Rich he has found the burdens of success to equal, if not exceed, the difficulty of getting there. Waylon can probably survive it all, if anybody can, but I think his old friends miss him, and I miss the open, free-wheeling spirit who at the end of our interview could write down his name and address on a piece of notebook paper and say, 'Thanks, hoss. Make sure you send me a copy.'

HANK WILLIAMS, JR.

Living Proof

I'm gonna quit singin' all them sad songs
Cause I can't stand the pain
The life I sing about now
And the one I live are the same.
When I sing them old songs of Daddy's
Seems like every one comes true
Lord, please help me, do I have to be
The living proof? . . .

TARZAN YELLS drift across the neatly manicured courtyard. Startled guests of the Hammond, Louisiana, Holiday Inn look up to see a burly-looking man with a towel around his head and cut-off dungarees, calling down to several long-haired young men lounging around the pool. The heat just rises off the pool perimeter. The Tarzan yells repeat themselves periodically and are answered in kind, until the powerful-looking man, his coarse features masked by dark glasses, beard, and the towel, reappears at the pool. 'Bwana juju?' says one of the members of the band. 'Bwana wanna,' says Hank Williams, Jr., somewhat mystifyingly. Everyone in the group watches as the piano player, Hollywood Jim, approaches two girls who are sunning themselves, not altogether innocently, in the steaming Louisiana sun. There is much talk and laughter, some grunts, an occasional jungle call. Hank junior tries to coax Merle Kilgore (author of 'Ring of Fire' and a startling lookalike for his old hell-raising buddy, Johnny Cash) out to the pool, because, he says, twenty years of booze and pills have done remarkable things to Merle's body. Some beer appears courtesy of the local promoter, a joint is casually passed around, the local promoter himself, fat and full of promises, arrives with lines he must have learned out of the movies and plans for everything from a borrowed Rolls Royce for a stylish arrival to 'something to open up your nose.'

'You think he's gonna be a bug?' someone asks Hank junior after the promoter leaves. 'I don't know, but he's already a squirrel. There's an old saying,' says Hank junior, maybe making it up on the spot. 'Promoter comes early, he's got to be squirrelly. Promoter comes late, okay date.' He laughs easily, pleased with the saying, pleased with himself, as invincible in his easy-going charm as he has proved to be by his sheer survival, both physically and psychologically, in a world that placed him among its royalty by birth, then waited for him to destroy himself simply to validate its claim.

The promoter comes back with a young woman who has been sitting in his car awaiting permission to say hello to Hank junior. She is, it turns out, very pregnant, and everyone laughs when Hank junior wonders where they could have met about nine months ago. Although he has failed to recognize her, she is the stepdaughter of a hunting friend, and Hank junior introduces her to his wife, Becky, cool, blonde, pretty, and impeccably polite, who has been traveling with her husband on all his road trips ever since their marriage nearly two years ago. There are some more jokes, reminiscences, Hank clamps a black cowboy hat on his head, prematurely bald like his father's before him, and goes back to the room to relax before a five o'clock sound check.

After a big seafood meal courtesy of Phil D'Antonio ('A big fan of yours,' says the promoter), the troupe arrives at the Columbia Theater, where Jimmie Rodgers once played a lifetime ago. In recent times the theater has been closed, and this is the first live show in many years.

Three and a half hours later it is over. 'Well, another promoter bites the dust,' says the star, as the band pack up their instruments. The statement is not cynical but realistic. The tickets have been priced too high, the promotion has turned out to be virtually nonexistent, and the size of the audience has reflected these two errors in judgment. Among the two or three hundred who have actually showed up, there is a hopeless division between the very young, who want to hear nothing but Hank junior's new Marshall Tucker-styled music, and the very old, who want to hear nothing but his father's songs. All of these problems are only compounded by a performance that is, not surprisingly, flat and by a subsequent refusal to abandon the stage until some spark is struck. The result is that when Hank junior does finally finish, after a valiant but futile attempt to involve himself and his audience, nearly everyone has left, and the keen edge of anticipation with which the evening started out—from the girls nervously hanging around the stage entrance to the local police flagging down the bus to offer an escort—is altogether dissipated. There are glum post-mortems, the band and the star have muffled words of criticism for each other, but soon the concert is forgotten for matters of more immediate concern. Such as where and if the party is going to be tonight, and whether a member of the troupe has wagered that he can get three girls *in* the bed or *on* the bed. There is another show tomorrow night in Ruston, some seven hours away, but the bus will not be leaving till morning and, aside from packing up, there's no more to be done tonight. The promoter

Father and son. Courtesy of Douglas B. Green.

is over in a corner, looking woebegone and small. He done everything, says someone wryly, except promote the show.

> *Why, just the other night after the show*
> *An old drunk came up to me*
> *He said, You ain't as good as your daddy, boy,*
> *And you never will be . . .*

Hank Williams, Jr., has been on the road ever since the age of eight. Possessor of one of the most famous names in country music (actually his name was Randall Hank until after his father died, of pills and alcohol, when he was three), he seemed destined to become heir not only to his father's music but to his father's legend and fate as well. Pictures show a wide-eyed baby looking up expectantly at his father, a miniature guitar strung around his neck, and he got his nickname Bocephus (the name originally belonged to ventriloquist Rod Brasfield's dummy) from his father's radio pledge, 'Don't worry, Bocephus, I'm coming home.' It has often been said that it was his late mother, Audrey, who pushed both her husband's and her son's careers, but while he concedes that she was certainly instrumental, Hank junior hotly denies that she was responsible for any of 'the legal abortions that happened in the Hank Williams estate' or for pushing him into a career that he didn't want.

'Oh, she was ruthless, Mother could take your head off if you got on the wrong side of her, but she was for *me* all the way, she wanted me to do my own thing, which was exactly the other way from lots of others. We started out in a car, an old Cadillac, the old routine, with a trailer and a rack. I'd fit on the back shelf, you know, back in the rear window, because I was small enough to curl up on it then. My first shows I didn't play, Mother wouldn't let me have a guitar for a while, but then I got me a little old three-quarter Gibson and started learning some chords. I had the best teachers in the business. Hell, everyone wanted to teach Hank Williams, Jr., a chord. And then I'd go out there, and those folks would just go berserk. I was doing maybe twenty, thirty shows a year, all during summer vacation. To tell you the truth, it didn't really matter what I did, they didn't really care. I could have gone out there and burped and still got a standing ovation. Just because I was Hank Williams, Jr. Oh man, Hank Williams was really hot back in those years, and they wanted anything they could get of him. That was just the law of the land.'

It remained the law of the land for quite some time. At fourteen Hank

Audrey, Lycretia, Hank Williams, Jr., and Hank, Sr.
Courtesy of Hank Williams, Jr.

junior made his concert-hall debut at Cobo Hall in Detroit and cut his first record for MGM, his father's company. The record was 'Long Gone Lonesome Blues,' a Hank Williams classic. 'I couldn't wait to get it out. My voice had changed early, and I was almost as tall as I am now, but I was just a snotty-nosed kid, really. Listening to it today, I guess it was a pretty sorry-sounding thing, but it sold a whole lot of records. I quit school then. The touring got so heavy I had to quit. Hell, I hated school anyway, I wanted to be out on the road. I felt so much older than all them kids, being on Ed Sullivan, Johnny Carson, every show there was, really, running around with broads and stuff. Shit, I felt like I was twenty-one at fourteen.'

From the time he was fourteen he headlined a caravan of stars put together by his mother, which frequently featured an up-and-coming singer named Waylon Jennings ('He had a Dodge motor home then, and I'd take every chance I could get to go over and drive it') and introduced an unknown named Merle Haggard at the bottom of the bill. Sometimes the caravan would join forces with Johnny Cash, who was in the middle of his pill-eating habit. Merle Kilgore, as skeletal then as Cash, and for the same reason, was a regular member of the troupe, keeping everyone loose as he cast spells and indulged in all kinds of wild, wired lunacy. At sixteen Hank Williams, Jr., became the youngest songwriter ever to win a BMI citation, and his soundtrack album for *Your Cheatin' Heart*, the movie of his father's life, went gold. Back home in Nashville he had his own combo, which played, he says, Jimmy Reed blues, Chuck Berry songs, King Curtis's 'Soul Twist' ('We wasn't doing "I'm So Lonesome I Could Cry," I'll guarantee you that'). On the road, though, it was nothing but the music of Hank Williams and the Drifting Cowboys, presented by Hank Williams, Jr., and the Cheatin' Hearts. The drinking and the pills undoubtedly started early. 'Even when I was eight or ten, they'd say, "Hey, have a drink, Little Hank." It turned those old guys on to be giving a drink to Hank Williams's son. I don't think they meant anything by it, to them it was really something. Of course I didn't mind. It was just a chance to get away from Mother, you know, but I guess I was thrown into it pretty quick.'

By the time he was twenty-five he had made several movies, overdubbed an album of duets with his father, had been married and divorced twice—and had no idea who he was. 'I was upset about all kinds of things. I was depressed about my management, Mother's health was failing real bad, then this divorce came along and I really hit bottom. I went down to Panama City and I stayed stoned on pills and booze for months at a time. I just felt all this loneliness and depression, I was all tore up about the direction I was heading, every time I'd play one of Daddy's records I'd just start to cry. I was really hurting pretty bad. I wasn't living anywhere regular. Sometimes I'd stay with Kilgore, sometimes I'd live with Lefty Frizzell, maybe I'd see Cash once in a while. I started seeing this doctor in Nashville, this psychiatrist—he was

On stage with his grandmother, Mrs. Stone (Hank senior's mother).
Courtesy of the Country Music Foundation Library and Media Center,
Nashville, Tennessee.

a hunting friend — it was the kind of thing where I'd call him up to get me out
of places in the middle of the night. A couple of times he put me in the
hospital to straighten out, just so I could get some food and sleep.'

He talked to the psychiatrist about the curse that he felt was hovering
over him, the false friends in Nashville who were just waiting for him to live
out his father's fate (his father's death at twenty-nine seems to have taken on
an almost numerological significance for Hank junior). The psychiatrist
wondered, did he like the people he was working with? Did he like living
surrounded by memories of his father, among his father's former business
associates and friends? No, Hank junior said, he had come to hate Nashville
and all that it stood for. Well, what *did* he like, in fact? Hunting and fishing
with his friends outside the music business. Well, said the psychiatrist, why
not do that then?

So in 1974 he moved down to Cullman, Alabama, not too far from his
grandparents' farm in Troy. His friends were nearby; his new manager,
J.R. Smith, whom he had met in Panama City, had a trucking business in
Cullman; the fishing and hunting were good; and he could get off the road,
take some time, and rethink his life and career. He put together one more
album for MGM, a total departure from anything he had previously done.

He cut it in Muscle Shoals with rockers Toy Caldwell and Charlie Daniels and contributed the wrenchingly personal 'Living Proof' and 'Stoned at the Jukebox.' He was getting ready to go out on tour behind the new album (*Hank Williams, Jr., and Friends*) when in August of 1975 he went mountain climbing with a friend of his, Bill Dyer, in preparation for a Canadian sheep hunt. That was when he fell 490 feet from a ridge on the Continental Divide. It nearly killed him, tore his face completely apart (his mouth, palate, nose, and forehead had to be completely reconstructed), left him with the fear that he could never sing again, but finally got him off the treadmill.

> *I'm feelin' better*
> *I got hurt, but I'm back on the road*
> *Getting it together*
> *Between Macon and Muscle Shoals*
> *It all came together*
> *In my sweet Alabama home*
> *And I'm through forever*
> *Trying to put everybody on . . .*

Ruston, Louisiana, is a complete change of pace. A sumptuous buffet has been set, the view of man-made D'Arbonne Lake is magnificent, and even the oppressiveness of the heat is incidental in the air-conditioned living room of Sam Thomas, local banker, real estate entrepreneur, recent acquaintance of John Mitchell 'on the banks of your beautiful Alabama River' (the Federal penitentiary is in Montgomery), and Merle Kilgore's first radio sponsor some twenty-five years ago when Merle was a college student in town. Thomas has sent a private airplane to pick up Merle and Hank and their party and has invited some of the town's most prominent citizens— Mayor John Perritt, a former state senator, a fresh-faced trucking tycoon— and their wives to join him and his guests for the afternoon at this exclusive lakeside retreat, which also boasts indicted representative Otto Passman among its residents.

Merle, who could charm the birds out of the trees, has charmed his hosts all afternoon, alternating stories of the big time with reminiscences of his college days at Louisiana Tech. He recalls the time he wanted to buy a $25 pair of shoes from John Perritt for a date with university president Ropp's niece and traded radio advertising time to get them. He recalls, too, the only time he ever met Hank Williams, Sr., when as a boy in Shreveport, just completing his paper route, he ran across Williams arriving at the local radio station at six-thirty in the morning for a broadcast. Because the elevator wasn't running, he asked if he could carry the singer's guitar, and his idol answered, 'Grab it, hoss.' 'Grab it, hoss,' Merle repeats with some bemusement. Like all of his stories, it is told with the same flair and good humor that characterize his stage act and many of his compositions.

By request he plays 'More and More,' the song he wrote while still a student at the university, which rocketed him to national fame at eighteen. 'The first thing I did was buy two Cadillacs. They sent me a royalty check for $30,000, and I blew it all. The government got the cars back for taxes. I didn't even *know* about taxes.' Apparently he still doesn't, since the government has only recently dropped a full-scale case against him ('Oh, my nerves,' says Merle in mock distress).

Merle has himself just moved to Cullman, taking over Hank junior's original A-frame, as Hank and Becky have built a larger house on the Cullman Reservoir. Because he goes back so far with Hank junior, there are some who think he is just along for the ride, but in reality he provides one of the few threads of continuity in Hank junior's life, and their friendship is based on an understanding and an intimacy that no outsider can breach. It doesn't hurt that Merle is able to ride with any of the younger man's moods and is the only one who can coax him out of his frequent fits of brooding obsessiveness. Their feeling for each other is mirrored in their actions and in their talk, as Hank junior continually applauds Merle for his new resolve to stay off alcohol and pills. As for Merle, when Hank junior had his accident, Merle flew out to the hospital right away, and, when it finally appeared as if Hank junior was going to pull through, simply declared, 'Another fine mess you've gotten me into. Think of my job before you ever do anything like this again.'

The talk drifts from Elvis to George Wallace to Earl Long ('Good ol' Earl'). Hank junior spends much of the afternoon calling local gun shops, as he does in every town, searching for rare models. Earlier in the day there has been some skeet shooting, at which Hank junior proved to be expert, shattering the clay targets with monotonous regularity, shooting from the hip, quick-drawing, firing equally well from either side, and seemingly unaffected by the deafening reports or the sore shoulders that eventually sent everyone else back inside.

Merle sings some more of his compositions, does 'Johnny Reb' and 'Wolverton Mountain,' and soon the whole room is singing along. Sam Thomas's wife, Anita, takes up 'Oh Lonesome Me' and Mayor John Perritt, a ruddy-faced heavy-set man who once played football at the university but is crippled now by a degenerative hip disease, leads the singing on 'Blue Eyes Crying in the Rain' and the perennial 'Cotton Fields.' There is talk of flying up to Reno to catch Hank junior's show in a few weeks. Everyone is having a good time, genuinely delighted to be around a star.

Isn't it nice, someone says, as ice cream and cake are served, that we can sit around eating ice cream and cake and having such a nice time, instead of smoking those funny cigarettes like Waylon and all those other outlaws do. A dark look comes across Hank junior's face. 'You just caught us at the wrong time,' he says. 'That kind of stuff comes later.' Then, in case they missed

Hank and Merle Kilgore, Ruston, Louisiana. NANCY BERGERON

the point, he tells them how proud he is of Merle, off the pills and booze after all these years, just boiling up that wacky-baccy marijuana in his tea. There is polite tittering, Merle seems somewhat discomfited, glancing at Hank with an 'Oh, my nerves!' look and then shrugging it off. Even this display fails to shake the bland composure of Ruston's leading citizens ('I thought they was like to shit,' says Hank junior afterwards. 'I hate that bullshit. I'm gonna tell 'em exactly what I do'), and they are all in the front row at the show held later that night in the Louisiana Tech gym for the benefit of the Ruston Beautification Foundation.

Unfortunately the show itself is something of a bust, and only the homecoming of Boogie King Merle Kilgore comes close to saving the day. The small audience is once again split about half and half between young kids and fans of the original Hank, and though Hank junior divides the show fairly evenly between the old and the new and runs through his usual crowd-pleasing tactic of playing piano, dobro, fiddle, and harmonica in addition to guitar, somehow none of it quite works, the older people in the audience sit sullenly with their arms folded, and the show is forced to end prematurely when it goes overtime. The only highlight comes when Hank junior sings 'Once and For All,' a song he wrote for Becky, with real feeling and a little bit of impishness as he interjects a line that isn't on the record:

I could have a woman every time I call
But I'd rather see you walking down the hall
Especially if you're wearing no clothes at all
Cause I'm gonna love you once and for all
Until the final curtain falls . . .

Everyone is frustrated afterwards. Only Merle Kilgore's good humor manages to keep up spirits, as he tells of similar disasters he has witnessed over the years and unexpected triumphs, too. Another bumsville, someone concludes, referring to the promoters as a bunch of yo-yos. 'Oh, I know it,' says Merle agreeably, with his sharp country boy's manner. 'Gol-lee. . . .'

> *I just ain't never made no superstar*
> *But I'm gonna keep on playing this white guitar*
> *Don't know how long or how far*
> *But I will keep on playing this white guitar.*

Things are going better, but obviously they're still not good enough. When Hank junior moved to Cullman, he freed himself not only of his old management ('I knew I was getting screwed, I just didn't know how'), but also of his old record company, which had been putting out Hank Williams records since 1947. With J.R. Smith as his manager, he feels confident that he is at last conducting his own career. With his new record company he has at least put out two records that he can be proud of, with the second, *The New South*, serving as a kind of hallmark of the brave new style (musically stark, lyrically straightforward, and above all, honest) pioneered by his friend Waylon Jennings, who also produced it. Nonetheless the question remains. Why? Why, after all that he has been through, is he still out on the road, twenty-one years after his public debut, still subject to the same doubts and the same stress that almost destroyed him once already? He's had number one records, he's won more than his share of awards and gained more than his share of recognition. It's hard to imagine, then, what he's doing playing in front of a few hundred people in Hammond or Ruston, Louisiana, putting up with the frustrations and indignities of the road, meeting people he doesn't want to meet, when the royalties from his father's song catalogue alone would make for a more than comfortable living.

Bad booking, is the official explanation; Warner Brothers, too (which will soon pass his contract to Elektra in a sophisticated corporate trade), has yet to figure out how to promote him right. There are still a few bugs in the system, and the organization is just getting cranked up to make Hank Williams, Jr., country star, into Hank Williams, Jr., Superstar. Because it's obvious that Hank junior is no longer interested in being number one in a field in which his name is almost bigger than the market. If he gets a big pop hit, he says, the country stations that are refusing to play his newer material will have to play him. Whereas if he stays with the country field, his career will undoubtedly be safe, successful—and very predictable. This ambition to conquer new worlds is something that has been on his mind for a while now, and to this end he has just cut Jackson Browne's 'You Love the Thunder,' with Neil Diamond's producer, which he says the company is very enthusiastic about and plans to rush out as the new single. We listen to the cut over and over in the bus, along with tapes of Marshall Tucker, Linyrd Skynyrd, and a masterful version of one of Hank junior's latest songs that Waylon has cut for his new album. Hank junior professes to make no distinction between recording his own compositions and someone else's ('We've done my stuff before. They're so gung-ho on this one, might as well give them something they want to work on'), but it's difficult to see how a Jackson Browne song is going to make Hank Williams, Jr., a superstar.

To some of the people around him, the picture he presents of himself is not altogether an accurate one. 'Living proof? Of what?' says one scornfully. 'He's put in time, not dues.' 'I know they been feeding you all this bullshit,' says someone else. 'Even Merle's probably been giving you the same line about his music and his daddy and the fall. He's probably been telling you his music's so important to him. Not true. If you went down to see him in Cullman, you wouldn't see him with a guitar in his hand. There's times he's gone for weeks without even picking it up, from the day he gets off the road until he goes back out again. He's more interested in his guns than he is in his music.'

It's understandable in a way. Hank Williams, Jr., by comparison to almost anyone else struggling to make a living in the music business, is the Fortunate Son. Certainly in one sense he had it all handed to him, but unlike many sons who inherit their father's business, he wasn't satisfied with what he was handed. Perhaps because he didn't know how to express this dissatisfaction, he very nearly threw away everything he had, including his own life, and he makes no bones about his passion for guns, sports, sex, military history, and similar indulgences. He has a voracious appetite for all kinds of experience, and he will not rest until that appetite is satisfied. Hank Williams, Jr., is used to getting his own way, and while he can be the most gracious of hosts, it is not surprising that he sometimes disregards the little niceties, that he can be rude, self-absorbed, and insensitive to the needs and weaknesses of others.

To members of the band, too, he can be enormously frustrating to work with. Like most sidemen they are musicians who have grown up on rock and are put off both by the slipshod musical quality of Hank junior's performance (because he uses a lead guitarist's light-gauge strings, for example, and he has an unusually heavy touch, his guitar is almost constantly out of tune) and by its very unpredictability. They would prefer a smoothly professional show. 'We try to get him to rehearse, and once in a while he'll actually sit down and run through some new songs. But he'll just play them once for us and then go on to the next. Which ain't rehearsing actually.' After the show in Ruston one band member kicks the wall in frustration. Not only has Hank junior altered the harmony on several of the songs, he has also introduced old songs in new keys and new songs with no mention made of

Lone Star Ranch, Reedsferry, New Hampshire (pre-accident). HENRY HORENSTEIN

the key. 'I hate it when he does that,' says the sideman, practically in tears. 'It embarrasses me as a musician, it makes me look bad. I told him that once, and he apologized, he said, I'm sorry, but there's nothing I can do about it.'

And it's probably true; there *is* nothing he can do about it, and very likely there is nothing he should do about it. When he gets out on stage Hank Williams, Jr., is transformed: he can either be galvanized or he can be brought down, but in order for the moment to catch fire he has to be free to improvise, to introduce new lyrics or harmonies, to maintain a direct link between feeling and performance. In the two concerts that I saw, the feeling never quite crystallized, but even on the evidence of two bad shows it's clear that Hank Williams, Jr., whatever his faults, is playing music from the heart. And that—not some sterile mimesis—is what the customers pay to see.

So what's left is Life on the Road, as usual. How much and how long is anyone's guess. Hank junior has always said he'll quit at thirty-five; now he thinks it may come earlier. Always in the back of his mind must be his stated *fear of the later years/When nobody's gonna want you around*, although the recent vision of crossover success has whetted his appetite for greater things. All kinds of projects are in the offing. More showcase bookings. Maybe he'll tour again with Waylon (as he did last year) or go out with

Marshall Tucker, thereby attracting the young audience that he needs to put his new music across.

For now, it's the life that he's always known. The sealed-off world of the highway. The 'bugs' that intrude and all the little favors that come with them. The '69 Silver Eagle careening through the countryside, tape deck going at full blast and everyone playing cards under the not-so-watchful gaze of the Polaroid snapshot of the Country Star naked, shown from the shoulders down. The walls in all the motels are stained or have holes punched in them. It's impossible to imagine how stifling a life it really is; the only diversions are getting high or getting laid, and after a while sleep — or the lulling comfort of the bus — is the best escape. Even in description it sounds more romantic than it is, because there's nothing romantic about it. The shows themselves are almost incidental. 'I enjoy the hell out of it when it's right,' manages Hank junior weakly. 'When it's wrong, well sometimes me and Becky talk about it and say, Fuck all of it. Why not just quit? Then the

At fifteen.

next night you can have two thousand people screaming, like we did in Pensacola. I guess as long as there are more good times than bad times, I'll keep on doing it. You know, as long as I've got my music, a little weed, some wine, my guns, a little pussy on the side now and then—' He winks in Becky's direction and grins. Becky comes over and puts her arm around him. She is supportive in a way that no one else in his life has been—or perhaps in a way that he has not allowed anyone else in his life to be—up till now.

> *I just ain't been able to write no songs*
> *Guess I stayed straight for a little too long*
> *I hate to, but I got to get back to getting stoned*
> *Cause I ain't been able to write no songs.*

The songs that he has written over the last three years, and the albums that he has recorded, have emerged almost as a diary of awakening consciousness. Dominated by a mood not so much of introspection as of increasing self-awareness, they dwell on familiar themes frequently restated and are filled with the details of real life. Becky is a living presence in many; so are Waylon and Toy Caldwell. On the *Friends* album, 'Montana Song' presages his fall, and 'Stoned at the Jukebox' speaks with a mixture of bewilderment and relief of the move down to Alabama (*Now I'm busted stone flat down in Huntsville / I got nothing but time and bottles to kill / And I never thought I could ever be like that*) and the painful conclusion of his second marriage. 'Once and For All' pays tribute to Becky's continued loyalty after the accident, when they had known each other for only a few months (*Cause you're the one that stuck it out*), and 'The New South' evokes a now-departed 'Boston girl' with precisely selected strokes. There is nothing quite like this in contemporary country music, there is nothing quite so unabashedly personal. And it seems to me no accident, despite the more optimistic tidings of the most recent album (*I'm feelin' better*, he announces to the world at large. *This here music from now on won't be nothing but home-grown, and my own*), that he has come to rely more and more on an idiosyncratic blues form (*I started turning up loud and looking at the crowd / And bending them guitar strings*), which allows him to express these feelings. It is no accident either that his father continues to be a dominant presence in his themes if not in his music or his writing, which is far more particular, or confessional anyway, than anything his father ever wrote. On *The New South* alone there are four songs that refer directly or indirectly to Hank Williams, and it seems an irony that Hank junior will never escape, that the more he tries to pull away the more he will be reminded of his father's name.

There is, really, no pulling away in any case. Just before the present tour begins, he has made a rare trip to Nashville for the opening of his newest business enterprise, the Hank Williams Museum, just across from the Wax

Museum. All of official Nashville is there for the opening; TV cameras catch Roy Acuff, Mac Wiseman, Faron Young, song publisher Wesley Rose, the original Drifting Cowboys, the venerable Duke of Paducah — all friends and associates of his father — and the one contemporary celebrity whose presence sets everyone in the room to buzzing, a man who modeled himself on Hank senior and serves as a model to Hank junior — Waylon Jennings. Hank junior handles all interviews with practiced ease, everyone is very polite, and no one pauses too long in front of the more grisly exhibits: a pair of tattered slippers ('Hank Williams Died In These Shoes Jan. 1, 1953,' it says on the sole of one), two pairs of pajamas ('Notice the cigarette holes in both pairs of pajamas'), and the powder-blue Cadillac convertible in which the guest of honor's father died ('Damn, someone must have stolen the lock buttons,' says Hank junior, who as a teenager drove the car around in a souped-up version and then had it restored). Yes, he and a very wan-looking Waylon tell a television interviewer, Hank was the first outlaw, he started it all. He was the only outlaw, declares Waylon defiantly, surveying a roomful of people who are just waiting to see him fall, before retreating to a locked room where he can be comfortable again. The 'billy world goes round and and round.

Hank Williams, Jr., manages to rise above it all. They condemned his father, and they applied the same judgment to him (though this was not, he hastens to add, his father's musical colleagues. It was the *businessmen*. It is always the businessmen) — but he has survived. More than anything else he seems to have finally accepted the fact that he is a survivor. Unlike his father. His thick, muscular body — in such sharp contrast to his father's rail-thin, almost consumptive appearance — proclaims it. His voice, too, which has lowered and coarsened, perhaps as a result of the accident, perhaps in emulation of Waylon, scarcely recalls the high, lonesome sound of emptiness and despair that his father brought to the music. He doesn't want to sing any more sad songs, he insists, but whatever songs he sings will no longer be in his father's voice.

The last I see of Hank junior, his bus goes racing by on the highway outside of Ruston. It is past midnight, and they will not get into Darlington, South Carolina, until mid-afternoon the next day. The lights from the bus remain visible for quite a distance along the darkened road and then become fainter until you can barely see the legend 'Hank Williams, Jr.' inscribed on the back, with 'Jr.' lit up in red.

MERLE
HAGGARD

In the Good Old Days
(When Times Were Bad)

Currently 'living' in Nashville with Leona Williams, [Merle Haggard]
does not consider it his home, hates the climate. . . . Feud with Buck
Owens is over. They just ignore one another. . . . Merle and Bonnie not
divorced but legally separated. Bonnie still travels with and performs in
Merle's show. Merle is Bonnie's biggest fan and is very concerned
about her career. He still has and will probably always have a great
dependence on her. (For instance, when Merle is sick he calls on Bonnie
because she'll know what to do.) Leona travels with Merle, too.

From a Merle Haggard press release put out through the
office of Frank Mull, 'close personal friend,' fall 1978

MERLE HAGGARD has been tied up in meetings for two days. There
are meetings with accountants and meetings with lawyers, there are
business managers and financial advisers to consult—all on the subject of
his rapidly approaching marriage. 'Country and western singing star Merle
Haggard will marry a former backup singer in his act,' I read in Tuesday's
Tahoe Tribune, while waiting for the phone call that will summon me to my
scheduled interview. 'A spokesman for Harrah's, Tahoe, where the forty-one-
year-old entertainer is performing through Thursday, identified the bride-
to-be as Leona Williams, who provided backup vocals for Haggard's act.
Acting as bridesmaid for the wedding Saturday will be Bonnie Owens,
Haggard's former wife and now singing as a member of the backup group
for her former spouse.'

When I am finally ushered into the Star Suite on the sixteenth floor of
Harrah's—where even an ordinary room has two bathrooms with a phone
and TV to go with each bath and the Star Suite itself occupies two floors as
well as offering a spectacular view of the lake, plus guacamole and M&Ms on
silver service and a tuxedoed butler on duty twenty-four hours a day—I sit in

Portrait. LEONARD KAMSLER

on what appears to be yet another meeting, having to do with some last-minute aspect of Merle's upcoming marriage and hastily arranged divorce settlement. Seated around an oval table are more than a dozen people, including Merle's lawyer, his agent, his seventeen-year-old daughter Kelly, his brother Lowell—a bluff, easy-going man who calls his baby brother Bud—plus the hotel publicist, assorted members of the band, and an older man scratching out marks on a legal-sized pad of paper. Manager Fuzzy Owen, described by one of the band as 'looking like Fonzie's dad,' wanders in and out. Fuzzy's cousin Lewis Talley, who gave his name to the record company for which Merle first recorded in 1961, and Dean Holloway, a skeletal-looking figure in cowboy hat and jeans, who has been friendly with Merle ever since they ran away from home together and were thrown in jail as kids, observe the proceedings quizzically. Meanwhile, Merle himself peers in from time to time, puts in a word, repairs to the kitchen, and wanders downstairs, where another half dozen people are gathered.

No one seems to know quite what the meeting is about, except that it has something to do with the wedding. 'There isn't going to be any wedding,' says Stew Carnall, Merle's agent, a lanky, white-haired man in loose-fitting jeans, 'if we don't get a goddamn divorce first.' 'Are you serious?' someone asks. 'I'm serious.' At this point the phone rings. Almost before Stew hangs up, the phone rings again. It is a minor hotel functionary, who will call a dozen more times in the next forty-five minutes over some obscure problem about Merle's registration. Wolf Man, one of the four miniature dogs prowling the suite, relieves himself on the carpet, but the maid refuses to clean it up. 'I was hired to cook. I wasn't hired to clean up dog shit,' she declares sensibly enough. Everyone seems to find this vastly amusing. The phone keeps ringing, and the other maid, Doris, turns on the TV in the middle of a sentence. 'I don't believe this,' says Stew with a cheerful show of disbelief. 'This is the single most important decision in his whole goddamn life, and she's got to watch the goddamn football game. Honestly, I can't believe this is happening.' The phone rings and is slammed down several times in quick succession, and finally all pretense of a meeting is abandoned. 'What was I supposed to be doing here?' asks fiddle player Gordon Terry, who has kicked off his shoes and made himself at home. 'You were supposed to be a witness,' says backup singer Ronnie Reno, glancing at the doodles that make up the meeting's 'minutes.'

Downstairs little knots of people form, as at a party. The original 'Roly Poly' by Bob Wills is on the record player, repeated over and over again. Merle sits down on the plush sofa beside me, his Abe Lincoln beard giving his already melancholy appearance an even more melancholy cast, unruffled apparently by all the turmoil around him. 'Well, what can I do for you?' he says with the utmost consideration. I am completely taken aback. I have been plunked down in the middle of some odd situations, but this is perhaps not just the oddest but the most inexplicable: what *am* I doing here? I am genuinely distressed to encounter one of my true heroes under these circumstances. For a moment all the questions that I have carefully prepared go out of my head. Merle's troubled boyhood (his mother first committed him to a juvenile home at fourteen, 'to frighten him'); his prison background ('I turned twenty-one in prison,' as the song says, and by the time he got out two years later he had spent nearly six years behind bars); growing up fatherless in a converted railroad car in Bakersfield; hitchhiking up and down Weedpatch Highway looking for a gig playing guitar — somehow at this point none of it seems like an appropriate topic of conversation.

'I don't know,' I murmur, 'maybe now isn't the best time —'

'No, I mean it,' says Merle, with a courteousness bordering on gallantry. 'You know, I'm a strange kind of person. The more that's going on, the more life I'm able to be involved with and learn about, the more it seems to replenish my well of ideas. I'm not patting myself on the back or anything, it's just the way it is, but you know, I've taken periods off and gone to the boat, gone incognito and been out of touch for two or three months at a time, and I couldn't write anything — and then I've been in situations even more confusing than this, and I've gotten a song. So go ahead, it really doesn't bother me.'

I continue to express some disbelief, but, sure enough, within a short period of time he is speaking of his plans to publish a book of poetry ('It's been in the works about a year, and now I think we've finally got a publisher. Some started out as songs but just weren't melodic enough. Some I shaped into poetry to begin with. It's called *A Poet of the Common Man*'), telling me of the two novels that he's worked at off and on for the last four or five years ('I never have completed them, but they're there; at least I think I have the stories in mind, but it's very time-consuming, it's kind of out of my bag for me. One of 'em's a semi-comedy, a novel of — what would I compare it to? It's called *The Sins of John Tom Mullen*, it's almost like *The Beverly Hillbillies*, it's just a hilarious story, except it's got some mystery areas, too'), and explaining how he first started writing ('I started trying to write when I was in grammar school. My grades suffered from it, it's right there in the comments on my report cards'). It is all engrossing in a soft-spoken, matter-of-fact kind of way, simply because Merle has the disarming knack of making his listener feel as if he or she is the only person on earth.

We are in the midst of talking about the undertaking he is currently most excited about — a projected movie on the life of Bob Wills ('I just finished writing a summary to present to Universal. I think everyone wants to see his story told as a legend carved out with pride and decency, I think it could be a big moneymaker in certain areas of the country, probably if the movie's done well it could go big all over') — when his lawyer bursts in with the news that Bonnie has arrived with *her* lawyer. Maybe I should leave, I suggest, but Merle dismisses my suggestion out of hand. Bonnie — who was

Street musicians, October, 1935. Courtesy of the Library of Congress. F.S.A.
BEN SHAHN

once married to Bakersfield's other superstar, Buck Owens, dated Merle's manager Fuzzy for a brief time in the fifties, and, after marrying Merle in 1965, raised the four children he had by his first wife (also named, coincidentally, Leona)—looks understandably frazzled and at one point bursts into tears and declares that she is not going to go through with it. Except for the financial figures, the scene is a common enough one, I suppose, between soon-to-be-ex-husband and wife, but I am led to question once again just what I am doing here. Evidently the same thought occurs to Bonnie not too much later. Back in the living room, she approaches me. 'You know, I just found out who you are,' she says. 'I hope you understand, all of that wasn't real, I'm not really like that. I'm a nice person. You see, we was just putting on an act. It wasn't for you, it was for someone else, do you understand? Have you met Dean Holloway?' she says, introducing me to Merle's boyhood friend. 'I believe this is the man who's gonna be my next husband.'

> *Merle Haggard is bored. He works on an average of 80–100 days a year, but out of those days he actually only works two hours a day. The rest of his day is spent waiting. He's achieved more success than he ever intended and cannot come to terms with this success. This, combined with the boredom, results in Merle's feeling lifeless and feeling that there is nothing in his life that's very important to him. His staff and the people close to him try to keep him busy. (For instance, Frank Mull recently gave Merle a bicycle to occupy some of his time.)*

Merle Ronald Haggard was born on April 6, 1937, in Oildale, California, a kind of Hoover camp that he has come to refer to euphemistically as a 'suburb' of Bakersfield. His family had arrived two years earlier from Checotah, Oklahoma (about twenty-five miles south of Muskogee), where his father James played fiddle and guitar at house parties and dances and his grandfather was a champion fiddler. By the time that the family moved to California, his mother had found religion and his father had long since given up music, 'to please my mother, I'm sure it was just to keep peace in the family.' When they first moved out, the whole family worked on a dairy farm, milking thirty head of cows for fifty dollars a month (Merle's brother Lowell was fourteen, his sister Lillian twelve at the time of the move). Soon his father got a job as a carpenter with the Santa Fe Railroad, and Merle grew up in a converted refrigerator car beside the Southern Pacific tracks. When his father died in 1946, his mother Flossie went to work as a bookkeeper for a meat-packing house ('Fortunately she had a good education'), leaving her nine-year-old son pretty much on his own.

It wasn't long afterwards that he first started getting in trouble, playing hooky from school (he finally quit in the eighth grade), getting picked up by juvenile authorities for any number of minor transgressions. At twelve or thirteen he started running away from home with friends like Dean Holloway and Bob Teague, 'picking hay, sacking potatoes, roughnecking it on oil rigs.' He liked to hop the freights, but he always had a sure way of getting home, because he had a free ride on the passenger trains (with a pass earned by his father's death) until he was twenty-one. About the only thing he really cared about was playing the guitar. When he was eleven, his brother Lowell, who was running a service station at the time, traded a man two dollars worth of gas for a guitar. 'He brought it to the house and set it up there. He didn't really get it for me, but I played that thing all the time. About the first guitar I can remember getting for myself was an old Bronson that me and Bob Teague bought for five dollars one time after we left our homes and more or less tried to go out on our own. We were harvesting hay in northern California, and we'd play Lefty Frizzell and Hank Williams songs all night long. I wrote several songs around that time, but mainly I wanted to be a guitar player. When I washed out at that, I tried singing things.'

When he was fourteen his mother committed him to a juvenile home, because, he told associate Bob Eubanks, 'she just couldn't handle me. She had a boy who was, uh, more than wild. I don't know what I'd a done with me if I had been the parent. I was a child that needed two parents – all children really do. My dad wasn't there, and my older brother tried to step in and of course I resented that. It just got all confused and mixed up. Mama certainly did try.'

In the next few years he was arrested on a succession of charges – car theft, bogus checks, burglary, breaking and entering. He escaped seven times from reform schools and youth institutions (the letters PSI, for Preston School of Industry, are still tattooed on his left wrist), moved briefly to Texas, set up housekeeping with a girl in Eugene, Oregon, married his first wife, Leona, at seventeen, and was without any direction of his own. 'Wild hair was all it was,' he has told writer Paul Hemphill. Today, he says, without seeking to excuse his behavior, it is unlikely that he would have spent a day in jail for the same crimes. 'The laws are so much more lenient now, you know. I just grew up too fast. I wanted to be on my own when I was fourteen, and the law didn't want me to.'

One of the high points in his life came in 1953, when he was invited up on stage by his idol, Lefty Frizzell, and sang Jimmie Rodger's 'My Rough and Rowdy Ways' at the Rainbow Garden in Bakersfield. The low point undoubtedly was reached when in 1957 at the age of twenty he was sentenced to San Quentin, 'hard time,' for a bungled burglary. San Quentin, he feels, made a man of him. He was faced with a clear choice between motivating himself and following a life of crime. He spent his twenty-first birthday in solitary, just a few cells down from Caryl Chessman, but shortly after that he started performing on the weekly Warden's Show. When he got out in 1960, he moved back in with his mother, who had been taking care of Leona and the children in the railroad car in which Merle had grown up. He went to work for his brother Lowell, who was now an electrical contractor, but he was determined to make a career in music. 'I was a victim of life's circumstances,' he says, looking back on an unprofitable life of crime. 'You know how it is, one thing led to another, you make friends on the inside that you wouldn't even want to have on the outside, and they taught me things—but then I finally wised up, and I got out of it.'

Bakersfield in 1960 was a jumping little scene. Buck Owens had just begun to enjoy the national success that would bring him eighteen number one country hits in the next decade. Dallas Frazier at twenty-one was already an established songwriter (his 'Alley Oop' was a smash hit that year for the Hollywood Argyles), and Tommy Collins, a prolific songwriter and sometime preacher, had been recording for Capitol since the early 1950s. Merle started playing guitar in the clubs around Bakersfield soon after his release—first at the High Pockets and Tex's Barrelhouse at ten dollars a night, then at the Blackboard and the Lucky Spot. He met Bonnie Owens (divorced from Buck since 1953), who worked as a cocktail waitress and sang on Tuesday nights, at the Blackboard; at the Lucky Spot he ran into Fuzzy Owen, a transplanted Arkansan who played steel guitar both at the club and on Cousin Herb Henson's TV show (Ferlin Husky and Glen Campbell had been recent guest stars on the show). Fuzzy and his cousin Lewis Talley had put out a number of records on their own Tally label, and Fuzzy more or less took Merle under his wing, recording him in the garage that served as the label's

Lefty Frizzell. Courtesy of the Country Music Foundation Library and Media Center, Nashville, Tennessee.

studio and guiding him in his career. 'He was willing to spend just about anything he could invest in my potential,' Merle told *Billboard* reporter Todd Everett. 'He's not one to elaborate on what he thinks, but I think that it's evident that he must have had quite a bit of confidence in me to spend his bankroll like that.'

The first Tally release, in 1963, sold two hundred copies. The next, 'Sing a Sad Song,' was a national hit. By the time that '(My Friends Are Gonna Be) Strangers' made the Top 10 in 1965, Capitol Records, whom Fuzzy had been trying to interest for some time (Capitol was the label that recorded Cousin Herb Henson as well as Buck Owens and almost every other prominent Bakersfield artist), finally decided to make a move and bought up Merle's contract along with the Tally masters. The following year Merle hit the number one position with his fourth Capitol release, 'I Am a Lonesome Fugitive,' and he had eight more number one hits before 'Okie from Muskogee' – the

Merle with Bob Wills. Courtesy of the Country Music
Foundation Library and Media Center, Nashville, Tennessee.

song that made him a hardhat hero and a symbol of the populist backlash (it
deplored the loss of traditional American values and, in a statement that was
intended as a semi-spoof, declared disingenuously, 'We don't smoke marijuana in Muskogee')—catapulted him to a new level of income and notoriety
in 1969.

Up to this point Haggard's career might be considered a more or less
conventional success story. If his background was a little seamier than that
of most pop stars, it reflected the ambience nonetheless that many like to
project. His return to the patriotic fold was only in keeping with the times,
when construction workers attacked anti-war demonstrators, and politicians
exploited the fears of the so-called Silent Majority. It would have been the
most natural thing in the world for Haggard, like his sometime model Johnny
Cash (whose network TV show put him in increasing conflict with his own
image of rugged independence), to have embarked upon a whole string of

profitable promotions, commercial and political. And yet his success led not to a repetition of flag-waving sentiments (he released only one follow-up, 'The Fightin' Side of Me,' and then only under pressure) but to an unlikely excursion into the past, his own and the country's, which remains the most vital strain in his music today.

It is the Depression that continues to excite Merle Haggard's imagination. 'There were so many things I loved about the thirties,' he says with a nostalgia for a time he could scarcely be expected to remember—and perhaps for a certainty that went out of his life when his father died. 'I could find many reasons for wanting to live back there. Such as trains was the main method of travel, the glamour of trains always appealed to me. And America was at the dawn of an industrial age. Coming out of a Depression into a war. Then again the music was young. So many things were being done in music, it was wide open back then, electronics had not yet been involved, and basically it was *real*. Sure, I'd have liked to have visited those days and at least seen it happen. For musicians of that generation such as Eldon Shamblin and Joe Venuti it was an unbelievable period to live in, they saw it all.'

The Eldon Shamblin to whom he refers is, it is worth noting, not just a name but a sharp and affable sixty-two-year-old man who is a member of Haggard's Tahoe band. Shamblin joined Bob Wills's legendary Texas Playboys in 1937 as arranger and nonpareil rhythm guitarist and was compared favorably in jazz journals of the time with black swing pioneer and fellow Oklahoman, Charlie Christian, who was featured in Benny Goodman's band. Merle met Shamblin when in 1970 he determined to make a tribute album to Wills, the originator of *western* swing, that unique fusion of jazz and hillbilly, two-steps and waltzes, which is the western (or Texas) half of country and western. Authenticity, musical and emotional, was Merle's goal in making this album, just as it had been when he earlier recorded a brilliant tribute to his first hero, Jimmie Rodgers. For the Wills album not only did he learn to play fiddle in a period of roughly three months; he also reassembled a good part of Wills's old band, which he subsequently kept together and incorporated into his own group, The Strangers. He then went out on the road with a new type of fusion music. 'We had a great band for a couple of years,' says Merle proudly. 'Of course we didn't make no money.' Which is why he couldn't keep the band together, and why it is reassembled only for special occasions, like the Harrah's engagement.

This augmented twelve-piece band is a wondrous sight to behold. With fellow Wills alumni Tiny Moore and Johnny Gimble, Wills disciple Gordon Terry, and two of Tiny Moore's students from Sacramento, the band can boast a front line of six old-time fiddlers when Merle picks up his bow. Sparked by the hot solos of long-time Strangers Roy Nichols and Norman Hamlet on lead and steel guitar respectively, the music moves with all the punch and speed of the great Bob Wills bands of the thirties and forties, refashioning the sound of the great Merle Haggard bands of the sixties and seventies. At each solo the attention of the entire band is focused on the soloist, and, very much in the manner of Wills, Merle directs the action, calling out the instrumentalist's name, emitting appreciative cries, and leading the whole ensemble into the toe-tapping unison sound of the swing era. It is a remarkable performance and an uncanny reconstruction, not just of the music but of the feeling conveyed by the music of Bob Wills. (Wills's own love for his early bands reached the point that he intended to buy a big ranch and divide it up among the band members, so that, according to his biographer, Charles Townshend, 'after they retired they would live close enough to each other to get together every few nights for a jam session.')

The only difference is that this is Harrah's, not Cain's Dancing Academy, the supper show, not an all-night dance. It is a difference of which Merle is keenly aware. 'Well, of course, Vegas and Tahoe are good security for an artist. These places are very stable, the money isn't bad, and Harrah's has been great to me. But it's very cramped, there's no way you can get loose like you can on the road. You just do the show, it's not really musical, what I mean by that is that the music lover could not be satisfied, whereas the people who are educated in this type of entertainment are probably satisfied. It's just not the most fun.'

Backstage anyway the talk is almost all of music – of Wills and his piano player, Al Stricklin, and legendary Texas fiddler J.R. Chatwell, who wouldn't go further west than Amarillo in pursuit of fame. 'He never gave a shit about money,' says someone. 'He'd rather play with a good rhythm section than make it big.' 'But he made it anyway,' says Johnny Gimble admiringly, referring not to material success but to peace of mind. In all the talk, the band shows itself to be a curious mixture of old and young, as grandfatherly-looking Eldon Shamblin, worldly-wise and unshockable, tells tales of the business and urges seventeen-year-old Mark O'Connor, Tiny's pupil, to get an education. The fiddlers go off by themselves to fiddle; a fairly universal scorn for Nashville is expressed ('There's a lot of people that want to meet me in Nashville?' says Roy Nichols in disbelief to the new bass player. 'I don't believe I ate that shit'); and everyone gets a laugh when a tuxedoed member of the Tahoe Philharmonic (Harrah's insists, like all the Vegas and Tahoe clubs, on an orchestral backing, no matter how inappropriate) comes back to work out a new arrangement for 'San Antonio Rose.' 'It is my favorite,' he says in a Viennese accent, as Eldon hums it out for him and looks over his shoulder to correct the notation. 'It is in C major, is it not?' 'Yeah, but Merle sings it in D sharp,' drawls Eldon to muffled snickers. There is also a good deal of speculation about Merle's marriage, whether or not it will take place ('I just don't think Merle'll do it,' says one of the musicians. 'Of course I've been wrong before.' 'Have you?' says Eldon with exaggerated politeness) and whether anyone will consent to be best man if it actually does. In all of this the tone is mostly one of respect, mixed with as much bemusement as anyone is likely to feel in the presence of Merle Haggard.

The small talk doesn't really matter, though; what this band wants to do is to play. They are almost champing at the bit to get back out on stage for the late show, and Merle himself seems noticeably more enthused now that his guitar teacher, and Nashville session man, Grady Martin, is in the audience ('Yeah, he's all jacked up to play guitar now,' says a band member cynically). Back on stage it is a palatable blend of the old and the new – 'Mama Tried' and 'Trouble in Mind,' Jimmie Rodgers's 'Hard Times Blues,' some fiddle breakdowns, and Merle's latest Wills-styled hit, 'It's Been a Great Afternoon' – all presided over with a combination of filial tenderness, paternal pride, and the greatest good will by the leader himself. The unison passages take off, Johnny Gimble leans into his solos and positively radiates his pleasure, the singing is effortless and light, and there is no evidence of strain as Merle emulates the easy-going charm of his mentors, Bob Wills and Bing Crosby. In the middle of the set there is the inevitable call for 'Okie,' but Merle never misses a beat, simply remarking, 'Let's play some music first.' When a persistent patron demands 'Just Between the Two of Us,' a hit for Merle and Bonnie at the beginning of their careers, Merle demurs weakly. 'You know, it's been thirteen years.' 'I know,' shouts back the man in the audience. 'Sing it.' Bonnie looks pained, and you wonder if the delicate line between art and life is about to be bridged. You wonder if Bonnie is going to cry.

But that's the kind of dualism only Merle Haggard could appreciate. His whole career has been founded upon just such paradox. As a young man barely out of prison, he crooned love songs, sounding very much like Marty Robbins, who was hot at the time. It was not even his own compositions that first drew upon the prison experience for him; instead he virtually stumbled upon the song, 'I'm a Lonesome Fugitive.' 'Liz Anderson [the writer] came to a show we were doing in Sacramento. She said she had some songs, but I wouldn't have listened if it hadn't been for my brother Lowell. It turned out she had six hits in her pocket. Well, that kind of opened up a whole trend of songs, such as "Branded Man" and "Sing Me Back Home." It gave me thought for writing. It gave me direction for writing. You see, what it was, with that song I was really and finally some way or another come together – musically and image-wise. I mean, it was a true song, I wasn't trying to shit nobody, because long ago I had made the decision not to try to hide my past, but then I found out it was one of the most interesting things about me.'

Nonetheless, when it looked as if the prison songs were becoming a trap, Merle neatly sidestepped that issue by embarking upon the first in his series of historical albums. And when 'Okie from Muskogee' hit in 1969, bringing undreamt-of fame and presidential invitations, Merle's first inclination (thwarted by his record company) was to release 'Irma Jackson,' a tale of interracial love, as the follow-up. His whole career in fact can be looked upon as a series of deliberate avoidances (walking out on the Ed Sullivan show, quitting a network production of *Oklahoma*), instinctive retreats from the obvious, and restatements of his central role as an outsider (remaining in Bakersfield, rather than moving to Nashville, was one very key element of his alienation; even his blues singing, a major component of his music, stresses over and over that 'I'm a White Boy,' a 'White Man Singin' the Blues').

Perhaps this is what has enabled him to create the astonishing body of work that represents the 'career' of Merle Haggard. There is no one in contemporary popular music who has created a more impressive legacy, or one that spans a wider variety of styles. In a genre that has always relied upon filler to round out the album coming off a country hit, Merle has written the vast preponderance of his material ('Without writing you have nothing,' says Merle, meaning both the royalties and the satisfaction) and has used each album as a vehicle for personal expression, sometimes not even leaving room to include the hit. He has written blues and folk songs, social commentary and classic love songs, protest and anti-protest, gospel and ballads, prison and train songs, drinking songs, and updates of Jimmie Rodgers's blue yodels. He has written just about every kind of song there is, in fact, except a convincing rock number, and while such prolificness is not without its price (some of the rhymes are less than fresh, some of the metaphors could have been worked out a little more fully, and sometimes you wish an idea had been left to simmer rather than having been incorporated immediately into a song), taken as a whole the body of work that he has created is absolutely staggering. His voice, which was originally compared to Lefty Frizzell's for its patented catch and tremulousness of tone, has deepened over the years to become the perfect vehicle not only for the weepers but for the toughness of the blues as well.

It is his band, though, the aptly named Strangers, that has given him the freedom to experiment, to cut across styles and try different forms of instrumentation. In the late sixties, for example, when he was cutting standards like 'Fugitive' and 'The Bottle Let Me Down,' the band consisted of Roy Nichols and James Burton alternating on lead guitar, Glen Campbell on rhythm and harmony, Glen D. Hardin on piano (soon to be recruited, along with Burton, for Elvis Presley's band), and Buck Owens alumnus Ralph Mooney on steel. 'That was our A-team recording crew. You can take a look at that line-up and see why we had some hits.' Just as you can listen to the steaming guitar solos of Roy Nichols today, the pealing steel guitar of Norm Hamlet (with Merle since 1970) or the honky tonk piano of Mark Yeary (present since '72) and hear the same energetic trading-off of ideas, always fresh, always to the point.

It is more like a traveling road show than a band, an encapsulated world in which the actors shuffle about, exchange positions, take on new roles, but always remain attached to the unique centrality. Which is Merle. Perhaps that is the point. 'These people are very close,' says one observer, who doubts that the inner circle will ever break ranks over anything less than World War III. And indeed Bonnie did act as bridesmaid when the wedding took place on Saturday. And indeed Lewis Tally did act as best man. . . .

> *Merle's favorite subjects are his houseboat, fishing, and Bonnie Owens. . . . Merle makes a substantial income. He has invested some of his money in farmland in Northern California and cattle with his brother. Merle enjoys gambling and spends a great deal of time in Las Vegas. . . .*

'I'm afraid for Dolly,' says Merle, referring to Dolly Parton's crossover success, though he might as well be speaking about himself. 'I know Dolly and admire her. At one time we were real close, but it remains to be seen whether this whole thing is going to work for her or against her. You see, the

With James Talley. J. CLARK THOMAS

Merle with Leona Williams, center, and Bonnie Owens as bridesmaid, far right.

thing is, if she wants to be a TV personality or a Raquel Welch, I have no doubt she can do it, knowing her like I do. I'm just wondering if possibly she might find it's not what she wanted after all. I mean, all the promotion and all the advertising they've done on her is fantastic, but I don't think all they can possibly do can make you a star. I think Dolly Parton *is* a star, and that does not depend upon the surge of promotion that's out on her, all the different things and gimmicks they've dreamed up to exploit Dolly Parton. Every superstar that has lived on through the years did it without that. I cannot call one name in which promotion played a major part, in which the lasting staying power was either there or was not to begin with. I just hope it don't irritate Dolly to the point where she won't be what she could have been without it—you understand? Because of this she may never become what she would have been. She could have been the biggest thing in the world. If she was just Dolly.'

In the same way he sees Elvis as having been 'a prisoner of success. I'm positive he was. I didn't know Elvis well, but I met him and I knew a lot of people who were close to him. Elvis, I believe, was just plain simply tired of it. He didn't want to live any longer. I don't know how you feel about these things, but the celestial life – if such a thing exists – I think that was what he was seeking, I think it released him. Either that or he didn't die at all. Had a face-lift and a fingerprint job – if you think about it, it isn't that far-fetched. A lot of people who were there swear it wasn't him in the coffin. I'm also convinced Colonel Tom Parker is capable of it. Kind of an interesting thought.'

It is indeed. In any case Merle Haggard is not going to let that happen to him. He isn't even going to write his autobiography at this point. Why not? He eyes you suspiciously, his craggy face skeptical and a little bit weary. *'It's not over yet.'*

POSTSCRIPT

On January 25, 1979, an item ran in *Radio & Records*, among other publications, entitled 'Splitsville?' 'The Merle Haggard and Leona Williams marriage is headed for divorce court,' it said. 'They married October 7; the divorce suit was filed this week. . . .' Merle wasted no time in responding with a press release of his own. 'In the process of hiring an attorney for business reasons, not necessary to disclose,' read Merle's statement, 'a misunderstanding came about in reference to the status of my marriage to Leona Williams. Just to set the record straight, we're not divorcing each other, on the record or off.'

JAMES TALLEY

Scenes from Life (A Triptych)

STARTING OUT: MEHAN, OKLAHOMA, 1976

> *I'm like that potbellied trucker drinkin' coffee*
> *I'm like that red-headed waitress named Louise*
> *I'm like every workin' man all across the land*
> *Just tryin' like the devil to be free.*

JAMES TALLEY's heroes are not unfamiliar ones. They include John Steinbeck, Woody Guthrie, Merle Haggard, James Agee, The Band, and Otis
Spann. Which would not be surprising if Talley were just another college-
educated rock musician, 'trying to look as if I didn't have anything, city folk
trying to be country.' He is, instead, a thirty-two-year-old country and western
singer with roots in Oklahoma, who went to college, got his degree in fine
arts, enrolled in a Ph.D. program in American studies with a concentration
in Depression art, and supported himself and his family when he first came
to Nashville by working for the Public Health and Welfare Service in rat
control and delivering health services to the poor. He has been a landscape
painter, written a book, as yet unpublished, on the Spanish rural culture of
the Southwest (*The Road to Torreon*), and, disillusioned with government
bureaucracy ('I gave up the idea of communism when I went to work for the
government. The civil service is enough to turn anyone off'), worked in
construction for the last few years. Not a conventional background in any
sense, much less for a young country singer seeking a real popular base.

What sets James Talley apart most of all is his earnestness. He speaks
slowly in a modest sort of drawl, measures his words with great care, and
believes altogether in the importance of what he is doing, the validity of
his art, and most of all in himself. He is explicitly populist in his politics,
almost pridefully so, and by his insistence on spelling things out, making
literally clear just where he stands and what the connections are, sometimes

248

he says things that a sophisticated audience might feel don't need to be said. Talley, however, while possessing a dry, self-described 'Okie' sense of humor, never doubts the necessity of reminding his listener that 'poverty is by design in this country,' and that, in reference to Indian rights, 'they have black reservations in this country, too. They call them ghettos.' He is writing songs for and about the working man and woman, and he steadfastly refuses to acknowledge any gap between himself and his audience. Perhaps he's right; maybe there isn't any. Because his songs have a simplicity and a clarity, an unprepossessing, almost matter-of-fact honesty that is at once disarming and instantly accessible. They are rooted in the specific, refer to comfortable, familiar musical forms, and open up in a craftsmanlike, understated way to tell you everything you will ever need to know about themselves and their author.

I went out on the road in early 1976 on the first leg of the promotion tour that was supposed to make James Talley a household name and, not coincidentally, publicize his second album. On this kind of tour the artist goes out with record company support, charging expenses against royalties and making contact with the endless array of program directors and disc jockeys at all the regional radio stations, big and small, who determine whether or not his record is going to get played. In this case Talley was accompanied by thirty-four-year-old Bill Williams, national promotion director for Capitol Records' country and western division, who has gone out on a limb before to promote artists he believes in (Charlie Rich and Stoney Edwards among others), but rarely so far out. If Talley's second record doesn't sell, it's Williams's reputation that suffers most, giving comfort to a lot of old-line Nashville fat cats who would just as soon see Talley and all the other young upstarts fall flat on their faces.

Top 40 radio, whether it's country or pop, is a land of perpetual youth, and the strain is apparent even to the casual visitor. What impressed me most in my brief foray into this world was Talley's ability not just to make contact with people but to find enough to interest him simply in the variations—of tone, of attitude, of orientation—which were encountered at each little country radio station we visited in Arkansas and Oklahoma. This managed to sustain him through interview after interview without his ever getting bored or losing patience. Much of the talk was the same, as Talley patiently led each interviewer through careful discussion of his Oklahoma background, his musical influences and aspirations, and his gratitude for their continued support, but he treated every individual with dignity and respect, no better and no worse than the waitress or the young Bar B Q proprietor to whom he proudly presented his album. 'I've always prided myself on the ability to walk up to some guy and make him feel at ease,' he says without irony. 'I think it's important to let people know that you're interested in them.' Nor is he reluctant to discuss his life and work, for

249

James Talley, like most artists, is more than willing to recount his story in precise and loving detail, so earnestly does he believe in it.

HE WAS BORN in Mehan, Oklahoma, outside of Stillwater, moved to the state of Washington, and grew up in Albuquerque, New Mexico. His father held every kind of job from working in a chemical plant manufacturing plutonium to selling refrigerators door to door to Mexicans. 'You talk about your hard-core rednecks. When him and my uncle got together, it was like turning two wild men loose. All they had to do was sniff the cork, and they were gone. My Uncle Jim ran a grader for the county, Payne County. I reckon that's why the roads are so messed up. My father picked a little guitar. He had a real beautiful tenor voice. He always sang, and he could tap dance real good, too. Sometimes he'd sing and do a little softshoe. He was quite a character, back when he was younger.'

His mother was a teacher, struggling to get her degree in the bleak post-Depression years. Summers James would go back to Mehan to visit his mother's parents, who had themselves emigrated from Kansas and Missouri. His grandmother's father had been in the Land Rush. James's parents 'courted to Bob Wills' at Cain's Academy Ballroom in Tulsa, a piece of personal trivia that informs his memorable 'W. Lee O'Daniel and the Light Crust Doughboys.'

He came to Nashville in 1968 with the idea of being a musician. He arrived 'in a 1949 Willys panel truck with four Goodyear Double Eagle recap tires.' He had left school two years earlier because 'I was studying all about the Depression, and all of a sudden I realized, Hey, there's something out there in the street that's really happening. I mean, I was driving along the street, and I just all of a sudden noticed this fucking shack in the middle of the barrio, and I said to myself here I am stuck in an academic cloister, studying what happened thirty years ago, and it's happening right here, right now. That's how I became a welfare caseworker in Albuquerque, but I was writing songs then, too.' He had been playing mainly folk music up until then and was inspired to some extent by the Kingston Trio. He was a little bit ashamed in his academic phase to be 'from the sticks' and is doubly ashamed, in looking back on it today, at his embarrassment at the time.

'When I got to Nashville, I was realistic about it, I believe. I didn't expect anybody to jump up and down and scream and rave about my songs. Although the first week I was there I started to try to take a little tape around. I didn't know anybody, though, and I didn't know anything about the rules. Before that I didn't even know what a commercial song was—you see, I had always considered music to be a means to express yourself that could encompass any subject. I didn't realize there were just a few narrow categories in commercial country music. Cheating songs, drinking songs, boy-girl songs, put the woman on a pedestal, that kind of thing. You see, I thought of myself

Mehan, Oklahoma. James Talley, in his grandmother's arms. Courtesy of James Talley.

as a songwriter then, but I never was worth a shit at pitching my songs. I worked for the Glaser Brothers for a while. I never did sell any songs, but I learned a lot from Chuck Glaser about what's commercial and what's not.'

Around 1973 he signed with Atlantic's country division, an ill-fated association that yielded only one single. Then, taking his cue from many aspiring writers as well as regional musicians, he decided to take matters into his own hands and record himself, on his own terms and at his own expense. He got the studio time in partial payment for construction work he had done on the studio itself. He put all of his money together to pay the musicians. The result was *Got No Bread, No Milk, No Money, But We Sure Got a Lot of Love,* which he released on his own Torreon label, pressing a thousand copies, all of which were distributed to radio stations and record companies. That was how the album was picked up by Capitol, where, if sales were not spectacular, critical notices were. It was these critical notices, along with Bill Williams's faith, which resulted in his contract being picked up and the second album getting made. Was he ever discouraged? DJ after DJ asks him, and James Talley always seems a little surprised. 'I was very single-minded about it. I just worked at it. People didn't know what to make of it. It wasn't pop, it wasn't country, who'd buy it? But I believed in the album, and I believe in my music. Well, you see, I'm a Scorpio, not that that maybe means anything. But they say that Scorpios are very determined people. If there's something that I decide on, then nobody's going to stop me, unless I die trying. I feel very proud of both these albums. If I never do anything else, I feel as if I can go to my grave with them.'

He has reason to feel proud. The two albums are a testament both to his faith and to the best that Nashville and country music have to offer. They are simple music, a self-conscious return to roots both in terms of musical form – Bob Wills, Hank Williams, and spare production techniques – and in terms of the values they represent. 'We need clarity and simplicity today more than ever. People are so fucking afraid of simplicity, but it seems to me that's part of the reason we're in the middle of an identity crisis in this country. It seems as if people have just lost their roots. And, you know, when a person's lost his roots, he's just adrift without an anchor.'

The first album is about Mehan and the southwestern past. It is sprinkled with references to his mother, his father, his aunt ('blue-eyed Ruth'), and his grandparents Og and Mary ('*Og in his khaki pants / Suspenders and straw hat / Chewing Beechnut tobacco to beat the band*'). It's a homey, comfortable record of deceptive simplicity and real profundity that was hailed by critic Greil Marcus as a potential classic in a review that Talley labels 'crucial' to everything that has happened since. The second album, *Trying Like the Devil*, is by contrast explicitly political. It is angry, ironic, exhilarated, and tender by turns, with songs about work, lack of work, love, and urban despair – and an outlaw number to end all outlaw numbers, in which Talley declares, with a conscious bow to Woody Guthrie:

> *Now there's always been a bottom*
> *And there's always been a top*
> *And someone took the orders*
> *And someone called the shots*
> *And someone took the beatin', Lord,*
> *And someone got the prize*
> *Well, that may be the way it's been*
> *But that don't mean it's right.*

'You know,' says Talley, as we ride along in his new Ford van, listening to a cassette of the just-released album, 'Chuck Glaser always says, "I'm not talking about breaking the law. I'm just talking about the music." I said to Bill Williams, "Right here in my song, I'm talking about breaking the fucking law."'

JAMES TALLEY and Bill Williams are funny traveling companions. My presence may make the situation odder, but life on the road is a succession of oddities, irritations, jokes, insults, and comments on one's place of origin – in Bill's case Waco, Texas (pronounced Wack-o), which Talley thinks is about the sorriest excuse for a city in a sorry excuse for a state. They battle back and forth about football teams, spilled coffee, and speech patterns, seeming to enjoy each other's company but also getting on each other's nerves.

Both Bill and Talley carry thick address books and check in with office and home, associates and friends, several times a day. Talley insists on calling up a friend at one o'clock in the morning from a deserted phone booth in Okemah, Oklahoma, Woody Guthrie's home town. We've turned off the highway to get a look at Guthrie's birthplace, which sits lonesome and tumbling down on a half-paved street in a not very prosperous section of town. The police cruise by several times, the friend is phlegmatic about the call, and Talley shivers in the phone booth, but he doesn't get off the phone for fifteen minutes.

'You know, I'm probably one of the few people in the country who has a Guthrie stone,' he volunteers as he gets back in the car. The Guthrie stone, it turns out, was presented to him by a friend, Henry Bumpkin, who somehow managed to remove it from the foundation of the house and promised, 'As long as you have this Guthrie stone you'll keep your luck.' Well, Talley still

Woody Guthrie. Courtesy of Marjorie Guthrie.

has the stone, and, with two self-produced albums out, he certainly feels that he's kept his luck. When they get back to Nashville, he promises Bill Williams a look at his Guthrie stone – but only if Williams shows the proper respect for its possessor.

In Stillwater, midway between Oklahoma City and Tulsa, Talley is greeted something like a returning hero. KSPI program director Gene Ragsdale has come into the station specially to tape an interview and hear the new album. The last record came in for a lot of play, he murmurs. Folks around Stillwater couldn't get enough of it, especially with all the local names and interest. Can't wait to hear the new one, he says, even as he slaps it down on the turntable, listens briefly and noncommittally to snatches from several cuts, and returns it to its sleeve. He is dressed in doubleknits, his gray hair is modishly styled, and he wears aviator glasses. After recording a brief interview, he and Bill Williams talk business; a promotional tie-in that Talley and Bill have come up with for the album is tentatively discussed; and Gene Ragsdale briskly puts his desk back in order and clears off the console before leaving for the day. The receptionist smiles at us on the way out. James Talley may be something of a celebrity in Stillwater, Oklahoma, but what Gene Ragsdale thinks – and the airplay he gives the new album – is important to the record's success.

We head out to Mehan, just a few miles outside of town. As we approach the dirt-road turnoff, Talley becomes more and more excited, pointing out the sign ('Mehan Road'), the red clay that in the spring would fill up the wheelwells of an old '47 Chevy, the sandstone foundations, the ripped-up tracks, across cow pastures and cornfields, where his grandfather, Og, used to hail the train to Cushing. As we come into Mehan, a crossroads with a population of forty-four at last count, there is almost a sense of déjà vu, for it is just as Talley has described it in his songs. There is the boarded-up grocery, where *I sang Jesus loves me for a dime one time / For soda pop and candy I could sing real dandy / Any time*. Inside it is dark and musty; at one time it must have been a church, but the church pews are broken and a backboard has been nailed up with a deflated basketball lying underneath on the concrete floor.

Next door two men work on a car in the yard. The older man wears a Sanitation Department insignia on his shirt and barely blinks in surprise as Talley approaches him. No, he doesn't remember Og and Mary, but he hasn't lived here very long. 'Those years go by,' he says philosophically. James presents both men with copies of his album, which they regard at first with surprise and then accept gratefully. Across the road sits the house where his grandparents lived. It has been 'improved' with siding and a closed-in back porch; the outhouse and storm cellar are gone, and there are no chickens in the yard. A little boy regards us curiously from the front porch; Talley explains himself to the boy's mother, but she does not invite us in. He gives

James Talley with friends Jerry LeRoy, left, and Henry Huddleston.
J. CLARK THOMAS

her an album, too, and just as we are leaving her husband, a painter named McKnight, drives up in his panel truck. He has just gotten off work and is wearing his white painter's overalls. It turns out that he has actually grown up around here, and he and James exchange reminiscences of old Og ('Yeah, ol' Og, he was a character') and the Field brothers, who grew up over by the grocery store. Mr. McKnight has heard the song, 'Mehan, Oklahoma,' several times on the radio and is anxious to listen to James on the Billy Parker show from Tulsa that night. It's probably too late for him, though, he concedes, a gentle slow-moving man who speaks with deliberation and dignity and looks clear-eyed at the world. It's a scene which in many ways is awkward, even for its chief protagonist (*You know it's hard*, Talley sings, *to get back home / To see things die that you once loved so*), but it is in no way inauthentic. This is where the music comes from, you realize suddenly. This is what Talley has been talking about all along.

255

We make one last stop at the Rosewood Manor Rest Home in Stillwater to see James's grandmother, Mary (*Mary in her Sunday best / Wearing flowers on her dress / Waiting on the train to Cushing in the sun*). Happily his Aunt Ruth is there, too, a warm expansive woman who, somewhat to his embarrassment, smothers James with affection and urges him to shave his beard. 'Can't you get Jimmy to cut his hair?' she implores Bill Williams, to whom she has taken an instant fancy. 'You know, he'd look so pretty if he'd just let people see his face. I don't know what he wants to go around for looking like a bear.'

We are back on familiar ground now; everyone is at home with Aunt Ruth. James's grandmother, Mary, enjoys the conversation, which is mostly about old times. As we are leaving, Aunt Ruth reminds her favorite nephew, 'You would have been better off if you had listened to me a long time ago. Now what did I tell you, Jimmy? Didn't I tell you to stop fooling around with that folk music? I knew it'd never come to anything, I told him, "You go out and do some good country music." Well, he didn't say anything, but the next thing I knew I got that record in the mail. And don't you go telling these people that you were poor either. Your mother was mad at you, Jimmy, for telling that other writer you were poor. His folks weren't rich, but his mother is a schoolteacher. You be sure and get that in your story.'

I left them that night in Tulsa. In two days we had traveled close to a thousand miles, hit half a dozen radio stations, and gotten a total of four hours' sleep. From midnight to five they appeared on the Billy Parker show, then drove back through Oklahoma City and four hundred miles on to Amarillo and Lubbock. Along the way they stopped off to see Charles Townsend, author of the definitive biography of Bob Wills, and pored over some of the Wills memorabilia he has collected over the years. It was well into the next night before they finally found a Holiday Inn and fell off to sleep for the first time in forty-eight hours. The tour had only begun – it was to continue for another ten days and several thousand miles – and James Talley was in his own words 'tryin' like the devil.' Like any other working man.

INAUGURATION DAY, JANUARY 20, 1977

INSIDE the Washington, D.C., Armory, preparations for the Inaugural Ball are casually chaotic, even while the Inauguration itself is going on. The cavernous, hangar-like building is decorated in red, white, and blue; shimmering blue-spangled streamers hang down from the ceiling, while golf carts and forklifts crisscross the heavily varnished floor. Charlie Daniels's equipment arrives in a big semi; the Marshall Tucker Band has a bank of amps; early in the afternoon Guy Lombardo's Orchestra pulls up in a shining

Silver Eagle that drives out onto the floor. In the midst of all this James Talley's six-man band and equipment show up in a Ford Econoline van. 'Well, now they'll know the hillbilly band has arrived,' Talley comments wryly, as he runs through a midafternoon sound check in preparation for his appearance at this most prestigious of the seven inaugural balls.

In a certain sense James Talley really has arrived, and he clearly feels buoyed by all the acclaim and critical hosannas that have come his way. At the same time neither of his albums has sold at all well, and more and more Talley has found himself in the dangerous position of being written off as a critics' favorite—someone who could sing about 'the people' but could not make contact with them. Then, just about the time of the Democratic convention, acting on his wife Jan's suggestion, Talley sent both his albums to another self-professed populist with a Plains, Georgia, address.

'I just knew that he would like Jim's music,' Jan Talley says. 'Both Jimmy and Rosalynn Carter were out of town at the time, but we got a follow-up note from Jeff Carter, thanking Jim for the albums and saying that he would pass them on to his parents.' Nashville friends scoffed at Talley, who has been nothing if not dogged in his search for popular acceptance. Even the mailman kidded the Talleys about the Plains postmark, and Talley himself was not completely sold on Jimmy Carter until he read an interview in the *Nashville Tennesseean* in which Carter cited James Agee's *Let Us Now Praise Famous Men*, a poetic documentary of rural poverty in the thirties, as one of his favorite books. That clinched it for Talley. 'Well, when I found out that James Agee was one of his favorite authors, I knew that he couldn't be all bad.'

It was in December, while he was finishing up his third album, *Blackjack Choir*, that Talley first heard that the Carters had not only gotten his records but had listened to them and liked them as well. Capitol Records got a call from Barbara Walters's office asking for information on just who James Talley was. Talley, it turned out, had been named by the Carters in their Barbara Walters interview as one of the musicians they listened to most. That portion of the interview was not actually aired when the special ran, but it set off a chain of reverberations that eventually led to an invitation for James Talley to appear at the People's Inauguration.

It's a picturebook story that probably photographs better from a distance. Capitol has had to be pushed to the limit before they will make any financial commitment to the Inauguration appearance. There have been continual foul-ups and confusions about when and where Talley will actually perform. And, as a consequence of his new political eminence, Talley has been badgered with political questions, all of which he refers to Jan, who, he says perfectly candidly, 'is the one who reads the newspapers.' By the time that he actually goes on stage, he has been hanging around the Armory for seven or eight hours, without anything to eat being provided by the Entertainment Committee. And the performance itself, for all the excitement and glamor surrounding the occasion, and though Talley is backed by a band tight enough to call themselves 'overrehearsed,' is if anything anticlimactic, coming at the beginning of an evening which would later see the Marshall Tucker Band removed in the middle of a rousing set, to make way for Guy Lombardo's patriotic salute to the President. There are elements of disorganization and confusion, none of the songs except 'Up from Georgia' gets much of a response, and there's no question that this audience has come to celebrate (the Armory party is designated as the Georgian and Minnesotan affair), not to listen to James Talley. So that by the time Talley and the band finish their brief set, there is more of a sense of exhausted release than the jubilant elation one might have expected.

Backstage in the dressing room, though (assigned by handwritten notice to James Talley and Guy 'Lumbardo,' and secured and designated as the President's escape exit), spirits noticeably pick up. Though he is exhausted, Talley is full of conviction and full of himself. It's almost like a party made up of true believers whose belief for once is being borne out. Bill Williams, the Capitol promotion man, who has worked as hard for James Talley as he did at Epic for Charlie Rich (but with markedly dissimilar results), is on hand, looking elegant in a gray western suit. Cavellière Ketchum, Talley's photographer friend, who provided the Walker Evans-like photographs for Talley's James Agee-like text to *The Road to Torreon*, beams with happy bemusement and shows a Secret Service man his camera equipment. Talley's new high-powered manager from the Coast finds a table on which to spread out some business papers; Secret Service agents and their dogs sniff for bombs in the hallway; and James Talley talks of his plans to produce a record by B.B. King, whom he persuaded to play lead guitar on one of the cuts from Talley's new album, marking King's first appearance in twenty years on a session other than his own. Talley hopes to record B.B. doing unadulterated blues with top Nashville musicians like Johnny Gimble and Josh Graves ('You know the first record that Josh Graves's father gave to him when he was a little boy? It was Blind Boy Fuller's "Step It Up and Go." Not many people know that. That's why he's such a good bluesman') and delights in telling the story of King's modesty and gentlemanliness. 'He just said, "Today I'm your man. I'll play anything you want me to play."' Photos are taken, the Leon Morris bluegrass band jams in a corner, Talley signs an album for one of the security agents and makes plans with the local promo man for radio interviews which will start at nine o'clock the next morning. . . .

Jimmy and Rosalynn Carter made their appearance at the Armory around midnight, just before a waxlike Greg and Cher Allman made their own regal entrance. A resounding cheer went up as the President and his wife slowly proceeded to the stage and repeated remarks that had probably been made at six other inaugural parties already. While they were still shaking hands and accepting congratulations, Talley's fiddle player, John Sayles, came clattering

Jan and James Talley with Jimmy Carter at the White House.
Courtesy of James Talley.

down the backstage stairs, leaping the last six steps and proclaiming jubilantly
to James and Jan Talley, who had stationed themselves there in hopes of
presenting the Carters with a copy of the new album: 'She wants to meet you!'

In a few moments the Carters came down, surrounded by the usual retinue
of aides, Secret Service, TV technicians, reporters, and Sally Quinn. At the
bottom of the steps President Jimmy Carter paused a moment, his face opening
up in the familiar smile. 'Hello,' he said, heading for Talley. 'I recognize you
from your albums.' 'I'm Rosalynn,' said his wife softly, shaking hands. 'We
just really enjoyed your records.'

They stood and talked, the two couples, while photographers snapped
pictures, microphones were extended, lights flashed, and backstage cynics
who had been acting very dubious about James Talley all evening all of a
sudden started crowding around. 'You don't really live on that place?' said
the President, referring to the first album cover, which showed James and a
nine-months-pregnant Jan sitting on the porch of a ramshackle grocery store

259

called Talley's. 'No,' said Talley. 'And she's lost a little weight since then.' 'You have the same favorite author,' said Jan, referring to Agee. 'Yes, that was one of the few books I brought up here.' They stood and conversed quietly about the gala, about James Dickey's poetry reading the night before, about Talley's albums—creating a real and surprisingly intimate moment in the midst of this demented mob scene.

Then the Carters were gone, and it was like a dream that everyone was trying to re-create. 'I didn't look excited?' protested Talley, who looks about as excitable as Gary Cooper at his most phlegmatic. 'You know, when Nixon was inaugurated,' Talley later reminisced, 'I was working construction, driving nails all day long from eight in the morning till five at night. When Carter was elected, I was playing the Inauguration. That's got to tell you something. Somewhere in there there's some symbolism to be sifted out.' He was reminded that he had written to Rosalynn Carter and promised her the new album. Talley laughed. 'You know, when I wrote to her and said that I'd personally make sure she got a copy, I didn't know then that it would turn out literally to be so.'

NASHVILLE SKYLINE, 1978–1979

I WISH I could say that everything had continued to go as smoothly for James Talley as it appeared that it might on Inauguration Day, 1977. There was, of course, a great deal of excitement and much press ballyhoo following his presidential performance. Capitol Records ran a national ad headed 'JAMES WHO?' repeating a quote from the *Washington Star* about Talley's unexpected appearance. Once again, however, excitement didn't translate into sales, and on his *new* new manager's advice (the hotshot manager from the Coast didn't work out), Talley left Capitol in November of 1977, in the middle of a tour to promote his fourth album. The new manager unfortunately soon lost interest, as did the 'progressive' young booking agency he had found for Talley, when it became apparent that another record deal would not be immediately forthcoming. For all the praise he had gotten, no one had ever said that James Talley was going to be the next Pop Superstar, and that's the kind of potential you need to sustain managerial enthusiasm without a steady income coming in.

So James Talley embarked on the second (or third) painful stage in his Music City education. It's a familiar enough story, I'm sure, and one not worth lingering on. How old friends disappear. How bookings dry up. How critics suddenly worry that perhaps they have gone out on a limb for a failure— and quickly hedge their bets. How connections, carefully nurtured, suddenly are no longer there. In Talley's case I'm not an objective observer, since I was, and am, one of the legion of the faithful (when you sign on with James Talley, you're signing on for a crusade), but I'm sure that one of the things that hurt him most was the gratuitous cruelty of some of the defections. To many, James Talley's principles had always smacked of self-righteousness ('If I hear about his suffering one more time,' said one fellow musician, 'I'm gonna scream'), and indeed there is a strain of self-absorption in James— 'mission' would be the more positive term for it—that sometimes does not allow much room for the possibilities of dialogue. Perhaps the funniest moment I've ever shared with James stemmed from another aspect of this same self-absorption. It came during DJ Convention, one of Nashville's more spectacular week-long affairs, when James was going out for a breakfast strategy conference with two of Capitol's highest high mucky-mucks from the Coast. James was driving, and as we took a circuitous route through Nashville's back streets and alleys I thought the terrain was beginning to look familiar. We ended up in front of Rat Control headquarters, where two very squeamish Capitol executives watched Larry Sharp, a caustic maintenance worker, dangle various examples of the different breeds of Nashville rat by their tails, while current supervisor Henry Murphy—the inspiration for 'Magnolia Boy,' one of James's most beautiful songs—held his sides and laughed. When I asked James afterwards why he had done it, he said he thought it would be good for their education, and perhaps it was.

Such behavior is not calculated, however, to win friends and influence people—unless you are so great a success that it is taken as an example of winning eccentricity. With James it has in a sense created a backlash—among disaffected band members, for example, who resent having someone else's vision imposed so strongly upon them (this, despite the fact that no one could be *fairer* than James, paying the musicians as much in many instances as he is likely to make himself and carrying them through slack periods with a conscientiousness that has sometimes been the despair of friends and family). Critics, too, have seized upon the unrelenting earnestness of his work (it's not fashionable), and perhaps a nadir in this regard was reached when a Xeroxed handbill was privately circulated by a West Coast writer announcing the 'James Talley School for Salt of the Earth Folk Singers' and promising that you, too, can 'be compared to Woody Guthrie and John Steinbeck! Rush . . . application and Talent Test today!'

It's been a difficult period, obviously, for someone who believes so un-reservedly in himself and who in a sense already grabbed the brass ring when his first album was picked up by a major label and when he appeared at the Inauguration. It's almost like being exhibited as a prize fish (if you want to dismiss capitalism with this kind of metaphor) and then being tossed back into the sea. The economics alone of survival are frightening. Payments still come due at the first of the month, but there is no fixed income, and many clubs are reluctant to book an artist like Talley who comes without any

James and son, Reuben James. J. CLARK THOMAS

record company support (print advertising, radio spots, a certain guaranteed attendance). Also, with work opportunities fewer, Talley has been forced to give up his band, and as a solo act the number of places he can play is reduced even more. In this kind of situation any opportunity is seized upon. For a while Talley joked that he might become the next Marlboro man, when he did a concert sponsored by Philip Morris for the American Auto Racing Grand Prix at Watkins Glen. Other promotional appearances have been discussed (Philip Morris was at one time talking about a European tour as well as an album of songs on the Old West), and though the world has yet to see James Talley singing in Macy's window, don't bet it couldn't happen.

Such buffeting has left Talley feeling understandably frustrated and confused. One week he is appearing at the White House (he has been invited twice since the Inauguration); the next he is standing, metaphorically, in the welfare line. For a while it seemed as if his writing suffered, as he cast about for commercial formulas that could put him on a competitive basis with Fleetwood Mac or Willie Nelson, and he occasionally descended into bitterness. *People trying to go somewhere,* one as-yet-unrecorded song declared, *They will hurt you / To get their share / They don't know / And they don't care / What it does to you.* More and more, though, he has been returning to the cheerful resignation of the blues. 'Remember,' he says with conviction, 'as long as there are people on this earth, there will be the blues.'

He remains committed to the goals he originally set for himself: to achieve something significant musically, to affect people in some meaningful way. He likes to speak of himself as a craftsman. 'I don't want people to think that I'm a poet or a politician. I want them to think that I'm telling their story. I paint a picture on a human level. The whole purpose of art, as I see it, is to move people off center, to make them feel something they've felt before or think about something they've never quite put into focus for themselves. My music is no different from any other art form. It's a means of communication. It's not political, it's just life and looking at life and telling a story. Humanism might be my cause.'

STONEY
EDWARDS

A Simple Little Dream

I CAN REMEMBER the first time I heard 'Blackbird' on a country music
station on the radio. I don't think I was really listening as a guitar picked
out notes over the stark, spoken introduction about a boy getting his first
guitar made out of 'orange crates and sticks.' The voice was cracked and
country with a suggestion of Merle Haggard in the phrasing, in its emotional
catch and sharp Okie twang. Then a drumbeat signaled the beginning of the
chorus. . . . *And he said, It won't be long, son / Till I rosin up my bow.* . . .
The other instruments fell in, a lonesome fiddle echoed the second line,
Donnie Brooks's harmonica hooted—*You and me and cousin Jesse going to ride
the train*—and I almost drove off the road. For the next few lines contained a
phrase I'd never heard on the radio before: *Just a couple of country niggers /
Stealing the radio / From Georgia / On up to Bangor, Maine.* . . .*

'You know, that really tickles me. I never asked anybody about the first
time they heard that record who didn't know what was coming. But to hear
you say that—' Stoney Edwards roars with appreciation. 'You really didn't
know what was coming, did you?'

Although it was beautifully produced by its composer, Chip Taylor, and
the message ('Nobody heard the fucking message of that song') turned out
to be one of racial pride, the song was not much of a hit, and I didn't hear it
often on the radio. Moreover, it was banned on many stations, even though
Stoney Edwards had enjoyed a string of recent hits and there was a strong
promotion campaign behind the record. Letters came in from all over the
country, expressing indignation, deploring the unnecessary racial epithet,
questioning the wisdom of even releasing the record. All of this furor ignored
the fact that the singer with the dusty country accent and impeccable country
credentials was black.

---

*'Blackbird' by Chip Taylor. Copyright © 1975 by Blackwood Music, Inc. and Back Road Music.
Used by permission. All rights reserved. International copyright secured.

Hold your head high, blackbird,
Sing your pretty song
Don't let no scarecrows chase you down . . .

'I'm getting pissed off,' Stoney Edwards announces to no one in particular. An impish smile plays about his lips. 'I get pissed off every four or five years. Well, you see me wearing my black hat, don't you?' What happens when you get pissed off? someone asks. 'Last time it happened I shot a man,' he says.

Looking at Stoney Edwards, you can almost believe that he is serious. A small, wiry, mocha-colored man with wavy, reddish hair and green-flecked eyes, he carries himself with a quiet assurance that is reflected in the expressive mobility of his worn, scarred face. From a disconnected and loveless childhood in which 'I grew up not knowing what I was, Negro, Indian, or white,' he has become in the last few years the second-ranked black country and western performer, behind Charley Pride. Quite aside from the implications of being categorized as a kind of freak, of being constantly compared to a singer with whom he has little in common (Edwards writes, Pride doesn't; Edwards rarely sings love songs, Pride presents himself as a kind of dusky matinee idol; Pride capitalizes on the anomaly of a black man singing Hank Williams, Edwards by inclination, heritage, and independent attitude stands proudly in the historical mainstream of country music), Stoney Edwards has never had an easy time of it, and perhaps it is the suffering and displacement he has undergone ('I know no one's suffered more pain than I have, I mean maybe in a war, but a war can't be helped') that has enabled him to put up with all the vicissitudes of the quest for stardom, not only with good grace but with good humor.

Stoney Edwards is a wealth of country philosophy, narrative art, pithy good sense, and what has often been called mother wit. In the time that I am with him he deals with fans, DJs, radio interviewers, record company executives, all with the same mixture of poise and deferential modesty that never fails to captivate his audience. It is Nashville's annual DJ Convention week, and there is business to be discussed, a contract to be renegotiated, a new album to be planned. Stoney spends two drawn-out afternoons rehearsing at the home of his new producer, legendary producer, songwriter, bon vivant, and would-be space explorer, 'Cowboy' Jack Clement, who has lent Stoney his band for an appearance at the progressive-oriented Old Time Picking Parlor. When rehearsals go badly and Clement loses himself in astral flights of fancy or declamatory rewriting of Shakespeare, Stoney simply accommodates himself to the prevailing mood, and in fact, the band still does not know his songs or changes by show time, when they appear before a select audience that includes Emmylou Harris, Jerry Jeff Walker, the Amazing Rhythm Aces, and Guy Clark.

Stoney. Courtesy of JMI.

'What do you think was wrong with the show?' he asks afterwards with a puzzled kind of glumness. 'Well, I know I didn't exactly chew the big fat off a rat's ass.'

Still, he manages to make the best even of that. He dutifully attends cocktail parties, regales out-of-towners, wheels his black Cadillac cautiously through unfamiliar streets, and generally manages to deflect all the corporate attention he is getting, both well intended and otherwise ('All these people grinning at each other like they're loving each other, and hating each other's fucking guts all the time. There's enough hate in the world. I don't hate nobody') with a good-humored grin, a good-natured put-on, and a sad-eyed charm, which only emphasize how very different he is from all the boosters who talk so easily of art as industry, music as product, and shifting demographics. 'My songs are true,' says Stoney Edwards emphatically. 'Every fucking song I write comes from my own experience.'

> *I ain't never had nothing*
> *Anybody else would ever want*
> *I ain't never had nothing*
> *But somebody else's old junk. . . .*

Just what that experience was would make a full-length novel, for Stoney Edwards is not exaggerating when he says, 'I can't see anything in my future to equal the pain I been through.' He was born on December 24, 1929, outside of Seminole, Oklahoma, and christened Frenchy after a bootlegger who 'just came by on Christmas Eve. I was supposed to look like him, but, you know, one time I guess I didn't have nothing else to do, I went and looked him up, and, you know, he was the ugliest sonofabitch I ever did see. My father had a lot of Irish, my mother had all Indian rights, her mother was a full-blooded Indian, and she came from people who were very wealthy in land.' His mother's land didn't do her much good, though, because 'she was beat out of it by my daddy and by her own sisters, too. My mother was a very highly educated person. She was a graduate music teacher with honors, but I never took a lesson from her. To tell you the truth, man, there was so much confusion I don't remember ever living with my mother. I just remember about four incidents. One time she baked a cake, one time we was eating something, one time—oh, I don't know, I don't talk about it that much, cause it was so unpleasant, really. My mother left my baby brother when he was nine months old. That's why I never did go to school. The ones ahead of me did, but I practically raised two sisters and a brother under me. We'd feed the baby sugar tit, my mother would just come by every now and then. I used to work, farm for people, when I was small I would plow or do any kind of farmwork, really. We used to hunt, fish, we caught rabbits, we used to walk barefooted in the snow. It was rough, but at least I knew how to handle that. My life has been happy days and sad days, and I take it all as being necessary to go through to be what I am. You see, I *know* there's nothing ahead so high I can't step over it, cause I crawled so fucking low I fell out of the basement—and that's hard to do.

'Really, I don't regret anything about my childhood days. When I look back on that time—and I look back on it a lot—I enjoy remembering even the worst times, cause it's something I overcame. The only thing that I regret—and this is something that's kind of hard to explain—is that I never did call anybody Mama, I never called anybody Daddy. I called my daddy Bub and my mother Red, that was what they was to all of us seven kids. I don't know *why*. I've wondered about that a lot. Some damn things you just can't explain.

I guess I had some no-good parents. How can you have feeling for people like that?'

I got over poverty
Got over what my childhood did to me
Finally made myself a name
Got no stones to throw and no one to blame.

He lived off and on with his father and various 'uncles and aunties' all through his teenage years. His father remarried and kicked him out of the house. His uncles' primary occupation was bootlegging, an activity in which he took part with some pride and enthusiasm. It must have been a profitable enterprise, since at one time the family was operating three stills in various locations throughout the county. What appealed to Stoney most, though, was the closeness of that rough-and-tumble life, the challenge of outrunning the feds, the sense of belonging to a society where 'a man was accepted as a man by what he was, what he did, not by what the law said he was supposed to be. Hell, the law knew everybody was violating the law back then, the sheriff was probably operating a little still himself. But times was hard, and people had hearts then. If you made a good crop farming, the sheriff knew it, everybody in town would know it, and the sheriff would just say, I don't want you selling too much of that corn this year. Hell, I never thought we was doing anything really bad, oh I mean it was a little wrong, but what I mean, there wasn't any conniving and jiving about it. We weren't screwing anybody out of anything. We were just giving people what they wanted. You know, I may go back to it yet. One damn thing about it, I ain't never found anything that was more exciting than making corn whiskey.'

The two other things that preoccupied him were music and race, and in a sense these, too, would eventually come together in a fairly surprising way. 'I was never really accepted by anyone until I started singing country music. I mean, being the color that I am, having the hair and the eyes that I do, I didn't really know where I belonged, I was never really accepted by any race. Sometimes I wished I was black as a skillet or white as a damned sheet, but the way I am it's always been a motherfucker. Sometimes I'd go in an all-white place and then just leave. I mean, nobody would say anything, but that's just the way I would feel about it. Other times I'd be with all black and I'd want to hide. To the Indians I was a kind of half-breed. A lot of it could have been in my mind, but I mean it was a goddamn problem!'

Music apparently was a kind of escape valve, for Stoney Edwards occupied himself with it even at an early age. 'I've always wrote songs. Oh, you know, they wasn't songs exactly, I don't think they rhymed or anything. They'd just be about a bug crawling through the sand, an ant maybe, some kind of foolishness—I don't know, what would you call it? They wasn't poems, more like daydreams, I guess. I mean, I used to wish I was a bug sometimes. Have you ever wondered when you saw a bug crawling across the floor just where that bug was going, why he was going there, did he ever come back? Well, that's the kind of thoughts that occupied my mind, foolishness really, but I don't think it was stupid or out of line. I wrote songs because I didn't know nothing else to sing, really. I got tired of "Old Joe Clark" and church hymns and the few Bob Wills songs I got off the radio—those were the only songs I knew all the way through. So I *had* to write, I had to make up my own.

'I made my first guitar out of a bucket and a piece of wire when I was just a little bitty kid. When I was fifteen or sixteen I worked about a week in Oklahoma City where my father lived, to make enough to buy my first guitar. He used to pick a little guitar himself, him and all my uncles would play guitar and banjo, square-dance type of stuff—they would just play strictly at home—but my daddy wouldn't even let me play guitar in the house when I was trying to learn. I'd just leave the house, go to a neighbor's, and then wait until he went to bed before I came home.

'Today? Today my father is very, very proud of me, but I can't feel toward him like I know I ought to. It's just something within you. You can forgive, but you can't forget. I mean, it's nothing to be proud of, but what's true is true, even if sometimes the truth hurts. I know he loves me a helluva lot more than I love him, but I just can't help but think if he could have given me that love when I needed it how much good it might have done me. Oh, I don't know. Maybe what they done is better in a way. I think of all kinds of excuses, and I've started believing them in a way. Maybe it made me stronger in myself, you know. Maybe if they'd been behind me more, it would have been harder for me to be what *I* wanted to be—which is a musician—they would have wanted me to be a doctor or a lawyer or an Indian chief. Today he comes to all my dances, but sometimes I don't even go to his table. Sometimes I wish he wouldn't even come.'

His mother died in 1950, just before he left for California when 'the feds got really rough' and persuaded him that 'there wasn't no future in corn whiskey. When she passed I didn't even shed a tear, but, you know, I just found out she was a very, very lonely woman. She had her whole family deny her, she had her husband beat her out of her rights, you know now there's not enough sadness in my heart for her. Every time I think about it I start getting pissed off. You know how miserable she was? Two weeks before she died she went out to see my sister in California. She hadn't never been to California before, but she told my sister, "Don't send me back to that same cemetery where all my family is buried. I don't ever want to see them again." So there she is buried out in some lonely cemetery out in Los Angeles. There's no end to how disappointed she must have been. Sometimes I think that's why she told us not to call her Mother.'

Daddy had a 1941 Ford
When I was just about ten years old
We used to listen to Hank and Lefty on the radio
'Why don't you love me like you used to do?'
And 'Just look what thoughts will do.'
Old Hank and Lefty raised my country soul. . . .*

He moved to Oakland and then to Richmond, California, where he worked in a car wash, then as a maintenance man, machinist, construction worker, and finally crane operator in a shipyard. In 1954 he married his wife, Rosemary, who, along with most of their friends, couldn't understand what drew him to country music. 'Oh, some of them would say, "Hey, man, I hear you're still singing that shitkicking music." And I would say, Yeah. But others would just say, "Hey, man, baby, more power to you, cause that's what it's all about, man, do *your* thing." See, the thing about it was, I always did listen to any kind of music. I could go out and have fun even if I went to a blues club where they was playing nothing but blues. I love good gospel music. Right today if a jazzman is playing his jazz and he's doing it well, I give him all the credit in the world, even though it's not my bag. But I knew what I liked, and, you know, my wife finally admitted to me, "You know, I've listened to you sing country music for fifteen years now, and I believe it's something you really want to do!"'

He never thought of making a career out of singing in any case, and few people even knew of his interest in it, since mostly he just fooled around in the garage, composing songs on a portable tape recorder. Because he cannot read or write, he learned to carry two or three songs in his head at once and would work on them at every possible opportunity. Occasionally he would get up and sing a song in a bar, and that was how he acquired the name Stoney, in about as cavalier a manner as he had become Frenchy, when a patron, forgetting his name, declared: '"I'm stoned, and he probably is, too." From that night on I was Stoney.'

Then in 1968 he suffered the disabling accident that would eventually lead to his career in music. While working as a forklift operator, he was trapped inside a sealed-up tank and suffered severe carbon dioxide poisoning. For almost two years he was either in a semi-coma or 'just out of my mind crazy. I didn't know what the fuck was going on, and they didn't give me nothing for it—I found this out afterwards—because there isn't any cure. The doctors said they was just waiting for me to die. You see, usually 8 percent will kill you, and they told me I had something like 80 percent in my bloodstream. I don't know, the only thing I can figure is that it was all that smoking I done all those years that worked to offset the carbon dioxide poison. Of course I don't know. That's just a theory.' He was unmanageable in any case, refused social security, could not be helped by anyone except his wife, and but for her would have been committed to a mental institution. When he recovered he had no job ('I still haven't been cleared to go back to work'), no money, no prospects. Six months later he was in the recording studio. 'I went from shipyard to graveyard to Capitol Records.'

He arrived at Capitol by an even odder series of coincidences. With no hope of going back to work, he apparently decided to concentrate more seriously on his music. He began writing songs again, though during his illness his daughter had inadvertently destroyed the tape that contained all his early compositions ('Sometimes a line or two will come into my head, but I racked my brains so much I got headaches, so I just kind of quit thinking about it'). He also got involved in a benefit that was being given for Bob Wills, who had only recently been incapacitated by the first in a series of

Bob Wills. Courtesy of Douglas B. Green.

271

strokes. Because Stoney had been such a fan of Wills as a boy, and probably because it's the kind of thing he would do for anyone in need, he helped to set up the benefit, throwing himself into all the details of organizing and publicizing the event. When the day came, someone remembered that Stoney Edwards, too, was something of a singer, and he was given a one-number spot on the program. He sang 'Mama's Hungry Eyes.' A Richmond lawyer named Ray Sweeney heard him and took him down to Capitol; it was just at this point that Charley Pride was really starting to happen. 'A week and a half after that I was on Capitol Records.' It seems hardly ironic to him that 'what I wanted to do all my life through Bob Wills, I got to do it by doing this for him.' He had been at his lowest point, feeling helpless, despairing, a drain upon his family. He had even determined to leave them, 'so that there would be one less mouth to feed.' Then the record contract came along and was reinforced by the success of 'Two Dollar Toy,' his first single and, like all his songs, based on a true incident.

> Last night I woke up
> Like I done many times before
> But this time I had evil on my mind
> I quietly packed my clothes
> And headed for the door
> But in the doorway stumbled and fell over a toy.
>
> My little girl says, 'Daddy, cover me'
> And 'Daddy, please don't go'
> That's when the love in my heart
> Overruled a thought I had in my mind
> Last night a two-dollar toy made a million-dollar daddy out of me.

Stoney Edwards's musical output from 1970 to 1977 (when he was dropped by Capitol) was considerable. There were five or six albums, a number of good-sized hits, and some enterprising choices for material, including Jesse Winchester's 'Mississippi, You're on My Mind' and Leonard Cohen's 'Bird on a Wire.' All of the songs are enhanced by Stoney's voice, a strong vibrato-laden instrument with a wide range, bass drop, and the sincerity to wring emotion even from otherwise pedestrian vehicles. The songs are oddly tinged as well by the listener's inevitable awareness of race. 'Mississippi, You're on My Mind,' for example, takes on different connotations when you realize that the singer is black. 'Yankee Lady' or even 'Hank and Lefty Raised My Country Soul,' with its explicit statement of debt to Hank Williams and Lefty Frizzell, are similarly affected. This despite the unmistakable twang in Stoney's voice that betrays nothing more than his origins as an Oklahoma dirt farmer. He has compiled in any case a solid body of achievement. Nothing that he has done to date, however, even hints at what Stoney Edwards is capable of.

The reasons for this are twofold. The first is that very few of the songs that Stoney Edwards has written have actually been recorded, and when they have been recorded they haven't been recorded right. This would not be particularly significant if it were not for the fact that Stoney Edwards is a great writer. I don't know if words set down on the printed page can convey the strength of his compositions, but after listening to Stoney run through recorded work, unpublished material, and songs in progress, it seems to me his writing can be compared favorably to that of two heroes of his, Merle Haggard and Lefty Frizzell. What is most impressive about it is the weight of his compositions, the wealth of detail, the selectivity of his art. Every story paints a picture, even novelty numbers like 'My Uncle Nupi' or 'Head Bootlegger Man' or 'The Fishing Song,' which depend for their effect on throwaway lines like, *With a $50 reel and a $40 pole / All I'm doing is catching cold / I'll never go fishing again.*

'What it is, I don't lose the strength of the song. I don't seem to lose any power, you know what I mean? Like some songs will have a good idea, they'll have a strong verse and then they'll just fade out into the chorus— well, my songs are strong all the way through.' His own assessment seems pretty much on the mark, and recognizing the care with which the songs are crafted, the painstaking selection of specifics, the occasionally startling use of metaphor, you wish sometimes that Stoney Edwards were able to read the poetry that he would obviously so much enjoy. Stoney takes another view. 'I'm glad I can't read,' he insists. 'It scares the shit out of me sometimes how close I came to being an educated man. What I'm saying is, when I think of how many things that's written about that's copied—well, I *can't* copy anybody else. What I write comes from a natural feeling inside myself. What I write has to be true.'

Perhaps he's right. Certainly what comes out in Stoney's writing, apart from its idiosyncrasy of structure (which can itself be a strength), isn't hindered by lack of education. What comes out on record, however, is quite a different story, and that is the other reason so little that Stoney Edwards has done to date reflects his real capabilities. Surprisingly none of the pat explanations apply. Capitol seems to have been behind him, and Chip Taylor is only the latest in a long line of producers who have honestly believed in Stoney Edwards. None, however, has known precisely how to serve him or how to bring out the eloquent simplicity of his style. There have been choirs; there has been unnecessary instrumentation; 'Talking About Jesus,' one of his most beautiful compositions, with the potential to be a religious standard, was recorded out of tune; *Valley of the Giants*, a concept album of tributes to the great figures in country and western, was never released; even Chip Taylor's impeccably produced *Blackbird* session, while well intended, did not leave enough room for Stoney Edwards.

'The trouble with Stoney is that he doesn't speak up,' one observer says.

Stoney Edwards with friends. Courtesy of JMI.

'He knows what's going on. He just doesn't say anything.' Seeing him on a day-to-day basis, you realize that this is indeed true. While he will blow up over all the 'bullshit' or express private skepticism about methods and/or results, when it comes to the sticking point, he will always go along. If you ask him about Capitol, despite any reservations or frustrations he may have had, despite all his disappointments, he will tell you, 'Capitol's not responsible for me being misused. A man uses himself. Other people may look at it differently, but I think I have not given *them* a fair shake. You see, the way I look at it, when they draw up a contract, it's merely guesswork, there's no guarantees on either side. I don't think I have anything coming from them. If I get a favor, fine—but *nobody owes me a damned thing.*' Such a policy of accommodation has made Stoney Edwards almost universally well-liked, but it has not necessarily helped him to realize his vision.

> *I had a simple little dream*
> *That got lost somewhere between*
> *My searching for fortune and fame*
> *Now after all of this confusion*
> *I done come to this conclusion*
> *That dreams are cheap if you keep 'em in your mind. . . .*

The last few years have not been easy for Stoney Edwards. Things were going well until he moved to San Antonio, to please his wife and because it offered a more central location for Nashville recording trips and the dances that he plays throughout Texas and Oklahoma. At that point he had a house in Oakland, a trailer, and a new home in Texas. Due to mismanagement and a run of bad luck, he had to sell the first two and very nearly lost the third. Subsequently his bus was on the verge of being repossessed and he 'came close to having a nervous breakdown,' doing singles and one-nighters to dig himself out of the financial hole that success had left him in. The irony of fate is not lost upon him. 'I discovered,' he says, 'that the ladder I climbed didn't have any steps on the way down.' He was depressed for a time and stopped writing songs, but after a while, true to his nature, he bounced back. 'You know,' he says, 'I learn something every time I make a mistake. I learn that I don't ever ever want to make that sonofabitch again.'

> *Never thought of it too much*
> *Till I started trying to touch*
> *The dream that I'm now reaching for . . .*

Today things are looking up again. For his regular gigs he is back to working with his own band, and in 1978 he signed a record contract with Jack Clement's newly revived JMI label. He has started writing again, too, and for the first time has begun to play a little guitar on stage, setting his own rhythm and, surprisingly, incorporating some blues into his act. The arrangement with Clement could be profitable for both, if Clement can only subordinate his storied eccentricity to his newfound faith in 'systems' and 'business.' The potential for crossover still remains. Nonetheless Stoney is hedging his bets. He has recently discovered a will that would invalidate his aunts' long-ago sale of his mother's land. With a lawyer from Oklahoma City he is investigating the possibility that 92 million barrels of oil have been taken out of what should be his (and his brothers', sisters', and cousins') land. If the lawsuit should succeed, and Stoney is fully confident that it will, he will become—not a rich man, because he isn't greedy, but comfortable. His eyes twinkle with excitement more at the intricacies of the case than at the prospect of the money.

How do you feel? someone asks him. 'Terrible,' Stoney characteristically responds, then grins and picks his teeth.

'I want to be remembered,' he sums up, 'as a good singer, as a good person, as someone that people loved, but most of all as someone that people miss. That's my goal in country music. If I can achieve those three things, I don't have to be the greatest star. The best can always be replaced, you know, has to be—but you never replace the good ones. I want to be remembered for a hundred years as a good man and as a good country singer. You see, I've had my shit together for a long time, man, it's just that up until now it's been too heavy to pick up.'

Part Four

THE BLUES
ROLL ON

T HE MUSIC that I first started writing about, and my first love (after
baseball), was the blues. It was certainly remote, and there was, to me,
something intensely romantic about it, when I first started listening, at the
age of fifteen. More than anything, though, it grabbed me at some gut level.
As Charlie Feathers's friend, Slick, said of Charlie's music: 'I don't care what
you say, you get the best music in the world in these little juke joints and
holes in the wall, because this is where they always sing from the heart.'
And that's what blues is: music from the heart.

There was a time when the blues was popular with white audiences. Of
course the blues started out as a popular music, but rock 'n' roll—which we
all hailed, along with Chuck Berry—delivered us not only from the days of
old but from most regional ethnic music (even though rock 'n' roll, when it
began, was little more than a regional ethnic music itself). In any case the
popularity of rock 'n' roll—and the opportunities it gave to black performers
particularly to dream of success on a much vaster scale—effectively killed off
the blues as a popular black music. However, there was a time in the mid-to-
late sixties, in the flush of good feeling that arose from the discovery of a

Mississippi dancers. VALERIE WILMER

so-called Woodstock nation, when the blues undeniably achieved a certain liberal cachet. There was a burst of recording activity, the most astonishing obscurities were unearthed, and artists like B.B. King gained the very real global popularity that they still enjoy to one extent or another today.

Looking back on it, or even examining the phenomenon at the time, one would have little hesitation in saying that it was an artificial flowering. Little good work came out of it (or perhaps it would be more accurate to say that the proportion of good work to bad was staggeringly small), and more often than not the musicians' raised expectations were only destined to be cruelly dashed after the first taste of celebrity. In the seventies the blues once again went underground. In fact they went so far underground that sometimes you suspected they were no longer around. With white critics, who had once paid lip service to 'the sufferings of a noble people,' the blues became almost an object of scorn, a running joke, with references scattered throughout all the trendy journals to 'da blooze,' and the popular success of the parodistic Blues Brothers only reinforcing the low esteem in which the music was now held.

My own feeling is that this kind of sophisticated mockery only represents a legitimization of the very racism that once fueled the blues' short-lived revival. Perhaps, though, that is too earnest a response, and I am giving more credit to intentional design than ought to be assigned. Indeed in the last few years, though the number of new blues releases is way down, and the major labels have all dropped their blues lines, there has been a real upgrading in the quality of what *has* been released and a resurgence of popular interest in established figures like Muddy Waters and new artists like Son Seals. My trip to Chicago in 1977 (documented here in JUKE JOINT BLUES) was a reaffirmation of faith in the face of my own doubts of the blues' survival. And, of course, Big Joe Turner, the Boss of the Blues, just rolls on, an impervious force of nature, while the music of Howlin' Wolf and Otis Spann will live on long after all the trends have disappeared.

One of the things that was most interesting to me in doing this book was to discover the extent to which the blues had invaded the lives and music of nearly every artist I was writing about. Ernest Tubb recalled listening to the records of Ethel Waters and Bessie Smith. For Mickey Gilley — growing up with his cousin, Jerry Lee Lewis, in rural Ferriday, Louisiana — Haney's Big House, a local black juke joint, was the source of his style. Elvis, of course, was the first widely successful white blues singer. Sleepy LaBeef credits gospel singer Sister Rosetta Tharpe with providing rock 'n' roll with its stylistic inspiration, and Johnny Cash and Carl Perkins echo this sentiment. Hank Williams, Jr. plays Jimmy Reed tunes for relaxation. Charlie Rich goes off to visit his father's sharecropper, C.J., who taught him how to play blues piano. There is scarcely any example of native American music that is altogether free of black influence, in fact, and that is why it really doesn't matter if the blues is or is not a fashionable item. If it isn't on the airwaves, it's always in the air, the most arresting, viscerally exciting music that I've ever known. As Rufus Thomas said, in a statement that can stand as an epigraph for this book: 'Blues will always be here. Of all the other music in the world, watch it—it'll tail out and change. But you'll always be able to hear twelve-bar blues. Always. It's the backbone of American music—blues and country, cause country and western and blues are right there together, just that close, and gospel. Everything else comes from that.'

THE HOWLIN'
WOLF

If you ain't thought about, you ain't talked about.
And they talks about me every day.

BIG FOOT CHESTER (courtesy of Dick Shurman)

H OWLIN' WOLF was larger than life in every respect. As an entertainer, as an individual, and as a bluesman, he was outsize, unpredictable, and always his own man.

He was a great blues singer whose music was always resonant with personal association. Like Jerry Lee Lewis and James Brown, great entertainers in other fields, he also possessed that quality of egocentric self-absorption which is the mark of the true showman. To many people this may seem contradictory, as if the task of 'entertaining' an audience could only dilute the emotional essence of the blues, but Wolf proved that to its natural audience blues is not all pain and suffering. It is instead a kind of release. When you listen to the blues you should be moved; doubtless you should take the 'deep' blues of a singer like Muddy Waters or Howlin' Wolf with the same sense of dignity with which they are intended. You should also come away with a smile on your lips.

The first time I met Howlin' Wolf he was as oblivious to my existence as he was every time thereafter. That was all right with me. I was honored to be in his presence. Someone was reading him an article I had written which described his performance. It spoke of vulgarity that carried with it its own conviction. It referred to his elephantine dance, the magnitude of his presence. It quoted lyrics from his songs, which Wolf repeated with great gusto, as if the thought had never occurred to him. 'Three hundred pounds of heavenly joy, mmm hmmm,' he would declare approvingly, savoring the phrase that had been meant to describe him. 'Where'd you get that from, boy? You make that up out of your own head?' I swallowed my embarrassment with relief. I had no idea what his perception of the situation was, but I felt that on some level we had connected.

Howlin' Wolf was a totally enigmatic personality. He was a man at once complex, driven, and altogether impossible to read. To his friends and con-

At home. PETE WELDING

temporaries I think he was as much of a mystery as to the casual outsider, an enormous man (six foot three, over 275 pounds in his prime) of great placidity, sudden explosiveness, and an infinite capacity for hurt. To Johnny Shines, who idolized Wolf so much that he followed him around as a young man and was himself called Little Wolf, 'I first met [him], I was afraid of Wolf. Just like you would be of some kind of beast or something. Because it was an old saying, you know, people thought about magic and all such things as that, and I come along and say, a guy that played like Wolf, he'd sold his soul to the devil. And at that time Wolf had the most beautiful skin anybody ever seen in your life, look like you can just blow on it and it'd riffle. And I was kind of afraid of Wolf, I mean just to walk up and put your hand on him. Well it wasn't his size, I mean what he was doing, the way he was doing, I mean the sound that he was giving off.'

Wolf was the kind of person around whom legends accumulate because of the belief he invested in those legends himself. As a young man he was

The Howlin' Wolf Band, 1954, with Hubert Sumlin,
Hosea Kennard, Jody Williams, and unidentified fan.
Courtesy of Dick Shurman and Jody Williams.

called 'Bullcow' and 'Foot,' but it was as the Wolf that he found his true persona. It was the mighty Wolf when he was feeling good. 'I'm a taildragger,' he would declare, quoting the song. 'I wipes out my tracks.' When he was feeling sorry for himself, though, which was often, he became 'the wolf that howls, trying to be satisfied.' He was a mountain wolf, a timber wolf, a lone wolf, a howlin' wolf. But always the Wolf. Always himself. He took his legend seriously.

He was born, improbably enough, Chester Arthur Burnett, after our twenty-first President, on a plantation between West Point and Aberdeen, Mississippi, on June 10, 1910. He grew up listening to Charley Patton, Son House, Willie Brown, and the Jackson school of Tommy Johnson with its delicate falsetto moan, in the midst of a Mississippi blues tradition so vital that it remains the underpinning for much of today's popular music. It is a tradition in which the question of authorship is almost moot, feeling is prized over originality, roots are extended but never abandoned, and oral transmission has been the sole means for keeping faith.

Wolf was well schooled in this tradition. Although he stayed on farming with his father ('He wasn't no blues singer, but he was a great ballplayer — country ballplayer') until he was nearly forty, he was known as a bluesman from an early age. 'I played in the South ever since 1928, the fifteenth day of January. Guitar and mouth organ both, cause that's what had me interested. The first piece I ever played in my life was by Charley Patton, was a tune about "Hook up my pony and saddle up my black mare."'

He is remembered singing on the streets and back out on the plantations and juke joints of countless little Mississippi towns all through the thirties, playing guitar and rack harmonica together, in a style, he said, like Jimmy Reed's. He was never much of a guitar player, and even his harp playing, encouraged though it was by his brother-in-law of the time, Sonny Boy Williamson (this was Sonny Boy II, Rice Miller, wizard of the mouth harp), was always fairly rudimentary. It was his voice that was his crowning glory, a voice that could fairly be called inimitable, cutting with a sandpaper rasp and overwhelming ferocity but retaining at the same time a curious delicacy of shading, a sense of dynamics and subtlety of approach which set it off from any other blues singer in that rich tradition. In addition it combined the rough phrasing of Patton with the vocal filigree of Tommy Johnson and its familial descendant, the blue yodel of Jimmie Rodgers, the white country singer whom Wolf always admired. This became Wolf's howl.

He moved to West Memphis in 1948 and put together a band, including a very young James Cotton and Little Junior Parker, which broadcast over station KWM, where Sonny Boy, too, had a spot. This was the time when B.B. King had first come to Memphis, Rufus Thomas was just beginning his broadcasts on WDIA, and Sam Phillips was opening up his Memphis Recording Service on Union Avenue. Ike Turner, then a teenage talent scout, brought Wolf into Phillips's studio, and the resulting records were sold to Chess. When the Bihari brothers, who had had a previous understanding with Phillips, started putting out records of Wolf on RPM, Leonard Chess came down to protect his investment and spirited Wolf away to Chicago. It was 1952.

His sound never really changed. It was the same in 1975 as it had been twenty-five years earlier. More than any other singer of his generation, he was indifferent to trends, both because he lacked the musical flexibility to take advantage of them and, more significantly, because he always knew his own mind. More than any other musician that I've known, Howlin' Wolf was determined to present his own music in his own way. His blues continued to reflect the conditions from which they first had sprung – for Howlin' Wolf there was little distinction between art and life.

His performances, as a result, were of an unpredictable nature, because, quite naturally, they reflected how he felt. His blues could be savage, doleful, elated, mournful by turns, depending on his mood, and the fascination of his performance, aside from the towering nature of the music itself, was his almost constant sense of engagement. I saw Wolf in just about every conceivable setting over the last ten years, and he nearly always managed to rise above his surroundings, not so much by the novelty of his act (despite the extravagant trappings, he was always recognizably Wolf, and his blues never departed from their traditional pattern) as by his wholehearted assent to the moment. He accepted the adulation of the Rolling Stones, with whom he appeared on the Shindig TV show in 1965, and the response of a South Side Chicago audience with equal aplomb. He put every bit of himself into his performance, whether it took place in a jammed concert hall or there were only ten people in the room.

This was something about which he rarely spoke. He just liked 'to entertain the peoples,' he would say disarmingly in interviews, but put him on a stage and a fierce drive took over. At Ann Arbor this led him to do his best to prevent his long-time Chicago rival, Muddy Waters ('I never did quit trying to be friends,' commented Wolf disingenuously), from even taking the stage by stretching out his act long past its allotted limit. At Newport it caused him to roll around on the stage, a broom between his legs, wearing overalls and singing Robert Johnson's 'Dust My Broom.' Like any great entertainer he sized up his surroundings and adapted himself accordingly. At Club 47 in Cambridge, his presence was awesome as he paced the tiny platform, laid a meaty hand against a support pillar, and proceeded to exert himself as if he were about to bring the building down around his shoulders. He acted out his songs, sometimes deliberately, as he would sight a train ('Smokestack Lightnin''), run alongside, and hop aboard; other times more broadly, as he tottered about the bandstand, stuck out his lips, let the microphone droop between his legs, popped his eyes, and declared, 'Great Googly Moogly.' He was beyond questions of taste and vulgarity. If you had asked him, and

Muddy and Wolf: a rare reunion. Ann Arbor, 1969. TOM COPI

he was in the right mood, he would have declared a fierce racial pride, and indeed he was scornful of Muddy—though it may only have been spite—for carrying white players in his band. What he did on stage, though, like his multiplicity of moods, transcended reason, had an interior logic of its own that made sense, but only if you knew Wolf.

His music was equally unpredictable. He played what he felt, just called out to the band for 'a slow blues in D,' and let them pick it up as they went along. The result was a musical performance that was often disorganized but was always somehow right, focused as it was on Wolf's presence, the force of his personality. He possessed, too, an almost limitless repertoire and musical memory, which could cast back over a period of fifty years and come up with no one knew what unlikely treasures—a Charley Patton tune, Robert Johnson's 'Hellhound on My Trail,' an unrecorded standard, a classic from his early years. He became in this sense a unique, and unlikely, repository of tradition, but more than that, at a time when other artists were content to settle on a fairly established routine, Wolf continued to challenge himself (and his band). He didn't care much about the words, but when he got hold of a verse that he liked he sang it over and over, chewing on it, taking it to the top of his range, creating an extraordinary tension, a unique dynamic, before he was willing to let go.

285

Portrait of Wolf, ca. 1970. Courtesy of Chess Records.

For the last few years of his life he was a sick man. He had several heart attacks, and in 1973 an auto accident sent him flying through the windshield of his car, causing the kidney damage that eventually contributed to his death. As soon as he got out of the hospital, he went back on the road again, and indeed he was performing until the final month of his life. I saw him often in the last few years, and I don't think it's romantic projection to imagine that he made a conscious choice that this was what he wanted to do and nothing short of dying was going to stop him from doing it. In every city where he was booked, he had to check around for a VA hospital (Wolf served in the army in World War II; it made him nervous, he said) to make sure he could get dialysis treatment for his kidneys. He wore a bandage over the catheter attachment in his arm. He was slower, and sometimes his eyes took on a benign, dreamy expression. He was unchanged.

The music that he made at the end was incomparable, the effort heroic. He was forced to pace himself, and Eddie Shaw, his bandleader-manager, firmly limited him to half a dozen songs in a set. Usually he took it fairly easy for the first two or three, but even when he was not singing he sat up on stage, his legs spread wide, head tilted back, orchestrating the music with a beautiful, beatific smile and an impatience to get on with his part of the show. Sometimes his body failed him, and sometimes he just overexerted himself, carried away by the enthusiasm of the moment. Then Shaw would take the microphone from him, and he would sit there, eyes cast down, color drained, shaking his head at this betrayal. It sounds grotesque, and it was often frightening, but Wolf was never an object of pity, and each time that I saw this happen he roused himself as if by some supernatural effort and seized the microphone back, singing and blowing his harmonica with a force and a determination that seemed unwilling ever to quit. It was a little like James Brown with his cape, but this was real life, a continuing and weird drama of affirmation.

He remained himself. In some ways he was more benign, but in others he was the same old Wolf, hurt and suspicious, sad-spoken, paranoid, reproachful. Why had his piano player, a veteran Chicago bluesman, been replaced? 'He wanted too much of the spotlight,' says Wolf with a mournful expression. 'He wanted to be equal with me, and you can't do that. He made an ass of himself. Age got nothing to do with it.' Did he still have land in Arkansas? 'I ain't selling that. You got to have some place to go when they kick you out.' Once I asked him if he had gotten a story I had written, which I had sent some months before. 'No,' he said, no more recognizing me this time than the first time we met. 'They done stole it from me.' That was his way, and I don't think anyone ever fully understood it. At the University of Vermont in 1974, Johnny Shines and I were wandering around backstage when we came across Wolf in a broom closet! Shines, I think, was as nonplussed as I, and, trying to make conversation, started talking about fishing in Alabama. Wolf just stared blankly ahead of him, until Johnny, whose admiration for Wolf never diminished, simply gave up the effort. I saw Wolf get really angry only once, when a young white girl danced around him, touching Wolf's face teasingly with her hand. Wolf's expression grew blacker and blacker, until at last he brushed her away with one huge paw, like a god swatting a fly.

I like to remember the last time I saw him, in the spring of 1975. Wolf looked well, thinner than he once had been, but he had been sick for so long now it seemed as if he might never die. He did the kind of set that had become characteristic over the last few years, starting out slowly, drawing out the songs to a comfortable length, generally rationing his energies but unquestionably involved, like a good schoolteacher holding class. The last song of his set was one of his earliest hits, a blues that by its title alone typifies many of the attitudes and concerns of Howlin' Wolf's music. 'I Asked for Water (She Gave Me Gasoline)' is an irony that goes back to Tommy Johnson and the era before the blues began. It is a song that is accompanied by Wolf's wordless falsetto moan and remains a most vivid example of the living tradition of the blues. This particular night Wolf caught fire for the first time all evening, singing the song with all the power and force that he had invested in it for the last forty years. Over and over he repeated the familiar verses, until at last Eddie Shaw attempted to intervene. 'The great Howlin' Wolf!' he announced. 'Let's hear it for the Howlin' Wolf!' Wolf just kept on singing, moaning softly in the background, interrupting every time Shaw tried to get him off the stage. In the end, of course, the song went on until Howlin' Wolf was through with it, and even Eddie Shaw had to smile.

OTIS
SPANN

Blues Is a Man's Best Friend

I CAN WORK with pretty near any blues singer there is, I don't care what kind. As long as they play the blues, and, uh, rock 'n' roll, I can work with them.'

Not many blues players could make that kind of claim, but Otis Spann, whose piano playing was the driving force in the Muddy Waters band for nearly twenty years, could speak with authority. More than almost any other blues instrumentalist, he brought a unique combination of forcefulness and sensitivity to his playing, and whether he was accompanying Chuck Berry or Little Walter or Sonny Boy Williamson or Buddy Guy, he always indicated his sympathy for their style by some subtle variation in his approach. He left his mark on every record on which he played, and when he died in 1970 at the age of forty, there was no one to take his place.

He was a mournful, diminutive, and slightly bewildered-looking man who seemed happiest when he was drinking or playing the piano. In recent years he had had a lot of problems with his health, but he always retained that gentle, almost innocent quality that characterized his musical presence as much as his personal manner. For years he was a fixture in his half-brother Muddy's band, and you could look forward to seeing him, whenever Muddy came to town, both in his role of accompanist and as a featured soloist. From his familiar position, half-hidden and pushed into a corner by the oversized grand piano, he would hold court, carrying on a running conversation with the tables around him and offering well-meant, gratuitous advice to an audience that could barely pick up his words. He played with his head flung back, swinging his legs loosely off the floor and facing the piano at an angle with a fine disregard for the microphone. Always he seemed lost in the music, and his vague speech and abstracted manner made an odd contrast with his powerful and impassioned singing and playing.

He always wanted to be a musician. From the time that he was a little boy in Jackson, Mississippi, he played the piano and sang. At eight he won a talent contest at the Alamo Theater, and after that he would appear with the stage show. 'Mr. Alamo, he used to send for me, you know, to play for the vaudevilles. Man, I had a little tuxedo and hat, it was really something.'

In 1951 he came to Chicago to join Muddy's band. The group consisted of Muddy, Jimmy Rogers, Spann, and Little Walter, and in addition to being the best group Muddy ever put together, it was undoubtedly one of the finest blues bands ever assembled. 'Little Walter broke that up. Little Walter broke that up when he made "Juke." See, we were down in Louisiana, and Little Walter had made it, but it hadn't been released. So he heard it on the radio one day, next thing you look up and Walter was gone. See, you get a record out, you figure, well, now I got something, now I can make it. But that's wrong, that record may go no further than across the street.'

Otis stayed with Muddy for the next fifteen years, assuming musical leadership of the group in the absence of another virtuoso like Little Walter. It was his piano that drove the band on the uptempo numbers like 'Mojo,' and on the slower songs he could always be counted on to provide a characteristically dark and somber mood. His vocals, too, came to be featured more and more, and his warm, hoarse, slightly boozy voice was a perfect vehicle for the kind of melancholy, intimate blues he had taken up from his idol, Big Maceo (after Maceo had a stroke, Spann occasionally played left hand for him).

Over the years he and Muddy worked out an almost perfect understanding. 'See, my blues is not as easy to play as most people think they are,' Muddy

Otis Spann with Smokey Smothers, guitar, Chicago, 1959.
Courtesy of *Living Blues.* GEORGE ADINS

Otis and Muddy, London, 1963. VALERIE WILMER

said. 'Cause here, this is it. The average man used to playing ordinary twelve-bar blues, but me, I makes my blues in different numbers, sometimes thirteen, fifteen, fourteen, you know, just the way I feel. So a man playing with me gotta follow me, don't follow hisself. Well, see, Spann, that's the way he was. If you playing blues, the man can play with you. He don't care what kind of time you break, he can break it with you. That's a man who was raised singing the blues, he was raised in Mississippi and he *knows* the blues.'

Otis always spoke of Muddy with the greatest admiration and respect. He lived for years in the basement apartment of Muddy's house, and when he died he was living just around the corner in a shabby apartment building that was in sharp contrast to his brother's immaculately kept home. He referred to Muddy frequently when I saw him the week before his death, and pictures of Muddy performing were the only evidence of his occupation. 'Oh, Muddy a good man. Muddy Waters the best bandleader that I know of. He really is. You know, Muddy used to drink hisself, oh man we used to have some good times out there.'

With admirer, Croydon, England, 1963. VALERIE WILMER

He went out on his own in the late sixties. 'See, things were kind of slow for a while. I told Muddy, I said, well, things are getting slower with the blues. You know how the blues do. They'll die down, and then they'll pick back up again. So I said, instead of both of us in the same band together playing the blues, let's split it up, and maybe what we're doing together, with the band split up, we still can make it. So he said okay.' Spann wanted to give his wife Lucille a chance to sing, too, and they had a fair amount of success together. But, he said, 'I changed my style of playing for a while, which I shouldn't have did. For a long time, you know, I fell back. But then I went back to my old gimmick.'

He was proud of his success. The ballrooms and college circuit may seem antiseptic, compared with the vitality of Chicago's South Side. But blues doesn't hold much of a living either, Otis said, 'unless you make it high as me and Muddy.' And he didn't really consider that he had strayed so far afield, since he continued to record with Muddy and to work—on record anyway—with a great many of the South Side singers like Walter Horton and Johnny Young and Junior Wells and Johnny Shines. For each of them Otis was the ideal accompanist because he always seemed to sense just what to put in and what to leave out, and he never did anything less than what was required.

When he died, everyone felt his loss. He was a popular singer and well liked by his fellow musicians. When I saw him he was very weak but talked about gaining his strength back so he could go out on the road again. He had played in Boston just the week before and was planning to work a solo gig in Wisconsin some time soon. We talked a little about the problem of material, since in the past year alone he had released at least a half dozen albums. What did he look for in a song? I asked him. 'Oh, that's easy,' he said, and his painfully emaciated face creased in a smile. 'You always looking for a hit. You *know* that.'

Otis never had a hit, but he left a body of music that was moving and deeply felt and, as he sang on one of his earliest records:

> *When you in trouble blues is a man's best friend*
> *Blues ain't gonna ask you where you going*
> *And the blues don't care where you been.*
>
> *We just can't let the blues die, the blues don't mean you no harm*
> *People, we can't let the blues die, blues don't mean no harm*
> *I'm gonna move back in the lowlands, that's where the blues come from.*

That's the strangely charged outlook of the blues—an optimism that springs paradoxically from the embrace of its opposite quality—but when you listen to Spann's music today, nearly ten years after his death, you know that his blues will survive.

Backstage at the Apollo, 1966. PETE LOWRY

POSTSCRIPT

In a way the picture suggested by this chapter may be too elegiac. Not as far as Otis Spann is concerned – Spann to my mind was the sweetest and gentlest of men. But how was it that I happened to interview him only four or five days before he died? The story of how this came about may modify a little the impression (perhaps engendered by the portrait itself) that in death, at least, Otis Spann received proper recognition.

Briefly what happened is that I received a telephone call from a friend at *Rolling Stone* who told me that Spann was dying and that *Rolling Stone* wanted to pay tribute to this great bluesman before it was too late. We both agreed that it was a ghoulish idea but not atypical. And yet I had been out to Chicago recently myself, had talked to Spann at the time, and had heard nothing about any serious illness. I called Muddy Waters, whom I had just done a story on. He said Spann might be a little under the weather but was fine as far as he knew. I called Bob Koester, then headquarters central for all Chicago blues news. He had heard nothing. I called back my friend and reported what I had learned. I'd be glad, I said, to do a story on Otis Spann, as long as he wasn't dying, but I didn't know if the magazine would want a story on a living blues singer. My friend checked with the editor. The editor was confident of his sources and for some reason had decided that Otis Spann was *the* major contemporary bluesman. If his information about Spann's illness was wrong, that would be the magazine's lookout. So I went out.

When I arrived at Spann's home, a dilapidated apartment whose walls were covered with pictures of dogs, I sat in the living room talking to a woman and a male neighbor. A skeletal-looking man in a bathrobe sat drowsily on the sofa half-asleep. We made small talk, I wondered to myself when Spann would be coming back, and then the man on the sofa, too weak to do anything more than mumble faintly, said something. It was only when I heard the ghost of his familiar, husky voice that I realized that this was Otis Spann.

I have never felt so acute a shock. Somehow I stumbled through a very brief interview, and when Otis died a few days later, *Rolling Stone* devoted a full page to him. Otis in his sweet way never even blinked at the intrusion. Though he seemed to be heavily sedated, he insisted he felt better that day. 'Since I been sick, man,' he said, 'people from all over come to see me. Bring me this, bring me that. Make you feel kind of—' His voice trailed off.... 'Especially people who don't even know you.'

BIG JOE TURNER

Big Joe Rides On

One moment of Joe Turner singing that 'it's your dollar now, but it's gonna be mine some sweet day' is worth more than all they [the Beatles] have ever said.

MURRAY KEMPTON, in a 1966 story on the Beatles

I'M IN A WORLD of trouble,' announced Big Joe Turner, who is so big now that he should be called Huge Joe Turner, as he lurched towards the stage on the cane that he uses as a walker ('my legs goofed up on me'). His voice, which emanates from a frame that has to be seen to be fully appreciated ('Since I got off my diet, I'm as big as a house again'), filled the club without accompaniment or amplification. The trouble, he explained when he got to the stage, came from a hot dog, which had made him 'sicker 'n a horse. A hot dog is really what you call a classical thing, and can you imagine, the guy put sauerkraut on it'—his voice registers indignation and disbelief, before dropping to a hoarse whisper—'and it didn't go down so good.' This last statement is accompanied by a shy, self-deprecating, almost intentional naiveté, garnished with a slight rolling of the eyes and a dismissive wave. After some moments of free-associating on the subject of the hot dog as a classical American dish, Big Joe, whose speaking voice is never far removed from melody, began to sing.

That was the way it was over a ten-day period when Big Joe Turner, Boss of the Blues, made his first Boston-area appearance in nearly fifteen years. Big Joe Turner, for those who don't know it, is a classical American institution himself, the man who brought boogie woogie to Carnegie Hall as part of John Hammond's historic 1938 Spirituals to Swing and then went on virtually to invent rock 'n' roll—or at least give it a good send-off—when his 1954 hit, 'Shake, Rattle and Roll,' was covered by a young country and western DJ from Chester, Pennsylvania, named Bill Haley. It was, says Big Joe, who was close to forty-five when he became white America's latest teen

Big Joe, 1930s. Courtesy of Valerie Wilmer

idol, 'like taking candy from a baby. Doing blues was a kick. I just do it different. You see, most people sing blues slow and draggy-like, but I put the beat to it. I've sung the blues all over the world, and I always got a good response. I never changed my style ever since I started in to singing. I been in the same style all my life.'

For an institution, Big Joe Turner shows few signs of encrustation or pretense, delivering all the sounds for which he is famous with great gusto, energy, and good humor, and proving in the process that his stentorian voice is still capable of blowing out windows and knocking down doors. From the chair into which he sank his great bulk, he stomped out the beat with his cane, displayed surprising vocal agility and range, and, when he really became involved in a song, hammered the notes flat by the sheer force of his voice. He also interpolated bass rumbles and falsetto screeches, did pop-eyed imitations, mugged shamelessly, and with his plaintive, still baby-faced good looks, slicked-back hair, and barbered mustache, generally played the part of the thirties cabaret performer.

Between songs he delivered monologues on subjects as varied as busing, the Bible, the mysteries of ancient Egypt, the Ku Klux Klan, the proper selection of useful wedding presents, the fate of the Concorde ('Ain't no use bucking it, you fighting a losing job, cause in the end they gonna land it'), plus a whole range of social and sexual issues — all strung together by the most tenuous of threads, each drawn-out, fascinating, hilarious, and obscure by turns, with the last quality definitely predominating. It is all, one suspects, a reflection of a fifty-year background in show business and more particularly a prolonged exposure to the sophisticated New York entertainment world, which Joe Turner entered with a five-year stand at Barney Josephson's Café Society immediately following his triumphant Carnegie Hall debut. His

Big Joe, 1977.

conversation is studded with references to Duke, Cab, Benny Goodman, Bill 'Bojangles' Robinson, Art Tatum, Bette Davis, Mae West, and the Mills Brothers ('They wasn't just a word,' he says in reference to them all, 'they was really here, and they brought a lot of life to the party'), and his hip talk and slightly mystifying line of jive are but another good-natured remnant of an earlier era.

Interviewing Big Joe Turner is not much different from watching him perform. His speaking voice is curiously soft and high-pitched, but he speaks only of what he wants to speak about; there are uncomfortable flashes of suspiciousness ('Don't put that in your script.' It's already in the script, points out a friend, indicating the tape recorder. 'Well, take it off. I don't want nothing to incriminate me'), and he has the cavalier manner of the grand seigneur when it comes to dates and eras. He has played with so many musicians and performed in so many settings that it would be impossible to have anything but anecdotal recall, but Joe Turner is not concerned with statistics so much as with the people who made the music and the feeling that went into it.

He was born in Kansas City in 1911, grew up wanting only to be a singer. 'I tried to play drums, but I had two left feet. I always admired piano players, but I never thought I had the good know-how to do something like that. I wanted to learn how to sing, I had a gross of singers I used to listen to, and I was fascinated with that.' As a boy he led around a blind blues singer, listened to records by Ethel Waters and Clarence Rand ('He was a beautiful man, a crooner, before Bing Crosby's time'), and tried to sneak into the clubs on Independence Avenue where eventually, after he painted a mustache on his face, he started singing.

'I'd been in nightclubs ever since I was a kid, and I knowed what was going on cause my brother-in-law worked at a nightclub, and I used to go down there in the daytime when he'd be down there and the janitor'd be cleaning it up and everything, and they had windows painted on the inside — so people couldn't see in? — so I'd go down and get me a razor blade and scrape off the paint so me and my bunch could see what's happening, you know. So I scraped maybe four or five peepholes, and then at night when they'd have the shows and the band and the people singing and going on, we be down there peeping through them windows!'

It was in joints like the Backbiters' Club, the Hole in the Wall, the Cherry Blossom, and Black and Tan that he first ran into such Kansas City stalwarts as Bennie Moten, George Lee, Count Basie, and Andy Kirk. At the Backbiters' he first encountered boogie woogie nonpareil Pete Johnson, with whom his signature piece, 'Roll 'Em Pete,' was conceived. At Piney Brown's Sunset Club he worked as a bartender, mixing drinks and singing without a microphone from behind the bar. At some point he got a paper megaphone to go out on the sidewalk to sing and drum up business, with the band wailing away inside. 'We was doing boogie woogie, we was singing all pop songs, "Swanee River," anything a sucker wanted to hear we done it. We didn't miss. If the people come and request, say, "I'm the Sheik of Araby" – BOOM, got you covered. Give me the money and we got it going for you.' When he went to New York for the first time in 1936, he claims, it was no different from the gigs he had been working, and when John Hammond tried to put him together with Count Basie, he vetoed the move both because 'Jimmy Rushing had been singing with him all along and because I didn't want to be worrying about the music. Jimmy Rushing knew how to lay out at certain times when the band gonna play them big raises and swells and all that kind of stuff. But me, I was just a free man. I was free in what I'd do. Well, I mean, I get to going good, I could just sing and not have to worry about them fine arrangements.'

He remained a free man. When boogie woogie fell into decline, Big Joe Turner became known as a blues shouter. When rock 'n' roll came into vogue, Big Joe Turner was a rock 'n' roller. He did it, as he explains, without ever changing his style, and 'I had two cooks, one bottle washer, and one chauffeur everywhere I traveled. I had four cats to help me with my clothes on, help me with my clothes off, and help themselves to my money.' In recent years he has lived in California in semi-retirement with his wife Pat and 'Our Dog Rhythm,' as his business card proclaims. In November of 1976 he was booked into New York for the first time in thirty-three years at Barney Josephson's new club, The Cookery, and he has been working steadily ever since, mostly with a well-spoken, dapper-looking pianist named Lloyd Glenn, who is actually two years his senior and provided the foundation for the West Coast style of blues exemplified by Lowell Fulson, Jimmy Witherspoon, and Ray Charles in the late forties.

'You want me to call him down here and let him tell you a few words?' says Big Joe in the motel efficiency apartment in which he is sipping 'bitters' and cooking up a pot of beans. 'Well, I mean, it would be nice, and he would be happy. . . . Talk to my cousin a little bit,' he says when Lloyd finally arrives. 'Say, Glenn, the man want to talk to you.'

Indeed Lloyd Glenn turns out to have a story every bit as interesting as the man he is accompanying. Born in San Antonio in 1909, 'coming up as a kid, the first thing I heard was the blues. I was born in it. My dad, my mother played, and all their friends. My uncle and my dad and one of Dad's friends all played ragtime, so I come up with all these different styles. Now if you want somebody to get behind a jump, I'll play some jump; you want some pop, I'll play some pop; don't make no difference what it is, I'll come up with it. See, when I got into the first band, I couldn't read any music, and I told them, "No, I don't want no band, cause I can't read no music." And they said, "Come on, you can play enough. Just come on, get in the band, we'll teach you the rest." So the first band was Millard McNeil, and he gave me a little music catechism, a little bitty thin book like that, and it had the beginner's. Well, I memorized, when you're young you can absorb that stuff real fast. Like Joe was saying, when he was young, he'd learn them songs, he could hear Pete Johnson, he could just hear music going through his head, and he could work with it. Well, when you're young, your mind is active, so when I got up to some age where I was playing everything, then I started jumping with the classics, and I learned about five of them, and I wish I knew more of them now, because it would be a real good variety for me, to go with my music. Not for here, but to break up the monotony like working at The Cookery with Joe—although I imagine here in Boston, too. Because I have always understood that Boston was sort of a cradle of background for conservatories. Matter of fact, the lady that taught me—no, the one that I wanted to teach me, she wouldn't—she'd come up here every year during that time to go to the conservatory. And she wouldn't teach me, say, "Glenn, I wouldn't dare teach you." I'd say, "Well, I want you to teach me." Say,

Lloyd Glenn.

"No, I wouldn't, I'd ruin your style." She could see how I was fingering things. I'd sit down, and she'd play "Rustle of Spring," and I'd sit down right behind her, see, she'd always hire me every year to play for the school-teachers, you know, the mucky-mucks. I was about the toughest around—'

'Nice boy,' gurgles Big Joe appreciatively.

'I was in school, I was still going to high school—'

'Nice clean-cut kid.'

'And I was wailing then. I was taking everybody's style. Man, I was stealing—I was imitating Earl Hines, they used to call me Fatha Hines. . . .'

With that they embark upon an exchange of reminiscence that takes in virtually all of the recent history of American popular music, from Benny and Buster Hill ('He's like an old grandmaw. Same droopy style') out of Dallas, Texas, to Wynonie Harris ('He was a dancer. He heard me, and he picked up blues singing. Pretty good at it, too') to Ray Charles chasing Jack Lauderdale around his record shop looking for payment on his first records. Oddly enough Lloyd never crossed paths with Big Joe till Glenn moved out to California in the forties and then became A&R man for Swing Time Records, Jack Lauderdale's label. Glenn had a few hits himself, 'but Jack didn't want me to leave, because I picked up good talent for the company, and when I did go out, it was too late for my own records.' Nonetheless he achieved a good deal of professional renown, put together bands for some of the most successful West Coast blues singers, and produced any number of sessions for any number of labels, including one—which he and Joe are still trying to pinpoint—on Big Joe Turner in the late 1940s. In recent years, like Joe, he hadn't been doing much and was discouraged not only about the future of the blues but about the lasting value of his own work.

'Even my boys—a few years ago I told 'em, "Look, I'm gonna teach you the blues, I'm gonna learn you my tricks that I know—all the other tricks of the trade, you can learn that from some other guys, but I'm gonna teach you the little things that people like about *my* style that I don't tell nobody." Say, "Your style's too old, Daddy." Yeah, that's their answer. I say, "Learn it anyhow. You don't like it, throw it away." "Your style's too hard, Daddy, I can't play it." I said, "I'll teach you!" "I don't want it, Daddy." Now about five years ago my youngest son wanted to play. I said, "Just think of how much you could have been doing up till now." He went out and got him a little group, they made a job, and it scared him. They got about five requests to play gigs, they played so well. I said, "Just think of how much I could have taught you, that you could play or not. See, you're young, you could add, that's what I did with my dad. I don't play exactly like my dad. I added on to what my dad played and what those guys played. See, you don't have to play what I play. I'm gonna teach you *my* tricks, and you play 'em *your* way."'

It was George Wein who saw in Lloyd and Big Joe a natural pairing of styles, and Glenn was happy to go out again. 'Well, everybody everywhere

Gene Phillips and his Rhythm Aces, ca. 1946; Lloyd Glenn, piano.
Courtesy of Dick Shurman and Lloyd Glenn.

knows Joe, and it wasn't no problem playing for Joe, because I knew what style would be required. You see, blues is blues, it's the same language, but Joe sings in an altogether different style from, say, T-Bone. I know just what to put behind that style. I have a style for him and a style for T-Bone and a style for any other bluesman. But Joe's a little different than the other bluesmen I've worked with. If you don't understand him, you gonna lose out, you gonna lose something rare. If you be around Joe for a while, you find out that he's a pretty interesting guy. You got to understand the big man.' Joe grunts his approval. 'Other bluesmen are all right, don't get me wrong, they all right, they're good men. But Joe's really different.'

'A lot of people,' says Big Joe Turner, 'come and go, but I'm still with 'em. I'm still as good as I ever was. I'm just older. Maybe I'm better, cause I know more about it. I ain't bragging, because that ain't my nature, and I don't mean it that way at all. But I have been doing this all my life, and I know how it goes, and I watch the response on people's faces, where I can tell when they're enjoying it and when they're not, and I keep working at 'em till I get 'em where they can be comfortable and where I can be comfortable, and then I go from there.'

At Sandy's on Boston's North Shore he was accompanied by a local rhythm guitarist, Glenn's agile piano, and assorted sitters-in. Although there was a distinct raggedness to his performance, and his sense of how to pace a set may well have loosened up in recent years (sometimes it was difficult to tell whether it was the introduction or the song that was the point), Big Joe's self-assessment is not far off, and when he leaned back in his chair, head thrown back, eyes closed, and teeth bared, it was certainly possible to imagine that this was the Big Joe Turner of twenty, thirty, or even forty years ago. His verbal inventiveness and fascination with sounds remain undiminished. Sometimes he will play with the lyrics, which he draws from a vast and seemingly inexhaustible pool, trying out paraphrases, substituting variations, twisting words into surprising and often comical shapes; sometimes he will slur to the point that sound alone is substituted for sense; his operatic-sized voice, thickened perhaps and a little lower with age, is still an awesome force of nature. His sense of rhythm, too, remains rock solid and enlivens all of his various excursions in the key of C.

'What all you got on that tape?' says Big Joe Turner.

Just what you said, it is explained.

'Well, don't you put nothing else on there then. Don't mention nothing about nothing else.'

'Do you understand this man?' interjects Lloyd Glenn. 'Do you understand what he's saying?' I nod, with about as much idea of what he's saying as if he were talking in Arabic. 'I don't think you do,' says Lloyd, perhaps unnecessarily. 'He's telling you, in song, his life. That's the subject. That's it. He's just not going into detail about what's going on in his life. You got it now. That's it.'

'I just sing what pops into my mind,' says Big Joe Turner approvingly. 'I don't like nobody telling me what to sing. It mess up my whole program. You see, I have it flashed in my mind what I'm gonna do. And when people holler, "Sing so and so and so and so," well, maybe I'm gonna sing it, but in another place, another spot, and that goofs me off. I make it up as I go along. I don't plan nothing. *I have no plans.* I live my whole life in music, and I don't tell nobody my secrets. That's the end of the program.'

JUKE
JOINT
BLUES

Chicago, 1977

THE CLUBS

OFTEN THE CLUBS bear the names of women. Theresa's. Queen Bee's. Ma Bea's. Josephine's. Sometimes a grandiose title belies the poverty of their appointments. Louise's Palace, for example, at 69th and South Park, is a postage-stamp-sized bar without even a stage for the musicians, and the restrooms out back are about as 'nasty' and down-home as the music itself. As likely as not, the clubs are not identified by name in any case but by address or by a title they have not borne for five or ten years. There are dozens of these little clubs in Chicago, most no better than corner bars, a few struggling towards naugahyde and carpeted respectability. There is no PA, the musicians start their set unannounced, at the end of a song there is little or no applause. 'Come on,' the singer may tease his audience. 'You ain't in *church*.' The audience needs no reminding of that fact. Church is not a place they are likely to be.

'Juke joints,' wrote blues historian Paul Oliver, of the country as well as the city variety, 'are English pubs and Western saloons without the charm of the former or the romantic appeal of the latter; they're social clubrooms to which the church members don't go, they're dance halls that are too small for more than a few couples to hully-gully. They are in fact unappealing, decrepit, crumbling shacks, which never seem to have been built yesterday, but always thirty or forty years ago, and unpainted since. They're the last retreat, the final bastion for black people who want to get away from whites, and the pressures of the day. It was in these juke joints that the blues found a home.'

FLORENCE'S on a Sunday afternoon on Chicago's South Side. Not far away in fashionable Hyde Park, weekend shoppers take advantage of the spring

Theresa's, 1971. VALERIE WILMER

weather and throng a brick-paved pedestrian mall. In the same general neighborhood, University of Chicago students attend to their studies, toss a Frisbee around, stop to talk with a friend on the way to the library. Inside Florence's it is another world. The din alone sets it apart, the smoky atmosphere, the sheer funk of all those closely-packed-together bodies, the shouts and laughter, above all the music, which serves not so much as a focus but as an accompaniment to all the raucous exchanges, all the various *business* that is going on. There is a buzzer at the door to let you in, and the doorkeeper surveys the passageway from behind a thick glass partition. A couple of years ago there was a shooting, and Florence's has gained a 'reputation,' which these security measures do little to dispel.

The last time I was here, more than six years ago, it was Hound Dog Taylor's gig, and then as now dancers filled the narrow aisle—mountainous women with their medusa wigs, young girls, skinny beanpoles, spry old men—dipping and swaying, scrunching down and grinding in place, with a natural grace and eloquence of movement that delights participant and onlooker alike. Then as now, streamers and balloons decorated the bare, low room in commemoration of some soon-to-be-forgotten occasion. Today it is 'Happy Birthday, Virginia,' but there is always some event to be celebrated, some anniversary to be noted, some excuse to dress up drab lives and surroundings in much the same way that the men and women who patronize this bar themselves dress up with some unexpected touch of color, a jaunty cap, a flashy suit, a glittering ring, some vivid combination of garish greens or reds or purples.

Up by the bandstand a stocky, middle-aged man who calls himself Mordez scribbles furiously in his notebook in indecipherable ideograms he claims alternately to be Japanese, Korean, or some private code. He is jotting down ideas for songs, he says; he is putting together a critique of the group on stage; he is recording his life and times, his discovery of one after another of all the blues greats and the ways in which they stole his best compositions from him. Which, it naturally follows, is why he writes in Japanese.

The bandstand itself is barely large enough for the band, which consists of four pieces. The band is Magic Slim and the Teardrops, made up of Magic Slim singing and playing lead, his brother Nick on bass, another brother, Lee Baby, on drums, and Junior Pettis, better known as Daddy Rabbit, on second guitar. The Slim brothers are enormous (their sister, just as big, is known as Hercules), but at six foot six, with his dirty polo shirt stretched tight across the belt of his heavy workman's pants, Slim himself is easily the most imposing. Like his predecessor at Florence's, Hound Dog Taylor, Magic Slim (born Morris Holt in Grenada, Mississippi, he was given the nickname by his more famous friend and contemporary, Magic Sam) puts out nothing but good rocking, good feeling, *danceable* music. Also like Hound Dog when I first saw him, Slim is virtually unrecorded and unknown

Magic Slim, in fez, his brothers Nick and Lee Baby, and Junior Pettis, far left,
at Houserockin' Social Club Dance, 1977. STEVE TOMASHEFSKY

outside the circuit of South Side clubs, where he is both ubiquitous and extremely popular. The vocals come out through his Kustom amp, and Slim beams good-naturedly, his heavy face sweating, as he calls out a high-spirited version of 'Dirty Mother Fuyer' unlikely to be heard on the radio, and the audience, recognizing a familiar showpiece, quiets down, then explodes in loud appreciation at the climax of each bawdy verse, which is in turn bawdier than the last. Then it's blues time again, and Slim settles back into a slow-rocking groove, his huge hands choking out the notes, his voice echoing that curious mixture of dirtiness and delicacy that characterizes the Albert King-styled blues so pervasive on the Chicago club scene today.

Besides Slim, this afternoon at Florence's will feature: Fred Below, the blues' premier drummer, sitting in and giving Lee Baby a percussion lesson; a dapper, zoot-suited Little Nick, who not only plays in the style of Albert King but uses King's Gibson Flying V model guitar as well; Joe Carter, an Elmore James disciple, who had a band in the fifties, has an album out on the collector Barrelhouse label, and plays in a slide-guitar style virtually identical to that of his idol. All are going on to play somewhere else later in the evening, and each announces the location several times, inviting the audience to join him there. Mordez takes it all down, nods approvingly, confers anxiously with Little Nick, puts off a disgruntled Alabama Red, a moon-faced professorial type who is trying without success to get the performers to plug his latest self-produced release and to peddle it himself from a bulging briefcase.

Magic Slim and his sister, 'Hercules,' Grenada, Mississippi, 1954.
Courtesy of Lucinda Holt, Dick Shurman, Steve Cushing.

The crowd responds differently to different singers. It is, strictly speaking, Magic Slim's gig, and Magic Slim is undoubtedly the most popular of all the performers, but there is no real star system in the blues. Neither reputation nor technical virtuosity has ever been prized so much as honest emotion and depth of feeling. It is the kind of music where if mistakes are made, they are made sometimes with such force and conviction that even the wrong notes can ring true. So that although the music may be wildly varying in quality—and you will encounter every variety of talent in the blues clubs, from naked genius to pathetic imitation—the one constant that remains is the environment itself. And within that environment there is a shared experience, and a shared faith, which is the underpinning of the blues.

Blues, it has been said over and over by its proponents, has kicked off every new movement in American popular music, will survive every trend.

'Blues,' says a younger singer in the club, 'is the foundation of it all. More than the foundation. Because you can come and tear the building down, but you can't destroy the ground it's built on.'

And as I sit in Florence's, as out of time and out of place as a person can be, confronted with my own memories and my rational disinclination to believe that things can still be the same after all the jarring dislocations and deaths of the last few years, I am nonetheless forced to agree. I consider then, as I do writing this now, that I may be allowing myself to be swept away by what I want to believe, but for myself anyway I've had it reconfirmed that when the music is felt and the atmosphere is right, there is no musical experience that can be compared with the blues. The names and faces may change, the words may alter and the beat get turned around, but the blues will never die. 'This is what it all came from,' says another observer, 'even before it got to wax. I mean, how about them old slaves and shit? They was hollering the blues. They wasn't hollering no rock 'n' roll.'

THE BLUES GOES TO COLLEGE

BLIND JOHN DAVIS, a courtly, white-haired, sixty-three-year-old man with a strange absence of pigmentation around the eyebrows and forehead, lives upstairs from Queen Bee's in a bad section of town. He doesn't like the noise, and he doesn't like the neighborhood, but he has lived here for over fifteen years and doesn't really want to move. 'I hear when they dance today it's more like fighting,' he says to his friend Charley, who grew up just a few blocks away from him, not far from the neighborhood where they both now live. The two laugh and take another sip of whiskey. It is

Blind John Davis. **Courtesy of** *Living Blues.* AMY O'NEAL

ten o'clock in the morning, and John is fortifying himself for a lunchtime engagement at the College of DuPage in suburban Glen Ellyn, Illinois.

A piano and organ, a record player and a stack of dusty records are all unmistakable evidence that John Davis is a musician. Propped up against the wall is a guitar. It is, John says, Tampa Red's guitar, worth $900 when it was new. Does he still see Tampa, I ask, for Tampa is confined to a nursing home these days. 'Oh my God, yes. Of course ain't nobody remembers him, except me and this boy here,' he says, indicating Charley. 'After all the guys he fed and gave shelter to. I bring him out to my house for dinner sometimes. You see, Tampa gave me my first break in making records, way back in 1937, I think it was, and we was buddy-buddies ever since.'

Blind John Davis was a premier Chicago session man all through the late thirties and forties. His piano can be heard on countless recordings by Big Bill Broonzy ('He was the strongest of all the male blues singers, don't you think, I mean for a musician that didn't have no musical knowledge'), Sonny Boy Williamson, Washboard Sam, all the Lester Melrose recording artists. He has been to Europe twelve times, going back as far as 1951 with Big Bill, and prides himself on his musical training and versatility. His two closest studio associates were Ransom Knowling, the bass player, and Judge Riley, the drummer, 'and they both got their bachelor degree in music.'

At the College of DuPage, John runs through his usual repertoire of blues, 'semi-blues,' and popular songs. He is playing on a stage set up in the middle of the cafeteria, and the sound bounces around inside the cavernous room as students purchase lunch and carry their trays back to the table. On the walls there are signs advertising the Campus Christian Fellowship and Veteran's benefits, madras-jacketed professors with white shoes walk back and forth in front of the piano in earnest discussion, students focus for a moment on this unexpected entertainment, and then return to their own conversations. None of it bothers John. Between sets he and Charley repair to the men's room, where they decorously sip from a brown paper bag. 'Don't you indulge?' says John with a sly grin.

After the concert is over we wait around for over an hour for John's check to be located. Several students come up shyly to say how much they enjoyed the concert, and the cashiers want John to know that they hope he will be back soon. 'Thank you so much,' says John with unfailing courtesy. 'We hope so, too.' Perhaps it is the result of years of playing the ballroom circuit in Wichita, Laramie, Denver, Terre Haute, but John seems impervious to it all. When we finally get the check, John nods and stands up immediately, a tall camel-backed man in a heavy black overcoat and a black preacher's hat.

Back at the apartment house Charley cashes the check at the liquor store across the street, while John fumbles with the rickety iron gate he has had installed at the bottom of the stairs. A ninety-seven-year-old friend of his was recently hit over the head and killed quite close by. 'I called him Dad.

They didn't have to do that.' John shakes his head. 'They could have just taken his money without hurting him.' He talks about buying a small house with a yard. He is a vigorous, intelligent man with an inquisitive mind. He has led an interesting life. His father was a prosperous bootlegger who had three or four joints. 'I was always a music fanatic, but I started playing more or less out of jealousy. My father would pay these guys to do the playing for him, and I asked him, "Paw, if I learned to play, would you pay me?"' His son is an electrical engineer, and he has two daughters who are schoolteachers. He was never able to teach them music, he says, but the great-grandbaby, who is seven, he thinks really has it in her to play.

A WORD ABOUT THE BLUES

That which I have myself experienced! That which
I, myself, have seen, heard, and done — and I am
an old man, veteran of the hard going, stupid
with sleepless nights, dicing to pay life's
hard account . . . I SING!
And these that squirm about my heart's garden
are my brothers (brothers of the soul). For they,
like I have known the hard way. Me? Well, I'm
the blues singer!

> Liner notes to an Elmore James 45 on
> Bobby Robinson's Fire label, mid-sixties
> (apparently inspired by Dzondira Lalsac's
> liner notes to *Blues Consolidated*, Duke LP 72)

I live across the street from a juke joint
And all night long they sing the blues

BIG JOE TURNER

SON SEALS at thirty-four is perhaps Chicago's most exciting new blues voice in a decade. He grew up not across the street but in the back of the juke joint which his father owned and operated in Osceola, Arkansas. A shy, very private man, he was born on August 13, 1942, the youngest of thirteen children. 'My daddy said I was the last pea in the dish, I guess that's why he was so crazy about me.' Son's father, Jim, also known as Son, had been with the Rabbit Foot Minstrels, played trombone, piano, guitar, and drums, and opened up the Dipsy Doodle Club in 1940. The Dipsy Doodle, like many juke joints, was a combination restaurant, candy store, dance hall, and gambling house. There were 'boarders' who paid for their meals by the week

Son Seals. Courtesy of *Living Blues.* AMY O'NEAL

and 'a great big old coal heater sitting in the middle of the floor. My father was especially noted for making hot tamales. Oh man, white people was crazy about it, every white person in town came out for his hot tamales, man. You'd be surprised who didn't come out. I don't want to put the mouth on no one, but you'd see the sheriff, the chief of police. You'd be surprised at what went on! Oh shit, man, what you talking about? They came out there to get boozed all up and shoot some dice!'

They came out to hear the music, too. Osceola native Albert King (he was Albert Nelson then, drove a tractor trailer, and played a 'great old fat Gene Autry type of guitar') performed during the week with the In the Groove Boys. So did Robert Nighthawk and Sonny Boy Williamson, and on the weekends Joe Hill Louis or Bill Harvey would come in from Memphis. 'Music,' says Son, 'was all I could think of. I was in a sense luckier than the average kid, growing up in that kind of environment. I mean, I wanted to play so bad I could taste it. I couldn't hardly stand school for wanting to get home and get to that guitar or bang around on the drums. There was a boy called Odell Mitchell who used to play drums with Albert. That guy was so good I'd just sit and watch him for hours when I was a kid. Well, he'd leave his stuff there through the day, and I'd get up there and fool with it, just try to follow the jukebox, that was the way I started, just playing behind everything that was on the jukebox. Those drums stayed in my mind until they nearly run me crazy.'

When he was fifteen or sixteen he started playing drums behind Joe Hill Louis, and shortly after that he formed his own group, The Upsetters, who played first at the T99 in Osceola and then the Chez Paris in Little Rock. They kept the Little Rock gig for four years off and on, playing a mix of material, frequently working white clubs and private parties where the group stuck mostly to Fats Domino and Elvis Presley hits. At some time during this period he traveled up to Cairo with Eddie Snow, another of the In the Groove Boys, and when he got stranded up there he went on the road as the drummer for a twelve-piece all-girl band that played everything from Count Basie to contemporary hits, 'all kinds of music—they were *tight*. What interested me about their music was it was so scientific.' All of this musical experience was invaluable, Son insists, both because it taught him how to play in any kind of musical setting—it taught him professionalism, that is—and 'when it was all over and all was said and done, it showed me what I *didn't* want to do. It helped me to know my own identity.' Which was, of course, the blues.

During all this time he never strayed from home for too long, moving briefly up to Chicago in 1962 at his sister's invitation ('She said, "I know I can't get you away from around Daddy," but I stayed a while'), going out briefly with Earl Hooker's Roadmasters, and, most significantly, rejoining Albert King—who had gone on by now not only to claim kinship with B.B., but to enjoy some of the biggest blues hits of the sixties with 'Born Under a Bad Sign,' 'Cross-Cut Saw,' 'Laundromat Blues'—as King's drummer and rhythm guitarist. He played with King at the Fillmore and on King's *Live Wire/Blues Power* album, and there is no question of the influence of Albert's style upon Son's work—his thick-toned, heavily amplified, 'dirty'-sounding guitar owes a debt to King in particular that many of Son's contemporaries share—but it was his father who taught him how to play and exerted the greatest influence upon him. 'My daddy was a well-respected man, both by black and by white. There wasn't a place in town he couldn't go through the front door, and it wasn't because he was overbearing or smart-alec or also at the same time Uncle Tom. It was the way he carried himself. He'd just go in as a man, and he never had no problem. People used to joke, everywhere

Albert King. VALERIE WILMER

you see him you see me, when I was a kid growing up. I used to wonder sometimes, how would I ever make it without him?'

It was only when his father died in 1971 that he moved to Chicago for good and began gigging around the South Side, where he sat in at first with friends from home, then joined Hound Dog Taylor, whom he had met in 1962, when Hound Dog had one of his periodic fallings out with second guitarist Brewer Phillips. In 1972 he took over Hound Dog's gig at the Expressway Lounge, and this was where Bruce Iglauer, a twenty-four-year-old shipping clerk at Delmark Records who had just recorded Hound Dog for his fledgling Alligator label, first saw him. Actually Iglauer had heard him earlier over the phone, when Wes Race, one of Chicago's premier blues fanatics, called from the Flamingo Club. '"Bruce, now I want you to listen," he hollered over the background noise, and turned the phone towards the bandstand. I thought I knew every bluesman in town, but this was something new, and something special—an incredibly fast, raw lead guitar and an urgent, intense singer. I must have listened ten minutes before I shouted back, "Who the hell is that?" "That? That's Son Seals."'

The songs that Son was doing at the time were the usual repertoire—Muddy, Wolf, B.B., Albert. 'No, I wasn't doing any of my own then. Because there wasn't any call for them. When Bruce asked me, was I ready to record, I said I was, but when I went in to do my own thing, I think he was kind of surprised, I mean when he came to rehearsal. Because it was different from what he heard me playing over there. Different tunes. Lots of 'em. He didn't know I had been working on my own tunes for years, just not for the public. But I knew how I *would* have played those tunes, had I the opportunity to. Then when the record came out it made me even more confident, just to know that the people accepted it.'

That first album, *The Son Seals Blues Band*, released in April of 1973, certainly bore out the promise that Wes Race and Bruce Iglauer, not to mention Son himself, had foreseen. What set it off from the average blues release was the strength of the original compositions, which combined real feeling, sometimes startling imagery ('Your Love is Like a Cancer'), and a contemporary, soul-influenced musical sound. It got good reviews, provided a fine forum for Son's instrumental strengths and a vocal style that owed a lot at that time to Magic Sam, but more than anything it gave him the excuse to develop his original style even further ('When I got into doing my own tunes, I knew I had to come up with something') and – though Son says, 'I don't just be thinking of the purpose of recording' – to continue with his writing.

By the time the second album, *Midnight Son*, came out in the winter of 1976–77, Son was in full command of his style. There was a new assurance in his voice, the guitar playing was as raw and dirty as any blues playing since Jimi Hendrix, and the songs continued to exhibit the wit, insight, and imagination of the first record. The album got rave reviews, sold accordingly, and prompted both a national tour and a widespread recognition of Son as perhaps the herald of a new blues generation. Son, who quit drinking a few years ago because of a mild case of epilepsy, takes his newfound stardom pretty much in stride and remains absolutely serious about his music. He writes his new songs in composition books rather than putting them on tape, because 'a thing like that seem so private to me, a tape player would be too exposed, and I don't even want my wife fooling with my stuff. You've got to give yourself plenty of time to fool around with the words, that's the most important thing. As long as there's the slightest doubt in my mind that I can improve this or I think I can improve but *one* verse, I can have ten tunes, but if there's that one verse I'm not satisfied with, I'm not ready to record yet. Because I don't care if that record don't hardly get off the shelf, at least I want my part of it to be right.'

When he has played in Europe or at the Bottom Line in New York, he has received widespread acclaim. In Chicago in 1977, though, he is still just another musician, differentiated from the rest only by the fact that he has finally reached the point of making a living from his music. When he's in town, he works seven nights a week at Queen Bee I and Queen Bee II, but you are unlikely to hear him do many of his songs or work with his own band in this setting. This is because the gigs are not strictly speaking his. He is instead part of a loosely organized house band which was hired by the management, so that often he is backing fright-wigged singers like Muddy

Waters, Jr., or Dennis Weaver, who are as inept as their names might suggest. This is where his training comes in handy, Son points out. 'About the only satisfaction I get from this is knowing I can play all these different kinds of music.' Like Magic Slim or Joe Carter, he sits in from time to time around town, and when he occasionally gets a booking at a prosperous (read 'white') Northside club like The Wise Fools, he will reassemble his full band of Snapper Mitchum on bass, Pete Allen on rhythm guitar, and Tony Gooden on drums. This is assuming that they don't have another gig, that the band's lineup remains stable, that any one of a thousand unforeseen circumstances doesn't intervene. It's not much different from when Muddy Waters and Wolf started out thirty years ago, and probably Son, like Muddy, will transcend this milieu eventually — but there is no guarantee he won't go back to it either. It's the notorious instability of the blues life, but Son shrugs it off, driving around town in his battered telephone company van.

The clubs are calmer now than they were five years ago, he says. 'Back then it wasn't nothing for you to be just sitting there and some guys to fall through the window and start a humbug in a minute. It seems a little better now in the way of trouble, you don't feel that intense feeling like something's gonna happen every time you walk in the door.' It is all, Son says, part of the general living conditions, 'but then that's what started the blues, I guess.' And yet even this stoicism, so strongly expressed, doesn't mask an element of nostalgia that remains at the center of the urban blues. It's almost as if an earlier time and a more innocent place were always on the verge of being invoked. 'People down home really knew how to enjoy themselves,' says Son. 'I tell you, man, I'd go back there today if I could just make it economically, you know, moneywise and shit. You can go down there right now, go out to them country juke joints and watch them shoot dice and cuss, fry their fish and barbecue and stuff, it's just wide open, you don't have to worry about being mugged, knocking heads or something all the time. If you want to get too high, you want to lie down over there and take your nap, you don't have to worry about waking up, all your money gone and all this stuff. It's just, let yourself go. Every Sunday is the Fourth of July.'

JIMMY JOHNSON'S RECORDING SESSION

THE RECORDING SESSION in tiny Studio B seems doomed almost from the start. To begin with, the scheduled drummer doesn't show, and then, when his replacement does, the recording console blows a fuse. The producer, sixty-six years old and one of the most flamboyant characters in the business, with his reddish blond hair worn long, a safari jacket open to bare his broad chest, and black platform heels, is talking once again about

Jimmy Johnson. STEVE TOMASHEFSKY

how he discovered James Brown and how 'they fucked me out of a million dollars, and I mean fucked me. But I'll tell you something, baby, every one of them motherfuckers is dead, that's the truth, and I'd rather have twenty dollars in my pocket and be above the ground than have a million and be pushing up flowers—ain't that right?' He chuckles heartily to himself and starts talking about Hank Ballard and Little Willie John.

Inside the glassed-in recording booth, the singer, a neat, youthful-looking man with a close-cropped Afro and a worried expression, appears increasingly uneasy. The singer is forty-eight-year-old Jimmy Johnson, brother of soul singer Syl Johnson and of Mack Thompson (actually the family name is Thompson), Magic Sam's old bass player. Although Jimmy Johnson has been around the scene for years, and was a fixture for a decade in some of the better soul bands in the city, he has only recently started playing the blues clubs, and, aside from an album that he recently cut for a French specialist label, this is to be his first record. It is part of a ten-volume blues series that has been undertaken, for reasons unknown, by a major soul label. They have left it in the hands of this Chicago-based independent producer, who, since he is not really in touch with the contemporary blues scene, has in turn gone to Jim and Amy O'Neal of *Living Blues* for suggestions. That is how Jimmy Johnson has come to find himself in the recording studio.

At last the session starts. They'll give it one more try, the producer decides, until another fuse blows: 'Then that's it, baby.' The drummer and piano player have never played with Jimmy Johnson before; the bass player,

David Matthews, a Buddha-like figure who resembles Solomon Burke, ordinarily plays rhythm guitar. All right, says the producer, we want to get real down home, chitlins and collard greens and all that kind of shit. 'And I want you to stretch out, baby, none of that three-minute shit, I want you to get that feeling. These cuts'll go around four minutes, so you just keep your eye on me, and I'll give you the signal to wind it up.'

The singer nods, lowering his eyes. What kind of material has he got? the producer asks. 'I can give you multiple choices,' says the singer and starts running through some of the titles, but the producer is obviously not interested. 'I just want you to play it country,' he says, nodding his leonine head. Could he, the singer ventures, get a little dirtier sound from his guitar? The way they have set it up, they have bypassed his amp to get a cleaner tone. 'I'd like to get the sound a little raggedier,' explains Jimmy Johnson, 'because the distortion give you better sustain on the notes.' No problem, no problem, says the producer, misunderstanding. 'I'll put those highs right back in the mix. Look, I want you to be happy, Jimmy, that's the whole thing, but I've got to make me a little happy, too, right? I'll tell you what, I'll meet you 75 percent of the way, but I've got to get my 25 percent, too, if you can dig where I'm coming from.' No, says Jimmy Johnson deferentially, he'll meet the producer halfway. 'All right. You said it, baby.' The producer, who obviously fancies himself a psychologist, beams. 'Okay. Let's do it.'

The songs are done without any real run-through. Jimmy Johnson sets the rhythm and provides a brief intro; then they cut. The piano player, who is thoroughly professional and very adaptable, glances back over his shoulder, keeping his eye on Jimmy Johnson the whole time. The drummer, who is young, long-haired, and chews gum to mask his nervousness, can't keep time and plays so tentatively that Jimmy Johnson tries to cover the rhythm, too. The songs are good, and Jimmy Johnson plays with the same delicacy and feeling that you hear in the clubs, his somewhat thin, sensitive voice always retaining a brittle edge. All the time that he is playing, the producer stomps around inside the glassed-in recording booth, clapping his hands, stamping his heels, raising his eyebrows and nodding encouragement, obviously attempting to instill confidence and that 'down-home' feel that in his view is the only standard you can apply to a blues record.

There are no second takes, playbacks are only grudgingly conceded, because, the producer insists, he wants nothing to take away from the spontaneity of feeling. All through the session he keeps looking at his watch; he wants to get out of here by nine o'clock. During one song the musicians get really hot, but Jimmy Johnson breaks off in the middle. 'What's the matter?' says the producer, caught in midbeat. 'You was blowing good, baby.' He had to stop, Jimmy Johnson explains, because he mixed up the verses. That don't matter, that don't matter, the producer shakes his head in disbelief. Ain't nobody gonna care what *order* you do the verses in. When they reach

the four-minute mark, the producer either gives an elaborate windup or signals with his fingers to stretch out for a fade. If he wants a solo in the middle
of a song he mimes playing the guitar, and if he wants Jimmy Johnson to
sing another verse, he goes to his mouth. At the end of two and a half hours,
they have a finished record, eight four-minute takes that are complete except
for one instrumental overdub that Jimmy Johnson will have to come back to
do. 'Well, that wraps it up,' says the producer. He has only two or three more
albums left in the series, and he is well pleased with the night's work.

Jimmy Johnson puts his guitar back in its case and quietly thanks the
other musicians. He has gotten no more and no less than he bargained for
probably. All he can hope for now is that the record will actually be released.

THE MUSIC BUSINESS IN CHICAGO

IN THE FORTIES AND FIFTIES, when blues was big business, Chicago was
the center of the blues recording world. Labels like Chess, Vee Jay, and
a host of lesser-known independents were all Chicago-based and indeed
became the focus of many a blues fan's pilgrimage to the city. The Rolling
Stones recorded '2120 South Michigan Avenue' (the old Chess address) as a
well-meant tribute to their roots and then cut much of two later albums at
the Chess studios. All the classic sides by Muddy, Wolf, Sonny Boy, Little
Walter, Buddy Guy, Jimmy Reed, and Otis Rush came out of Chicago studios.

Today the major labels are all gone, either out of business or in a temporary
holding pattern. The two principal labels that are left to document the Chicago
blues tradition are a far cry from Chess and Vee Jay. They put out albums,
not 45s, and would have been dismissed in the heyday of Chicago recording
as eccentric 'collector' labels. They are now just about the only vehicle by
which a locally popular bluesman can acquire status, not only in the world
outside but in the indigenous milieu of the South Side clubs. Son Seals sells
his Alligator albums off the bandstand; Junior Wells is known as a recording
artist, not just by twenty-year-old hits like 'Little By Little' or 'Hoodoo Man'
but by his three Delmark albums as well.

Delmark is the dean of blues collector labels, going back twenty years
to Delmar Avenue in St. Louis, where its first two albums, by Speckled
Red and Big Joe Williams, were recorded. It was founded by Bob Koester,
a dedicated midwesterner with equal passions for jazz, movies, and the
blues, which he sometimes manages to combine. Koester had recorded
mainly country and traditional blues and jazz until 1966, when he put out his
first Junior Wells album, *Hoodoo Man Blues*, featuring Buddy Guy under the
pseudonym of Friendly Chap on guitar (Guy was an exclusive Chess artist at
the time). Not only was the record Delmark's best-selling album, which it

Buddy Guy at Theresa's, Chicago, 1971. VALERIE WILMER

remains; it was among the first long-playing records to make a serious attempt to document this living blues tradition (Pete Welding's enterprising Testament label was first with *Modern Chicago Blues*, and Sam Charters's *Chicago / The Blues Today!* on Vanguard was released almost simultaneously). The effect, though perhaps less than cataclysmic, was considerable enough. Delmark went on to record Magic Sam, Mighty Joe Young, Luther Allison, Jimmy Dawkins, J.B. Hutto, all legends on the South and West sides but virtually unknown outside of the city except on the basis of a few 45s. The albums went on to create a whole new audience and in many cases whole new careers for the artists.

Alligator Records was started almost as an offshoot of Delmark. Its founder, Bruce Iglauer, describes himself as 'fresh out of college and ridiculously overconfident' when he went to work for Bob Koester as a shipping clerk in 1970. 'I honestly didn't know much about the blues (of course I thought I did), but I was thrilled just to be around the real honest-to-goodness bluesmen.' After two years at Delmark, Iglauer decided to start his own label when Koester showed little interest in recording the music of Hound Dog Taylor, one of the most popular club performers and a personal favorite of Bruce's. The first album, *Hound Dog Taylor and The HouseRockers*, came out in late 1971 and documented the kind of loose, joyous, foot-stomping, crazy music that rarely finds its way onto record. It is probably the best-selling small-label blues release of all time and made Hound Dog, an indefatigable veteran of the club scene, into a small-scale international star. Alligator's third album represented Son Seals's debut, and in the spring of 1979 the label released a three-volume set called *Living Chicago Blues*, which included Magic Slim and Jimmy Johnson, among others.

Along with the record labels (and there are certainly others that have put out significant Chicago blues releases, including Barrelhouse, Chris Strachwitz's Arhoolie Records in California, and the various recording ventures of Steve Weisner, who is seeking to document some of the more obscure aspects of the club scene), one other Chicago blues institution should be mentioned, and that is *Living Blues*, a periodical expressly devoted to 'the Black American Blues Tradition,' which was founded in 1970 by Iglauer, surrealist spokesperson Paul Garon, and editors Jim and Amy O'Neal. Passionate, opinionated, at times myopic, *Living Blues* is an ideal propagandist for a tradition that has otherwise been almost altogether ignored. Over the years it has done almost as much as the record labels not only to straighten out some of the tangled history of the blues but to help the musicians both to become better known and to find jobs and recording opportunities. In fact the small coterie of dedicated Chicago blues advocates, which includes Koester, Iglauer, the O'Neals, Steve Tomashefsky, Dick Shurman, and premier blues fan Wes Race, has exerted a not inconsiderable influence on the blues community itself. For outsiders they have opened up a window to another world, but more important, for musicians like Son Seals and Hound Dog Taylor, they have opened up the opportunity to lead altogether different lives.

THE BLUES NEVER DIE

EVERY NIGHT of the week you can hear the blues until four in the morning at any one of a dozen Chicago clubs. Everywhere you go you run into history, whether it's in the form of Rufus Foreman, the grave professorial-looking saxophone player who first hired Buddy Guy, or you catch a glimpse of the elusive Left Hand Frank or the even more mysterious Egyptian lady, who ululates one unearthly soprano trill, then runs out of the club. You may run into Willie Cobbs or Earring George, Mad Dog Lester, or a red-suited Lovey Lee; Luther Tucker is in town for the funeral of his son, and Sammy Lawhorn, Muddy's old guitar player, a sad figure since losing his wife and children in a fire, sits in all over town and plays brilliantly each night until each night he gets too drunk to play. If I were to go back in six months it could all be changed. Eddy Clearwater, Bobby King, and Hip Lankchan would be back at their regular gigs, Lonnie Brooks, once one of the many Guitar Jrs., would

Wolf. Courtesy of Chess Records. RAY FLERLAGE

be laying down his country and western-influenced blues, and Otis Rush and Fenton Robinson, the stars of another generation, might be gigging around regularly. It makes no difference, because in the world of the blues, everyone is a celebrity in one way or another. Singers surface and disappear, go to prison, join the church. It's a transient world struggling for some kind of permanence, in which gesture is all, judgments are infrequently made, and even the most brutal personal losses are suffered with a sweet, sorrowful tolerance that shrugs at the unpredictable vagaries of life and human behavior.

The last night I was in Chicago we went out to the 1815 Club on the West Side, which Howlin' Wolf's old bandleader, Eddie Shaw, has bought and fixed up to attract a 'nice' mixed crowd. The band is the Wolf Gang, which has remained more or less intact since Wolf's death, and throughout the evening of good-time, lighthearted music there are references to Wolf and even a few imitations thrown in for good measure. Eddie Shaw is an amiable MC who keeps things moving, going from one table to another between sets and greeting old friends, black and white. Towards the end of the evening he announces proudly that they have just completed paving the parking lot, a small fenced-in yard in which trash still peeks up through ungraded tar, and that soon they will have a guard, 'so that those bad boys won't be ripping us off any more.' In addition, he announces, he has commissioned a 'six-foot-five lifesize' statue of Howlin' Wolf, which will be set in place on June 10 and dedicated by a Chicago city alderman. A cheer goes up, and Eddie Shaw beams. 'I wonder,' says someone, 'how long it'll be before they pull that statue down.'

Epilogue

SAM PHILLIPS TALKING

J UST AS I was finishing up this book, the opportunity arose to do something I had dreamt of for what seemed like a lifetime — well, fifteen years
anyway. Through a combination of luck, timing, and the good will of Knox
Phillips, with whom I had been in touch off and on by letter and phone since
1968, I got to meet Knox's father, Sam, the somewhat reclusive founder of
Sun Records (despite the mania for information on Sun, he has given out
only two or three interviews since his retirement from the record business
over a decade ago), and the man who almost single-handedly authored one
of the most remarkable chapters in the history of American popular music.

You've got to understand what the prospect of meeting Sam Phillips
meant to me. Some kids dream of curing cancer, some of growing up to be
President. As for me I dreamt of playing in the major leagues, winning the
Nobel Prize for literature, becoming Elvis Presley's adviser and chief confidant,
and — as I grew older and only slightly more realistic — meeting Sam Phillips.
From the time that we first discovered Sun Records, my friends and I had
constructed elaborate fantasies not just about Elvis but about the man who
had recorded Elvis, Jerry Lee Lewis, Carl Perkins, and before that the great

Sam Phillips, the man who started it all, ca. 1957. Courtesy of Sam Phillips.

Memphis bluesmen (Howlin' Wolf, B.B. King, Bobby Bland) who were just as much our heroes. As I got to know Charlie Rich, and other Sun artists to a lesser degree, the way in which they spoke about Sam Phillips—his astonishing persuasive powers and force of mind—the way in which they recalled his ability to inspire, even as they complained about royalty rates and the eventual necessity for their leaving Sun, only fueled my vision of this behind-the-scenes Machiavellian genius who had discovered so many of the unique talents of a generation and seemingly gotten the very best out of them while they were still on his label.

The day I met Sam Phillips was momentous in several respects other than the meeting itself. I was doing a story for the *New York Times Magazine* (momentous for me) on the legendary Million Dollar Quartet, an impromptu session in which Elvis had joined Carl Perkins, Johnny Cash, and Jerry Lee in the Sun studio in 1957. Sam's new radio station, WWEE in Memphis, where I was due to meet Sam for what Knox said might be no more than a fifteen-minute interview ('With Sam you can't ever tell,' said Knox, to whom the founder of Sun is 'both my father and Sam'), was flooded that day by a frozen sprinkler system, and as a result I spent about nine hours out at the station stacking tapes, sponging off audio equipment, and doing my best to help out. And, it just so happened, the day that I met Sam Phillips was also the day that the first real attempt at a rock 'n' roll film documentary was aired on national TV, with rare early footage of Elvis, Jerry Lee, and other familiar figures from the dawn of rock 'n' roll.

It was a peculiar way to meet a lifelong hero. Almost all the pictures that I had ever seen of Sam Phillips showed a young, slick-haired businessman with a sly, almost foxy smile and the slit-eyed look of one of his most self-aware artists, Jerry Lee Lewis. The man that I encountered briefly from time to time all through the course of that day, padding about on carpeting so saturated with water that it soaked up through your shoes, had the look of an Old Testament prophet in tennis sneakers, his long hair and long reddish beard only matching the oracular tone and language that came out in the cadences of a southern preacher. He was totally in charge, flattering the contractor who had built the studio for him, following the sprinkler system man's explanation of just what had happened with courtly good humor, assigning specific tasks to each of the employees of the 50,000-watt station until they could get back on the air, fending off the good wishes of friends and family who had gathered around for support, dispatching Knox and his other son, Jerry, on various errands to pick up emergency equipment around town, and charming members of the local press corps (TV, radio, and newspapers all had their representatives on the scene of the disaster) with no apparent strain or impatience. With each individual he focused the full force of his personality for just as long as it took to get that individual moving in the proper direction, and—for all the differences of circumstances and setting—I felt for one brief moment as if I were getting a glimpse of the inspired chaos that was Sun.

The radio station, like the original Sun studio, is a testament to Sam Phillips's vision. According to Knox, Sam built 'every square inch' of the old studio with his own hands, installed the acoustic tile, built the speakers, rigged up all the audio equipment, even calculated the precise advantage of a control booth raised to a particular height (with his training as a radio engineer, his intimate knowledge of recording methods and equipment was not as surprising as it might at first seem). Similarly, he personally supervised every aspect of the new radio station's construction, 'like to drove the contractors crazy' with his exacting specifications, alone conceived its unique design—which might best be described as pyramidally modernistic (it features turrets and a brown cedar and stone facade)—and spent nearly every waking moment at the studio while the building was going up. Which was, as everyone remarked, the shame of it all, since the studio had only been in operation a few months, and now much of the equipment and the expensive carpet that Sam had specially ordered from New York would have to be replaced. No one seemed quite sure how Sam was going to react—since it is generally agreed that Sam has always been careful with a dollar—but like the southern diplomat that Chuck Berry has sung about, Sam had nothing but cheerful words of encouragement for everyone and thanks for their kind thoughts. In fact, he seemed almost to thrive on the crisis atmosphere, and his commander's role seemed only to animate him.

During one of our frequent encounters in passing at the coffee machine, he explained briefly the format of his new station (he also owns the largest station in the tri-city area around his hometown of Florence, Alabama, plus several smaller stations), which he hoped would set a new trend in contemporary radio. Basically WWEE follows a Top 40 format, but it mixes in music from all eras as well and seeks to emphasize the *connectedness* that Phillips feels is missing from today's tight Top 40 playlists. 'It's different,' he gladly admits, 'but I never have been one to do the same as everyone else. If I've got to do the same, I'd just as soon not do it.' Then he was off to attend to some fresh problem.

I wasn't sure if I was going to get any more than these occasional nuggets, the unwavering focus of Sam Phillips's gaze, and the opportunity to observe him under somewhat trying circumstances. If it had been no more than that, I think I still would have felt privileged, so compelling was my own vision of Sam Phillips. When we finally sat down at the end of that long afternoon and evening, after things finally seemed to be under control and the maintenance crew had finally succeeded in mopping up most of the water with suction cleaners, Sam Phillips seemed scarcely even winded, and I realized as he talked that he was speaking to every fantasy I had ever had about him, that he was telling the story of how one man, and one group, had made history.

He wasn't much interested in facts and dates, though he seemed secure in the knowledge that these would be noted by future chroniclers. What Sam Phillips was interested in was *feeling* and people—the very variousness of human nature. 'My mission,' he said, 'was to bring out of a person what was in him, to recognize that individual's unique quality and then to find the key to unlock it.' As I listened, I heard from him what my friends and I had so carefully constructed for ourselves, and I had a glimmer for the first time in a long time of the unlikely notion that history is not necessarily an accident, that the self-willed individual can affect his environment, and his times, in ways that we cannot even calculate.

Sam Phillips was born on January 5, 1923, on a farm outside of Florence, Alabama, in a family of eight children. This is where he first encountered black music, particularly in the person of Uncle Silas Payne, a blind, elderly sharecropper who used to tell him stories and sing him songs that have stayed with him all his life.

'I was raised by two great Southern parents. They were in the great Southern tradition. They were genuine people. Their beliefs were sustained by generation after generation of acceptance of what, quote unquote, *the norm* is. That's how people, life, circumstances, situations, especially color and the gradation of economic income were judged. Would you believe that that had a lot to do with life, black and white—your economic *income*, whether you had patches on your pants? My father was—and I hate to say this, because my father was probably the truest human being that I've ever met in my life, to the feel that I had—but at the same time he wouldn't break, bless his heart and God rest his soul, with the tradition, other than he would see that no one went hungry, even if we didn't have much more than the poorest sharecropper.

'But I saw—and I don't remember when, but I saw as a child—I thought to myself: suppose that I would have been born *black*. Suppose that I would have been born a little bit more down the economic ladder. So I think I felt from the beginning the total inequity of man's inhumanity to his brother. And it didn't take its place with me of getting up in the pulpit and preaching. It took on the aspect with me that some day I would act on my feelings, I would show them on an individual, one-to-one basis.'

Although, Sam says, he would have liked to have been a criminal defense lawyer, he went into radio when his father died, going to work as an announcer for Muscle Shoals station WLAY, where as a high school student he had set up broadcasts for the Coffee High marching band (Sam played drums and sousaphone and composed the school's drum march, which is used to this day). At WLAY he also met his wife, Becky—a ukeleleist who sang and played duets with her sister on piano—and got his certification as a radio engineer through a correspondence course. He went on to work as

706 Union Avenue. Miss Taylor's Restaurant is on the corner, just to the right of the original Sun Studios. PAT RAINER

an engineer in Decatur, then at WLAC in Nashville, arriving in Memphis at WREC (this was the station whose announcers, Rufus Thomas said, all spoke in an impressively 'big, booming voice') in the winter of 1944–45. Starting in June, he began to engineer live broadcasts of big bands like Glenn Miller, Jimmy or Tommy Dorsey, from the Hotel Peabody Skyway, and the following year these programs started going out nightly on the CBS network. It was a prestigious job, obviously, but it left him feeling frustrated and dissatisfied because 'it had gotten where with stock arrangements and everything, the creativity actually just was not there for those people. Don't get me wrong, I loved the forties bands, but when you're scheduled you just don't have that instinctive intuitional thing, and these dudes—I can remember well—they might have played the damned song 4000 times, and they were *still* turning the pages. Well, in those bands really you were numbered.'

What Sam Phillips heard in his head was the black blues he had been listening to from childhood on, the same music that you could hear in Memphis every day on Beale Street, the thoroughfare of the blues. In 1950 he determined to record these blues singers. He built his own studio in a converted radiator shop on Union Avenue, which was so small there was no room for an office aside from the receptionist's area and all business was conducted at Miss Taylor's Restaurant next door ('third booth by the window'). At first he leased sides to the Chess brothers in Chicago and the Biharis in Los Angeles (who owned the Modern and RPM labels), and at the radio station he was frequently met by fellow workers with greetings like,

Sam Phillips, 1978. PAT RAINER

'Well, you smell okay. I guess you haven't been hanging around those niggers today.' By his own account, though, Sam Phillips wasn't fazed in the least.

'I have *never* been conventional. I don't know if that's good, but it set me apart in the sense that I had a certain independence and individuality. And I knew one thing: believe and trust in what you're doing or don't do it. I just knew that this was great music. My greatest contribution, I think, was to open up an area of freedom within the artist himself, to help him to express what *he* believed his message to be. Talking about egos – these people unfortunately did not *have* an ego. They had a desire – but at the same time to deal with a person that had dreamed, and dreamed, and dreamed, looked, heard, felt, to deal with them under conditions where they were so afraid of being denied again – it took a pure instinctive quality on the part of any person that got the revealing aspects out of these people. It took an 'umble spirit, I don't care whether it was me or someone else. Because I knew this – to curse these people or to just give the air of, "Man, I'm better than you," I'm wasting my time trying to record these people, to get out of them what's truly in them. I *knew* this.'

Phillips knew, too, that he didn't want to spend the rest of his life working for someone else, and so in June of 1951, after recording what many consider to be the first rock 'n' roll hit ('Rocket 88' by Jackie Brenston, which appeared on Chess, had a driving beat, a booting sax, and celebrated the automobile), he quit his job at WREC and some six months later started the Sun label, its distinctive yellow logo designed by a fellow alumnus of the Coffee High School band. For the next two years Sun's roster was made up almost exclusively of black artists (including Rufus Thomas, who gave the label its first hit), and Phillips has nothing but the fondest memories of the blues singers he recorded. Joe Hill Louis, Dr. Isaiah Ross (the good doctor's specialty was the Boogie Disease), and Jimmy DeBerry are names that come up frequently in conversation, but it is the Howlin' Wolf (in real life Chester Burnett) whom Phillips remembers in particular, not only as the most distinctive blues singer he recorded but as the most distinctive stylist, the most unique *individual* whom he ever met in all his years in the record business.

'Ah, Chester—the vitality of that man was something else. Just to see that man in the studio—God, what I would give to see him as he was in my studio, to see the fervor in his face, to hear the pure instinctive quality of that man's voice. Once he felt at home, once you made him feel that he was in his own indigenous surroundings, Chester could not put anything on, there was no way he could be anything other than himself. Also, he had the ability to read people without even letting you know he was doing it. He gave the appearance of being almost totally unconcerned, but this was just a facade that he kept until such time as he knew you were truly interested in what he was all about. Once he knew that, once you broke that barrier, then you had all he had to offer.'

Only with Elvis's breakthrough success in the summer of 1954 did Phillips abandon his black constituency—and then evidently not without a great deal of soul-searching.

'This is a regrettable thing on my part, but I saw what I was doing as not deserting the black man—God knows, there was no way I could do that, because without the black man I don't know if I would have had the thoughts go through my mind that I did—but when I started out there was nobody on the scene recording black music, and by this time there was an awful lot of good black music that was being recorded by Atlantic, Specialty, Chess, Checker, and I felt they could handle it real good. And I saw what I was trying to do with white men was to broaden the base, to try to get more radio stations to play this kind of music, to give it more widespread exposure. I knew we had a hard trip for all of us. The Southern white man had an expression for his basic roots in country music in the Grand Ole Opry, but we didn't have that for the black man—and yet without those people there would have been no idea for us that was free of great encumbrance.'

What he was looking for from the beginning was the same unique quality he had found in Howlin' Wolf, the same *differentness* that he continues to prize to this day. Talk to Sam for any length of time and you will hear countless homiletics on the dangers of conformity ('I could have become a conformist and gone the, quote unquote, *beaten path*, and if that had happened I would have been a very unhappy man'), the glories of individuality ('You can be a nonconformist and not be a rebel. And you can be a rebel and not be an outcast. Believe in what you believe in, and don't let *anybody*, I don't care who it is, get you off that path'). As his son, Knox, says, 'If a guy came into the studio with a unique, distinctive sound and was himself, Sam heard it immediately, where most people would wince at it at first. Jerry Lee Lewis told me—and he had been up to Nashville, and they all said to him, "Man, get you a guitar"—Jerry Lee told me, Sam took one listen to his tape, and he didn't listen but halfway through, and he said, "You are a rich man." And he didn't mean in money, but in talent.'

It was with Elvis that the Sun era as we know it really began, and it was Elvis's music, of course, that gained him entrée to the Sun studio in the first place, but you wonder in talking with Sam Phillips if it wasn't Presley's unformed personality—his virtually unconsidered strengths and almost equally instinctive weaknesses, the *contradictions* that were never even partially resolved—which fascinated Phillips just as much as the music. 'He tried not to show it,' Phillips told writer Bob Palmer, 'but he felt so *inferior*. He reminded me of a black man in that way; his insecurity was so *markedly* like that of a black person.' There was never any question in his mind, Sam says, of Elvis's gifts, but there was a good deal of question about

Sam Phillips and Jerry Lee Lewis, 1958.

his acceptance by the public. Phillips recalls accompanying Elvis on his first trip to the Louisiana Hayride after the debacle at the Grand Ole Opry (when Elvis was advised to go back to truck driving).

'I didn't let anybody know, but when it came time for Elvis and Scotty and Bill to go on stage, I went out and got me a seat in that audience. Because I'll tell you what, we didn't have any idea how this thing was going to turn out—and I was going to do anything I could to help out, but I'll tell you the power of communication. When he got through his first number, and I don't remember what it was, those people were up on their feet. I mean, all types—old people, fat people, skinny people, listen, honey, it was just one of those things that just come up, and you say, "Man, I'm not believing this." Some big fat lady, I mean it took an effort for her to get up, and she got up and she didn't stop talking, right in the middle of the next number, she didn't know who I was, I didn't know who she was. She said, "Man, have you ever *heard* anything that good?"'

And then, of course, Elvis Presley took off, his contract was sold to RCA almost before the world was fully aware of his existence (in all, Phillips put out five singles on Presley in the year and a half that he was on Sun). The $40,000 that Phillips got for his contract—including $5000 in back royalties—provided working capital for the tiny company, and Sam insists to this day that he had no second thoughts in the wake of Presley's massive popular success. 'If I've been asked once,' he told Bob Palmer, 'I must have been asked a thousand times, did I ever regret it? No, I did not, I do not, and I never will.'

What followed in any case was a period of extraordinary ferment and productivity that has rarely been matched in American popular culture, a time when, as Sam Phillips says, it was possible 'to establish something and get the good old capitalist system out of the way just a little bit to let creativity take its place.' With the money provided by the sale of Elvis's contract, Phillips was free to concentrate on the careers of Carl Perkins, Johnny Cash, Jerry Lee Lewis, Charlie Rich, and other lesser-known but equally luminous talents. The effort paid off not only in sales but in the forging of a new style, the creation of a genuinely original, and lasting, body of music.

'I believe so much in the psychological. I think this had an awful lot to do with it. Number one is that caring figure. Number two is knowing what in the hell you're doing. I think at the time of our relationship there was a true trust. It was almost like a father–son or big brother–little brother relationship. And I think that adequately describes the feel, because—and I'll say this without any equivocation whatsoever—good or bad, I was always in charge of my sessions. Definitely in charge. But at the same time, when I say in charge, it was a type of thing that I made them know I was a part of the total effort. Because they didn't *need* anybody else looking down their nose,

they'd had *enough* of that in their life. That would have been the one thing
that would have kept them exactly where they were—*nowhere.'*

Y OU CAN HEAR an example of Phillips's psychologizing on the Dutch
bootleg LP, *Good Rockin' Tonight,* which contains alternate takes of
several of Elvis's earliest sides as well as a studio conversation between Jerry
Lee Lewis and Sam Phillips that came about in the midst of recording 'Great
Balls of Fire,' one of Lewis's biggest hits. Lewis apparently was reluctant to
record the song because of what he saw as its blasphemous attitude towards
the 'fire' prophesied in Revelations. He and Phillips got into a heated theo-
logical discussion, in the course of which Sam declared in measured tones,
'Now look, Jerry, religious conviction doesn't mean anything resembling
extremism. You mean to tell me you're gonna take the Bible and revolutionize
the whole universe?' It is a revealing exchange—revealing both of the anti-
nomian doubts that fueled rock 'n' roll from the start, and of Sam Phillips's
skill as an advocate—and, needless to say, Phillips prevailed.

A similar crisis occurred when Billy Lee Riley, a very talented artist who
never quite achieved a fame commensurate with his talents, felt slighted by
the attention that Sam was paying to his new artist, Jerry Lee Lewis. Riley
came into the studio drunk one night and started tearing it up. Knox Phillips,
who is today recording Riley for his own Red Rooster label but was no more
than fourteen at the time, called his father—he told Bob Palmer—and 'Sam
said, "Lock the studio door, and don't let him leave till I get there."'

'Sam got there,' Riley told Palmer, 'and we went back in his little cubby-
hole and talked all night till sun-up. Sam told me, "'Red Hot' [Riley's latest
single] ain't got it. We're savin' you for something *good.*" When I left I felt
like I was the biggest star on Sun Records.'

Carl Perkins remembers when Sam Phillips showed up unexpectedly for
Perkins's first appearance on Dallas's Big D Jamboree. 'I was just about to go
on the stage when he said, "Wait a minute, cat"—he always called me "cat"—
he had this box under his arm, and he took out a pair of blue suede shoes
that he'd had made—well, he didn't have them made, he'd had somebody to
put blue sparkles all over them, man, they was good-looking shoes, and
when the lights hit them things, that house went wild. And Sam flew from
Memphis to Dallas to put them shoes on my feet.

'Sam, he got a kick out of doing things like that. You got to remember
that Elvis, Cash, none of us had anything. We were very poor, came from
poor people, and it was Sam—I know he did for me—bought me the first
clothes I ever had to wear on stage. Well, you see, he really had the knack, he
just seemed to know—when we'd be making a record, he'd step out from
behind that little old glass window, and he'd say, "All right, boys, we just
about on it now." He'd say, "Do it again. Do it one time for Sam." Oh yeah,
he did me that way all the time. It was just that type of thing, you just forgot

about making a record and tried to show him. It was things like that that'd cause me—I'd walk out on a limb, I'd try things I knew I couldn't do, and I'd get in a corner trying to do it and then have to work my way out of it. I'd say, "Mr. Phillips, that's terrible." He said, "That's original." I said, "But it's just a big original mistake." And he said, *"That's what Sun Records is. That's what we are."'*

And yet one by one they left him. Elvis, of course, was the first. Then Johnny Cash and Carl Perkins went to Columbia. Jerry Lee Lewis eventually signed with Mercury, and Jack Clement and Bill Justis (Sun's chief engineer and arranger) were both fired on the same day for 'insubordination.' Some say all these defections were the normal sort of fallout for any small company; others point to a low royalty rate, problems with distribution, and Sam Phillips's notorious fiscal conservatism.

'Now what happened was that some of the artists—now I'm not a person that's real easy to get close to in certain areas, and I wish I weren't that way, but I know this—and some of the artists later on, I think, felt that maybe I was devoting a little more time to this new artist that needed nurturing like I had tried to nurture the early ones. So there was a little friction, and they got a little mad at me, but I think they trusted me even though they left me when a bunch of bullshitters started talking big money and this sort of thing. It's kind of like a family. Some children can feel that just because you feel this one needs a little more attention—well, they've forgotten that *they* got attention and love. But for that reason I have never felt hard at any of the people that left me.'

Almost without exception, each of the artists went on to a painful history of guilt and inner turmoil, and Sam Phillips has given much thought to just what it was that caused so much unhappiness in the later lives of his protégés. It was not, he is firmly convinced, rock 'n' roll itself that was the culprit.

'Well, to me the entertainment of people—the *ability* to entertain with the spiritual qualifications of these people—is just almost boundless. I'll tell you what, there is a lot of spirituality out on that stage that just like religion— or anything else in church when it's used the wrong way—is going to hurt some people. But that doesn't mean that rock itself was bad. It never was. It's just that people got so wrought up in the idea of making millions of dollars. And the managers and the bookers, they didn't give a damn, man, it's another product, it's another number, milk it for what it's worth. And so it was difficult for these people to undergird themselves, and then, of course, it happened so fast. So the first thing that started in their minds was: when am I going to be rejected?'

Knox Phillips remembers vividly the day when the Million Dollar Quartet was both formed and disbanded (what happened was that Elvis, already under contract to RCA, wandered down to the Sun studio during a Carl Perkins session on which Jerry Lee Lewis was playing piano; it was, as

Sun sale closing, 1969; Shelby Singleton, center, Sam Phillips, left.
Courtesy of John and Shelby Singleton.

Sam Phillips says, a momentous 'happenstance,' but one which, because
Elvis was an RCA recording artist, had still not been heard by the public as
of 1979). Elvis hugged Knox and his brother, Jerry, then twelve and nine
respectively. 'He said, "Stay with me, boys, stay with me." And at the time
I didn't know that had any real significance, because I didn't know Elvis
intimately or anything, but evidently he was a very insecure person, and us
having long hair and looking a little bit like him represented some kind of
reinforcement.'

'Well, he was torn,' says Sam. 'Elvis — if he had had the proper love ratio
with someone that he truly loved and felt and trusted — this would never
have befallen Elvis. Because Elvis in so many ways was an extremely strong
person, but in other ways, without that ability to communicate with somebody
that he felt truly felt him and knew him and understood him, this is where
Elvis's problem came. Where it comes in with all of us. So I can tell you one
thing. All of the artists that I had, if they had stayed with Sam Phillips, we
might have starved to death together. But — and I like a drink as good as
anybody, but I'll tell you what — there would have been no great extremes,
because I would have shown them one way or the other *that I loved them.*'

EVENTUALLY SAM PHILLIPS, too, lost interest in his creation and then got
out of the record business altogether.

With protégé Jack Clement, 1973. Courtesy of Jack Clement.

'I thank myself for having the good judgment to get out of the business rather than trying to compete against certain economic blocs that I just could not control. Number one, I knew I couldn't compete with the giants, and number two, I saw the business falling apart at the seams to where I couldn't live with it and make a living in an honest way. So rather than to lose my respect for myself and to cheat people, instead of just folding my tent and running away and being bitter at anybody and not doing anything, I just proceeded to do something else. We get a little fulfillment day by day.'

Sam Phillips went on to become a wealthy man (he is an original share-holder in Holiday Inns), but he remains a Memphian through and through (Memphis, always a haven for eccentrics and individualists, is the only locale I know that actually boasts of its craziness). He still lives in the same modest house he has inhabited for the last twenty years, busies himself with his radio stations, expresses nothing but contempt for the Nashville establish-ment, whom he sees as 'a bunch of bullshitters' for the most part, and remains 'as strong in the faith of reason' as he has always been.

When we met, he was waiting for the latest Arbitron ratings to determine if the new radio station format had a chance of catching on. At the end of a long day we sat in a waterlogged office watching rock 'n' roll history on a tiny black and white TV, mostly with the sound turned off. For a moment there was Jerry Lee Lewis, and Sam perked up. 'Ah, Uncle Gerald,' he chuckled appreciatively. 'You think that guy isn't dynamic? That man can play more piano in a minute than anyone I've ever seen!' Then Elvis came on the screen, looking impossibly young, impossibly expectant. The show was called 'The Heroes of Rock 'n' Roll.'

'Ah, wasn't he something. Let me tell you something about him. Elvis—you looking at him now, back then—he looks so clumsy and so totally un-coordinated. And this was the beauty of it, he was being himself. Well, he had that little innocence about him, and yet he had, even then he had a little something that was almost impudent in a way. That was his crutch. He certainly didn't mean to be impudent, but he had enough of that, along with what he could convey, that he was just beautiful and lovely—and I'm not talking about physical beauty, because he was not that good-looking then. Really, by conventional standards he was supposed to have been thrown off that stage, and I—listen, I calculated that stuff in my mind. Are they going to resent him? With his long sideburns? That could be a plus or a minus. But I looked at it as this. When he came through like he did, it was neither. *He stood on his own*.

'Let me say this. I don't want to come off as the poor ole country boy that made good or anything like that. I'm just trying to come over with what I know deep in my heart to be the truth, as I relayed it to myself then. I may have some dates wrong, and some facts and figures, but the material aspects of it is not wrong. Cause I will see it in my mind's eye until the day I die—and then I'm not so sure I won't see it after that. I'm not looking for any heroism or anything at all, but I think that music is a part of a very spiritual aspect of people. And I just think that it has gotten out of hand a little bit today, scientifically trying to analyze everything that you do, and if it doesn't have that stamp, then nobody can peddle it. I don't say there's a thing wrong with disco, but when you drive so much of the same thing and people get into too much of a pattern, I want to tell you that if that is giving of yourself in a way that you can be fulfilled, then I just don't have the ability to interpret it in that way. Listen, they're talking about that you've got to have—well, what is the trend now? Well, *Jesus God*, now if there's anything we don't need, it's a trend.

'One of these days, though, I may not live to see it, maybe you all will, but one of these days that freedom is going to come back.'

Sam Phillips's voice rises, it is like a flood, and you can hear him telling Elvis that yes, his music will prevail. It will.

'Because look, the expression of the people is almost, it's so powerful, it's almost like a hydrogen bomb. It's going to get out.

'Now let me just tell you one other thing, Peter, and I'll get out of here. I'm not just saying go back to the fifties and this sort of thing. But if it could be worked—and it will be worked—to where just a few like Elvis could break out, then I would preach, I would become an evangelist if I were alive, saying,

For God's sake, *don't* let's become conformists—*please*. Just do your thing in your own way. Don't ever let fame and fortune or recognition or anything interfere with what you feel is here—*if* you feel you are a creative individual. Then don't let the companies get this going real good and buy up all the rights of the individual some way or the other. That's not right. We'll go back in another circle. Till it gets so damn boring that your head is swimming. And I'll tell you, I hope it's not too long coming, because of the fact as we go longer and longer into the lack of individual expression, as we go along, if we get too far we going to get away from some of the real basic things. All of us damn cats and people that appreciate not the fifties necessarily but that freedom are gonna forget about the feel. We gonna be in jail, and not even know it.'

SELECTED
DISCOGRAPHY

O BVIOUSLY a selection of this sort is bound to be arbitrary and is very much a reflection of personal taste. It is intended, however, to suggest a basis for listening from which the interested reader can go on to make his or her own choices. I have tried to pick records that are, or have been, generally available, but record companies come and go, conglomerates absorb whole catalogues and spit out new identifying numbers, and once an artist has been dropped by his label, there is no telling how long his records will stay in catalogue. In addition, with the CD revolution of the last few years, the whole business has been thrown into a state of even greater confusion, with a surprising profusion of reissues in some areas and a surprising dearth in others. Here's how I've tried to solve a virtually insoluble problem in what amounts to an age of technological transition. I've listed the best available selection that I know of in compact disc format as of spring 1992, along with the latest catalogue numbers. If, however, a particular album has not been translated to CD, and no suitable substitute is available, I have simply included the original, or most familiar, LP version with an asterisk to indicate its antediluvian status and appropriate identifying information. What I have not done is to substitute an anomalous Greatest Hits package for a carefully thought-out idiosyncratic classic by Merle Haggard, say, simply because the former is currently available and the latter is not. If you want to pursue the matter further, Roundup Records, Roots & Rhythm (formerly Down Home Music), and Red Lick Records are matchless mail-order repositories for roots music of all kinds and issue extensive catalogues. Write to Roundup at P.O. Box 154, Cambridge, MA 02140. Roots & Rhythm's address is 6921 Stockton Ave., El Cerrito, CA 94530; Red Lick's is P.O. Box 3, Porthmadog, Gwynedd, Wales.

PART ONE: HONKY TONK HEROES

The recordings of Jimmie Rodgers have been made available in countless anthologies and combinations. Any of them are good. My favorites are: *Never No Mo' Blues* (RCA LPM 1232), *Train Whistle Blues* (LPM 1640), and *My Rough and Rowdy Ways* (LPM 2112), which provide a fine selection of Rodgers's blues, railroad ballads, and sentimental favorites. In 1992 Bear Family issued a beautifully illustrated and annotated 6-CD set of the

Brewton, Alabama, 1973. VALERIE WILMER

complete recordings called *The Singing Brakeman* (BCD 15540), while Rounder completed its own individually packaged 8-volume set (Rounder 1056-1063). You can't really go wrong.

ERNEST TUBB

Country Music Hall of Fame (MCA D-10086) A good many of the hits, 1941–1965, nicely selected and annotated by Tubb's biographer and archivist, Ronnie Pugh.

*Honky Tonk Classics (Rounder SS14). Probably an even better selection. Wonderful, uncluttered, idiosyncratic versions of just what the title plainly states, once again selected by Ronnie Pugh.

Live, 1965 (Rhino 70902-2). A wonderful recent find. The only legitimate representation of Tubb's live show on record, with all the warmth and all the homespun charm that he routinely dispensed pretty much on a nightly basis.

HANK SNOW

*Just Keep A Movin' (Detour 33-004). It's hard to imagine improving on this non-hit selection. Great sound, great music, great package. The unheralded birth of rock 'n' roll.

The Singing Ranger (Bear Family BCD 15426). All of his American recordings from 1949–1953, a 4-CD set. I wouldn't recommend this with most artists (certainly not with Ernest Tubb, who does have his own multiple-CD Bear Family set), and even with the Singing Ranger there is a dismaying amount of dross. But there is so much that is wonderful, and the sound and packaging are so exemplary. . . If you really love this set, you can go on to Volumes II and III (and, probably, more). If you want to start with a less daunting package, try either *I'm Movin' On* (RCA 9968-2) or *16 Top Tracks* (RCA [UK] 90106), both Greatest Hits collections.

DEFORD BAILEY

*Harmonica Showcase (Matchbox 218). DeFord's complete output on one side, including 'Pan American Blues.'

RUFUS THOMAS

The Blues Came Down from Memphis (Charly CD 67). A good selection of Sun's blues material, including representative cuts by Dr. Ross and Joe Hill Louis as well as Rufus's 'Bear Cat' and 'Tiger Man.'

Walking the Dog (Atlantic CD 82254). Rufus's newly reissued first album remains his best representation on record. Here Rufus sings the blues, does the Sophisticated Sissy and performs at least two versions of the Dog.

BOBBY 'BLUE' BLAND

The 3B Blues Boy (Ace CD CHD302). The earliest Duke sides, from 1953 on. Raw, untutored, more like B. B. King than you would expect – but indispensable.

The Voice (Ace CD CHD323). A lesson in sophistication. This is Bobby at his creamist, most soulful, and riveting best, with 26 selections and the best sound you're ever going to get from Duke masters. 1959–1969 recordings. Classic.

Two Steps from the Blues (MCA D-27036), **Here's the Man* (MCA 27038), **Call On Me/That's the Way Love Is* (MCA 27042), **Ain't Nothing You Can Do* (MCA 27040). These are the individual albums from which the above was derived. Bobby at his best – all the hits, all the feeling. Finally *Touch of the Blues* and *Spotlighting the Man* (Mobile Fidelity MF CD770), two good 1969 albums packaged on one superior-sounding CD, would make a nice secondary selection.

His California Album (MCA D-10349). The best of his '70s recordings. Very nice, despite a somewhat misleading title. *Together for the First Time . . . Live* (MCA D-4160); *Together Again . . . Live* (MCA D-27012). With B. B. King. Interesting both for the music and the implicit rivalry. Bobby wins, but the victory is a little hollow.

PART TWO: HILLBILLY BOOGIE

For rockabilly background there are countless sources, but Arthur Crudup, Bill Monroe, and Sister Rosetta Tharpe are three who have been constantly cited. Crudup's *That's All Right Mama* (RCA 61043) contains a good selection (22 cuts) of his influential early recordings, including 'Mean Old Frisco,' 'Rock Me Mamma,' and of course 'That's All Right.' Bill Monroe has innumerable top-notch albums out. Probably the most logical place to start would be *The Country Music Hall of Fame* (MCA D-10082), which includes 'Blue Moon of Kentucky' among 16 classic sides. Sister Rosetta Tharpe's **Gospel Train* (MCA 1317) features the rockabilly gospel of 'Strange Things Happening Every Day' as well as the folk standard, 'This Train,' which she originated.

CHARLIE FEATHERS

Rock-A-Billy (Zu Zazz ZCD2011). Close to the (still unrealized) Charlie Feathers collection. Strongest on the early Sun sessions with fascinating demos, singles, and alternate takes from 1954 on, through four classic King sides and an assortment of oddities up till 1973. Greil

Marcus has called 'One Hand Loose' from the 1956 King session 'everything rockabilly was meant to be . . . fast, hard, simple, straight, and utterly impassioned.' With a wonderfully (and typically) eccentric early version of 'Frankie and Johnny,' wherein bluegrass meets the blues.

Good Rockin' Tonight (Barrelhouse 03). 1973 recordings which Charlie said he hated but I think are great.

Live in Memphis, Tennessee (Barrelhouse 06). More of the same in a club setting. Not as good, but with Charlie's brother, Lawrence, rocking away as well.

ELVIS PRESLEY

Here the going gets rough. I could include a dozen pages on Presley alone, but I won't. I've left out the hits, the oddities, and the gospel albums and concentrated on my secular favorites. In recent years, through the unstinting efforts first of Gregg Geller and then of Ernst Jorgensen and Roger Semon, RCA has finally caught up with the bootleggers, so almost all the albums listed here will be official (and current) RCA releases.

The Sun Sessions CD (RCA 6414-2-R). All of the titles, most of the alternate takes and studio conversation, all the experiments and all the dogged failures on a single-CD set. About as close as we're going to get to what Elvis and Sam Phillips were really aiming for in the beginning.

The King of Rock 'n' Roll (RCA 66050-2). The complete '50s master recordings in a 5-CD box, completely remastered and researched by Ernst Jorgensen. This includes both sides of the acetate an 18-year-old Elvis made for his mother in the summer of '53, as well as a fifth CD of rarities, with astonishing live performances from 1955.

Elvis: A Golden Celebration (RCA CPM 6-5172) A monumental 6-record collection, which includes all of the 1956–57 TV appearances, an almost inaudible but fascinating homecoming performance at the Mississippi-Alabama Fair and Dairy Show in Tupelo, and outtakes from the 1968 TV special. More of a resource than a listening experience, but invaluable in that respect.

Elvis . . . The Beginning Years (Louisiana Hayride 3061). Live from the Louisiana Hayride, 1954, 1955, and into 1956. Startling and familiar both, at one and the same time. Only nine selections.

The Million Dollar Quartet (RCA 2023-2). Actually a trio. Over an hour of Elvis, Carl Perkins, and Jerry Lee Lewis fooling around in the Sun studio in 1956 with gospel, country, blues, and rock 'n' roll. There are many illuminating moments, but perhaps the most illuminating of all occurs when Elvis describes Jackie Wilson's performance of 'Don't Be Cruel' in Las Vegas with the Dominoes and imitates Wilson emulating him. 'He tried so hard until he got much better, boy, than that record of mine,' says Elvis, with true conviction.

Stereo 57: Essential Elvis Vol 2 (RCA 9589-2). An archaeological find. Wonderful alternative takes in a relaxed and illuminating setting – and in true stereo (binaural) to boot.

Elvis – NBC Special (RCA 61021-2). A good document of a great moment in history, but if you want the whole picture, see if you can find **The Burbank Sessions* Vol. 1 (Audifon AFNS 62768), a bootleg which offes a complete record of the small-group (trio for the most part) concerts from which snippets of the '68 special were taken. Scotty was there, D.J. was there, and *Elvis* was there, all the way.

The Memphis Record (RCA 6221-2R). The 1969 Chips Moman sessions. His finest studio recordings since Sun. Indispensable.

Reconsider Baby (RCA 5418-2). Elvis sings the blues, ranging in time from 1954 to 1972. Might be something of a revelation to the Elvis neophyte.

Elvis Country (RCA 6330-2). The other side of the coin. A 1971 attempt, largely successful, to recreate some of the ambience of the Sun recordings, with a small group version of Bill Monroe's 'Little Cabin on the Hill' and a rocking 'Whole Lotta Shakin'' standing in for 'That's All Right' and 'Blue Moon of Kentucky.'

CHARLIE RICH

*Original Hits and Midnight Demos (Charly Sun CDX 10). The issued Sun sides are fine, with some classics and some duds, but the 'midnight demos' are the treat.

The Complete Smash Sessions (Mercury 314 512 643-2). The sessions that Charlie was most satisfied with musically from the early part of his career. Brilliant original material.

*Charlie Rich (English RCA NL 89999). A facsimile of his RCA Groove album, produced by Chet Atkins. Nearly as good as the Smash material, not quite as moody but jazzier and a little more swinging.

*The Fabulous Charlie Rich (Epic 26516). My favorite; includes 'Life's Little Ups and Downs.'

Behind Closed Doors (Epic EK 32247). The hits that made him a superstar, with a good selection of additional material.

*Silver Linings (Epic 33545). The gospel side of Charlie Rich. Beautiful and heartfelt (if occasionally gimmicky) versions of old favorites, sung in the inimitable manner.

Rockabilly Stars, Vol. I (Columbia Special Products 37618). Includes the original demo version of 'Feel Like Going Home.'

Pictures and Paintings (Sire 9 26730-2). I've got to admit to more than a soft spot in my heart for this. The album that Charlie wanted to make from the time that I first met him – blues, jazz, soul, and beautiful new originals from Charlie and Margaret Ann, in 1992. I can't even pretend to be objective about it – I think the highlights for me are 'Mood Indigo' and 'You Don't Know Me,' which would have been an equally apt title for the album.

SLEEPY LABEEF

Sleepy LaBeef: Early, Rare, and Rockin' Sides (Baron 102). Sleepy at his earliest and rarest (includes a couple of his pseudonymous cover versions as well as previously unissued demos), but not necessarily his rockingest. Great 'Baby, Let's Play House' and a couple of other storming cuts which feature the legendary Charlie Busby and thirteen-year-old Wendell Clayton on bass.

1977 Rockabilly (Sun 1004), *Beefy Rockabilly* (Charly 30145). The Sun years. Good feeling, poor production – lacking the wit, variety, and crackling lead guitar of Sleepy's live show.

Downhome Rockabilly (Sun 841-063-2). This is more like it. The last of Sleepy's Sun sessions, and the first to feature his own lead guitar. About half the album is Sleepy at close to his studio best, and 'There Is Something On Your Mind' is alone worth the price of admission.

It Ain't What You Eat, It's the Way How You Chew It (Rounder 3052), *Electricity* (Rounder 3070). Wonderfully eclectic and deeply felt. *It Ain't What You Eat* is a selection of the most wide-ranging material – perhaps a little *too* wide-ranging – which catches fire on selections like 'Shake a Hand' and a wonderful 'Tutti Frutti.' *Electricity* is a little more consistent, with a classic 'Ain't Got No Home' and an inspirational title cut. It's all Sleepy, though, guts and guitar and those unpredictable moments when everything comes together.

Nothin' But the Truth (Rounder CD3072). *The* Sleepy LaBeef album. Live at Harper's Ferry, 1985, with all the crazy music, and all the unlikely juxtapositions, that no studio album could ever do more than suggest. 'Let's Talk About Us' is something like the Mighty Clouds of Joy meet Rockabilly.

MICKEY GILLEY

Mickey Gilley Story, Vols. I and II (Collector 1013 and 1014). Gilley in the early years. 'I Ain't Bo Diddley.'

Mickey Gilley's Greatest Hits, Vol. I (Epic EK 34743). Just like it says.

Room Full of Roses, *Gilley's Smokin'* (Columbia PE 34736,34749). The best of his numerous individual albums.

JACK CLEMENT

All I Want to Do in Life (Elektra 6E-122). *The* Jack Clement album (still the only one to date).

The recordings of Hank Williams and Lefty Frizzell are available in a number of different forms. Probably the best overall Hank Williams package is *The Original Singles Collection* (Polydor 847-194-2), which collects all the singles and a number of rarities in a beautifully annotated 3-CD set. In addition, Polydor has issued an 8-volume double-album set which includes all of Hank Williams's studio recordings, and a good many previously unreleased ones from studio and demo sessions, with exemplary sound and exemplary notes. This is a priceless treasury. The titles are: *I Ain't Got Nothin' But Time* (Polydor 825 548-2), *Lovesick Blues* (825 551-2), *Lost Highway* (825 554-2), *I'm So Lonesome I Could Cry* (825 557-2), *Long Gone Lonesome Blues* (831 633-2), *Hey, Good Lookin'* (831 634-2), *Let's Turn Back the Years* (833 749-2), and *I Won't Be Home No More* (833 752-2). Finally, for the person just looking for an introduction, *40 Greatest Hits* (Polygram 821 233-2) is undoubtedly the best place to start. *The Best of Lefty Frizzell* (Rhino 71005-2) pretty much runs the gamut of Lefty's hit-making career, while two Rounder anthologies, **Treasures Untold* (SS 11) and **Lefty Goes to Nashville* (SS 16), document the time when 'Hank and Lefty crowded every jukebox,' though for the most part avoiding the hits. **Lefty Frizzell Sings the Songs of Jimmie Rodgers* (Columbia C32249) is a faithful and deeply moving tribute. If you're really feeling ambitious and want to get a sense of the scope (as well as some of the depressing commercial troughs) of Lefty's work, save your money and get *Life's Like Poetry* (Bear Family 1550), a completist's 12-CD tribute (along with a 152-page biographical book by Charles Wolfe) to a great talent.

The Bob Wills Anthology (CBS Special Products 32416) is a start towards an appreciation of Wills's monumental and far-ranging achievement, and six volumes of radio transcriptions (*The Tiffany Transcriptions* Vols. I–VI, Tiffany 16, 19–21, 25, and 27) give a fine idea of how the band actually worked outside the somewhat stiff confines of the commercial recording studio. If you like these, there are even more!

WAYLON JENNINGS

*Honky Tonk Heroes (RCA APL 1-0240). The classic Waylon Jennings. Though he had been recording for years when he made this album in 1973, this was where it all came together.

*This Time (RCA APL 1-0539). Waylon and Willie – sung, produced and written by the two original Outlaws. Far better than the platinum-selling Outlaw anthologies.

*Dreaming My Dreams (RCA APL 1-1062). Waylon with his then brother-in-law, Cowboy Jack Clement, producing. A dream team.

*Waylon Live (RCA APL 1-1108). Not the ultimate, but a pretty fair representation of the Waylon Experience live in Texas in the mid-'70s.

Ol' Waylon (RCA APL 1-2317). The best of his post-Outlaw excursions. Thoughtful and somewhat introspective.

I've Always Been Crazy (RCA APL 1-2979). Interesting more as psycho-drama than as music.

HANK WILLIAMS, JR.

Hank Williams, Jr. And Friends (Polydor 831 575-2) The first of his breaking-free statements. Includes some of his most moving autobiographical songs.

One Night Stands (Elektra 5E-538). Post-accident, nowhere near as revela-tory, but nice musical feeling.

The New South (Elektra 5E-539) My favorite, even though it doesn't have quite the impact of *And Friends*. Hopeful, anxious, quirky, self-aware. Like a running diary of his life.

Family Tradition (Elektra 194-2). Some great new compositions, disappoint-ing production. For all of its extraordinary impact in live performance and on demos by Waylon and Hank junior, 'I Just Ain't Been Able (To Write No Songs)' seems to have been thrown away in the studio. Nonetheless, the album is almost worth it for the title cut alone.

In the last ten or twelve years Hank Williams, Jr., has achieved an ex-tremely high level of visibility. He has come out with one strong album after another, which has seen him taking on blues, rock'n'roll, popular standards, the libertarian mystique, and personal demons. He is always interesting, if not always (perhaps no longer even often) in the best of taste, and is perhaps the most broadly popular figure in contemporary country music. Nonetheless, I would still argue that the above albums – which are marked by a kind of naked vulnerability rarely on display today – are the place to start.

MERLE HAGGARD

Merle Haggard is probably the most difficult artist to sum up both because of the breadth of his work and his prolific output. His recordings reveal so many different facets of Merle and his music that it's difficult to select a representative few. For that reason I've tried to group some of his best records in generic categories. Unfortunately, as of spring 1992, virtually none of his Capitol output remains in print. Rather than try to update the catalogue numbers with new numbers that have themselves become ob-solete, or replace classic albums with perfectly respectable but relatively random, homogenized anthologies, I have retained the original listing data.

*I'm a Lonesome Fugitive, *Branded Man, *Sing Me Back Home, *Mama Tried
(Capitol ST 2702, 2789, 2848, 2972). The best of his prison recordings.
*For the Last Time (UA LA 216-J2), *A Tribute to the Best Damn Fiddle Player in
the World (Capitol ST 638), *I Love Dixie Blues (Capitol ST 11200). Merle's
tribute records. The first is kind of a ringer, a Bob Wills reunion in
which Merle played only a peripheral part (he sings three tunes and
plays a little fiddle). The record is enhanced by the limited participation of Wills himself, already incapacitated by a stroke, and remains a
brilliant and moving document. Merle's A Tribute to the Best Damn
Fiddle Player, for which he reassembled much of Wills's band and for
the first time took over Wills's role as bandleader, is as sincere and
genuinely creative an hommage as anything but Merle's Jimmie Rodgers
record. I Love Dixie Blues is another lesson in history, recorded live in
New Orleans with a horn section and honoring both New Orleans jazz
(another forerunner of the blues) and Emmett Miller, an enormously
influential predecessor of Jimmie Rodgers, who is today virtually
unheard and unheard of.
*Same Train, Different Time (Capitol SWBB 223). Merle's masterpiece – an
odd statement, considering the quality of his original work, but somehow everything comes together here on the classic songs of Jimmie
Rodgers.
*Pride in What I Am (Capitol SKAO 168). A beautiful set of originals with an
acoustic emphasis.
*Okie From Muskogee (Capitol ST 384). Live in Muskogee. Functions as a
kind of Greatest Hits.
*Someday We'll Look Back, *Let Me Tell You About a Song (Capitol ST 835, 882).
A pair of albums which do look back, this time on personal history, on
Oklahoma and Bakersfield roots. The latter includes 'They're Tearin'
the Labor Camps Down' and Merle's mild paean to interracial love,
'Irma Jackson.'
*Merle Haggard Presents His Thirtieth Album (Capitol ST 11331). Consciously
sets out to display the kind of variety and musical enterprise that
Merle's whole career has been built on.
*A Working Man Can't Get Nowhere Today (Capitol ST 11693). Put together
after Merle left Capitol, this is one of Merle's best – an amazing
collection, including 'I'm a White Boy,' the ultimate redneck song (in
both good and bad senses).
*The Way It Was in '51 (Capitol SW 11839). Like the latter, post-Capitol, and
made up of songs already out on various LPs. Nonetheless, as true and
deeply felt a tribute as any of the others, this time to Hank and Lefty.
*Serving 190 Proof (MCA 1645). A thoroughly beat and altogether moving
autobiographical statement (as of 1979), in which the singer's age (41)
and spiritual malaise are mentioned often.
*That's the Way Love Goes (Epic FE 38815). The best of Merle's '80s albums,

349

focusing more on the failure of romance than the failure of politics. The Lefty Frizzell title cut is an eloquent expression of Merle's natural (and frequently touching) tendency towards melancholy.

JAMES TALLEY

Got No Bread, No Milk, No Money, But We Sure Got a Lot of Love/Tryin' Like the Devil (Bear Family BCD 15433). James Talley's first two Capitol albums on a single Bear Family CD. The first is Talley's statement about roots and raising and Mehan, Oklahoma. The second is Talley's political statement. Like rock'n'roll, they will stand.

Blackjack Choir/Ain't It Somethin' (Bear Family 15435) The third and fourth combined. These are more uneven. Between the two there is a single great album, with 'Magnolia Boy' from the first and 'Richland, Washington' from the second, equaling in emotion, conciseness, and accessibility anything Talley has ever done.

STONEY EDWARDS

*Mississippi You're On My Mind (Capitol 11401). A nice conventional country collection which includes 'Two Dollar Toy' and 'Hank and Lefty.' Stoney's voice is great, production isn't.

*Blackbird (Capitol ST 11499). More Chip Taylor (author of 'Blackbird' and producer of the record) than it is Stoney, but a definite step in the right direction. Two good Stoney originals, but the real Stoney Edwards has yet to be heard on record. Both Jack Clement and Asleep at the Wheel's Chris O'Connell have recorded interesting (and very different) material on Stoney, but so far none of it has seen the light of day.

PART FOUR: THE BLUES ROLL ON
HOWLIN' WOLF

Memphis Days, Vol. I (Bear Family BCD 15460), *Howlin' Wolf Rides Again* (Ace CHD 333). The early Memphis sessions; crude, raucous, overamplified, powerful, and, all-in-all, simply astonishing. The first is the find.

Moanin' in the Moonlight (Chess CHD 5908), **Rocking Chair* (Chess 9183). Early hits. Probably his best. They appeared together for a time on a two-for-one Chess CD, though the sound wasn't very good.

The Real Folk Blues (Chess CHD 9273). Mostly middle-period material; a little uneven.

Change My Way (Chess CHD 93001). Some of his best middle- and late-period singles (1958–66), brought together in an attractive package.

*The Back Door Wolf (Chess 50045). Wolf at the end. Some great moments, not the least of which is a heartfelt 'Coon on the Moon.'

Howlin' Wolf (Chess CHD 3-9332). A brilliant 3-CD compilation, by far the best of the Chess Boxes to date and a paradigm example of how an anthology of this sort ought to be put together. It covers all of the high spots, with enough rarities to compel interest – but it remains listenable throughout because for once the music alone is the first (and last) consideration, and neither completeness nor collector's myopia stands in the way of a uniformly high aesthetic standard.

OTIS SPANN

The Blues Never Die! (Original Blues Classics 538). An historical document – the Muddy Waters band, 1965. Some of Spann's best numbers, with additional vocals by harmonica player James Cotton.

*Half Ain't Been Told (Black Cat 001). Recorded a year earlier in England with pared-down backup (but still including Muddy as 'Brother'). Titles equally good.

Otis Spann Is the Blues, Otis Spann and His Piano (Candid CD 9001,9025). Otis Spann solo and in rare duets with Robert Jr. Lockwood on guitar (Lockwood contributes four classic vocals on the first album). The first is the best, but both are worth looking for.

*The Blues Is Where It's At (Bluesway 6003 [also as **Nobody Knows Chicago Like I Do*, Charly 1062]); *The Bottom of the Blues* (BGO CD92). Not quite as fresh as the preceding, but well worth a listen. Some great Muddy and Spann originals.

Chicago/The Blues/Today! Vol. I (Vanguard VMD 79216). Spann alone with drummer S. P. Leary and a frog in his throat. Strangely affecting atmosphere. The album also features nice sides by Junior Wells and J. B. Hutto.

BIG JOE TURNER

I've Been to Kansas City (MCA D-42351). A fine collection of great early sides.

Rhythm and Blues Years (Atlantic 81663-2). Nothing can really take the place of the classic Atlantic collection, the aptly named **Rockin' the Blues* (Atlantic 8023), but this comes close. It doesn't have the hits, but it has the ambience and includes Big Joe's collaboration with slide guitarist Elmore James on 'TV Mama' ('the one with the big wide screen'). For the hits try the eponymous *Greatest Hits* (Atlantic 81752-2), an exemplary collection.

JUKE JOINT BLUES

*Son Seals Blues Band (Alligator 4703). Great original material, with a Magic Sam wobble in the voice. Not yet fully realized.

Midnight Son (Alligator CD 4708). *The* Son Seals album. Commanding.

Live and Burning (Alligator 4712). More of the same. Which could also be said for Son's subsequent Alligator work. Start here.

Johnson's Whacks (Delmark DD 644). *Not* the slipshod Jimmy Johnson album that was being recorded for a Miami label the day I happened to visit the studio. Rather, this is *the* Jimmy Johnson album. Funny, inventive, musically adventurous, tough and lyrical, a breath of fresh air after all the clichés that often masquerade as Chicago blues. Jimmy has since made a number of other fine albums, but to my ears this remains his best to date.

Living Chicago Blues (Alligator CD 7701-7703). Jimmy Johnson, Magic Slim, Lonnie Brooks, Left Hand Frank, plus more. Beautifully recorded, with soul and imagination – perhaps just a little too clean for the joints. Delmark and Alligator between them pretty much cover the range of contemporary Chicago blues from the mid-'60s on (from Otis Rush and Junior Wells to Magic Sam, Hound Dog Taylor, and Fenton Robinson). Support them!

EPILOGUE: SAM PHILLIPS

The Charly series in England for some time represented Sam Phillips's legacy writ large. With well over 100 albums at its peak, it was on occasion pretty indiscriminate (as Phillips never was) and offers a classic illustration of the collector's mania for completeness to the frequent exclusion of good taste. Its present status seems up in the air, with LPs in the final stages of deletion and CDs not yet in hand. Both Rhino and Rounder have put out pretty good samplers, and Bear Family seems to be gearing up for a massive CD release. With all of these factors of shifting availability in mind, here are the best collections of blues, country, and rockabilly that I know of as recorded by Sam Phillips from 1950 on. *The Sun Story*, Vols. I and II (Instant 5039 and 5040: this was the old 3-LP *Sun Box* on Charly) is the best overall survey of the label. *Sun Records: The Blues Years* (Charly Sun Box 105), a 9-record set, is astonishing for its breadth and range, whereas *The Sun Country Years* (LP only at this point but still available on Bear Family 15211), a 10-record set, and *The Rocking Years* (Charly Sun Box 106), which weighs in at no less than 12 records and 221 selections, are probably for fanatics only. *Jerry Lee Lewis: The Definitive Edition of his Sun Recordings* (Bear Family 15420), on the other hand, is the one comprehensive boxed set indispensable to any rock 'n' roll (or blues, or country) record collection. It is nothing less than monumental (as Jerry Lee himself might say).

For a complete Bear Family catalogue, write P.O. Box 1154, 2864 Vollersode, West Germany. I really don't know what's going on with Charly, but watch for further developments.

GENERAL
BIBLIOGRAPHY

T HE MAGAZINES *Living Blues* (Center for the Study of Southern Culture, University of Mississippi, University, Mississippi, 38677), *Blues Unlimited* (36 Belmont Park, Lewisham, London, England), and *New Kommotion* (3 Bowrons Ave., Wembley, Middlesex, England) have been helpful in their entirety for their documentation of blues and rockabilly music. *Old Time Music* (33 Brunswick Gardens, London, England) is essential reading for any insight into what country music was before Nashville became an industry. *Picking Up the Tempo* (P.O. Drawer 150, Alice, Texas 78332) is long defunct, but a glance through its back pages will illuminate the outlaw ethos in country music, as no slick commercial venture has been able to. *Country Music* (342 Madison Ave., Suite 2118, New York, N.Y. 10173) is the most successful of the latter publications and in its fifteen-year existence has continued to prove an invaluable barometer of country trends, as will be evident from the chapter bibliography.

The bibliography which follows is a selective listing of books of general interest, books I like, and books which have been specifically useful in the preparation of *Lost Highway*. Obviously there can be no pretense of completeness (I have left a blues bibliography almost entirely to *Feel Like Going Home*), but this listing, like the discography which precedes it, is intended to give the reader a jumping-off place to pursue his or her own purely idiosyncratic inclinations.

John Atkins, ed. *The Carter Family*. London: Old Time Music, 1973.

Michael Bane. *The Outlaws*. New York: Country Music Magazine/Dolphin Press, 1978.

Johnny Bond. *The Recordings of Jimmie Rodgers: An Annotated Discography*. Los Angeles: John Edwards Memorial Foundation Press, 1978.

John J. Broven. *Walking to New Orleans*. Bexhill-on-Sea: Blues Unlimited Press, 1974.

Johnny Cash. *Man in Black*. Grand Rapids: Zondervan, 1975.

Steve Chapple and Reebee Garofalo. *Rock 'n' Roll is Here to Pay*. Chicago: Nelson-Hall, 1977.

Ray Charles and David Ritz. *Brother Ray: Ray Charles' Own Story*. New York: Dial Press, 1978.

Diego Cortez. *Private Elvis*. Stuttgart: FEY, 1978.

Fred Dellar, Roy Thompson and Douglas Green. *The Illustrated Encyclopedia of Country Music.* New York: Harmony Books, 1977.

Colin Escott and Martin Hawkins. *Catalyst: The Sun Records Story.* London: Aquarius Books, 1975.

——. *The Complete Sun Label Session Files.* Self-published.

John Goldrosen. *Buddy Holly: His Life and Music.* Bowling Green: Popular Press, 1975.

Douglas Green. *Country Roots.* New York: Hawthorn Books, 1976.

John Grissim. *Country Music: White Man's Blues.* New York: Paperback Library, 1970.

Tony Heilbut. *The Gospel Sound: Good News and Bad Times.* New York: Simon and Schuster, 1971.

Paul Hemphill. *The Nashville Sound: Bright Lights and Country Music.* New York: Simon and Schuster, 1970.

Jerry Hopkins. *Elvis.* New York: Simon and Schuster, 1971.

Michael Hrambalos. *Right On: From Blues to Soul in Black America.* London: Eddison Press, 1974.

Jack Hurst. *Nashville's Grand Ole Opry.* New York: Abrams, 1975.

Zora Neale Hurston. *Their Eyes Were Watching God.* Urbana: University of Illinois Press, 1978.

Charles Keil. *Urban Blues.* Chicago: University of Chicago Press, 1966.

Hans Langbroek. *The Hillbilly Cat.* Self-published.

Michael Lydon. *Rock Folk.* New York: Dial Press, 1971.

Joe McEwen. *Sam Cooke: The Man Who Invented Soul.* New York: Chappell Music, 1977.

Bill Malone. *Country Music U.S.A.: A Fifty Year History.* Austin: University of Texas Press, 1968.

Bill Malone and Judith McCulloh. *Stars of Country Music.* Urbana: University of Illinois Press, 1975.

Greil Marcus. *Mystery Train.* New York: Dutton, 1975.

Bill Millar. *The Coasters.* London: W.H. Allen, 1975.

Albert Murray. *South to a Very Old Place.* New York: McGraw-Hill, 1971.

Hank O'Neal. *A Vision Shared.* New York: St. Martin's Press, 1976.

Mike Paris and Chris Comber. *Jimmie the Kid.* London: Eddison Press, 1977.

Carl Perkins. *Disciple in Blue Suede Shoes.* Grand Rapids: Zondervan, 1978.

Jan Reid. *The Improbable Rise of Redneck Rock.* Austin: Heidelberg Publishers, 1974.

Ger Rijff. *Faces and Stages.* Amsterdam: Tutti Frutti Productions, 1986.

——. *Long Lonely Highway: A 1950's Elvis Scrapbook* (reprint edition). Ann Arbor: Pierian Press, 1988.

Jerry Rivers. *Hank Williams: From Life to Legend.* Denver: Heather Enterprises, 1967.

Mrs. Jimmie Rodgers. *My Husband, Jimmie Rodgers.* Nashville: Country Music Foundation Press, 1975.

Mike Rowe. *Chicago Breakdown.* London: Eddison Bluesbooks, 1973.

Tony Russell. *Blacks, Whites and Blues.* London: Studio Vista, 1970.

Arnold Shaw. *The Rockin' 50s.* New York: Hawthorn Books, 1974.

———. *Honkers and Shouters.* New York: Macmillan, 1978.

Robert Shelton and Burt Goldblatt. *The Country Music Story.* Indianapolis: Bobbs-Merrill, 1966.

Irwin Stambler and Grelun Landon. *Encyclopedia of Folk, Country, and Western.* New York: St. Martin's Press, 1969.

Jimmy Swaggart. *To Cross a River.* Plainfield, N.J.: Logos, 1977.

Nick Tosches. *Country: The Biggest Music in America.* New York: Stein and Day, 1977.

Charles Townsend. *San Antonio Rose: The Life and Music of Bob Wills.* Urbana: University of Illinois Press, 1976.

Alfred Wertheimer. *Elvis '56: In the Beginning.* New York: Collier Books, 1979.

Paul Vernon. *The Sun Legend.* Self-published, London, 1969.

Hank Williams, Jr. (with Michael Bane). *Living Proof: An Autobiography.* To be published by G. P. Putnam's Sons, Fall 1979.

Roger Williams. *Sing a Sad Song: The Life of Hank Williams.* New York: Doubleday, 1970.

Valerie Wilmer. *The Face of Black Music.* New York: Da Capo, 1976.

———. *Jazz People.* Indianapolis: Bobbs-Merrill, 1970.

Charles Wolfe. *The Grand Ole Opry: The Early Years.* London: Old Time Music, 1975.

———. *Tennessee Strings.* Knoxville: University of Tennessee Press, 1977.

Christopher Wren. *Winners Got Scars, Too.* New York: Dial Press, 1971.

THE FOLLOWING ARTICLES and monographs were specifically helpful in the preparation of this book and/or would make good supplementary reading. Many were made available through the resources of the Country Music Foundation in Nashville.

ERNEST TUBB

Norma Barthel. 'Ernest Tubb Yearbook and Discography.' An Ernest Tubb Fan Club publication.
Marshall Fallwell. 'E. T. Remembers.' *Country Music*, April 1974.
Joe Gracey. 'Ernest Tubb.' *Picking Up the Tempo*, No. 8.
Ed Linn. '"Country Singer" – The Ernest Tubb Story.' *Saga*, May 1957.
Red O'Donnell. 'Do What You Do Do Well.' Nashville *Tennessean*.

HANK SNOW

Dick Brown. 'Hank Snow's Lament.' *The Canadian Magazine*, March 1, 1975.
Jo Durden-Smith. 'Nashville Gothic.' *Maclean's Magazine*, May 1972.
'Hank Snow, The Singing Ranger.' Publicity biography put out by Hank Snow Enterprises, 1970.
Stewart MacLeod. '"My Gawd, You've Got to Be the Greatest, Hank."' *Weekend Magazine*, No. 36, 1967.

DEFORD BAILEY

Frye Gaillard. 'An Opry Star Shines On.' *Country Music*, March 1975.
———. 'Sour Notes at the Grand Ole Opry.' *Southern Voices*, May/June 1974.
David Morton. 'Every Day's Been Sunday.' *Nashville!*, 1974.
Bengt Olsson. 'The Grand Ole Opry's DeFord Bailey.' *Living Blues*, No. 21, 1975.

BOBBY BLAND

John J. Broven. 'The Success Story of Duke and Peacock Records.' *Blues Unlimited*, No. 12, June 1964.
J. B. Figi. 'Time for Bobby Bland,' *downbeat*, August 7, 1974.
Russell Gersten. 'That's the Way Soul Is.' *Real Paper*, November 22, 1973.
Gary Giddins. 'Bobby "Blue" Bland Meets the White Folks.' Village *Voice*, September 1, 1975.
Howard Husock. 'Blue As Ever.' Boston *Phoenix*, November 23, 1973.
Mike Leadbitter. 'Don Robey.' *Blues Unlimited*, No. 46, September 1967.
———. 'Memphis.' *Blues Unlimited*, Collectors Classics 13, 1966.
Jim O'Neal. 'Bobby Bland!' *Living Blues*, No. 4, 1970–71.
Doris Worsham. 'Saga of Bobby Bland.' Oakland *Tribune*, March 8, 1975.

ELVIS PRESLEY

Stanley Booth. 'A Hound Dog to the Manor Born.' *Esquire*, February 1968.

Philip Buckle. 'All Elvis.' A London Daily *Mirror* publication, 1962.

'Elvis.' *Rolling Stone* memorial edition, September 22, 1977.

'Elvis.' *TV Radio Mirror* special edition, 1956.

'Elvis Presley Special Edition.' *Country Music*, December 1977.

Albert Hand. 'Meet Elvis.' An *Elvis Monthly* special, 1962.

C. Robert Jennings. 'There'll Always Be an Elvis.' *Saturday Evening Post*, 1965.

CHARLIE RICH

Bob Allen. 'Charlie Rich: Just Rollin' With the Flow.' *Country Music*, April 1979.

Michael Bane. 'The Silver Fox Is Back in His Den.' *Rambler*, September 23, 1976.

Charlie Burton. 'The Ups and Downs in the Life of a Sun Record Legend: Charlie Rich.' *Country Music*, February 1973.

Hank Davis. 'Too Much Talent Hurt Charlie Rich.' *The Ontarion*, January 11, 1973.

Peter McCabe. 'Charlie Rich: Portrait of a Late Bloomer.' *Country Music*, June 1974.

Carol Offen. 'Home Is Where You Start From.' *Country Music Beat*, January 1975.

Mike Saunders. 'Charlie Rich.' *Phonograph Record*, 1973.

'The Silver Fox.' *Newsweek*, November 26, 1973.

MICKEY GILLEY

Bob Claypool. '14 Years on Spencer Highway.' Houston *Post*, April 28, 1974.

———. 'Mickey Gilley's Year of Stardom.' Houston *Post*, July 13, 1975.

———. 'The Boys From Ferriday.' Houston *Post*, June 27, 1976.

JACK CLEMENT

Patrick Carr. 'Swinging Cowboys!! It's Jack Clement.' *Country Music*, November 1974.

Harvey Magee. 'Cowboy.' *Hank*, October 1976.

Lola Scobey. 'Can an Adult Grow Up to Be a Child Star?' *Hitting the Note*, March 1977.

———. 'Let's Help Cowboy Sing.' *Picking Up the Tempo*, No. 20.

WAYLON JENNINGS

Patrick Carr. 'I Couldn't Go Pop With a Mouthful of Firecrackers.' *Country Music*, April 1973.
Dave Hickey. 'In Defense of the Telecaster Cowboy Outlaws.' *Country Music*, January 1974.
———. 'Waylon: More and Better, Faster and Stronger.' *Country Music*, December 1974.
Chet Flippo. 'Waylon Jennings.' *Creem*, July 1973.
———. 'Waylon Jennings Gets Off the Grind 'Em Out Circuit.' *Rolling Stone*, December 6, 1973.

HANK WILLIAMS, JR.

Michael Bane. 'Hank Jr.' *Country Music*, June 1976.
———. 'Hank Williams, Jr.: Long Gone From Daddy.' *Hustler*, 1976.
John Escow. 'The Son Also Rises/Oedipus Rocks.' *New Times*, May 29, 1978.
Jack Hurst. 'Hank Williams, Jr.' Chicago *Tribune*, February 12, 1978.

MERLE HAGGARD

Alice Foster. 'I Take a Lot of Pride in What I Am.' *Sing Out*, March-April 1970.
Paul Hemphill. 'A Restless Aries Loses His Devils.' *Country Music*, November 1972.
'Lord, They've Done It All.' *Time*, May 6, 1974.
Peter McCabe. 'A Candid Conversation with Merle Haggard.' *Country Music*, February 1974.
Earl Paige, ed. 'Merle Speaks His Mind.' *Billboard*, February 19, 1977.
Donn Pearce. 'The Improbable Ballad of Merle Haggard.' *Penthouse*.
'Penthouse Interview: Merle Haggard.' *Penthouse*, 1976.

JAMES TALLEY

Jon Bream. 'James Talley.' Minneapolis *Star*, February 16, 1977.
Doug Green. 'James Talley: Country's Angry Young Man.' *Country Music*, June 1977.
Nat Hentoff. 'James Talley: Tryin' Like the Devil to Be Free.' Village *Voice*, October 10, 1977.
Greil Marcus. 'Message From the Country.' Village *Voice*, August 11, 1975.
Jeannette Smythe. 'James Talley, Blue Collar Bard.' Washington *Post*, October 21, 1977.

STONEY EDWARDS

Glenn Hunter. 'Stoney Edwards.' *Country Music*, March 1976.
David Phillips. 'Stoney Edwards and Friends Talk.' *Picking Up the Tempo*,
    No. 18.

HOWLIN' WOLF

Harper Barnes. 'Honey, Don't You Hear Me Howling?' *Real Paper*, May 30,
    1973.
Howard Husock. 'Moanin' in the Moonlight.' Boston *Phoenix*, June 5, 1973.
Bruce Iglauer. 'Interview with Howlin' Wolf.' *Living Blues*, No. 1, 1970.
Pete Welding. 'Interview.' *downbeat*, December 14, 1967.
Paul Williams and Peter Guralnick. 'Interview.' *Crawdaddy!*, No. 5, 1966.

OTIS SPANN

Sheldon Harris. 'An Otis Spann Record Date.' *Jazz & Pop*, 1968.

BIG JOE TURNER

Whitney Balliett. 'Majesty.' *The New Yorker*, November 29, 1976.
Gary Giddins. 'Big Joe Turner Cooks Up a Shrine.' Village *Voice*, November
    29, 1976.
Mike Kempton. 'Big Joe Turner: He Started Boogie Woogie and Rock 'n'
    Roll.' Boston *Globe*, ca. 1965.

JUKE JOINT BLUES

Howard Mandel. 'Midnight Son-Rise.' *downbeat*, April 4, 1978.
Robert Palmer. 'Son Seals: Born into the Blues.' *Rolling Stone*, March 23, 1978.
Dick Shurman. 'Magic Slim.' *Crazy Music*, No. 8

SAM PHILLIPS

Walter Dawson: 'Interview with Sam Phillips.' Memphis *Commercial Appeal*,
    August 20, 1977.
Claude Hall. 'Phillips, Presley, Cash, Sun.' *Billboard*, December 27, 1969.
Robert Palmer. 'Sam Phillips: The Sun King.' *Memphis*, December 1978.
John Pugh. 'Rise and Fall of Sun Records.' *Country Music*, November 1973.

INDEX

Page numbers set in *italic type* refer to photographs.

Ace, Johnny, 75-76
Acuff, Roy, 50
Alan's Fifth Wheel Lounge, 163, 173
Albright, Richie, 213, *214*
Allen, Jules Verne, 27
Anderson, Liz, 243
Atkins, Chet, 97, 190, 201, 209-10

Bailey, DeFord, 4, 20, 49-56, *53*, *55*, *56*
Bane, Michael, 164
Bass, Ralph, 123
Bate, Dr. Humphrey, 52
Beale Streeters, 74-75
Beasley, Alcyone Bate, *50*
Below, Fred, 307
Bennett, Wayne, 81, 84, 91
Big Maceo, 290
Big Slim, 42
Binder, Steve, 138
Black, Bill, 96, 99-105, *101*
Bland, Bobby, 3, *15*, 21, 61, 68-91, *71*, *83*, *86*, *89*
Blue Yodels, 20
Booth, Stanley, 128
Bowman, Don, 209
Brasfield, Rod, 219
Brooks, Don, 213
Broonzy, Big Bill, 310
Brown, Mel, 81, 91
Burke, Solomon, 150
Burnett, Chester, *see* Howlin' Wolf
Burns, Hal, 31
Busby, Buzz, 189
Byrd, Billy, 36

Campi, Ray, *107*
Captain Midnite, *214*, 216

Carlisle, Bill, 22
Carnall, Stew, 234
Carson, Martha, 168
Carter, Jimmy and Rosalynn, 257-60, *259*
Carter, Joe, 307
Carter, Wilf, *see* Montana Slim
Carter Family, the, 19-20
Cash, Johnny, 209-12, 221
Chapman, Clete, 166
Charles, Ray, 20
Chatwell, J. R., 242
Chess, Leonard, 284
C. J., *4*, *155*, 159-60
Claypool, Bob, 182
Clement, Jack, 186-99, *188*, *191*, *194*, *197*, *198*, *210*, 265, 275, *337*
Collins, Tommy, 22, 238
Colter, Jessi, *210*
Counts, Robert, 60-61
Crudup, Arthur, 125, *126*, 127
Cryer, Sherwood, 178, 180, 182-84, *185*
Curtis, King, 208

Daily, Pappy, 170
Dalhart, Vernon, 39
Davis, Blind John, 309-11, *309*
Davis, Danny, 209
Davis, Oscar, 31
Dean, Dizzy, *40*
Dean, James, 118
Delmark Records, 319-21
Duke of Paducah, *131*

Edwards, Stoney, 194-95, 264-75, *266*, *274*
Emerson, Billy, 136

Feathers, Charlie, 4-5, 106-15, *107*, *113*, *114*
Feathers, Lawrence, 113-14
Fernwood Records, 189-90
Ferris, John, 192
Fields, Ernie, Jr., 84-85
Floyd, Harmonica Frank, 99
Foley, Red, 25, 122
Fontana, D. J., 102-3, *103*, 128
Frank, Joe, 31-32
Franklin, Rev. C. L., *76*, *77*
Frazier, Dallas, 238
Frizzell, Lefty, 168, 238, *239*

Gilley, Mickey, 171, 176-85, *177*, *185*
Gilley's Club, 178, *179*, 180-82, *182*
Gimble, Johnny, 241-43, 258
Glaser, Chuck, 252
Glaser, Tompall, 91, 201, 214-15, *216*
Glenn, Lloyd, 299-303, *300*, *302*
Graves, Josh, 258
Green, Silas, *59*
Greene, Jack, 26, 36
Grissim, John, 215
Groover Boy, 167
Guthrie, Woody, 252, *253*
Guy, Buddy, 320

Haggard, Merle, 6, 202, 221, 232-47, *233*, *240*, *245*, *246*
Haley, Bill, 295
Hall, Bill, 190
Hamlet, Norman, 241
Hammond, John, 295, 299
Hammond, Wayne, 34
Harkreader, Sid, 24
Hay, George D., 49, *50*, 51-52, *53*, 54
Hemphill, Paul, 119, 238
Holloway, Dean, 234, 236
Holly, Buddy, 204-6, *206*, 208
Hopkins, Jerry, 140
Houston, David, 45
Howlin' Wolf, *viii*, 5, 110, 167, 280-88, *281*, *282*, *285*, *286*, 322, 331

Iglauer, Bruce, 314, 321

Jackson, Al, Sr., 60
Jackson, Mel, 69-70, 82, 84-86, 88-90
Jarvis, Felton, 142

Jennings, Waylon, 6, 20, 201-16, *205*, *206*, *210*, *211*, *214*, *216*, 221, 231
Johnson, Jimmy, 316-19, *317*
Johnson, Pete, 298
Johnson, Tommy, 283
Jones, George, 170
Jordanaires, *132*, 134
Joseph, Hugh, 40-42
Justis, Bill, 153, 335

Kapp, Dave, 30, 32
Keil, Charles, 78
Keisker, Marion, 100, 125, 129, 134
Kempton, Murray, 2, 295
Kesler, Stan, 108, 112
Ketchum, Cavellière, 258
Kilgore, Merle, 217, 221, 223-27, *225*
Kilroy, Eddie, 184
Kimbrough, Junior, 109
King, Albert, 90, 312-13, *314*
King, B. B., *58*, 60-61, *62*, 72, 124, 258
King Records, 111
Koester, Bob, 294, 319-21

LaBeef, Sleepy, *xi*, 14-15, 163-75, *165*, *168*, *169*, *171*, *174*
Lauderdale, Jack, 301
Law, Don, 171
Lee, Bob, 51
Lee, Dickey, 190-91
Lewis, Furry, 54
Lewis, Jerry Lee, 9, 166-68, 176-80, *177*, 184-85, 187, *332*, 334
Linn, Ed, 28
Little Richard, 5-6, 144
Little Walter, 290
Living Blues, 321
Louis, Joe Hill, *58*
Luman, Bob, 119, 129
Lydon, Michael, 123

Macon, Uncle Dave, 49, *50*, 53
Magic Slim, 306-8, *307*, *308*
Marcus, Greil, 139, 252
Martin, Grady, 243
Mattis, David James, 65
McWilliams, Elsie, 28
Meaux, Huey, 178
Monroe, Bill, 109-11, *110*
Montana Slim, 40

Mooney, Ralph, 213, *214*
Moore, Lattie, 93
Moore, Scotty, 96-105, *101, 103*, 126
Moore, Tiny, 241
Morse, Steve, 173
Morton, David, 51, 54, *56*
Muddy Waters, 284-85, *285*, 289-92, *291*, 294
Mull, Frank, 232, 236
Murchison, Harold, 147, 152-53

Neal, Bob, 102, 129-30
Nelson, Willie, 201-2, 212-13, 215
Nichols, Roy, 241-42, 244
Nudie, *135*

O'Donnell, Red, 28
Oliver, Paul, 304
Olsson, Bengt, 51
O'Neal, Jim and Amy, 317, 321
Opry, Grand Ole, 20-22, *30, 43*, 45, 49-50, 53
Orbison, Roy, 94
Otis, Johnny, *78*
Owen, Fuzzy, 234, 238-39
Owens, Bonnie, 232, 235-36, 238, 243, *246*
Owens, Buck, 236, 238

Palmer, Bob, 332-34
Parker, Colonel Tom, 45, 102, 104, 130, *131*, 138
Parker, Junior, 77, *79*
Parton, Dolly, 245-47
Patton, Charley, 283
Peer, Ralph, 19
Perkins, Carl, 94, *133*, 334-35
Phillips, Dewey, 128
Phillips, Knox, 325-26, 334
Phillips, Sam, 63, 94, 99-102, 104-5, 108-12, 123-25, 130, 134, 190, *324*, 325-39, *330, 332, 336, 337*; *see also* Sun Records
Phillips, Tom, 112
Poindexter, Doug, 99-100, 102
Presley, Elvis, *3*, 4, 6, 9, *44*, 45, 94, 96-97, 100-4, *101*, 108, 111, *116*, 117-44, *121, 122, 131, 132, 133, 135, 137, 141*, 169-70, 247, 332-33, 335-36, 338

Presley, Gladys, 120, *121, 122*
Presley, Vernon, 120, *121, 122*
Pride, Charley, 191, 198, 265, 272

Quinn, Bill, 171, 178

Rabbit Foot Minstrels, 59
Race, Wes, 314-15
Ragsdale, Gene, 254
Ray, Nicholas, 119
Reeves, Del, 33-35
Reno, Ronnie, 234
Reynolds, Allen, 190
Rich, Allan, 150, 161
Rich, Charlie, 3-4, *4*, 80, 145-62, *148, 151, 155, 158, 159*
Rich, Margaret Ann, 4, 145-62
Riley, Billy Lee, 190, 334
Robbins, Pig, 160
Robey, Don, 76, *78*, 79-82
Rodgers, Jimmie, *18*, 19-20, 27, 39
Rodgers, Mrs. Jimmie, 28-29, *40*
Rosenberg, Natalie, 157
Rosenberg, Seymour, 146, 160
Russell, Tony, 21
Ryman Auditorium, 22

Schillaci, Mike, 171
Scobey, Lola, 187
Scott, Joe, 78-82, 84, 85
Scott, Ray, 148
Seals, Son, 311-16, *312*
Shamblin, Eldon, 241-42
Shaw, Eddie, 287-88, 323
Shawnee, 42
Sherrill, Billy, 149, *159*, 162
Shines, Johnny, 282, 287
Sholes, Steve, 42-44, 133
Short, Jimmie, 30
Singleton, Shelby, 163, 172-74, *336*
Sleepy-Eyed John, 189-90
Smith, Fay, 30
Smith, J.R., 222, 226
Smith, Ray, *92*
Snow, Eddie, 313
Snow, Hank, 21, 26-27, 37-48, *38, 40, 44, 47*
Solemn Ol' Judge, *see* George D. Hay
Spann, Otis, 289-94, *290, 291, 292*, 293
Staples, Roebuck, 57

Starlite Wranglers, 99, 102, 125
Starrett, Charles, 30
Stewart, Dick, 110
Stoker, Gordon, 128
Stone, Harry, 44
Stoneman, Ernest, 189
Stuart, Dick, 110
Sumner, J. D. and the Stamps, 140
Sun Records, 63, 94, 108, 111, 123, 130,
    133-34, 163, 330; *see also* Sam Phillips
Swaggart, Jimmy Lee, 176-79

Talley, James, 6, 49, 54, 203, *245*, 248-63,
    251, 255, 256, 257, 259, 262
Talley, Jan, 257, 259-60, *259*
Talley, Lewis, 234, 238-39
Tampa Red, 310
Taylor, Chip, 264, 273
Taylor, Hound Dog, 306, 314
Terry, Gordon, 234, 241
Terry, Sonny, 53
Tharpe, Sister Rosetta, 168, *170*
Thomas, Carla, 63-64, *64*, 66
Thomas, Rufus, 20-21, 57-67, *59, 61, 62,
    64, 65, 66*, 279
Townsend, Charles, 256
Travis, Merle, 97, *98, 211*
Troubadours, the, 23, 33-34
Tubb, Ernest, 2-3, 6, 7, *10*, 19, 21, 22-36,
    23, 29, 31, 32, 35, 39-40, *40*, 42-43
Tubb, Justin, *10*, 22, *23*, 26

Turner, Big Joe, 5, 295-303, *296, 297*
Turner, Grant, 22

Vanderpool, John, 147
Van Zandt, Townes, 187

Walker, Charlie, *116*
Walker, T-Bone, 73, *80*, 85
Wallace, Slim, 189
Waters, Muddy, *see* Muddy Waters
WDIA, *58*, 62
Wein, George, 301
Williams, Audrey, 219-21
Williams, Becky, 218, 230
Williams, Bill, 94, 159, 249, 251-54, 258
Williams, Burnett, 69, 72, 90
Williams, Hank, Jr., *200*, 203, 217-31,
    219, 220, 222, 225, 228, 229
Williams, Hank, Sr., 202-3, *219, 220,
    225,* 231
Williams, Leona, 232, *246, 247*
Williams, Professor Nat D., 58-61, *58*
Williamson, Sonny Boy, 283
Wills, Bob, 93, 235, *240*, 241-42,
    271-72, *271*
Wolf, Howlin', *see* Howlin' Wolf
Wolfe, Charles, 50
WSM, 20
WWEE, 326-27